MOLECULAR BASIS OF THE IMMUNE RESPONSE

ANNALS OF THE NEW YORK ACADEMY OF SCIENCES
Volume 546

MOLECULAR BASIS OF THE IMMUNE RESPONSE

Edited by Constantin A. Bona

The New York Academy of Sciences
New York, New York
1988

Q11
.N5
v. 546
1988

Library of Congress Cataloging-in-Publication Data

Molecular basis of the immune response / edited by Constantin A. Bona.
    p.   cm.—(Annals of the New York Academy of Sciences, ISSN 0077-8923 ; v. 546)
    Based on a conference held Jan. 11–13, 1988 in New York City by the New York Academy of Sciences.
    Includes bibliographies and index.
    ISBN 0-89766-486-8 (alk. paper).—ISBN 0-89766-487-6 (pbk.)
    1. Immune response—Molecular aspects—Congresses. I. Bona, Constantin A.   II. New York Academy of Sciences.   III. Series.
    [DNLM: 1. Genes, Immune Response—congresses.   2. Genetics, Biochemical—congresses.   W1 AN626YL v. 546 / QW 541 M718 1988]
Q11.N5 vol. 546
[QR186]
500 s—dc19
[599′.029]

SP
Printed in the United States of America
ISBN 0-89766-486-8 (cloth)
ISBN 0-89766-487-6 (paper)
ISSN 0077-8923

ANNALS OF THE NEW YORK ACADEMY OF SCIENCES

Volume 546
December 30, 1988

MOLECULAR BASIS OF THE IMMUNE RESPONSE[a]

Editor
CONSTANTIN A. BONA

Conference Co-Chairs
C. A. BONA and M. L. GEFTER

CONTENTS

[a]This volume is the result of a conference entitled Molecular Basis of the Immune Response, which was held by the New York Academy of Sciences on January 11–13, 1988 in New York, New York.

Major funding was provided by:
- BURROUGHS WELLCOME CO.
- GENENTECH, INC.
- HOECHST-ROUSSEL PHARMACEUTICALS, INC.
- HOFFMAN-LA ROCHE, INC.
- LILLY RESEARCH LABORATORIES
- MERCK & CO., INC.
- NATIONAL INSTITUTE OF ALLERGY AND INFECTIOUS DISEASES/NIH
- NATIONAL SCIENCE FOUNDATION
- PFIZER CENTRAL RESEARCH
- PFIZER PHARMACEUTICALS
- RIKER LABORATORIES, INC.
- THE UPJOHN COMPANY

Preface

CONSTANTIN A. BONA

Department of Microbiology
Mount Sinai School of Medicine
New York, New York 10029-6574

Understanding the genetic mechanisms through which the diversity of lymphocytic receptors is generated has long represented an attractive subject for immunologists and molecular biologists.

In the case of immunoglobulins, in early studies of allotypes of the V region in rabbits, and of idiotypes, it clearly appeared that a V gene can recombine with various constant regions. These observations strengthened Dryer and Bennet's hypothesis that variable regions were used with a single constant region gene by different lymphocytes producing antibodies.

For many years the inability to isolate antibody genes did not permit real progress in the understanding of the intricate mechanisms that govern the immune response. A breakthrough was achieved with the discovery of restriction enzymes. Almost immediately, this allowed the elucidation of the mechanism of recombination during B-cell development of different DNA segments encoding immunoglobulin molecules.

The ensuing 10 years have seen extraordinary progress in all fields of immunology: the organization of immunoglobulin, T-cell receptor and MHC genes, the mechanism of somatic recombination as an important source of diversity, and molecular mechanisms that control the expression of these genes. Important progress has been made in cloning and understanding the expression of genes encoding cytodifferentiation antigens, lymphokines, oncogenes, and viruses with a particular tropism for lymphocytes such as some lentiviruses.

The application of synthetic peptides in cellular immunology has opened the way for delineating the biochemical processes associated with antigen recognition, the heart of the immune response.

This conference was planned to review topics currently at the forefront of molecular immunology. They will all be discussed during this meeting and I hope that their significance for the progress of medicine and public health will be better understood.

The conference has brought together distinguished scientists whose work sets the pioneering pace of our progress in molecular immunology.

Dr. Malcolm Gefter and I are pleased to welcome you to this conference organized by the New York Academy of Sciences.

Differentiation of a Precursor Cell with the Germline Context of Immunoglobulin Gene into Immunoglobulin-Producing Cells in Vitro[a]

TATSUO KINASHI,[b] KAYO INABA,[c] TAKESHI TSUBATA,[d]
KEI TASHIRO,[b] RONALD PALACIOS,[e]
AND TASUKU HONJO[b]

*Department of Medical Chemistry[b]
and Department of Internal Medicine[d]
Faculty of Medicine
Department of Zoology,[c] Faculty of Science
Kyoto University, Kyoto 606, Japan
and
Basel Institute for Immunology[e]
Basel, Switzerland*

T and B lymphocytes are believed to differentiate from a common precursor cell that is derived from a bone marrow stem cell. The VDJ recombination, which brings the variable, diversity, and joining segments together to form a complete V gene, is a decisive step in B- or T-cell differentiation and thus provides a genetic marker of commitment to either B or T lineage.[1,2] The pre-B cell that has accomplished a successful V_H-D-J_H recombination produces the μ chain in the cytoplasm. Subsequent rearrangement in the light chain locus (kappa or lambda) is required for pre-B cells to become mature B cells expressing IgM on the surface.

Growth factors or lymphokines are often involved in differentiation of the bone marrow stem cell into various cell types. For example, granulocyte-macrophage colony stimulating factor (GM-CSF) stimulates differentiation of precursor cells into granulocytes and monocytes.[3] Interleukin-5 was found to be essential for generation of eosinophil colonies in *in vitro* culture.[4] We are therefore interested in the possible involvement of lymphokines in the regulation of B-lymphocyte differentiation.

To investigate regulation of the decisive step of B-cell differentiation, it is important to establish an *in vitro* system that allows induction of the VDJ and VJ recombination in a cell line containing the germline context of the immunoglobulin gene. Long-term cultured lines of pro-B cells were established from bone marrow cells.[5] These cells grow in the presence of interleukin-3 (IL-3), and detailed characterization of the Ly cell line and clones derived from it was described elsewhere.[6] The Ly clones, including the LyD9 clone that was used in this study, can differentiate into mature B cells, and they contain the immunoglobulin genes in the germline configuration. The phenotype of the LyD9 cells is B-220$^+$, Lyb8$^+$, BP-1$^+$, Lyl$^+$, IgM$^-$, Thyl$^-$, Lyt2$^-$, L3T4$^-$, Ia$^-$, Pgp-1$^+$, and LFA-1$^+$.[6] To induce differentiation of LyD9 cells into mature B cells *in vitro*, we first cultured LyD9 cells with mitogens, lymphokines (IL-4

[a]This work was supported by grants from the Ministry of Education, Science, and Culture, Japan.

1

and IL-5), or various combinations of the two. So far, none of these stimuli has been found to induce the differentiation of LyD9 cells into IgM-bearing cells.

CO-CULTURE OF LYD9 CELLS WITH BONE-MARROW FEEDER CELLS

We co-cultured LyD9 cells with bone-marrow accessory cells[7] for 10 days. The co-cultured LyD9 cells were analyzed with flow cytometry after being stained with antibodies against IgM and B220, a surface antigen specifically expressed on B-cell lineage. The uninduced LyD9 cells were negative for surface IgM, but 17% of the induced pro-B cells were stained with anti-IgM (FIG. 1A). We used the bone-marrow accessory cells of NZB mice, which have the IgM molecule of the e allotype, so that we could distinguish IgM-bearing cells of LyD9 (a allotype) from those of NZB mice with the use of the MB86 monoclonal antibody, which reacts with IgM molecules of the b and e allotypes but not with those of the a allotype.[8] Cells bearing IgM derived from NZB mice were few (at most 4%), indicating that LyD9 cells differentiated in vitro with high frequency (FIG. 1B). Expression of the B-220 antigen increased during co-culture (data not shown).

Bone-marrow accessory cells were prepared by removal of B cells and their precursor cells by the panning method; therefore, it was difficult to obtain many bone-marrow accessory cells for a scale-up of the culture for preparation of DNA and RNA from induced pro-B cells. To overcome this problem, we prepared bone-marrow stroma cells and used them as feeder cells. Bone-marrow cells taken from BALB/c mice were cultured for 5 days, and nonadherent cells were gently removed. The removing adherent stroma cells used might contain kinds of cells similar to the bone-marrow accessory cells just described. LyD9 cells were layered on the stroma cells together with mitogens. LyD9 cells were loosely associated with the feeder cells and grew on their surface. After 10 days of culture, LyD9 cells formed a monolayer sheet over the stroma cell layer, and floating cells increased in number. Few floating cells appeared without the addition of LyD9 cells. The surface of floating cells was stained with anti-IgM antibody, and DNA and RNA were extracted. Flow cytometry analysis of IgM-bearing cells showed that about 16% of the LyD9 cells thus induced were IgM positive (FIG. 1C).

The number of cells producing IgM increased greatly when LyD9 cells were treated beforehand with 5-azacytidine, which induces gene expression by demethylation of methylcytosines in DNA.[9] About half the LyD9 cells treated with 5-azacytidine became IgM-bearing cells when co-cultured with bone-marrow stroma cells (FIG. 1D). Demethylation of DNA is probably associated with gene activation[9]; therefore, 5-azacytidine treatment of LyD9 cells might activate the genes involved in the immunoglobulin rearrangements.

CO-CULTURE OF LYD9 CELLS WITH CLUSTERS
OF DENDRITIC AND T CELLS

Spalding and Griffin[10] reported that IL-3-dependent pre-B cells (cytoplasmic μ-positive cells) can be induced to differentiate into immunoglobulin-producing cells in vitro by co-culture with dendritic and T cells stimulated with concanavalin A. We prepared dendritic and T cells as described by Nussenzweig and Steinman.[11] Dendritic cells (DC) were mixed and incubated with T cells to make DC-T clusters. LyD9 cells were co-cultured with DC-T clusters, and portions of the cells were collected over a

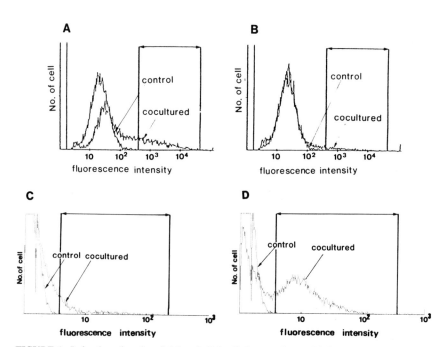

FIGURE 1. Induction of surface IgM on LyD9 cells by co-culture with bone marrow cells. In **A** and **B**, LyD9 cells were co-cultured with bone-marrow accessory cells. LyD9 cells were cultured in RPMI 1640-10% fetal calf serum (FCS)-5% WEHI-3B-conditioned medium. Bone-marrow accessory cells were prepared as described elsewhere.[7] Briefly, bone marrow cells were isolated aseptically from adult NZB mice. Bone-marrow accessory cells were prepared by removal of B cells and their precursors by the panning method with the use of antiimmunoglobulin and anti-B220 antibodies. LyD9 cells (1×10^5) were co-cultured with bone-marrow accessory cells (5×10^5) in 1 ml of RPMI 1640 medium containing 10% FCS, 50 μM β-mercaptoethanol, 1 mM sodium pyruvate, 2 mM glutamine, and nonessential amino acids (GIBCO) together with 50 μg of lipopolysaccharide and 50 μg of agar-extract mitogen. After 10 days of culture, cells were harvested for immunofluorescence staining with polyclonal rabbit antimurine IgM antibody (**A**) or MB86 monoclonal anti-μ antibody (**B**). Both antibodies were labeled with fluorescein isothiocyanate (FITC). The anti-μ antibody used in **A** does not distinguish *a* and *e* allotypes, but the one used in **B** recognizes the *b* and *e* allotypes. Uninduced LyD9 cells were used as a negative control. Stained cells were analyzed with a cell sorter (ABCAS100 for **A** and **B**, and EPICS5 for **C** and **D**). In **C** and **D**, LyD9 cells were co-cultured with bone-marrow stroma cells. Bone-marrow stroma cells (1×10^6) isolated from adult BALB/c mice were incubated in 1 ml of the co-culture medium just described. After 5 days, nonadherent cells were removed by washing three times with modified Eagle's medium containing 5% FCS and once with the co-culture medium. LyD9 cells (1×10^5) were layered on the remaining adherent cells in the co-culture medium (1 ml) together with 50 μg of lipopolysaccharide and 50 μg of agar-extract mitogen. After 10 days of co-culture, nonadherent cells were harvested for staining with FITC-labeled anti-μ antibody. In **D**, LyD9 cells were cultured first with 10 μg · ml^{-1} 5-azacytidine for 36 hours and rinsed twice before co-culture. Positively stained cells are indicated by *horizontal arrows*.

period of 7 days for assays of the presence of IgM-bearing cells by surface staining. Samples collected on days 5 and 6 were studied by flow cytometry. As a negative control, DC-T clusters were incubated without LyD9 cells and harvested on day 6 for immunofluorescence staining. The preparation of dendritic and T cells was contaminated by few, if any, B cells (FIG. 2A). The co-cultured LyD9 cells were 13% and 24% IgM-bearing cells after 5 and 6 days, respectively (FIG. 2B and C). These results indicate that DC-T clusters could induce LyD9 cells to differentiate with high frequency into IgM-bearing cells.

MOLECULAR EVIDENCE OF DIFFERENTIATION

To confirm expression of the immunoglobulin by induced LyD9 cells, we measured immunoglobulin mRNA in LyD9 cells co-cultured with either DC-T clusters or

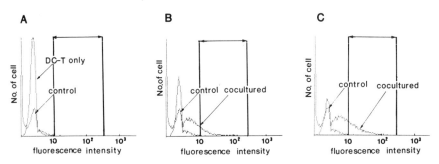

FIGURE 2. Induction of surface IgM on LyD9 cells by co-culture with dendritic and T cells. Dendritic cells were prepared from spleens of DBA/2 mice as described elsewhere.[11] T cells were prepared from spleens of DBA/2 mice by passage of splenocytes through a nylon wool column, followed by treatment with anti-Ia and anti-Lyt 2.2 antibodies together with complement. Dendritic cells were mixed with T cells at a ratio of 1:50 and incubated at 37°C with 3 μg · ml^{-1} concanavalin A. Dendritic and T-cell clusters were formed and separated from the rest of the cells by sedimentation through a 50% FCS cushion. LyD9 cells (1.5×10^5) were co-cultured with DC-T clusters derived from 5×10^4 dendritic cells and 5×10^5 T cells in 1 ml of medium containing RPMI 1640-10% FCS-50 μM β-mercaptoethanol-2 mM glutamine-2 μg · ml^{-1} concanavalin A. DC-T cells cultured without LyD9 cells for 6 days were stained with anti-μ antibody **(A)**. LyD9 cells were harvested on day 5 **(B)** and day 6 **(C)** for immunofluorescence staining with anti-μ antibody.

bone-marrow stroma cells. RNase mapping showed that C_μ transcripts first appeared on day 5 in LyD9 cells co-cultured with DC-T clusters (FIG. 3A); no C_μ transcripts were detected in DC-T clusters *per se*. The use of T cells from the mesenteric lymph nodes produced the same results (data not shown). LyD9 cells induced by bone-marrow stroma cells also contained C_μ transcripts (FIG. 3B). Northern blot hybridization showed that the C_μ and C_κ transcripts in differentiated LyD9 were full-length mRNAs and not sterile transcripts of immunoglobulin-C genes.

Finally, we tested whether these IgM-bearing cells had rearranged selected V_H and V_K segments of the immunoglobulin gene. Southern blot filters of restricted DNA from LyD9 cells co-cultivated with bone-marrow stroma cells were hybridized with the J_H or

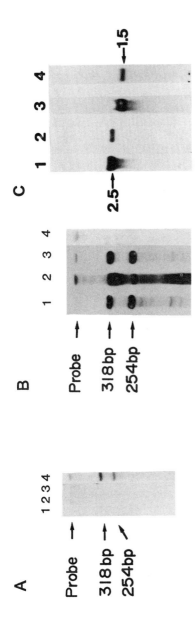

FIGURE 3. Detection of immunoglobulin mRNAs in LyD9 cells induced by co-culture with either DC-T clusters or bone-marrow stroma cells. RNase mapping (**A** and **B**). Cells (5×10^5) were harvested on the days indicated, rinsed with the phosphate buffer twice, and suspended in the lysis buffer (140 mM NaCl, 1.5 mM MgCl$_2$, 10 mM Tris [pH 8.5], and 10 mM vanadyl ribonucleoside complex) containing 0.1% NP-40. The cell suspension was vortexed briefly and incubated on ice for 5 minutes. After centrifugation of the suspension, an equal volume of proteinase K buffer (0.2 M Tris [pH 7.4], 25 mM EDTA, 0.3 M NaCl, 2% SDS, and 0.4 mg · ml^{-1} proteinase K) was added to the supernatant and the mixture was incubated for 30 minutes at 37°C. Samples were extracted with phenol and chloroform-isoamyl alcohol (24:1). To the extracts were added three volumes of ethanol to precipitate the RNA. RNAase protection analysis was performed as described elsewhere.[13] The riboprobe for the C$_\mu$ sequence was the genomic C$_\mu$ segment containing the C$_{H3}$ sequence (318 bp) and part of the C$_{H4}$ sequence (254 bp) in addition to the intron. The probe and the protected fragments are indicated by *arrows*. **A**, RNA extracted from DC-T clusters cultured without the addition of LyD9 cells and harvested on day 6 (*lane 1*). RNA extracted from LyD9 cells co-cultivated with DC-T clusters and harvested on day 3 (*lane 2*), day 4 (*lane 3*), or day 5 (*lane 4*). **B**, RNA extracted from LyD9 cells co-cultured with bone-marrow stroma cells. LyD9 cells treated with 5-azacytidine (*lane 1*) or not (*lane 2*) were harvested on day 6. RNA from 70Z/3 (pre-B cells) was used as a positive control (*lane 3*), and RNA from uninduced LyD9 cells was used as a negative control (*lane 4*). Northern blot analysis (**C**). RNA was prepared from LyD9 cells co-cultured with bone-marrow stroma cells on day 10 (*lanes 1–4*). RNA used in *lanes 2 and 4* was prepared from induced LyD9 cells cultured first with 5-azacytidine as described in the legend to FIGURE 1. RNAs were treated with glyoxal and dimethylsulfoxide at 50°C for 1 hour, electrophoresed in agarose gels containing 10 mM sodium phosphate buffer (pH 7.0), and transferred to nitrocellulose filters.[14] The filters were hybridized with the C$_\mu$ (*lanes 1 and 2*) or C$_K$ (*lanes 3 and 4*) probe. The probes were prepared as described before.[15]

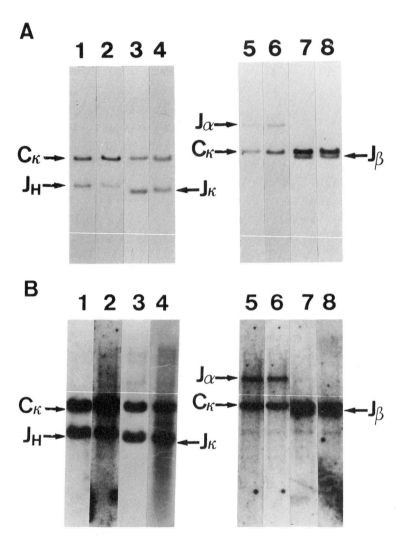

FIGURE 4. Southern blot analysis of immunoglobulin gene loci and T-cell receptor loci in DNA of induced LyD9 cells. DNA was extracted from LyD9 cells co-cultured with bone-marrow stroma cells for 9 days, 15% of which expressed IgM on their surface, and digested with $XbaI$. Because the $XbaI$ site is between the J_K and C_K genes, the size of the C_K fragments should not be changed by the immunoglobulin gene recombination. Uninduced LyD9 DNAs were used as controls. Filters were exposed briefly to quantitate relative intensity of bands (**A**) and longer to see if smeary bands appeared (**B**). Origins of DNA used are: uninduced LyD9 in *lanes 1, 3, 5, and 7;* induced LyD9 in *lanes 2, 4, 6, and 8.* Probes used are J_H and C_K probes in *lanes 1 and 2;* J_K and C_K probes in *lanes 3 and 4;* J_α and C_K probes in *lanes 5 and 6;* J_β and C_K probes in *lanes 7 and 8.*

J_K probe together with the C_K probe as an internal reference (FIG. 4A, lanes 1–4). We did not find any discrete rearranged bands hybridized with either the J_H or the J_K probe. After longer exposure (FIG. 4B, lanes 1–4), smears of both larger and smaller sizes appeared, and the germline J_H or J_K band had reduced intensity. The relative intensity of the germline J_H and J_K bands compared with that of the C_K band was 61% and 65% at day 9, respectively. The results indicate that the J_H and J_K segments were associated with heterogeneous V_H and V_K segments to yield J_H and J_K fragments of different lengths. The results excluded the possibility that the co-culture procedure selected preexisting IgM-bearing clones in LyD9 cells. No rearrangement at T-cell receptor loci occurred in induced LyD9, as the relative intensity of germline J_α and J_β segments was unchanged (FIG. 4A, lanes 5–8), and no significant smears appeared even after a long exposure (FIG. 4B, lanes 5–8).

DISCUSSION

One central question about lymphocyte differentiation is when and how T and B lineages segregate. Two alternative hypotheses on DNA rearrangement and T-B lineage commitment were proposed. Model 1 assumes that DNA rearrangement itself is a determining step of the commitment. Because VDJ recombinase seems to be common for immunoglobulin and T-cell receptor gene rearrangements, two loci may compete for recombination, and successful recombination of either locus simply determines the lineage. Model 2 assumes that commitment to the T or B lineage takes place before DNA rearrangement begins. Our results seem to be contradictory to model 1, because we have never found rearrangement of the T-cell receptor locus in the induced LyD9 cells.

However, we are not completely sure whether the LyD9 cell is destined to the B lineage only. Under different conditions, LyD9 cells may differentiate into other lineage cells including T cells. Palacios and Steinmetz[5] reported that IL-3-dependent pro-B cells similar to LyD9 can give rise only to B cells but not to T cells or granulocytes-macrophages when these cells were injected into irradiated syngeneic animals. Therefore, they concluded that these cells are pro-B cells. However, evaluation of *in vivo* experiments is limited because of competition for clonal expansion with endogenous cells.

Few systems for the study of rearrangement of the immunoglobulin gene *in vitro* have been described. In pre-B-cell lines transformed by Abelson murine leukemia, virus immunoglobulin gene rearrangement may take place spontaneously at low frequency.[12] Pro-B-cell lines dependent on IL-3 that were derived from murine fetal liver differentiate into IgM-producing cells when co-cultured with bone-marrow stroma cells[7]; unfortunately, molecular characterization of the differentiated cells was not provided in the report, and the efficiency of differentiation appeared low. The systems that we describe herein have several advantages over the foregoing systems. LyD9 is a continuously proliferating nontransformed cell clone, and it rearranges both the J_H and the J_K segments with high frequency only when induced.

ACKNOWLEDGMENTS

We thank K. Hirano for help in the preparation of this manuscript.

REFERENCES

1. TONEGAWA, S. 1983. Nature **302:** 575–581.
2. HONJO, T. & S. HABU. 1985. Ann. Rev. Biochem. **54:** 803–830.
3. GOUGH, N. M., J. GOUGH, D. METCALF, A. KELSO, D. GRAIL, N. A. NICOLA, A. W. BURGESS & A. R. DUNN. 1984. Nature **309:** 763–767.
4. CAMPBELL, H. D., W. Q. J. TUCKER, Y. HORT, M. E. MARTINSON, G. MAYO, E. J. CLUTTERBUCK, C. J. SANDERSON & I. G. YOUNG. 1987. Proc. Natl. Acad. Sci. USA **84:** 6629–6633.
5. PALACIOS, R. & M. STEINMETZ. 1985. Cell **41:** 727–734.
6. PALACIOS, R., H. KARASUYAMA & A. ROLINK. 1987. EMBO J. **6:** 3687–3693.
7. MCKEARN, P. J., J. MCCUBREY & B. FAGG. 1985. Proc. Natl. Acad. Sci. USA **82:** 7414–7418.
8. NISHIKAWA, S., Y. SASAKI, T. KINA, T. AMAGAI & Y. KATSURA. 1986. Immunogenetics **23:** 137–139.
9. JONES, A. P. 1985. Cell **40:** 485–486.
10. SPALDING, M. D. & A. J. GRIFFIN. 1986. Cell **44:** 507–515.
11. NUSSENZWEIG, M. C. & M. R. STEINMAN. 1980. J. Exp. Med. **151:** 1196–1212.
12. ALT, F. W., N. ROSENBERG, S. LEWIS, E. THOMAS & D. BALTIMORE. 1981. Cell **27:** 381–390.
13. MELTON, A. D., A. P. KRIEG, R. M. REBAGLIATI, T. MANIATIS, K. ZINN & R. M. GREEN. 1984. Nucl. Acids Res. **12:** 7035–7056.
14. MAKMASTER, G. K. & G. G. CARMICHAEL. 1977. Proc. Natl. Acad. Sci. USA **74:** 4835–4838.
15. YAOITA, Y. & T. HONJO. 1980. Nature **286:** 850–853.

Control of Recombination Events During Lymphocyte Differentiation

Heavy Chain Variable Region Gene Assembly and Heavy Chain Class Switching[a]

FREDERICK W. ALT, PIERRE FERRIER,
BARBARA MALYNN, STUART LUTZKER,
PAUL ROTHMAN, JEFFREY BERMAN,
KEITH BLACKWELL, SCOTT MELLIS,
ROBERTA POLLOCK, ANDREW FURLEY,
GARY RATHBUN, GEORGE YANCOPOULOS,
TON LOGTENBERG, MAUREEN MORROW,
WENDY COOK, BRUCE HEINKE, AND HEIKYUNG SUH

Howard Hughes Medical Institute and
The Departments of Biochemistry and Microbiology
Columbia University, College of Physicians and Surgeons
New York, New York 10032

The basic unit of an immunoglobulin (Ig) molecule is a complex of two identical heavy (H) and two identical light (L) polypeptide chains. Both types of chains contain a region of variable amino acid sequence at the amino terminal end (V region) in which reside the primary determinants of antigen binding specificity and a region of constant amino acid sequence (C region) comprising the remainder of the chain. Multiple classes and subclasses of immunoglobulins have been defined in mammals, each determined by a distinct heavy chain C region. There are two different families of light chain (κ and λ), each complete Ig molecule being composed of only one type of heavy and light chain. The V region of Ig heavy and light chain genes is assembled from component gene segments. The heavy chain V region gene is assembled from three different elements: the variable (V_H), diversity (D), and joining (J_H) segments; the complete $V_H D J_H$ heavy chain variable region gene is assembled just upstream of the C_μ region gene.[1] Assembly of light chain genes involves the joining of a V_L segment to a J_L segment to form a complete $V_L J_L$ variable region. For both heavy and light chain genes, transcription of the mRNA is initiated upstream of the V region and terminated downstream of the C region; intervening sequences are removed by standard RNA processing mechanisms.[1,2]

All immunoglobulin variable region gene segments are flanked by conserved recognition sequences that appear to direct the activity of a site-specific recombination system,[1] referred to as the "Ig recombinase." T-cell receptor genes are flanked by the same conserved recognition sequences[3]; this observation and others suggest that TCR

[a]This work was supported by grants from the Howard Hughes Medical organization and NIH grants AI-20047 and CA-40427. P.F. is an EMBO fellow, B.A.M., G.R., and R.P. are Leukemia Society Fellows, P.R. is supported by a Physician Scientist award, S.M. is a Pfizer Fellow, J.B. was a Damon Runyon-Walter Winchell Fellow, and A.F. is a Jane Coffin Childs Fellow.

9

V region genes also are assembled by the same "Ig recombinase."[4] Ig variable region genes are assembled in precursor (pre)-B lymphocytes in an ordered process. The first event in heavy variable region gene assembly involves D to J_H joining; subsequently V_H segments are appended to the preexisting DJ_H complex.[5] Heavy chain variable region assembly and expression of the heavy chain generally precede the assembly and expression of light chain genes.[6] This rearrangement and expression process culminates in the generation of primary B lymphocytes, each of which expresses a unique species of immunoglobulin (containing a unique species of heavy and light chain) on its surface. The production of only a single species of immunoglobulin in an individual B lymphocyte results from a unique regulatory mechanism referred to as allelic exclusion; allelic exclusion appears to be regulated at the level of the rearrangement process so that only a single "functional" heavy chain and a single "functional" light chain variable region gene are assembled in any given pre-B cell. These early stages of B-cell differentiation occur in primary B-cell differentiation organs such as the fetal liver or adult bone marrow. Subsequently, B lymphocytes migrate to peripheral lymphoid organs such as the spleen where upon contact with cognate antigens they can mature into antibody-secreting effector cells.[7]

The C_μ gene can be replaced by other, downstream constant regions during the maturation of a B cell[8]; this phenomenon, termed heavy chain class switching, appears to be mediated by a specific "recombinase" system[9] distinct from that which mediates V gene assembly. The class switch process allows the same heavy chain variable region (specificity) to be expressed in association with a different constant region effector function. The order of murine C_H genes has been determined to be $5'(V_H DJ_H)$-C_μ-C_δ-$C_{\gamma 3}$-$C_{\gamma 1}$-$C_{\gamma 2b}$-$C_{\gamma 2a}$-C_ϵ-C_α. Long stretches of repeated sequences (S regions), which lie upstream of each C_H gene, apparently mediate the switch event. Recombination between S_μ and downstream S regions deletes intervening sequences and places the assembled V region gene just upstream of the new C_H gene.[8] The class switch process also may be regulated. Thus, treatment of B lymphocytes with different combinations of mitogens and lymphokines can induce the appearance of terminally differentiated cells that have switched to the production of different constant region subsets.[10,11]

RESULTS AND DISCUSSION

Organization of V Gene Families

In the mouse genome, a cluster of four J_H segments lies 7 kb upstream of the μ constant region exons (C_μ). Approximately 10 D segments are located directly upstream of the J_H cluster.[1] An estimated 100 to 1,000 V_H segments lie at an unknown distance upstream from the D cluster.[12,13] These V_H segments have been subdivided into nine distinct families on the basis of nucleotide sequence homology. In the few murine strains examined, V_H families often are organized into discrete clusters; deletion and recombinant-inbred strain mapping have allowed ordering of V_H families in several strains.[12] The size of known murine V_H families varies from as few as four to hundreds of members in the case of one family.[12,13] Recent data suggest that the order of the families defined in BALB/c mice may not be uniform in all mouse strains. (For review, see reference 2.) Our most recent studies used pulsed field gradient gel electrophoresis to link the most proximal known murine V_H segment ($V_H 81X$) to within 200 kb of the D and J_H clusters.[14]

Most studies on primary repertoire development have focused on the heavy chain locus of the mouse, in part because of the wealth of knowledge concerning the organization of the murine V_H locus. To clearly elucidate organizational factors that may be involved in repertoire development and to extend these studies to humans, we have determined the organization of the human variable region locus in detail.[15] Previous work demonstrated that the organization of the human J_H region resembles that of the mouse; thus, six functional J_H segments lie in a cluster approximately 6 kb 5′ from the C_μ gene, and a D segment homologous to the most 3′ murine D lies just 5′ to this cluster.[16] Multiple additional D segments, some homologous and some divergent from the other known murine D segments, lie in the approximately 80 kb upstream from the J_H locus (FIG. 1). Previous work had defined three human V_H families (V_H1 through V_H3).[17,18] To further define the content of the human V_H locus, we have isolated numerous human genomic V_H genes on the basis of homology to murine V_H genes and have also isolated V_H genes from $V_H D J_H$ rearrangements in human B-cell tumors. Analyses of these gene segments have allowed us to define three novel human V_H gene families (V_H4 through V_H6). The V_H4 and V_H5 families also were independently identified by others.[19,20] On the basis of the number of unique hybridizing

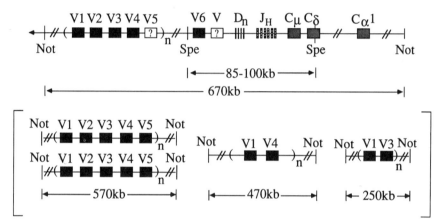

FIGURE 1. Organization of the human V_H locus. The organization and linkage of the various segments were determined by pulse field gel electrophoresis. The four Not 1 restriction fragments on the bottom have not been linked to each other or to the 670-kb Not 1 fragment that contains the rest of the locus (*top*). Details are in reference 15.

fragments in genomic blotting assays, we estimate that the V1 and V3 families are the largest with more than 20 members, the V2 and V4 families have approximately 10 members, the V5 family has less than 5 members, and the V_H6 family a single member. However, on the basis of other types of analyses,[15] we believe that these are minimum estimates and that the human genome probably contains between 100 and 200 unique V_H sequences, of which a significant proportion are pseudogenes. With the exception of the largest murine V_H family (J558,13), there appear to be relatively similar numbers of related V_H genes in mice and humans.

The organization of human V_H genes differs from that of the mouse.[15] Thus, we have isolated multiple cloned genomic DNA segments of about 15 to 20 kb that contain either V3 and V1 or V3 and V4 genes on the same segment. We also have employed pulsed field gradient gel electrophoresis to demonstrate that the human V_H locus encompasses more than 2,000 kb of DNA and also have demonstrated that the multimember V_H families are interspersed over much of this locus. In addition, we have

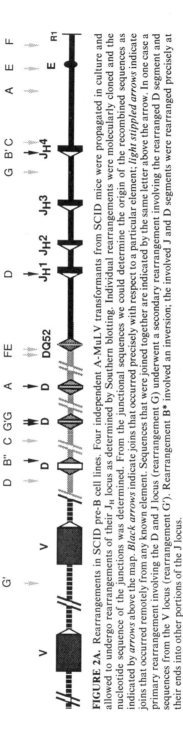

FIGURE 2A. Rearrangements in SCID pre-B cell lines. Four independent A-MuLV transformants from SCID mice were propagated in culture and allowed to undergo rearrangements of their J_H locus as determined by Southern blotting. Individual rearrangements were molecularly cloned and the nucleotide sequence of the junctions was determined. From the junctional sequences we could determine the origin of the recombined sequences as indicated by *arrows* above the map. *Black arrows* indicate joins that occurred precisely with respect to a particular element; *light stippled arrows* indicate joins that occurred remotely from any known element. Sequences that were joined together are indicated by the same letter above the arrow. In one case a primary rearrangement involving the D and J locus (rearrangement G) underwent a secondary rearrangement involving the rearranged D segment and sequences from the V locus (rearrangement G'). Rearrangement B* involved an inversion; the involved J and D segments were rearranged precisely at their ends into other portions of the J locus.

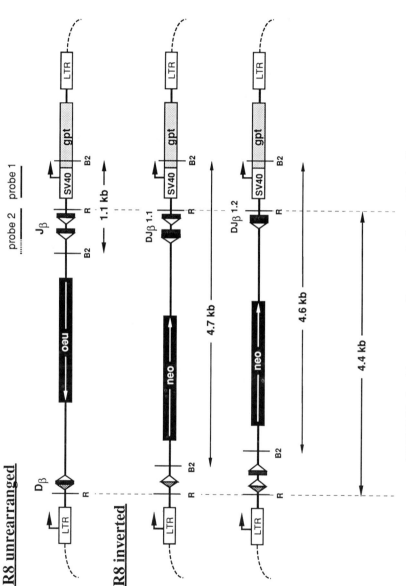

FIGURE 2B. Inversion constructs. See text and reference 2 for details.

linked the most proximal known human V_H segment, V_H6, to within 85 kb of the J_H locus (FIG. 1). This linkage and our more recent linkage of the murine V_H and J_H loci represent the first reported linkage of the variable and constant region portion of the Ig locus in mammals. Surprisingly, the distance between V_H and J_H is much closer than that estimated by classical genetic analyses.[15]

The use of V_H gene segments for V_H to DJ_H rearrangements is highly position dependent in murine pre-B cells; the J_H-proximal segments and particularly the most proximal segment are used highly preferentially.[21,22] This preferential V_H rearrangement results in a primary heavy chain repertoire in pre-B and B cells of the fetal liver that is also highly biased towards utilization of proximal gene segments; the repertoire of peripheral B cells in the adult, however, is "normalized" in that, with respect to families, representation is correlated with the number of members.[22] We also find similar biased use of J_H-proximal V_H gene segments in primary human B-cell differentiation organs; thus, the V_H6 segment comprises a significant portion of the fetal liver μ mRNA, but it is hardly detectable in the μ mRNA of peripheral B cells in the adult.[23] It has been proposed that the V_H locus may have evolved in the context of function; thus, more proximal V_H segments could have a role early in development, perhaps in establishing the mature repertoire.[24,25] Although this notion remains unproven, it is of interest to note that certain murine autoreactive antibodies were found to preferentially employ proximal V_H gene segments.[25,26] In this regard, our preliminary data indicate that the V_H6 segment is disproportionately represented in certain sets of human autoantibodies (Logtenberg & Alt, unpublished results).

Analysis of the Ig Recombination Mechanism in SCID Mice

The genetic defect in mice with severe combined immune deficiency (SCID) is manifested by the absence of functional B and T cells.[27] Because SCID mice seem to have as many early precursor B cells as do normal mice, the SCID defect appears to operate at the pre-B stage.[28] In addition, developing T cells and B cells in SCID mice make highly aberrant rearrangements (deletions) at the respective J loci.[27] These findings suggest that the SCID defect involves some function of the Ig recombinase system.[27] To further define the nature of this defect, we have analyzed the rearrangements made by A-MuLV transformed pre-B cell lines derived from the adult bone marrow of either SCID mice or their normal CB-17 counterparts.[29] Like many A-MuLV transformants from other normal strains, the CB-17 transformants that we analyzed had DJ_H rearrangements and appended V_H segments to these DJ_H intermediates during propagation in culture; the transformants from the SCID lines had either aberrant rearrangements or deletions of the J_H locus (to be discussed), but many of these also continued to undergo further rearrangement in culture. Therefore, transformants from both sources still apparently have active recombinase activity.

We isolated and determined the nucleotide sequence of multiple primary and secondary J_H-associated rearrangements from four independent SCID A-MuLV transformants. All of the primary rearrangements involved joining of sequences within or near the J_H locus to sequences within the D locus; we could identify the exact origin of all sequences (FIG. 2). Normal D to J_H joining involves fusion of sequences just downstream of the J_H heptamer to sequences just upstream of the 3'D heptamer.[1] Strikingly, none of the joints isolated from SCID pre-B lines involved normal ligation of a D sequence to a J_H sequence. Three involved joining of distal 5' D flanking regions to sequences 90 or more bp 3' to various J_H segments; three, precise joining of the D coding region to sequences downstream of a J_H segment; and one, precise joining of a J_H sequence to sequences upstream of a D segment (FIG. 2). Finally, one of the joints involved inversion of a segment of the J_H region (precisely joined), and a secondary join involved precise joining of the 5' end of a D segment to a sequence within the V_H region (FIG. 2). In the joint that we analyzed, the joining breakpoint was often found to be precise for one partner, but never for both.

The ability to append V_H to DJ_H segments in normal pre-B cells correlates with transcription of the germline V_H segments[4]; both the CB-17 and SCID transformants showed similar and normal levels of germline V_H transcription.[29] This result suggests that normal targeting mechanisms are also operative in the SCID pre-B cells. Furthermore, normal pre-B cells preferentially rearrange V_H segments to DJ_H complexes rather than replacing a DJ_H complex by joining an upstream D to a downstream J_H.[30] This finding suggested that recombinase is preferentially targeted to the V_H locus once a DJ_H complex is formed. Significantly, analysis of a secondary rearrangement in a line that had made an abortive D join into the region between $J_H 3$ and 4 demonstrated that the rearrangement involved precise joining of the 5' side of the D (at the normal position for V to DJ_H joining) to a sequence flanking a $V_H Q52$ gene[29] (FIG. 2). Thus, once SCID pre-B lines produce an abortive DJ_H rearrangement, they seem to undergo the normal process of searching the V_H locus for the next segment to rearrange.

Together, our findings indicate that most aspects of the mechanism and control of Ig recombination function normally in SCID pre-B cells. Thus, targeting of the recombinase is normal, as evidenced by the production of appropriate germline segments and the sequential attempts to make first D to J_H and subsequently V_H to DJ_H rearrangements. In addition, most aspects of the mechanism of rearrangement appear normal. D to J_H (V_H to DJ_H joining) is postulated to involve a two-step mechanism in which one step involves a precise break between the involved segments and their flanking heptamers followed by ligation of the heptamers. The other step is the joining of the two coding strands, which may involve loss of several bp by one or both and the addition of novel nucleotides at the point of joining (N regions), again followed by their subsequent ligation. Loss of bases could occur by multiple mechanisms including exonuclease activity, whereas the addition of bases is thought to involve the activity of terminal deoxynucleotidyl transferase.[31] We propose that recognition and cutting functions of the recombinase system are intact in SCID pre-B cells, because so many of the joins are precise with respect to one or the other involved segment (but not both). The occurrence of many precise joints relative to one partner suggests (but does not prove) that the putative exonuclease activity may also be normal; the occurrence of extra bases in some of the SCID joints and the fact that the SCID pre-B lines are also TdT-positive[29] suggest that N-region activity is normal. Thus, the most obvious possible defect would be a defect in ligation activity, although other explanations remain possible.

The nature of the SCID joints could have a logical explanation in the context of a ligase defect; the free ends resulting from endonucleolytic activity would have to be resolved if the chromosome remained intact. This resolution could occur if one of the free ends was involved in an illegitimate recombination event with the other strand. If the recombination event never occurred precisely at the junctions, this could explain why precise joining of both partners is never found, whereas precise joining of one partner occurs frequently. A similar mechanism was recently invoked to explain the structure of the joints that occur in Ig/oncogene translocations in B-cell malignancies.[32] The fact that the joins are often into nearby flanking sequence may result from the relative proximity of the recombining sequence, perhaps because they are held by the abortive recombination complex. This scenario could also result in inversions if both of the free ends simultaneously attacked the opposite strand of the other partner.[29] If, in fact, the defect does involve ligation, it will be of interest to examine the activity of known ligases in these cells and also to test the SCID pre-B cells for any potential defect in repair activities and for an increased frequency of translocations and large deletions similar to those observed in the oncogene translocations.

A current goal is to employ SCID pre-B lines or other Ig recombinase negative lines to isolate sequences encoding portions of the recombinase system via complementation

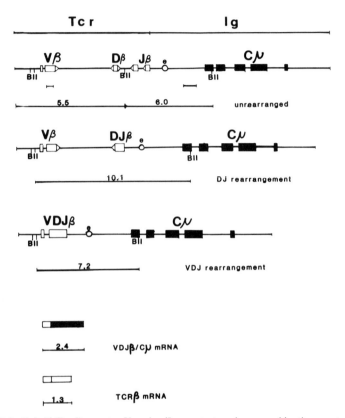

FIGURE 3. Hybrid T-cell receptor V region/Ig constant region recombination construct. The diagrammed construct was introduced into transgenic mice and analyzed for rearrangement as discussed in the text and outlined in the *lower portion* of the panel. An identical construct in which the Ig enhancer (e) was specifically deleted was also injected. Genomic DNA from the trangenics was digested with *Bgl*II and assayed by Southern blotting for hybridization to the indicated V_b probe. Unrearranged and DJ- or VDJ-rearranged genomic constructs were detected by this assay as outlined. The *bottom panels* represent the hybrid mRNA sequence that is made upon rearrangement of the construct.

of the defect. We have prepared inversion recombination substrates that undergo inverted joining to activate a neo gene at relatively high frequency in normal pre-B lines (FIG. 3). Thus far, such substrates, when introduced into SCID pre-B lines, do not undergo normal inversion at high frequency. In fact, the most common mechanism for activation of the neo gene that we observed is amplification. Perhaps of significance, several lines that have independently amplified the construct also had rearrangements around the J segments. One possibility is that nicking of the construct at the J segment occurs normally but that the inability to resolve the ends by the Ig recombinase system somehow predisposes the sequences to amplification. If so, further analyses of these variants may also yield important information relevant to the amplification process. Because of the relatively low frequency of inversional activation of the neo gene in SCID lines, we are also trying to restore the normal activity by complementation. In this regard, we have purified dozens of low abundance pre-B cell specific cDNA sequences by subtractive hybridization.[33] The subtraction was based on our previous findings that pre-B cells but not myeloma or L cells contained Ig recombinase activity.[34] With the hopes that pre-B specific sequences may include recombinase, we are currently constructing expression libraries to introduce them into the SCID lines containing the inversion substrate.

REGULATION OF V REGION GENE ASSEMBLY

The assembly of Ig genes appears to be regulated both at the level of the developmental stage (i.e., heavy before light) and at the level of allelic exclusion. In addition, it seems likely that assembly of these genes is regulated in a tissue-specific manner; thus, Ig V genes are not assembled in nonlymphoid cells and are not completely assembled in T-lymphoid cells, even though the latter assemble that highly related T-cell receptor variable (TCR) region genes. Thus, if all of these specific recombination events are performed by the same recombinase, a higher level of control is required to regulate specificity. One proposed mechanism is that assembly of V gene segments is regulated by relative accessibility to recombinase. Initial support for this accessibility model came from observations that unrearranged Ig and TCR V gene segments are transcribed and in an "active" chromatin configuration during or before their rearrangement (reviewed in reference 4). Strong support for this model has been provided by gene transfer and recombination substrate studies.[2]

To further define the mechanisms responsible for controlling tissue- and stage-specific variable region gene assembly, we have introduced a variety of different recombination substrates into the germline of transgenic mice. The most informative studies involved a vector that contained the T-cell receptor V_β, D_β, and J_β segments separated from the Ig C_μ gene by a DNA segment in which the Ig heavy chain enhancer sequence was either present or absent[35] (FIG. 3). We constructed 10 independent lines of mice with the enhancer-negative construct and 6 with the enhancer-positive construct. Individual strains contained 2 to 20 copies of the construct; copy number had no apparent effect on the results obtained. To assay for rearrangement and expression, we prepared DNA and RNA from a variety of tissue samples from a given strain. Expression of the transgenic RNA resulting from a $V_\beta D_\beta J_\beta$ rearrangement within the construct was readily detectable because it resulted in the production of a novel 2.4-kb transcript that hybridized to the V_β probe (FIG. 3). Likewise, $D_\beta J_\beta$ and $V_\beta D_\beta J_\beta$ rearrangements within the construct could readily be detected by probing appropriate genomic DNA restriction digests with the V_β probe (FIG. 3). Strikingly, we found absolutely no evidence for rearrangement of the enhancer-negative construct in any tissue, but found readily detectable $D_\beta J_\beta$ and/or $V_\beta D_\beta J_\beta$ of the enhancer-positive construct in various lymphoid but not nonlymphoid tissues (TABLE 1). In particular, $V_\beta D_\beta J_\beta$ rearrangements were most predominant in the thymus, whereas $D_\beta J_\beta$ rearrangements were observed in all lymphoid tissues (fetal liver, thymus, bone marrow, spleen, and lymph nodes). These results suggested that V_β to DJ_β rearrangement within the enhancer-positive construct may occur preferentially in T cells. To test the possibility of tissue-specific V_β rearrangement, B and T cells were

TABLE 1. Rearrangements of the T-Cell Receptor/Ig Hybrid Construct in Various Tissues[a]

	Enhancer +		Enhancer −	
	DJ	VDJ	DJ	VDJ
Lymph nodes	+ + +	+	−	−
Skin	−	−	−	−
Spleen	+ + +	+	−	−
Liver	−	−	−	−
Kidney	−	−	−	−
Thymus	+ + + +	+ + + +	−	−
Brain	−	−	−	−
Bone marrow	+	−	−	−
T cells	+ + + +	+ + + +	WD	WD
B cells	+ + + +	−	WD	WD

[a]Determined as outlined in FIGURE 3.

NOTE: The number of pluses indicates the relative level of a given type of rearrangement in the different tissues. A minus indicates no detectable rearrangement. ND indicates not done. The results are the composite of multiple independent strains with each type of construct. See text and FIGURE 3 for other details.

purified from lymph nodes and spleen and assayed for rearrangement of the construct. Strikingly, purified B-cell populations made DJ_β rearrangements but not $V_\beta D_\beta J_\beta$ rearrangements, whereas purified T-cell populations contained both DJ_β and $V_\beta D_\beta J_\beta$ rearrangements (TABLE 1).

To confirm the results with normal cell populations, we also introduced a similar vector that contained the herpes thymidine kinase gene between the D and J_β segments into Ig recombinase-positive pre-B-cell lines and tested for their ability to make rearrangements.[35] Only $D_\beta J_\beta$ rearrangements were observed in these cultured pre-B lines. In addition, we prepared A-MuLV transformed B cells from adult bone marrow and fetal liver and A-MuLV transformed immature T cells from adult thymus. In the pre-B lines the construct was either not rearranged or rearranged to the $D_\beta J_\beta$ stage, but the immature T-cell lines made both DJ_β and $V_\beta D_\beta J_\beta$ rearrangements.[35]

Together these results demonstrate that the Ig enhancer can serve as a recombinational enhancer; the activity of this element was necessary to achieve rearrangement in either T or B cells. It should be pointed out that although the IgH enhancer is involved in Ig heavy chain expression in B cells, it is also active in T cells. Thus, the enhancer may be a prerequisite to achieving general access to the locus by recombination enzymes. However, other elements, apparently associated with the V_β gene, provide the tissue specificity of the recombination event. This finding is consistent with the notion that the V to DJ joining step is the regulated step in the context of endogenous allelically excluded and tissue-specific variable region gene assembly.[5] We have not defined which portion of the V_β-containing DNA segment is responsible. In the context of transcription as a potential activator of recombination,[34] a likely candidate is the promoter; however, it is possible that other upstream or downstream enhancer-like elements are involved. Similar constructs that employed heavy chain V_H and DJ_H segments were rearranged in B cells (not shown). Therefore, the elements that provide the specificity must be contained within the hybrid construct and should be readily elucidated by appropriate modifications.

Also of interest, we have found high level expression of the rearranged construct in the thymus, but very low level expression in the spleen or lymph nodes (despite the substantial proportion of T cells found in those organs in normal mice); $V_\beta D_\beta J_\beta$ rearrangements were also not observed at the predicted levels in those tissues (relative to thymus) if they contained the same percentage of T cells as did normal mice. However, the *purified* T-cell population from lymph nodes and spleen contained a similar proportion of rearrangements as those of the thymus (not shown). These results suggest that T cells that rearrange and express the construct in the thymus are not proportionally present in peripheral lymphoid tissues compared to the number of T-cell counterparts in nontransgenic mice. There could be several explanations for this finding: among the most interesting is that rearrangement and expression of the construct leading to the expression of a hybrid protein somehow interfere with normal T-cell maturation.

REGULATION OF HEAVY CHAIN CLASS SWITCHING IN PRE-B CELLS

As already noted, a second type of recombination event, referred to as H-chain class switching, allows the progeny of a given B cell to maintain the parental H-chain antigen binding specificity (encoded by the V region gene) while varying its effector function (encoded by different C_H genes). Spontaneous switching to $\gamma2b$ seems to be a high frequency event in A-MuLV transformed pre-B cell lines[4]; spontaneous switching to other isotypes is a rare event in these lines. We find that preferential switching to

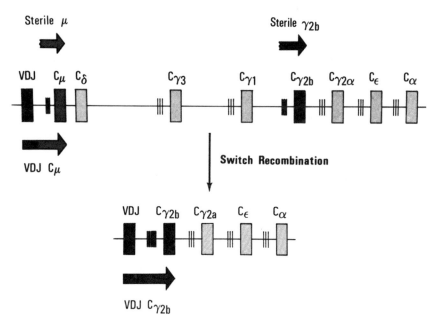

FIGURE 4A. Regulation of heavy chain class switching. The general organization of the Ig constant region locus is indicated. In the outlined diagram, transcription through the $C\mu$ and $C\gamma2b$ constant regions directs a class switch from μ to $\gamma2b$ production as indicated and described in the text. Germline transcription through other constant regions in response to treatment with mitogens or lymphokines could similarly target switching to those constant regions (see text).

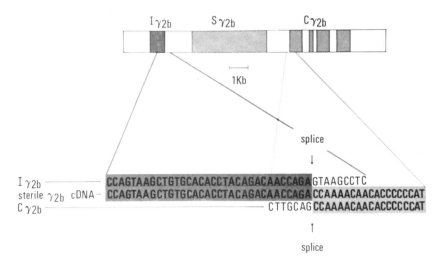

FIGURE 4B. The structure of the germline γ2b transcript is diagrammed; see reference 37 for details.

C Epsilon Probe

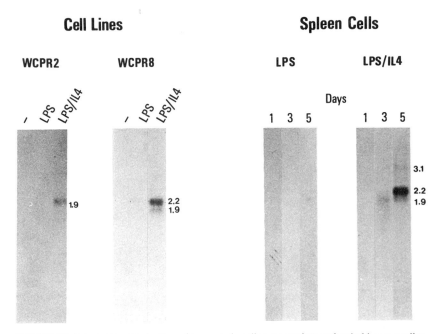

FIGURE 4C. Interleukin-4 induction of truncated epsilon transcripts and switching to epsilon. The cell lines were derived as described in the text and treated with LPS or IL-4 as described in reference 39. Normal spleen cells were also treated with LPS or LPS plus IL-4 for the indicated number of days as previously described.[39] Total RNA was prepared and assayed by Northern blotting for hybridization to a C_ε-specific probe. The 1.9-kb transcript is the putative germline transcript and the 2.2-kb transcript is the normal epsilon mRNA.

γ2b production in pre-B cell lines is correlated with specific transcription of the germline γ2b locus[36,37]; these transcripts initiate from multiple sites that lie several kilobases upstream of the γ2b switch region, and the primary transcript is terminated at the normal site downstream of the γ2b gene[37] (FIG. 4B). This primary transcript is processed to yield a polyadenylated "sterile γ2b" RNA sequence that has a small upstream exon attached to the body of the C region (FIG. 4B). The transcript does not appear capable of encoding protein. We and others previously proposed that this transcription may reflect a specific increase in the accessibility of a specific constant region locus to switch-recombination enzymes[36,38] (FIG. 4A), targeting pre-B cells to switch to γ2b production; the apparent lack of coding potential for these transcripts is again consistent with a direct role for transcription in the process.

The association of germline $C_{\gamma 2b}$ transcription in pre-B cells and preferential class-switching raised the intriguing possibility that a transcriptional (and recombinational) element active in pre-B cells is located near the $C_{\gamma 2b}$ locus. This possibility also suggests that mitogen and lymphokine-mediated class-switch events could be directed to a specific isotype by a similar mechanism. Treatment of splenic lymphocytes with the B-cell mitogen bacterial lipopolysaccharide induces B cells to mature into secreting cells, many of which have switched to the production of γ2b or γ3.[10] However, treatment of spleen cells with LPS plus interleukin-4 (IL-4) abrogates switching to these isotypes and results in predominant switching to γ1 and ε constant regions.[10] To test the predictions of the regulated switching model, we tested the effect of LPS and IL-4 on germline γ2b expression in A-MuLV transformed pre-B cells and in splenic lymphocytes.[39] LPS treatment of A-MuLV transformants rapidly induced the production of germline γ2b transcripts; nuclear run-on assays indicated that this induction occurred, at least in large part, at the transcriptional level.[39] Similarly, LPS treatment of splenic lymphocytes induced germline γ2b transcripts in these cells. In both pre-B lines and normal spleen cells, induction of the germline transcripts was followed by switching to those isotypes, suggesting a cause and effect relationship.[39] Strikingly, treatment with LPS plus IL-4 resulted in the complete abrogation of the induction of germline γ2b transcripts; in parallel, switching to γ2b was also abrogated. We have also defined a sterile γ3 transcript analogous in structure to the γ2b transcript. Treatment of certain A-MuLV transformant or spleen cells induces sterile γ3 transcription, which is also followed by switching to this isotype (not shown).

As previously described, LPS plus IL-4-treated cells switch to γ1 and ε. We have most recently defined a germline ε transcript. A prediction of the regulated switching model is that LPS plus IL-4 treatment should induce germline ε (and γ1) transcripts followed by switching to those isotypes. We tested this prediction in two ways. First, we derived A-MuLV transformed pre-B cells by A-MuLV infection of adult marrow cells propagated in the presence of IL-4; we did this to attempt to derive an IL-4 responsive A-MuLV transformant because many of the existing A-MuLV transformants had low levels of IL-4 receptors. Subsequently, we tested two such A-MuLV transformants for germline constant region gene transcription after IL-4 and/or LPS treatment (FIG. 4C). LPS alone induced γ2b as previously described and had no effect on ε expression (FIG. 4C), but IL-4 plus LPS specifically induced ε transcripts in such lines, including a 1.9-kb putative germline transcript in both lines and a mature ε mRNA (as a result of a switch) in the other (FIG. 4C, right). In addition, IL-4 plus LPS treatment of normal spleen cells induced first truncated (putative germline) ε transcripts by day 3 of treatment and subsequently normal ε mRNA transcripts by day 5 (FIG. 4B, left). These kinetics were similar to those of sterile and normal γ2b induction in spleen cells induced by LPS alone,[38] again suggesting a cause and effect relationship.

Our results support a model in which regulatory elements, under the control of different trans-acting factors, may be associated with the various C_H regions; differential activation of these elements (by treatment with lymphokines and mitogens) may allow a single-switch-recombinase to differentially perform isotype-specific switches. Thus, the distinct recombinational systems in lymphocytes that perform variable region gene assembly and H-chain class switching may both be directed by the "accessibility" of their substrate gene segments. In heavy chain class switching, the recombination event appears to be directed in specificity by treatment of cells with external agents. To our knowledge, this is the first potential example of such a phenomenon.

SUMMARY

Our recent studies have focused on the organization of immunoglobulin genes in mice and humans and the mechanism and control of the recombination events that are involved in their assembly and expression. This report describes our progress in this area with particular focus on elucidating factors that influence the generation of the antibody repertoire in normal and diseased states. We present a detailed analysis of the organization of the human V_H locus, studies that help to elucidate the nature of the recombination defect in mice with severe combined immunodeficiency, and studies of transgenic mice that focus on the mechanism that regulates tissue-specific variable region gene assembly. In addition, we also characterize mechanisms that control the heavy chain class-switch process. Although the latter process apparently involves a recombination system distinct from that involved in variable region assembly, we find that the two recombination events appear to be controlled by similar mechanisms.

ACKNOWLEDGMENTS

We would like to gratefully acknowledge the efforts of our collaborators: V_H organization—Charles Cantor, Cassandra Smith, and Urvashi Surti; SCID studies—Gabrielle Fulop and Robert Philips; transgenic studies—Bernie Krippl, Alistar Winoto, Lee Hood, and Frank Costantini; and class-switch studies—Yvonne Rosenberg and Bob Coffman.

REFERENCES

1. TONEGAWA, S. 1983. Somatic generation of antibody diversity. Nature 302: 575.
2. ALT, F. W., T. K. BLACKWELL & G. D. YANCOPOULOS. 1987. Development of the primary antibody repertoire. Science 238: 1079–1087.
3. KRONENBERG, M., G. SIU, L. HOOD & N. SHASTRI. 1986. The molecular genetics of the T-cell antigen receptor and T-cell antigen recognition, Ann. Rev. Immunol., 4: 529.
4. ALT, F. W., T. K. BLACKWELL, R. D. DE PINHO, M. G. RETH & G. D. YANCOPOULOS. 1986. Regulation of genome rearrangement events during lymphocyte differentiation. Immunol. Rev. 89: 5.
5. ALT, F. W., G. YANCOPOULOS, K. BLACKWELL, M. BOSS, E. THOMAS, R. COFFMAN, N. ROSENBERG, C. WOOD, S. TONEGAWA & D. BALTIMORE. 1984. Ordered rearrangement of Ig heavy chain variable region gene segments. EMBO J. 3: 1209–1219.
6. RETH, M., E. PETRAC, P. WIESE, L. LOBEL & F. W. ALT. 1987. Activation of $V\kappa$ gene rearrangement in pre-B cells follows the expression of membrane-bound immunoglobulin heavy chains. EMBO J. 6: 3299–3305.
7. KINCADE, P. W. 1987. Experimental models for understanding B lymphocyte formation. Adv. Immunol. 41: 181.

8. SHIMIZU, A. & T. HONJO. 1984. Immunoglobulin class switching. Cell **36**: 801–803.
9. OTT, D. E., F. W. ALT & K. B. MARCU. 1987. Immunoglobulin heavy chain switch region recombination within a retroviral vector in murine pre-B cells. EMBO J. **6**: 577.
10. PAUL, W. E. & J. OHARA. 1987. B-cell stimulatory factor-1/interleukin 4[1]. Ann. Rev. Immunol. **5**: 429–459.
11. WINTER, E., U. KRAWINKEL & A. RADBRUCH. 1987. Directed Ig class switch recombination in activated murine B cells. EMBO J. **6**: 1663.
12. BRODEUR, P., M. A. THOMPSON & R. RIBLETT. 1984. The content and organization of mouse IgH-V families. *In* Regulation of the Immune System, UCLA Symposia on Molecular and Cellular Biology, New Series, Vol. 18: 445. Alan R. Liss, New York.
13. LIVANT, D., C. BLATT & L. HOOD. 1986. One heavy chain variable region gene segment subfamily in the BALB/c mouse contains 500–1000 or more members. Cell **47**: 461.
14. MORROW, M. & F. ALT. In preparation.
15. BERMAN, J., S. MELLIS, R. POLLOCK, C. SMITH, U. SURTI, L. CHESS, C. CANTOR & F. ALT. 1988. Structure and organization of the human V_H locus: Linkage of the C_H and V_H regions. EMBO **7**: 727–738.
16. RAVETCH, J. V., U. SIEBENLIST, S. KORSMEYER, T. WALDMANN & P. LEDER. 1981. Structure of the human immunoglobulin μ locus: Characterization of embryonic and rearranged J and D genes. Cell **27**: 583.
17. GIVOL, D., R. ZAKUT, K. EFFRON, G. RECHAVI, D. RAM & J. B. COHEN. 1981. Diversity of germline immunoglobulin V_H genes. Nature **292**: 426.
18. KODAIRA, M., T. KINASHI, I. UMEMURA, F. MATSUDA, T. NOMA, Y. ONO & T. HONJO. 1986. Organization and evolution of variable region genes of the human immunoglobulin heavy chain, J. Mol. Biol. **190**: 529.
19. KODAIRA, M., T. KINASHI, I. UMEMURA, F. MATSUDA, T. NOMA, Y. ONO & T. HONJO. 1986. Organization and evolution of variable region genes of the human immunoglobulin heavy chain. J. Mol. Biol. **190**: 529–541.
20. SHEN, A., C. HUMPHRIES, P. W. TUCKER & F. R. BLATTNER. 1987. Proc. Natl. Acad. Sci. USA. Human heavy-chain variable region gene family non-randomly rearranged in familial chronic lymphocytic leukemia. **84**: 8563–8567.
21. MALYNN, B., J. BERMAN, G. D. YANCOPOULOS, C. A. BONA & F. W. ALT. 1987. Expression of the immunoglobulin heavy chain variable gene repertoire. Curr. Top. Microbiol. Immunol. **135**: 75–94.
22. YANCOPOULOS, G., B. MALYNN & F. ALT. 1988. Development-stage and strain-specific V_H gene repertoires. J Exp. Med. **168**: 417–435.
23. BERMAN, J. & F. ALT. Biased utilization of human V_H gene segments in primary differentiation organs. In preparation.
24. RAJEWSKY, K., I. FORSTER & A. CUMANO. Evolutionary and somatic selection of the antibody repertoire in the mouse. Science **238**: 1088–1094.
25. HOLMBERG, D. *et al.* 1986. The high idiotypic connectivity of "natural" newborn antibodies is not found in adult mitogen-reactive B-cell repertoires. Eur. J. Immunol. **16**: 82.
26. PAINTER, C., M. MONESTIER, B. BONIN & C. BONA. 1986. Functional and molecular studies of V genes expressed in autoantibodies. Immunol. Rev. **94**: 75–98.
27. SCHULER, W., I. J. WEILER, A. SCHULER, R. A. PHILLIPS, N. ROSENBERG, T. MAK, J. F. KEARNEY, R. P. PERRY & M. J. BOSMA. 1986. Rearrangement of antigen receptor genes is defective in mice with severe combined immune deficiency. Cell **46**: 963–972.
28. FULOP, G. M., G. C. BOSMA, M. J. BOSMA & R. A. PHILLIPS. 1987. Early B-cell precursors in Scid mice. Normal number of cells transformable with Abelson murine leukemia virus (A-MuLv). Cell. Immunol. **113**: 192–201.
29. MALYNN, B. A., T. K. BLACKWELL, G. M. FULOP, G. A. RATHBUN, A. J. W. FURLEY, P. FERRIER, L. B. HEINKE, R. A. PHILLIPS, G. D. YANCOPOULOS, & F. W. ALT. 1988. The SCID defect affects the final step of the immunoglobulin VDJ recombinase mechanism. Cell **54**: 453–460.
30. RETH, M. G., S. JACKSON & F. W. ALT. 1986. $V_H DJ_H$ formation and DJ_H replacement during pre-B differentiation: Non-random usage of gene segments. EMBO J. **5**: 2131.
31. ALT, F. W. & D. BALTIMORE. 1982. Joining of immunoglobulin heavy chain gene segments, implications from a chromosome with evidence of three D-J_H fusions, Proc. Natl. Acad. Sci. USA **79**: 4118.

32. BAKHSHI, A., J. J. WRIGHT, W. GRANINGER, M. SETO, J. OWENS, J. COSSMAN, J. P. JENSEN, P. GOLDMAN & S. J. KORSMEYER. 1987. Mechanism of the t(14;18) chromosomal translocation: Structural analysis of both derivative 14 and 18 reciprocal partners. Proc. Natl. Acad. Sci. USA **84:** 2396–2400.
33. ALT, F. W., V. ENEA, A. L. M. BOTHWELL & D. BALTIMORE. 1979. Probes for specific mRNAs by subtractive hybridization; anomalous expression of immunoglobulin genes. *In* Eukaryotic Gene Regulation. R. Axel, T. Maniatis & C. F. Fox, Eds. Academic Press, New York.
34. BLACKWELL, T. K., M. W. MOORE, G. D. YANCOPOULOS, H. SUH, S. LUTZKER, E. SELSING & F. W. ALT. 1986. Nature **324:** 585–589.
35. FERRIER, P., B. KRIPPL, A. FURLEY, A. WINOTO, H. SUH, L. HOOD, F. COSTANTINI & F. ALT. Tissue and lineage-specific rearrangement of T cell receptor variable region gene segments introduced into the germline of transgenic mice. In preparation.
36. YANCOPOULOS, G. D., R. A. DEPINHO, K. A. ZIMMERMAN, S. G. LUTZKER, N. ROSENBERG & F. W. ALT. 1986. Secondary genomic rearrangement events in pre-B cells: $V_H DJ_H$ replacement by a LINE-1 sequence and directed class switching, EMBO J. **5:** 3259.
37. LUTZKER, S. & F. W. ALT. 1988. Structure and expression of germline gamma 2b constant region. Mol. Cell Biol. **8:** 1849–1852.
38. STAVNEZER-NORDGREN, J. & S. SIRLIN. 1986. Specificity of immunoglobulin heavy chain class switch correlates with activity of germline heavy chain genes prior to switching. EMBO J. **5:** 95.
39. LUTZKER, S., P. ROTHMAN, R. POLLOCK, R. COFFMAN & F. ALT. 1988. Mitogen- and IL-4 regulated expression of germ-line Ig γ2b transcripts: Evidence for directed heavy chain class switching. Cell **53:** 177–184.

Transcriptional and Processing-Level Control of Immunoglobulin Gene Expression

ROBERT P. PERRY, MICHAEL L. ATCHISON,
DAWN E. KELLEY, AND MARTHA L. PETERSON

Institute for Cancer Research
Fox Chase Cancer Center
Philadelphia, Pennsylvania 19111

The regulation of immunoglobulin gene expression during B-lymphocyte development occurs at various levels. Transcriptional control is responsible for the tissue specificity and sequential activation of heavy and light chain genes, whereas alternative processing of RNA is used to determine the relative production of the membrane and secreted forms of heavy chain. Our laboratory is attempting to elucidate the molecular mechanisms of these regulatory phenomena. In particular we have studied the requirements for establishment and maintenance of transcriptional competence at the κ light chain locus and have investigated the role of cleavage/polyadenylation and splicing in the processing-level regulation of μ mRNA synthesis. The following is a brief summary of our recent findings.

ROLE OF THE κ ENHANCER AND CHROMATIN RESTRUCTURING IN THE DEVELOPMENTAL REGULATION OF κ GENE EXPRESSION

The importance of enhancer elements in transcriptional regulation of eukaryotic genes is well established; however, the mechanism by which these elements exert their effect is still poorly understood. There is abundant evidence demonstrating that enhancer function is required for efficient transcription of transfected immunoglobulin genes.[1] Thus, it was surprising to find that endogenous immunoglobulin genes continue to be transcribed in plasmacytoma cells when their enhancers are deleted[2-4] or are rendered nonfunctional by the loss of a critical nuclear protein factor.[5] These findings led to the idea that the immunoglobulin enhancers are essential in establishing transcriptional competence but not in maintaining the activity of constitutively transcribed genes.

According to this view of enhancer function, the activity of the Igκ enhancer should be crucial during the pre-B to B-cell transition when cells shift from heavy chain expression only to expression of both heavy and light chains. In fact, the enhancer may serve not only to establish transcriptional competence at the κ locus, but also to render the J_κ–C_κ region accessible to the DNA recombinases that catalyze Igκ gene rearrangements. Direct evidence implicating the enhancer in the developmental activation of the κ locus was provided by studies of its role in mediating lipopolysaccharide (LPS)-induced precocious κ transcription in a variety of pre-B cell lines.[5-7] This inductive effect, which can occur in the absence of protein synthesis, renders the nuclear protein NF-κB capable of binding to, and activating, the κ enhancer.[5,8] After transcription is established at the κ locus, the importance of the κ enhancer would presumably diminish during further maturation of the B lymphocyte.

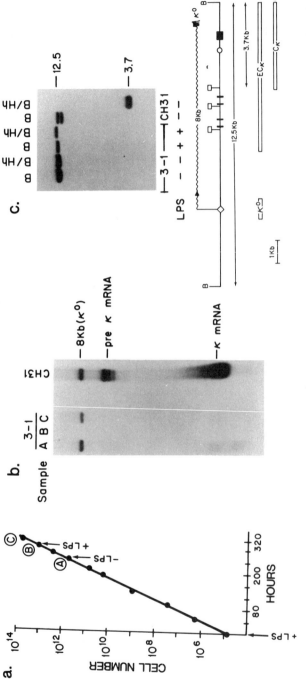

FIGURE 1. Analysis of κ RNA transcripts and methylation status of κ loci in an LPS-treated pre-B cell line (3-1) and B-cell lymphoma cells (CH31). (a) Growth curve of a culture of 3-1 cells maintained for 2 weeks at a concentration of 6×10^4 to 1.8×10^6 cells/ml by periodic dilutions. Except for the period between 238 and 282 hours, the medium contained LPS at a concentration of 10 μg/ml. A, B, and C indicate the times at which samples of cells were harvested for RNA and DNA analyses. (b) Northern blot of 5 μg poly(A)⁺ RNA from 3-1 cells harvested at times A, B, and C and 0.5 μg poly(A)⁺ RNA from CH31 cells, probed with the EC_κ fragment. The positions of the 8-kb κ^0 transcripts and the products of the CH31 κ^+ allele are indicated at the left; from CH31 cells. (c) Southern blot of DNA from uninduced 3-1 cells (−); from LPS-treated 3-1 cells harvested at point A (+); and from CH31 cells. DNA was digested with *Bam*HI (B) or *Bam*HI and *Hha*I (B/Hh) and probed with the C_κ fragment. The diagram below depicts the κ^0 locus with J_κ and C_κ exons as *solid bars*, the promoter as a *diamond*, the enhancer as a *circle*, and the κ^0 transcript as a *wavy line*. The *Hha*I sites are denoted by □ symbols and the probe fragments shown as rectangular bars. Resistance of the 12.5-kb *Bam*HI fragment to *Hha*I digestion indicates that each of the three *Hha*I sites is fully methylated; when these sites are entirely unmethylated, the *Bam*HI/*Hha*I digest yields a 3.7-kb fragment when analyzed with the C_κ probe.

What is the mechanism by which Ig enhancers become increasingly superfluous as B-lymphocyte maturation proceeds? One possibility is that the enhancer function is superseded by developmentally controlled structural alterations of the Ig genes. Indeed, a comparison of constitutively expressed and LPS-induced κ genes indicated that such an alteration might include a propensity for hypomethylation.[6,7] These observations also indicated that enhancer activation alone might not be sufficient to engender an altered methylation pattern, suggesting that the coupling of such structural alterations to enhancer activity might itself be a developmentally regulated phenomenon.

To gain a deeper understanding of these relationships, we introduced unmethylated κ genes into cells characteristic of early and late developmental stages and compared their expression and methylation status with that of the endogenous κ genes under defined conditions of κ enhancer function.[9] We observed that the endogenous κ locus in a pre-B cell chronically exposed to LPS remains fully methylated and dependent on enhancer function for its transcriptional activity even after it has been maintained in a transcriptionally active state for over 20 successive cell doublings (FIG. 1). Furthermore, this property was also manifested by transfected κ genes that were stably integrated into the pre-B cell genomes and that exhibited LPS inducible (enhancer-dependent) transcription. In contrast, the transcriptionally active endogenous κ genes in B cells and plasma cells are invariably hypomethylated[6,10] (FIG. 1). Moreover, stably transfected κ genes do not become methylated in these cells unless their enhancer is rendered nugatory by a lack of NF-κB.

These results are incorporated in the model depicted in FIGURE 2. In pre-B cell lines the unrearranged endogenous κ genes (κ^0) tend to be fully methylated and transcriptionally silent. These characteristics can also be acquired by initially unmethylated rearranged κ genes (κ^+) that are transfected into the cells and integrated at neutral chromosomal loci. In these cells the κ enhancer element is essentially nonfunctional because of the lack of a critical *trans*-acting factor NF-κB, whereas the factors necessary for proper functioning of the κ promoters are not limiting.[5] NF-κB becomes available when these cells are treated with various agents such as LPS or phorbol ester, which are believed to activate a posttranslational modification system—possibly protein kinase C—that converts an inactive form of the factor (NF-κB*) to a form with appropriate enhancer-binding properties.[5,8] Thus, transcription of both endogenous and exogenous κ genes is induced when the cells are exposed to LPS. These genes remain fully methylated despite their transcriptionally active state; moreover, they remain continuously dependent on NF-κB, as evidenced by the rapid cessation of transcription when LPS is withdrawn. Clearly, in these pre-B cells, enhancer-mediated transcriptional activity per se is not sufficient to cause hypomethylation of the κ gene.

In B-cell lymphomas, plasmacytomas, and hybridomas, the endogenous κ genes are generally hypomethylated and constitutively transcribed, irrespective of their rearrangement status [κ^+ or κ^- (nonproductively rearranged) or κ^0]. Furthermore, when exogenous κ^+ genes are transfected into such cells, they acquire these characteristics, provided the cell is permissive for the κ enhancer function, which presumably establishes their transcriptional competence. In a variant plasmacytoma cell that lacks NF-κB, the transcriptionally active endogenous κ genes are entirely unmethylated, whereas an inert transfected κ^+ gene becomes largely methylated at the very same set of restriction sites. It therefore appears that the linkage of hypomethylation to enhancer-dependent activation of κ transcription develops during the pre-B to B-cell transition. This property, together with associated changes in the chromatin structure of the κ locus,[11] may be sufficient to render the enhancer function dispensable or at least considerably less important for the maintenance of the transcriptionally active state. In general terms, this model implies that heritable alterations of methylation pattern and chromatin structure at a particular developmental stage can supersede the function of a regulatory element that was critical for expression at an earlier stage.

DEVELOPMENTALLY REGULATED PROCESSING OF IMMUNOGLOBULIN mRNA

The mRNAs encoding the membrane-associated (μ_m) and secreted (μ_s) forms of μ heavy chain are derived from transcripts of the same gene by differential RNA processing. The mode of processing is developmentally regulated, so that μ_m mRNA is predominant in pre-B and B cells, whereas μ_s mRNA production is heavily favored in

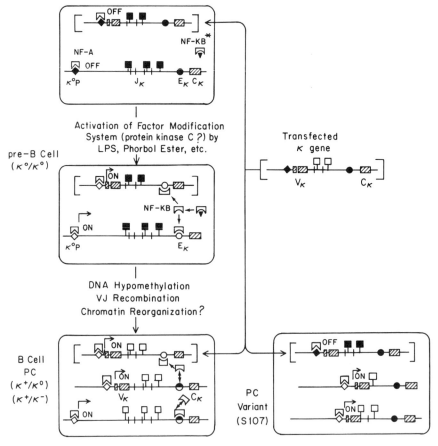

FIGURE 2. Model for the developmental regulation of κ gene expression and the predicted fate of a transfected κ^+ gene. Symbols for the transfected κ^+ gene (brackets) and the endogenous κ^0, κ^+, and κ^- alleles follow the conventions of the diagram in FIGURE 1c. Exons are *hatched boxes*. Inactive enhancer and promoter elements and methylated *Hha*I sites are designated by *filled symbols;* active elements and unmethylated sites by *open symbols.*

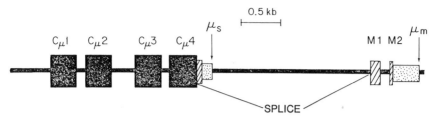

FIGURE 3. Diagram of the Cμ–μ_m region showing the possibility of competition between the splicing reaction that joins the Cμ4 and M1 exons and the cleavage reaction at the μ_s poly(A) addition site. The μ_s and μ_m cleavage/polyadenylation sites are marked with *vertical arrows*. The large *solid boxes* represent the gene segments that encode the four constant region domains common to both secreted and membrane forms of μ heavy chain. The *hatched* and *stippled* boxes, respectively, represent the tailpiece-encoding and 3′ untranslated regions of the μ_s and μ_m mRNAs.

IgM-secreting plasma cells. Regulation involves a choice between use of the μ_s poly(A) site versus splicing of the Cμ4 and M1 exons and use of the μ_m poly(A) site (FIG. 3). An initial series of transfection experiments with modified μ genes[12] clearly demonstrated that regulation is not the result of a stage-specific difference in the relative stability of the μ_m and μ_s mRNAs. We also observed that the relative production of μ_m and μ_s mRNA was very sensitive to the length of the Cμ4-M1 intron. Elongating this intron reduced the μ_m/μ_s ratio, whereas shortening it dramatically increased the μ_m/μ_s ratio. The effect of these substitutions and deletions was similar in both early and late-stage cells. These findings led us to propose that regulation involves a competition between cleavage/polyadenylation at the μ_s site and splicing of the Cμ4 and M1 exons, events that are mutually exclusive as far as μ mRNA production is concerned.

To help elucidate the basis for the developmental shift in competitive advantage, we carried out additional transfection experiments with genes in which the μ_s or μ_m poly(A) sites are replaced by various other poly(A) sites, whereas the splice junction sequences remain unperturbed. In one set of constructs (FIG. 4) we deleted a 313 nucleotide segment spanning the μ_s poly(A) site and inserted in its place fragments containing the μ_m or SV40-late or α_s poly(A) sites. The effects of these substitutions were basically the same in plasmacytomas and pre-B cells: the ratio of spliced (m) to cleaved (s) product was decreased by the μ_m and SV40 substitutions and increased by the α_s substitution. These effects were also observed when the poly(A) site substitutions were made in constructs containing a deletion that reduced the length of the Cμ4-M1 intron; in these cases the effects of the substitution and deletion on the m/s ratio were additive, indicating that the two types of perturbation act independently. Most importantly, the developmental regulation, defined as the difference in m/s production between pre-B cells and plasmacytomas, was achieved with the substituted poly(A) sites. This indicates that regulation does not depend on the recognition of some structural element unique to the μ_s region by a stage-specific processing factor. Rather, regulation may simply involve a general shift in overall cleavage/polyadenylation or splicing activity, the response being governed by the relative strengths of the signals that recognize critical constituents of the cleavage and splicing apparatus. Presumably, such strengths or affinities are ultimately determined by the sequence and conformational properties of the pre-mRNA. Our results indicate that the strengths of the substituted cleavage/poly(A) signals are in the order:

$$\mu_m \simeq \text{SV40-late} > \mu_s \gg \alpha_s.$$

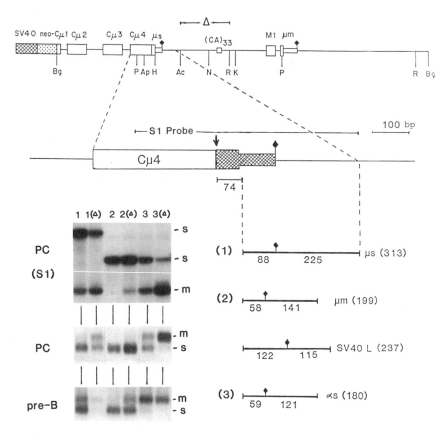

FIGURE 4. Effect of μ_s poly(A) site substitutions on the relative production of μ_s and μ_m mRNA. A previously described[12] recombinant plasmid, pSV5C$\mu_{s-m'}$, bearing a 6-kb segment of the μ constant region linked to an SV40-neo promoter (*top*) and a set of derivatives containing μ_s poly(A) site substitutions (*lower right*) with or without a deletion in the Cμ4-M1 intron (⊢Δ⊣) were transfected into S194 plasmacytoma cells (PC) or 3-1 pre-B cells (pre-B) and transient expression assayed by S1 nuclease protection and Northern blot analysis (*lower left*). The S1 nuclease probe (S1) consisted of a 610 nucleotide fragment spanning the 5' splice junction and the μ_s poly(A) site; the band corresponding to spliced product (m) is 223 nucleotides; those corresponding to cleaved products(s) are 410 nucleotides for the normal μ_s poly(A) site and 297 nucleotides (the limit of probe homology) for the substituted μ_m and α_s poly(A) sites. The Northern blots were probed with a fragment of SV40-neo sequence.[12] The *upper band* (m) is RNA that is spliced and terminated at the μ_m poly(A) site; the *lower band* (s) is RNA that is terminated at the μ_s or substituted poly(A) sites. *Lane 1:* the normal μ_s sites; *lanes 2 and 3:* the μ_s site replaced by the μ_m and α_s sites, respectively; *lanes 1 (Δ), 2 (Δ), and 3 (Δ):* the corresponding constructs also containing the intron deletion. The 5' splice junction is marked with a *vertical arrow* (↓); poly(A) sites by a *filled diamond* (♦); the numbers in *parentheses* and *below the lines* are segment distances in nucleotides; other symbols are described in reference 12.

As a further test of these ideas, we made a second set of constructs (FIG. 5) in which the μ_m poly(A) site was substituted by the μ_s or SV40-late or α_s poly(A) site. If regulation involves competition between cleavage/polyadenylation at the μ_s site and splicing of the Cμ4-M1 intron, altering the strength of the cleavage/poly(A) signal at the μ_m site should have little or no effect on the m/s ratio. This was in fact observed when constructs containing the μ_m site substitutions and either normal or shortened $C\mu4$-M1 introns were expressed in plasmacytomas. However, when these same constructs were expressed in pre-B cells, the yield of spliced product diminished as the strength of the μ_m site was reduced, although this diminution was not accompanied by a corresponding increase in μ_s mRNA. To account for this latter finding, we considered an additional possibility, namely, that transcripts from these constructs might be wasted (degraded without being processed to mRNA) when the cleavage/polyadenylation efficiency falls below a certain critical level. A diminished overall cleavage activity in pre-B cells coupled with the relatively weak strength of the μ_s or α_s poly(A) signal would presumably lower the efficiency sufficiently to engender this effect. For transcripts of native immunoglobulin genes, such wastage would be minimized by the stronger μ_m cleavage/polyadenylation signal and the possibility of splicing to the $C\delta1$ exon.

Our present model for μ_s versus μ_m regulation is depicted in FIGURE 6. According to this model, the overall cleavage/polyadenylation activity is relatively low in pre-B and B cells, thus permitting a high proportion of transcripts to pass through the comparatively weak μ_s cleavage/poly(A) signal without being cleaved. These transcripts can then undergo splicing of the $C\mu4$-M1 intron and cleavage/polyadenylation at the μ_m site. The temporal order of these two processing reactions is apparently variable, as indicated by our recent finding that pre-B and B cells contain nonpolyade-

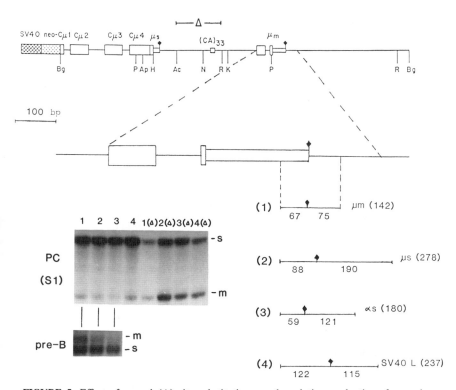

FIGURE 5. Effect of μ_m poly(A) site substitutions on the relative production of μ_s and μ_m mRNA. Experimental details and symbols are the same as in FIGURE 4. *Lane 1:* the normal μ_m site; *lanes 2–4:* the μ_m site replaced by the μ_s, α_s, and SV40-late poly(A) sites, respectively.

nylated, spliced intermediates [pre-$\mu_m(A^-)$] as well as unspliced, polyadenylated transcripts that are terminated at the μ_m site and subject to the same splicing versus cleavage option as are the original unprocessed transcripts [pre-$\mu_m/\mu_s(A^+)$]. An increase in the overall cleavage/polyadenylation activity in plasma cells would increase utilization of the μ_s poly(A) site and diminish the possibility of the competing reactions. This model resembles the "endase" model previously proposed by Blattner and Tucker[13] in that it involves a developmental change in overall cleavage/polyadenylation activity. However, in contrast to that model, we believe that the critical competition is between splicing and cleavage/polyadenylation rather than between cleavages at alternative poly(A) sites. The superior strength of the μ_m cleavage/

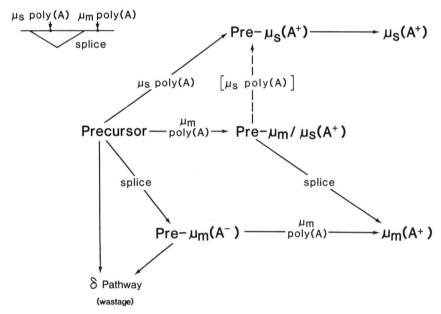

FIGURE 6. Model for the processing pathways regulating the production of μ_s and μ_m mRNA. See text for explanation.

poly(A) signal may be exploited to help regulate the commitment to the μ and δ mRNA pathways and to reduce potential wastage of pre-$\mu_m(A^-)$ components in early-stage lymphocytes.

REFERENCES

1. CALAME, K. L. 1985. Mechanisms that regulate immunoglobulin gene expression. Ann. Rev. Immunol. **3**: 159–195.
2. WABL, M. R. & P. D. BURROWS. 1984. Expression of immunoglobulin heavy chain at a high level in the absence of a proposed immunoglobulin enhancer element in *cis*. Proc. Natl. Acad. Sci. USA **81**: 2452–2455.
3. ZALLER, D. M. & L. A. ECKHARDT. 1985. Deletion of a B-cell-specific enhancer affects transfected, but not endogenous, immunoglobulin heavy-chain gene expression. Proc. Natl. Acad. Sci. USA **82**: 5088–5092.

4. KLEIN, S., F. SABLITZKY & A. RADBRUCH. 1984. Deletion of the IgH enhancer does not reduce immunoglobulin heavy chain production of a hybridoma IgD class switch variant. EMBO J. **3:** 2473–2476.
5. ATCHISON, M. L. & R. P. PERRY. 1986. Tandem kappa immunoglobulin promoters are equally active in the presence of the kappa enhancer: Implications for models of enhancer function. Cell **46:** 253–262.
6. NELSON, K. J., E. L. MATHER & R. P. PERRY. 1984. Lipopolysaccharide-induced transcription of the kappa immunoglobulin locus occurs on both alleles and is independent of methylation status. Nucl. Acids Res. **12:** 1911–1923.
7. NELSON, K. J., D. E. KELLEY & R. P. PERRY. 1985. Inducible transcription of the unrearranged κ constant region locus is a common feature of pre-B cells and does not require DNA or protein synthesis. Proc. Natl. Acad. Sci. USA **82:** 5305–5309.
8. SEN, R. & D. BALTIMORE. 1986. Inducibility of κ immunoglobulin enhancer-binding protein NF-κB by a posttranslational mechanism. Cell **47:** 921–928.
9. KELLEY, D. E., B. A. POLLOK, M. L. ATCHISON & R. P. PERRY. 1988. The coupling between enhancer activity and hypomethylation of κ immunoglobulin genes is developmentally regulated. Mol. Cell. Biol. **8:** 930–937.
10. MATHER, E. L. & R. P. PERRY. 1983. Methylation status and DNase I sensitivity of immunoglobulin genes: changes associated with rearrangement. Proc Natl. Acad. Sci. USA **80:** 4689–4693.
11. ROSE, S. M. & W. T. GARRARD. 1984. Differentiation-dependent chromatin alterations precede and accompany transcription of immunoglobulin light chain genes. J. Biol. Chem. **259:** 8534–8544.
12. PETERSON, M. L. & R. P. PERRY. 1986. Regulated production of μ_m and μ_s mRNA requires linkage of the poly(A) addition sites and is dependent on the length of the μ_s–μ_m intron. Proc. Natl. Acad. Sci. USA **83:** 8883–8887.
13. BLATTNER, F. R. & P. W. TUCKER. 1984. The molecular biology of immunoglobulin D. Nature **307:** 417–422.

Mechanism of Class Switching[a]

BARBARA K. BIRSHTEIN, DANIEL R. KATZENBERG,
ARI WEINREB, SANDRA GIANNINI, JONATHAN BARD,
CHARLES-FÉLIX CALVO, AND NANCY MARTINEZ

Department of Cell Biology
Albert Einstein College of Medicine
Bronx, New York 10461

The primary immune response is dominated by the expression of the IgM and IgD classes. The expression of these two classes is governed by differential RNA processing. With continued exposure to antigen and the influence of T cells, other isotypes, namely, IgG, IgE, and IgA, are produced, that is, heavy chain class switching occurs. Almost invariably, class switching is achieved through DNA rearrangement events that shift the heavy chain variable region, VDJ (V_H), from its position upstream of the most proximal C_H gene, $C\mu$, to a new site upstream of one of the other six heavy chain constant region genes. (For review, see reference 1.) This shift is suggested to occur either through a looping out-deletion mechanism or through unequal sister chromatid exchange. Both mechanisms account for the progressive loss of upstream C_H genes that is observed during the course of the switch event. However, in certain instances, upstream genes are not necessarily deleted and the relative 5'–3' order of C_H genes may be altered. For example, Honjo and colleagues[2] noted that MC101, an IgG1-producing myeloma, has evidence of a $\mu \rightarrow \alpha \rightarrow \gamma 1$ switch recombination. Similarly, Rajewsky and colleagues[3] described "back switches" in the MOPC 21 (IgG1, κ) (P3) myeloma cell line: $\gamma 1 \rightarrow \gamma 2b \rightarrow \gamma 1$. These observations are most easily explained through unequal sister chromatid exchange (USCE) occurring between heavy chain genes. Recently, Kipps and Herzenberg[4] detected a class switch that occurred through recombination between homologous chromosomes. Thus, at least three molecular mechanisms may account for class switch recombination in different systems. We have documented the action of USCE on immunoglobulin heavy chain genes in the MPC11 mouse myeloma cell line and characterized one exchange event and the DNA sequences that mediate it. These experiments will be discussed.

Many workers have investigated the DNA sequences involved in heavy chain class switching, with especial focus on the role of tandemly repeated segments of DNA, located 5' of each of the C_H genes, except for δ. These DNA segments comprise 1–3 kb of isotype-specific repeated elements. For example, the $C\mu$-associated tandem repeats are comprised solely of two pentamers: GAGCT and TGGGG. Other motifs include tandem arrays of unique 49-mers, with each motif isotype specific and potentially available for separate regulation, perhaps mediated through the action of T-cell factors.

In what was perhaps the first model system for heavy chain class switching in cultured cells, Preud'homme, Scharff, and Birshtein[5] observed IgG2b $\rightarrow$ IgG2a

[a]This work was supported by grants from the National Institutes of Health (AI13509, AI10702, and P30CA13330) and from the Irvington House Institute for Medical Research. B.K.B. is an Established Investigator of the American Heart Association. A.W. and D.R.K. were supported by training grant T3 2GM7288, from the National Institutes of Health, S.G. by 2T 32CA09173-13, C.F.C. by AI10702, and J.B. by Irvington House Fellowship 610-3543.

TABLE 1. Hybridomas Used in Mapping Study

Hybridoma	Heavy Chain Isotype	Antigen-Binding Specificity
AR 13	IgG2b	*p*-azophenylarsonate
RP 379	IgG2b	phosphorylcholine
RP 203	IgG2b	phosphorylcholine
RP 98	IgG2b	phosphorylcholine
RP 93	IgG2a	phosphorylcholine

switching in the MPC11 mouse myeloma cell line. A molecular description of the class switch rearrangement events in the laboratory[6] showed no role for tandem repeats in this process. Because this finding was contrary to observations in a variety of other systems, we studied the role of tandem repeats in heavy chain class switching in hybridomas, presupposing that the fusion process (with the myeloma fusion partner X63.653) has captured intact the switch event that occurred in the spleen of a normal mouse.

HEAVY CHAIN CLASS SWITCH RECOMBINATION

We studied five hybridomas that produce either IgG2b or IgG2a, as depicted in TABLE 1. Our strategy for defining the class switch rearrangement sites was through genomic Southern analysis, at least in part to avoid secondary rearrangements of Cμ-associated tandem repeats that are known to occur on cloning and propagation of these sequences in bacteria. The strategy is depicted in FIGURE 1. In a primary class switch rearrangement, sequences upstream of Cμ become associated with sequences upstream of Cγ2b (or Cγ2a). We studied the rearrangement through detection of non-germline restriction fragments that hybridize with both Cμ- and Cγ2b-associated probes. Detailed analysis of the rearrangement breakpoints was carried out through the use of several restriction digests and probes.

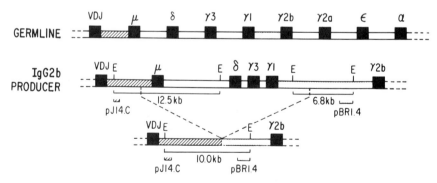

FIGURE 1. Strategy for mapping switch sites. In this schematic diagram, class switch recombination from IgM to IgG2b brings μ-derived sequences, indicated by *shading,* into juxtaposition with γ2b-derived sequences, depicted as *dotted.* Southern blot analysis using either a μ-derived (pJ14.C) or γ2b-derived (pBR1.4) probe shows loss of germline fragments and the appearance of a rearranged fragment. In a simple, direct class switch, the novel band detected is the same size with both probes.

FIGURE 2 shows eight maps of rearranged heavy chain genes from the five hybridomas. For RP98 and RP93, the single maps are necessarily the expressed chromosome. For AR13, RP379, and RP203, the assignment of the expressed map could not be made because both maps showed rearrangement to the same isotype, IgG2b. This observation is consistent with findings by Radbruch et al.[7] on lipopolysaccharide (LPS)-stimulated B cells and Hummel et al.[8] on hybridomas, in which rearrangement to the same isotype on both alleles was documented. Our data are consistent with either an isotype-specific recombinase, in this case γ2b-specific, that acts on both alleles, or a common recombinase whose accessibility to DNA sequences is governed by other, isotype-specific, mechanisms. For example, Stavnezer-Nordgren and Sirlin[9] and Yancopoulos et al.[10] documented transcripts of downstream genes before class switch rearrangement events to those genes. Transcripts are indicative of the "opening" of the DNA, which could be directed, perhaps, through the action of T-cell factors, such as IL-4 for IgG1 and IgE, or gamma-interferon for IgG2a.

For five of the eight maps, we detected DNA segments interposed between Cμ-associated and γ2b-associated sequences. In three of these instances we did not identify the origin of these DNA segments (although they are *not* derived from tandem repeats associated with γ3, γ1, γ2a, ε, or α). In two of the maps, AR13 and RP379, the interposed DNA sequences derive from γ1-associated tandem repeats. Consequently, AR13 and RP379 represent μ → γ1 → γ2b switch events. A limited number of other secondary switch events *in vivo* have been documented. These include the aforementioned MC101 (IgM → IgA → IgG1) and an IgE-producing hybridoma shown by

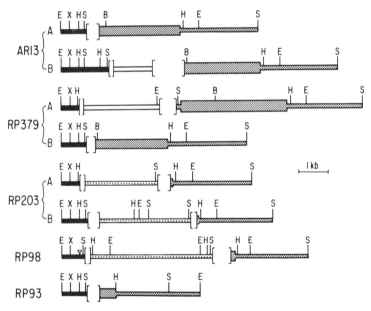

FIGURE 2. Maps of rearranged IgH loci in the hybridomas. Maps of the rearranged heavy chain loci in the five hybridomas. *Blackened regions* are derived from μ, *shaded regions* from γ2b or γ2a, *clear regions* from γ1, and *dotted regions* from an unknown source. *Bracketed regions* indicate the areas in which the switch sites lie. Tandem repeats are depicted as a *thicker segment.*

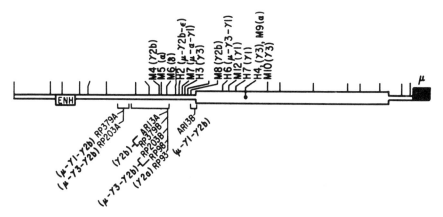

FIGURE 3. 5' Switch sites in the hybridomas and other systems. This figure, adapted from Katzenberg and Birshtein,[13] shows the location of the eight 5' breakpoints by brackets below the map. Switch sites in other model systems are indicated by bars above the map. An M or H marks the switch site in a myeloma or hybridoma, respectively, which occurred *in vivo*. Switches in cultured cells, either myelomas, hybridomas, lymphomas, or splenic blasts, are represented by unlabeled bars and are described in the text. Regions containing repeated pentamers are shown as *thicker* portions of the map.

Nikaido *et al.*[11] to have undergone IgM → IgG2b → IgE switch recombination, and an IgM → IgG3 → IgG1 switch in a hybridoma identified by Petrini *et al.*[12]

Interestingly, our characterization of switch recombination from IgG2b to IgG2a in the MPC11 cell line shows deletion of all γ2b-associated sequences. Thus, the IgG2b → IgG2a switch variants resemble direct IgM → IgG2a DNA switches with no evidence of their actual IgM → IgG2b → IgG2a lineage. These results imply that other switch recombination events that appear to be direct switches from μ may also result from subclass switch recombination. Together, these data suggest that subclass switching *in vivo* may occur at a significant frequency and should be taken into account when cellular regulation of isotype production is considered.

With respect to the original question on the role of tandem repeat sequences in mediating the recombination process, all 3' rearrangement breakpoints, with one exception, RP379, lie within γ2b- or γ2a-associated tandem repeats. However, the same is not true for the 5' breakpoints. FIGURE 3 shows that in the five hybridomas, the 5' rearrangement breakpoints lie upstream of and adjacent to μ-associated tandem repeats. 5' breakpoints for other switch recombination events that have occurred *in vivo* are named in this figure and show a similar trend. All exceptions, except one, produce either IgG3 or IgG1, the two isotypes immediately 3' to Cμ. Perhaps expression of IgG3 or IgG1 can occur during the process of a loss of μ-associated tandem repeats, but expression of downstream isotypes, such as IgG2b, IgG2a, IgE, and IgA, occurs through switch recombination outside the tandem repeat region.

A variety of model systems have been used to study the DNA sequences that mediate class switching. In addition to the study of hybridomas and myelomas that represent switches *in vivo*, several cultured cell systems have been used including the MPC11 system in our laboratory, Abelson-transformed pre-B cells, the I 29 lymphoma line that switches predominantly from IgM to IgA, and LPS-stimulated spleen cells. FIGURE 3 depicts the location of the 5' switch sites in these model systems. In efforts to consider generalization from these data, we noted that only lymphomas, that is, transformed immature B cells, have a majority of the 5' breakpoints within μ-associated tandem repeats, whereas switches in more mature cultured cells fall even further 5' than *in vivo* switches. The 5' breakpoints extend so far as to delete the heavy chain enhancer in a class switch variant of MPC11,[6] leading to the observation of Zaller and Eckhardt[14] that the expression of an endogenous gene is independent of the continued presence of the enhancer. Extension of these original observations implies that the enhancer element may act in the initiation of expression of the locus and therefore suggests that other sequences may be important in the maintenance of expression.

One can reflect on these data to propose three hypotheses. The first is that switch recombination commences within μ-associated tandem repeats, which are progressively deleted during further maturation of the cell, perhaps accompanied by further subclass and class switching. A second possibility is that the 5' breakpoints for switch recombination are qualitatively different in pre-B and more mature B cells, implying the action of two different recombinases. A third possibility is that class switches in more mature B cells require the initial loss of μ-associated tandem repeats. This idea is supported by experiments by Hurwitz and Cebra[15] that showed that in LPS-stimulated B cells, loss of μ-associated tandem repeats preceded class switching. In addition, the 18-81 pre-B cell line shows a deletion of μ-associated tandem repeats before the $\mu \rightarrow$ γ2b switch event repeatedly observed.

If loss of μ-associated tandem repeats precedes class switch rearrangement, one might suppose that this segment of DNA, through its specific motif, is involved in regulation of class switching, with its presence coupled to continued expression of $C\mu$, perhaps due to higher affinity for a necessary transcription factor. As loss of these sequences occurs, downstream regulatory sequences may bind the transcription factor, become activated, and set the stage for class switching.

UNEQUAL SISTER CHROMATID EXCHANGE

The heavy chain constant region cluster in BALB/c mice shows a single gene for each isotype. In the MPC11 cell line, there has been a tandem duplication of the Cγ2a gene on the expressed chromosome, postulated to occur through a USCE mechanism.[16] The duplicated γ2a genes in MPC11 undergo further USCE in variant heavy chain producers, that is, variants that make short heavy chains, hybrid γ2b-γ2a heavy chains, or γ2a class switches. A minimum of 60% of the variants show accompanying USCE, as evidenced by the reciprocal outcomes of either increased γ2a copy number (up to 5- to 10-fold) or loss of the non-germline γ2a gene form. It is the formal genetic evidence from the ongoing USCE events that lends further support to the argument that the same mechanism has led to the initial γ2a gene duplication in MPC11.

We have mapped the site of USCE through genomic Southern blot analysis, initially confining it to an 800-bp segment extending from a *Hind*III site 3' of Cγ2a to an *Eco*RI site that lies 3' of Cγ2b.[16] Recently, we determined the DNA sequences that mediate the USCE.[17] FIGURE 4 shows that about 30 bp 3' of the *Hind*III site present in γ2a-3' is a tract of TC and TG repeated dinucleotides. A similar motif is also located 3' of the Cγ2b gene (FIG. 5). With the exception of loops of 4, 7, 30, and 22 bp introduced into the γ2b 3' sequence, the two sequences are 95% identical.

Further genomic Southern analysis localized the USCE event to the region of repeated dinucleotides.[17] The tracts of dinucleotides are interesting in that they have been shown to be capable of assuming novel DNA conformations. For example, the TG dinucleotide tract represents alternating purine-pyrimidines and can assume the left-handed or Z conformation. The TC dinucleotide tract was shown to have a non-B, non-Z DNA conformation, termed H or triplex.[18]

One can estimate the size of the USCE joint if it were to derive from breaks at analogous positions in the two germline sequences and rejoining. However, the actual size of the USCE joint is 50 bp larger than the predicted size. To account for the extra DNA, we postulated a staggered DNA cut, as shown in FIGURE 5.

The USCE joint has been cloned and sequenced from an MPC11 variant that has amplified the γ2a genes (and the accompanying USCE joint) about four- to eightfold.

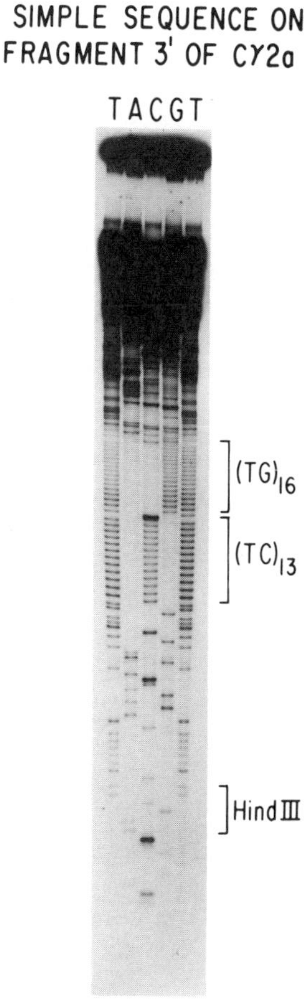

SIMPLE SEQUENCE ON
FRAGMENT 3' OF CY2a

FIGURE 4. Sequence of γ2a-3'. This autoradiogram of a sequencing gel of the germline region 3' to Cγ2a involved in the USCE shows the *Hind*III site along with the TC and TG dinucleotide repeats. Sequencing was performed by the dideoxy chain termination method.

As shown in FIGURE 6, the sequence of the USCE joint shows γ2a-3' sequences joined with γ2b-3' sequences through the TC dinucleotide stretches. However, these segments are not directly juxtaposed. Instead, a DNA segment of 64 bp, containing additional TC dinucleotides and two short DNA sequences of 6 and 8 bp, is interposed between the two donor sequences.

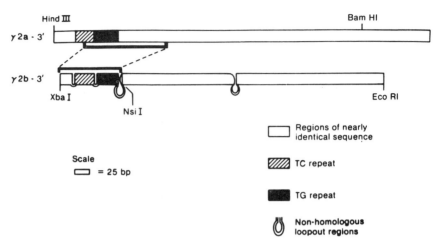

FIGURE 5. Schematic representation of the USCE germline sequences. Schematic diagram showing the sequence identity between fragments γ2a-3' and γ2b-3'. Loops 1, 2, 3, and 4 have sequence lengths of 4, 7, 36, and 22 bases, respectively. Southern blot analysis localized the USCE breakpoints to the regions in each sequence indicated by brackets, which show a "stagger" of approximately 50 bp.

The origin of the 64-bp tract is not known. It may possibly be a separately encoded piece of DNA not present in either γ2b-3' or γ2a-3' sequences. It may also represent expansion of TC dinucleotide sequences, as shown for similar, but not identical, short repeats in telomeres of Tetrahymena,[19] and "N" sequences as described in the VDJ joining events of V_H regions.[20] Both telomere expansion and N sequence interposition have been ascribed to individual terminal deoxynucleotidyl transferase enzymatic activities.

This is the first molecular description of a USCE event and to what degree it is a paradigm for such events is not known. Interestingly, TG dinucleotide repeats have been shown in the μ-δ intron, whereas TC repeats have been found in an intron within the δ gene itself.[21] Whether these repeats occur at a high frequency in the Ig cluster is not known.

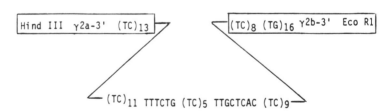

FIGURE 6. Schematic sequence of the USCE joint. The *top line* shows that γ2a-3' sequences are present from the *Hind*III site to the TC dinucleotide tract and that γ2b-3' sequences are present from the TC dinucleotide tract to the *Eco*RI site. The *bottom line* depicts the intervening 64 bp, of unknown origin. DNA sequence was determined by the chemical modification method.

SUMMARY

We have documented the action of unequal sister chromatid exchange on antibody genes, and our studies provide the first molecular description of an unequal sister chromatid exchange event.

We delineated the sequences that mediate class switch recombination in normal B cells through genomic Southern analysis of five IgG2-producing hybridomas. Successive subclass switching was documented in two of eight maps and may possibly account for interposed DNA in three additional maps, implying that subclass switching may be a relatively frequent occurrence in normal B cells. As in most other myelomas and hybridomas, the 5' breakpoint of switch recombination in our panel of hybridomas falls 5' to $C\mu$-associated tandem repeats, whereas the 3' breakpoint falls within $C\gamma$-associated tandem repeats. We consider various hypotheses in the text, the most interesting of which is that deletion of $C\mu$-associated tandem repeats is a necessary first step before class switch recombination in mature B cells. This hypothesis suggests that $C\mu$-associated tandem repeats may be a separately regulated DNA element.

REFERENCES

1. RADBRUCH, A., C. BURGER, S. KLEIN & W. MULLER. 1986. Control of immunoglobulin class switch recombination. Immunol. Rev. **89:** 69.
2. OBATA, M., T. KATAOKA, S. NAKAI, H. YAMAGISHI, N. TAKAHASHI, Y. YAMAWAKI-KATAOKA, T. NIKAIDO, A. SHIMIZU & T. HONJO. 1981. Structure of a rearranged γ1 chain gene and its implication to immunoglobulin class-switch mechanism. Proc. Natl. Acad. Sci. USA **78:** 2437.
3. BEYREUTHER, K., J. BOVENS, R. DILDROP, H. DORFF, T. GESKE, B. LIESEGANG, C. MULLER, M. S. NEUBERGER, A. RADBRUCH, K. RAJEWSKY, F. SABLITZKY, P. H. SCHREIER & S. ZAISS. 1981. Isolation and characterization of class switch variants of myeloma and hybridoma cells. *In* Immunoglobulin Idiotypes.: 229–244. Academic Press, New York.
4. KIPPS, T. J. & L. A. HERZENBERG. 1986. Homologous chromosome recombination generating immunoglobulin allotype and isotype switch variants. EMBO J **5:** 263.
5. PREUD'HOMME, J.-L., B. K. BIRSHTEIN & M. D. SCHARFF. 1975. Variants of a mouse myeloma cell line that synthesize immunoglobulin heavy chains having an altered serotype. Proc. Natl. Acad. Sci. USA **72:** 1427.
6. ECKHARDT, L. A. & B. K. BIRSHTEIN. 1985. Independent immunoglobulin class-switch events occurring in a single myeloma cell line. Mol. Cell. Biol. **5:** 856.
7. RADBRUCH, A., W. MULLER & K. RAJEWSKY. 1986. Class switch recombination is IgG1 specific on active and inactive IgH loci of IgG1-secreting B-cell blasts. Proc. Natl. Acad. Sci. USA **83:** 3954.
8. HUMMEL, M., J. K. BERRY & W. DUNNICK. 1987. Switch region content of hybridomas: The two spleen cell IgH loci tend to rearrange to the same isotype. J. Immunol. **138:** 3539.
9. STAVNEZER-NORDGREN, J. & S. SIRLIN. 1986. Specificity of immunoglobulin heavy chain switch correlates with activity of germline heavy chain genes prior to switching. EMBO J. **5:** 95.
10. YANCOPOULOS, G. D., R. A. DEPINHO, K. A. ZIMMERMAN, S. G. LUTZKER, N. ROSENBERG & F. W. ALT. 1986. Secondary genomic rearrangement events in pre-B cells: V_HDJH replacement by a LINE-1 sequence and directed class switching. EMBO J. **5:** 3259.
11. NIKAIDO, T., Y. YAMAWAKI-KATAOKA & T. HONJO. 1982. Nucleotide sequences of switch regions of immunoglobulin Cϵ and Cγ genes and their comparison. J. Biol. Chem. **257:** 7322.

12. PETRINI, J., B. SHELL, M. HUMMEL & W. DUNNICK. 1987. The immunoglobulin heavy chain switch: Structural features of γ1 recombinant regions. J. Immunol. **138**: 1940.
13. KATZENBERG, D. R. & B. K. BIRSHTEIN. 1988. Sites of switch recombination in IgG2b and IgG2a-producing hybridomas. J. Immunol. **140**: 3219.
14. ZALLER, D. M. & L. A. ECKHARDT. 1985. Deletion of a B-cell specific enhancer affects transfected, but not endogenous, immunoglobulin heavy-chain gene expression. Proc. Natl. Acad. Sci. USA **82**: 5088.14.
15. HURWITZ, J. L. & J. J. CEBRA. 1982. Rearrangements between the immunoglobulin heavy chain gene JH and Cμ regions accompany normal B lymphocyte differentiation in vitro. Nature **299**: 742.
16. TILLEY, S. A. & B. K. BIRSHTEIN. 1985. Unequal sister chromatid exchange: A mechanism affecting Ig gene arrangement and expression. J. Exp. Med. **162**: 675.
17. WEINREB, A., D. R. KATZENBERG, G. L. GILMORE & B. K. BIRSHTEIN. 1988. A site of unequal sister chromatid exchange contains a potential Z-DNA forming tract. Proc. Natl. Acad. Sci. USA **85**: 529.
18. LYAMICHEV, V. I., S. M. MIRKIN & M. D. FRANK-KAMENETSKII. 1985. A pH-dependent structural transition in the homopurine-homopyrimidine tract in superhelical DNA. J. Biomol. Struct. Dynamics **3**(2): 327.
19. GREIDER, C. W. & E. H. BLACKBURN. 1985. Identification of a specific telomere terminal transferase activity in Tetrahymena extracts. Cell **43**: 405.
20. ALT, F. W. & D. BALTIMORE. 1982. Joining of immunoglobulin heavy chain gene segments: Implications from a chromosome with evidence of three D-J$_H$ fusions. Proc. Natl. Acad. Sci. USA **79**: 4118.
21. RICHARDS, J. E., A. C. GILLIAM, A. SHEN, P. W. TUCKER & F. R. BLATTNER. 1983. Unusual sequences in the murine immunoglobulin μ-δ heavy-chain region. Nature **306**: 483.

Self-Nonself Discrimination
in the Immune System

A Broken Idiotypic Mirror[a]

J. URBAIN, F. ANDRIS, M. BRAIT, D. DE WIT,
F. MERTENS, AND F. WILLEMS

Laboratoire de Physiologie Animale
Département de Biologie Moléculaire
Université Libre de Bruxelles
Brussels, Belgium

Before a general theory of immunoregulation can be put forward, the research worker is faced with at least three major problems to solve. The first is understanding the mechanisms allowing self-nonself discrimination. A self-antigen (S) is one that is continuously present from the beginning and exposed to the immature immune system, whereas a foreign antigen is present only transiently and is usually absent when the immune system matures. Many persons term self-antigens all antigenic structures that are encoded by the individual's germline. However, no one knows, for example, if a ribosomal protein is considered a self-antigen by the immune system. Are some internal cellular constituents processed and continuously exposed on the cell membrane, as suggested by recent work?[1,2]

Until now, two major concepts have been used to explain natural tolerance. One theory holds that immature B cells (or T cells) are especially sensitive to negative signaling. Immature B lymphocytes are inactivated as soon as they encounter self-antigens. (For a review, see reference 3.) This "clonal anergy" of early B lymphocytes could be followed by activation of suppressor circuits that will allow maintenance of the "tolerant state."[4] In another theory, every B lymphocyte, whether immature or not, is paralyzable or inducible. Transduction of one signal, induced by antigen or antiidiotype, would lead to unresponsiveness, whereas the same signal associated with a second signal (cooperative help) would promote differentiation of the B lymphocyte.[5–8]

The exquisite sensitivity of immature B lymphocytes to negative signaling is well documented.[5,28] Some facts support the occurrence of suppressor circuits. Whatever the correct theory, the network theory seems to stand in sharp contradiction to the self-nonself discrimination phenomenon. The idiotype network rests on the assumption (which is demonstrated experimentally) that complementary partners (idiotypes and antiidiotypes) coexist within the repertoire of a single individual.[9–23] Therefore, as complementary lymphocytes emerge, they will cancel each other by virtue of self-recognition, leading to the paradox of the empty repertoire: diversity disappears as soon as it appears. Cohn[9,10] has repeatedly stressed that no network theory is possible because there is no way to distinguish a self-epitope from a self-idiotope. One goal of this report is to suggest that a network theory is possible on the basis of the self-nonself discrimination phenomenon.

The second problem of immunoregulation is the selection of actual and available

[a]This work was funded by contracts A.R.C. and CEE ST2J-0385-C (GDF).

repertoires. Before antigen arrival, the presence of so-called "natural immunoglobulins" must be explained. Do these natural immunoglobulins represent the constitutive synthesis of the total repertoire.[20,25,26] Are they synthesized by a special subset of B lymphocytes (Lyl subset)? These natural Ig are claimed to be polyspecific, autoreactive, and highly connected. Here we have a tautological problem, because being polyspecific, these immunoglobulins are autoreactive and highly connected.[20,25,26] The problem of the actual repertoire of "internally activated lymphocytes" is one of the most fundamental questions.[20]

As soon as the immune system is confronted with one antigen, the problem arises of the selection of available repertoires from a larger potential repertoire. In classical immunological thinking, it is often stated that this problem does not exist, because after establishment of self-nonself discrimination, the rest is due to clonal selection of the anti-nonself repertoire. On the basis of experimental data, we will argue that the selection of available repertoires is connected to both self-nonself discrimination and idiotypic circuitry.

The third problem of immunoregulation, which will only be touched here, is the regulation of ongoing responses or the dynamics of one immune response (understanding the increase and decrease of binding affinity, the isotype switching, the appearance of memory cells, the induction of suppressor circuits, and the like. (See reference 24 for discussion.) Before proposing a new network theory designed to explain self-nonself discrimination and the selection of available repertoires, we will describe some old and new findings that support the concept that idiotypic games are used by the immune system in the selection of available repertoires.

For years we have been investigating the selection of available repertoires and idiotypic choices using a tool called the idiotypic cascade.[29-36] In the initial experiments, we start with an idiotype "à la Oudin" (a private idiotype).[37,38] Then, conventional antiidiotypic antibodies are obtained (Ab2). These purified Ab2 are injected into normal naive recipients who, as a result, develop an Ab3 response. The major part of Ab3 antibodies share idiotypic specificities with Ab1, but they do not bind the antigen (subset id$^+$, ag$^-$). A small subset of Ab3 (Ab1') is strikingly similar to Ab1: they share idiotopes and bind antigen.

If the animals that have been immunized with Ab2 are subsequently challenged with antigen, the subset of Ab1' antibodies is largely expanded. Using the idiotypic cascade to probe potential repertoires, we demonstrated that it is possible to induce antibacterial or antiviral antibodies in rabbits or mice that have never seen either the bacteria or the virus.

A particularly striking experiment used a rabbit Ab2 directed against a private rabbit idiotype (antitobacco mosaic virus) (TMV). BALB/c mice dendritic cells were then pulsed *in vitro* with the rabbit Ab2, and these pulsed dendritic cells were injected into syngeneic mice that had never seen the virus, which synthesized Ab3 antibodies including anti-TMV antibodies. The treatment led to a striking priming effect: after the first virus injection, the antiidiotype-treated mice synthesized 300 g (average) of specific anti-TMV antibodies per milliliter (as compared with 10 g in the controls).[29]

The results of the idiotypic cascade can be explained in two ways that are not mutually exclusive: (1) The whole set of data can be interpreted in terms of double clonal selection: selection by antiidiotypic antibodies followed by antigenic selection. (2) Conversely the induction of third-order antibodies (Ab3) by Ab2 could suppress the internal auto-Ab2 and relieve the complementary Ab1 from suppression. In other words, the idiotypic cascade could interfere with the inner life of the immune system. This second interpretation not only is an idiotypic dream, but also is supported by some experimental data.

For example, we induced Ab3 antibodies in female rabbits by injecting them with an Ab2 directed against a private anti-*Micrococcus luteus* idiotype. These female rabbits were crossed with naive males. Two months after birth, offsprings, mothers, and fathers were immunized with *M. luteus*. All mothers responded by the synthesis of large amounts of Ab1' antibodies (id$^+$, ag$^+$) sharing idiotypic specificities with the starting private Ab1. The fathers produced unrelated anti-Micrococcus idiotypes. The surprising result was that half the offspring were synthesizing the same idiotype as were the mothers. These animals have assimilated "the learning" of the mother by being exposed to maternal Ab3 immunoglobulins. In this system, the interpretation cannot be simply clonal selection, because Ab3 (id$^+$ ag$^-$, id$^+$ ag$^+$, id$^-$ ag$^-$) cannot select Ab1.

The reverse experiment (crossing of Ab3 fathers with naive mothers) produced expected results: no idiotype cross-reaction was seen between the fathers, mothers, and offspring.[22] Similar results have been obtained by others.[3,36]

PRIVATE AND RECURRENT IDIOTYPES IN THE ARSONATE SYSTEM

The immune response Ars-KLH (arsonate coupled to hemocyanin) in mice from the A/J strain is characterized by a major recurrent idiotype whose code name is CRI A. (For a review see reference 14.) The molecular basis for this recurrent idiotype has been unraveled. During the primary response, the antiarsonate antibodies are characterized by the expression of a V-gene segment, VH id CR11, which can be associated with different D segments. As the response proceeds, the selection of a major canonical combination is observed: the recurrent idiotype, which is mainly associated with the heavy chain, is made up of the VH id CR11, the DF1 16.1, and the JH2 segments. (For details, see references 22, 28, 31, and 33.) Most other strains of mice, which belong to other IgH haplotypes, do not express this idiotype when immunized with the same antigen. Using a panel of monoclonal antiidiotypic antibodies and a panel of hybridoma, which are somatic variants of the germline combination, we were able to distinguish at least five idiotopes in the CRI A molecules.[18] For simplicity, we will not discuss the problem associated with the light chain. BALB/c mice immunized with Ars-KLH usually do not express appreciable amounts of this idiotype and do not harbor in their genome the VH id CR11 segment. F1 mice (A/J × BALB/c) express in a recurrent fashion the CRI A idiotype as well as the congenic mice CAL20. So at first sight the situation seems to be very simple. Either the relevant genetic segments are present and the idiotype is expressed or some genetic elements are absent and the idiotype is absent.[33] Recurrent expression of the CRI A idiotype could be due to clonal selection of the antigen of relevant precursors able "to sustain the generation of useful somatic variants."

However, the phenomenon of idiotypic recurrence is apparently more complex, because the idiotypic dominance of the CRI A idiotype is lost when irradiated A/J mice are repopulated with syngeneic bone marrow or spleen cells. This disappearance is also observed in long-term radiation chimeras or in partially shielded irradiated A/J mice. Detailed analysis of the response in immunized BALB/c mice (Willems *et al.,* in preparation) revealed that some mice (a small percentage) synthesize significant amounts of a strongly cross-reactive idiotype, which was designated CRI A-like. Four of five idiotopes were shared between CRI A and CRI A-like idiotypes.[34–36]

Furthermore, when BALB/c mice are pretreated with a polyclonal Ab2 directed against the CRI A idiotype and immunized with Ars-KLH, all BALB/c mice synthesized large amounts of antiarsonate antibodies characterized by CRI A-like idiotypic specificities. Thus, the CRI A-like idiotype is expressed as an idiotype "à la

Oudin" in BALB/c mice immunized with antigen alone and, as a recurrent idiotype, as a result of the idiotypic cascade.

Investigation of the molecular basis of CRI A-like idiotype 23 showed that the used V_H segment was very different from the VH segment of the CRI A: the V_H segment from CRI A-like molecules belongs to the V_H IX family. However, the D segment and the light chains are nearly identical in CRI A and CRI-like idiotypes.[35] We next turned our attention to recombinant inbred strains of mice AXC1, AXC2, and so forth. We will discuss only the data obtained from AXC1 mice, which harbor part of the V_H locus of BALB/c mice and the C_H locus of A/J mice. These AXC1 mice do not contain the V_H id CR11 gene segment used in the CRI A idiotype. When these mice are immunized with Ars-KLH alone, the CRI A-like idiotype, which is expressed as an idiotype "à la Oudin" in BALB/c mice, is now expressed in a recurrent fashion. This can be deduced from both serologic analysis and sequence analysis (using hybridomas from AXC1 mice). However, and this is the most significant fact suggesting that the selection of one available idiotype is not just a matter of antigenic selection, when F1 mice obtained from the cross between AXC1 and BALB/c mice are immunized with the same antigen (Ars-KLH), expression of the recurrent idiotype disappears. Results obtained in the backcross experiments clearly show that expression of this idiotype is under the control of genes that are unlinked to the Igh and IgK loci (Mertens *et al.*, submitted).

THE BROKEN MIRROR HYPOTHESIS

Let us consider the potential repertoire of one individual towards given epitope E. Epitope E is able to bind to Ig receptors of several idiotypic clones, designated Ab1a, Ab1b, Ab1c, ... Ab1i ... Ab1n. According to the network assumption,[39] and as a result of diversity, the repertoire of the same individual will contain complementary (or antiidiotypic) clones that we shall call Ab2a, ... Ab2i, ... Ab2n.[16,17]

With respect to antigens, Ab1 is considered the idiotype and Ab2 the antiidiotype. However, in the absence of antigen and for reasons of symmetry, we could say that Ab1 is the antiidiotype of Ab2 which is the idiotype of antigen X. Complementary partners (Ab1a and Ab2a, Ab1i and Ab2i, and the like) can be viewed as antagonistic. Ab1 suppresses Ab2, and Ab2 suppresses Ab1. The number of nonimmunoglobulin self-antigens (somatic self) is large; therefore, a significant fraction of the potential immune repertoire should be endowed with antiself specificity. Hence, some Ab1 and some Ab2 are often anti-S (antiinsulin, antihemoglobin, etc.) in addition to their idiotypic properties.

Let us suppose, for example, that Ab2i is antiself. The clones bearing antiself Ab2i receptors will be inactivated. As a result, the weight of suppression on Ab1i will be less than that on Ab1a, ... Ab1n. If antigen E is introduced, lymphocytes bearing Ab1i idiotypic receptors will escape suppression more easily than will clones Ab1a, Ab1b, and the like, still counteracted by those clones bearing Ab2a and Ab2b receptors.

Therefore, the idiotype Ab1i will tend to be a recurrent idiotype in one inbred strain of mice or a dominant idiotype in one individual from one outbred species, if the S antigen is polymorphic, within the species. In the beginning, everything is suppressed by virtue of symmetry. When the symmetry is broken by self-nonself discrimination, some clones escape suppression and determine the available repertoire. As such, the model explains why it is so difficult to induce syngeneic autoantiidiotypic antibodies (being antiself) or the results of the idiotypic cascade (the induction of Ab3 antibodies "knocks" down the complementary Ab2 and creates "blind spots" in the Ab2 repertoire). However, in this state, the model does not consider the distinction between self-epitopes (somatic self) and self-idiotopes (immunologic self). Furthermore, the network is represented in an oversimplified way by describing a collection of n pairs of complementary partners. There is no reason why one Ab1 should be connected to a single Ab2 and so on.

Let us imagine a developing immature immune system. It is important to realize that at this stage there is no endogenous synthesis of idiotypes (or antiidiotypes). With the exception of idiotopes present on maternal immunoglobulins or on immunoglobulins introduced by the research worker, the endogenous idiotopes are present only on membrane immunoglobulin receptors. We assume the functional inactivation of early B lymphocytes stems from the encounter with self-antigens that have been picked up by special presenting cells that we call self presenting cells (SPC). SPC could be immature normal antigen presenting cells (APC) or a special kind of cell whose main function is tolerance induction. Therefore, the immune system will not become tolerant to most idiotopes (except those of maternal immunoglobulins). These SPC can migrate to the thymus and present to T cells the total array of self-antigens that is accessible to B lymphocytes. Therefore, the library of developing B lymphocytes can be subdivided into two subsets. One subset does not meet self-antigens and will give rise to conventional B cells (BN). The other subset, as a result of SPC meeting, will be diverted from the normal differentiation pathway (BN). They will not die and will become long-lived lymphocytes unable to transform into normal antibody-producing cells (clonal anergy) but endowed with regulatory properties. We will call them BR (B regulatory lymphocytes).

The main function of these BR is to deliver positive signals of amplification to normal B lymphocytes, bearing receptors antiidiotypic to BR. Idiotypes, which will be favored in an immune response, are antiself antibodies. Ab1i will be favored because Ab2i is antiself. As the immune system matures, a first repertoire (antiself) is established. This repertoire is long-lived and will shape, by positive loops, the available repertoires to nonself-antigens. As such, the model has very precise implications: (a) "Tolerant" B lymphocytes are long-lived. Eventually they can be rescued and pushed to antibody secretion by LPS. (b) The induction of "anergy" in an antiself-lymphocyte is not due solely to the encounter of the lymphocyte with the self-antigen. This self-antigen must be on the surface of the SPC. (c) The somatic self and the immunologic self are treated the same way. Therefore, maternal idiotypes (or idiotypes introduced by the research worker at some critical period) should have dramatic effects in the shaping of available repertoires.

It is known that immature B lymphocytes are specially sensitive to tolerance induction, but the meeting of the B lymphocyte with the antigen is not sufficient to induce tolerance. For example, arsonate coupled to human immunoglobulin is an excellent tolerogen in neonatal mice, but arsonate coupled to mouse gammaglobulin is a very poor tolerogen in mice (De Wit *et al.,* in preparation).

Let us consider the case in which an immature immune system is exposed to maternal idiotypes. These maternal idiotypes will be treated as self-antigens (id S). The complementary lymphocytes bearing anti-id S (or Ab2) will be exposed to id S presented by SPC. As a result, B lymphocytes bearing Ab2 receptors will be transformed into B regulatory lymphocytes, favoring the emergence of complementary BN lymphocytes bearing anti-Ab2 or Ab1 receptors. Therefore, the young animal will have a tendency to produce the same idiotype as the mother, which makes sense in evolutionary terms. This is precisely the result we have shown in the experimental data just presented.[22,40,41]

The properties of regulatory B lymphocytes described herein look similar to properties exhibited by Lyl B lymphocytes[42,44] (long-lived, antiself-repertoires, regulatory properties, and so forth).[15] However, an alternative view is that these Lyl B lymphocytes represent a special lineage of B lymphocytes, expressing a special repertoire of great protective value to the individual.

This network model is very precise, is testable, and does not avoid the problem of self-nonself discrimination. Recent data from Dorf and his group[32] strongly support the idea of the existence of regulatory B lymphocytes helping complementary partners.

ACKNOWLEDGMENT

The authors are greatly indebted to L. Neirinckx and A. Tassin for typing the manuscript.

REFERENCES

1. CLAVERIE, J.-M. & P. KOURILSKY. 1986. The peptidic self model: A reassessment of the role of the major histocompatibility complex molecules in the restriction of the T cell response. Ann. Inst. Pasteur 137D: 425–442.
2. DE PLAEN, E., C. LURQUIN, A. VAN PEL, B. MARIAMÉ, J. P. SZIKORA, T. WÖLFEL, C. SIBILLE, P. CHOMEZ & T. BOON. 1988. Immunogenic (tum) variants of mouse tumor P815: Cloning of the gene of tum-antigen P91A and identification of the tum-mutation. Proc. Natl. Acad. Sci. USA 85: 2274–2278.
3. NOSSAL, G. 1983. Cellular mechanisms of immunologic tolerance. Ann. Rev. Immunol. 1: 33.
4. BRUYNS, C., URBAIN-VANSANTEN, C. PLANARD, C. DE VOS-CLOETENS & J. URBAIN. 1976. Ontogeny of mouse B lymphocytes and inactivation of antigen of early B lymphocytes. Proc. Natl. Acad. Sci. USA 73: 2462.
5. BRETSCHER, P. & M. COHN. 1970. A theory of non-self discrimination. Science 169: 1042–1049.
6. COHN, M. 1981. Conversation with Niels K. Jerne. Cell. Immunol. 61: 425–436.
7. COHN, M. 1985. Diversity in the immune system: Preconceived idea or ideas preconceived? Biochimie 67: 9–27.
8. COHN, M. 1986. The concept of functional idiotype network for immune regulation mocks all and comforts none. Ann. Immunol./Inst. Pasteur 137C: 57–100.
9. BONA, C., H. HEBER-KATZ & W. E. PAUL. 1981. Idiotype-antiidiotype regulation. I. Immunization with a levan-binding myeloma protein leads to the appearance of autoanti-(anti-Id) antibodies and to activation of silent j clones. J. Exp. Med. 153: 851–967.
10. CAZENAVE, P. A. 1977. Idiotypic-antiidiotypic regulation of antibody synthesis in rabbits. Proc. Natl. Acad. Sci. USA 74: 5122–5125.
11. JERNE, N. K. 1984. Idiotypic networks and other preconceived ideas. Immunol. Rev. 79: 1–29.
12. KEARNEY, J. F. & M. VAKIL. 1986. Functional idiotype networks during B cell ontogeny. Ann. Immunol. (Inst. Pasteur) 137C: 25–30.
13. SLAOUI, M., O. LEO, J. MARVEL, M. MOSER, J. HIERNAUX & J. URBAIN. 1984. Idiotypic analysis of potential and available repertoires in the arsonate system. J. Exp. Med. 160: 1–11.
14. TASIAUX, N., R. LEUWENKROON, C. BRUYNS & J. URBAIN. 1978. Possible occurrence and meaning of lymphocytes v bearing autoantiidiotypic receptors during the immune response. Eur. J. Immunol. 8: 464–468.
15. URBAIN, J., M. WIKLER, J.-D. FRANSSEN & C. COLLIGNON. 1977. Idiotypic regulation of the immune system by the induction of antibodies against antiidiotypic antibodies. Proc. Natl. Acad. Sci. USA 74: 5126.
16. URBAIN, J., P. A. CAZENAVE, M. WIKLER, J.-D. FRANSSEN, B. MARIAMÉ & O. LEO. 1980. Idiotypic induction and immune networks. In Immunology 80. J. Dausset & M. Fougereau, Eds. Academic Press, New York, NY.

17. URBAIN, J., C. WUILMART & P. A. CAZENAVE. 1981. Idiotypic networks in immune regulation. Contemp. Top. Molec. Immunol. **8:** 113.
18. URBAIN, J. 1986. Idiotypic networks: A noisy background or a breakthrough in immunological thinking: The broken mirror hypothesis. Ann. Immunol. (Inst. Pasteur) **137**C: 57–100.
19. UYTDEHAAG, F. & A. OSTERHAUS. 1986. Vaccines from monoclonal antiidiotypic antibody. Poliovirus infection as a model. Curr. Top. Microbiol. Immunol. **119:** 31.
20. VAZ, N. M., C. MARTINEZ & A. COUTHINO. 1984. The uniqueness and boundaries of the idiotypic self. *In* Idiotypy in Biology and Medicine. Köhler, ed.: 43–59.
21. WIKLER, M., J.-D. FRANSSEN, C. COLLIGNON, O. LEO, B. MARIAMÉ, P. VAN DE WALLE, D. DEGROOTE & J. URBAIN. 1979. Idiotypic regulation on the immune system. J. Exp. Med. **150:** 184–195.
22. WIKLER, M., C. DEMEUR, G. DEWASME & J. URBAIN. 1980. Immunoregulatory role of maternal idiotypes. Ontogeny of immune networks. J. Exp. Med. **152:** 1024.
23. WIKLER, M. & J. URBAIN. 1984. Idiotypic manipulations of the rabbit immune response against *Micrococcus luteus*. *In* Idiotypy in Biology and Medicine. : 219–241. Academic Press, New York.
24. KAUFMAN, M., R. THOMAS & J. URBAIN. 1985. Towards a logical analysis of the immune network. J. Theoret. Biol. **114:** 527.
25. DIGHIERO, G., P. LYMBERI, D. HOLMBERG, I. LUNDQUIST, A. COUNTINHO & S. AVRAMEAS. 1985. High frequency of natural autoantibodies in normal newborn-mice. J. Immunol. **134:** 765.
26. SOUROUSON, M., E. WHITE-SCHARF, J. SCHARTZ, M. GEFTER & R. SCHWARTZ. 1988. Preferential autoantibody reactivity of the preimmune B cell repertoire in normal mice. J. Immunol. **140:** 4173–4179.
27. LEO, O., M. SLAOUI, J. MARVEL, E. MILNER, J. HIERNAUX, M. MOSER, D. CAPRA & J. URBAIN. 1985. Idiotypic analysis of polyclonal and monoclonal anti-p-azophenylarsonate antibodies of Balb/c mice expressing the major cross-reactive idiotype of the A/J strain. J. Immunol. **134:** 1734.
28. SIEKEWITZ, M., M. GEFTER, P. BRODEUR, R. RIBLET & A. MARSHAK-ROTHSTEIN. 1982. The genetic basis of antibody production: The dominant anti-arsonate idiotype response of the strain-A mouse. Eur. J. Immunol. **12:** 1023.
29. FRANCOTTE, M. & J. URBAIN. 1984. Induction of anti-tobacco mosaic virus antibodies in mice by rabbit antiidiotypic antibodies. J. Exp. Med. **160:** 1485–1494.
30. ROTH, C., J. ROCCA-SERRA, G. SOMME, M. FOUGEREAU & J. THEZE. 1985. The gene repertoire of the GAT immune response: Comparison of the VK and D regions used by anti-GAT antibodies and monoclonal antibodies produced after antiidiotypic immunization. Proc. Natl. Acad. Sci. USA **82:** 4788–4792.
31. GURISH, M. F. & A. NISONOFF. 1984. Structural properties and genetic control of an idiotype associated with antibodies to the p-azophenylarsonate hapten. *In* Idiotypy in Biology and Medicine. H. Köhler, J. Urbain & P. A. Cazenave, Eds.: 63–88.
32. MANSER, T., S.-J. HUANG & M. GEFTER. 1984. The influence of clonal selection on the expression of immunoglobulin variable region genes. Science **226:** 1283.
33. RATHBUN, G., I. SANZ, K. MEEK, P. TUCKER & D. CAPRA. 1988. The molecular genetics of the arsonate idiotypic system of A/J mice. Adv. Immunol. **42:** 95.
34. MOSER, M., O. LEO, J. HIERNAUX & J. URBAIN. 1983. Idiotypic manipulation in mice: Balb/c can express the crossreactive idiotype of A/J mice. Proc. Natl. Acad. Sci. USA **80:** 4474–4479.
35. MEEK, K., D. JESKE, M. SLAOUI, O. LEO, J. URBAIN & D. CAPRA. 1984. Complete amino acid sequence of heavy chain variable regions derived from two monoclonal anti-p-azophenylarsonate antibodies of Balb/c mice expressing the major crossreactive idiotype of the A/J strain. J. Exp. Med. **160:** 1070–1086.
36. JESKE, D., E. MILNER, O. LEO, M. MOSER, J. MARVEL, J. URBAIN & J. D. CAPRA. 1986. Molecular mapping of idiotopes of antiarsonate antibodies. J. Immunol. **136:** 2568.
37. OUDIN, J. & M. MICHEL. 1969a. Idiotypy of rabbit antibodies. I. Comparison of idiotypy of antibodies against other bacteria in the same rabbits or of antibodies against *Salmonella typhi* in various rabbits. J. Exp. Med. **130:** 595.
38. OUDIN, J. & M. MICHEL. 1969b. Idiotypy of rabbit antibodies. II. Comparison of idiotypy

of various kinds of antibodies formed in the same rabbits against *Salmonella typhi*. J. Exp. Med. **130:** 619.
39. JERNE, N. K. 1974. Towards a network theory of the immune system. Ann. Immunol. Inst. Pasteur **125C:** 373–389.
40. BORDENAVE, G., C. BABINET & M. MICHEL. 1981. Idiotypic relationships between allotypically different rabbit antibodies. Molec. Immunol. **24:** 177–185.
41. STEIN, K. & J. SÖDERSTRÖM. 1984. Neonatal administration of idiotype or antiidiotype primes for protection against *Escherichia coli* K13 infection in mice. J. Exp. Med. **160:** 1001–1011.
42. SHER, D., M. DORF, M. GIBSON & C. SEDMAN. 1987. Lyl B helper cells in autoimmune viable motheaten mice. J. Immunol. **139:** 1811.
43. POLLOCK, B. & J. F. KEARNEY. 1984. Identification and characterization of an apparent germline set of autoantiidiotypic regulatory B lymphocytes. J. Immunol. **132:** 114–119.
44. HAYAKAWA, K. & R. HARDY. 1988. Normal autoimmune and malignant CD5 + B cells: The LyB lineage. Ann. Rev. Immunol. **6:** 197.

Expression of Immunoglobulin Genes in Transgenic Mice and Transfected Cells[a]

URSULA STORB,[b] PETER ENGLER,[b] JOANNA MANZ,[b]
KATHERINE GOLLAHON,[b] KATHLEEN DENIS,[c]
DAVID LO,[d] AND RALPH BRINSTER[d]

[b]Department of Molecular Genetics and Cell Biology
University of Chicago
Chicago, Illinois 60637

[c]Howard Hughes Medical Institute
University of California
Los Angeles, California 90024

[d]School of Veterinary Medicine
University of Pennsylvania
Philadelphia, Pennsylvania 19104

During the development of B lymphocytes, immunoglobulin (Ig) genes are rearranged apparently in an ordered fashion: first H genes, then L genes. Mature B cells demonstrate allelic exclusion of Ig genes, that is, only one H chain and one L chain are produced. The studies reported herein are concerned with the molecular mechanisms that govern allelic exclusion of H and L genes.

DETERMINATION OF REARRANGEMENT COMPETENCE BY A REARRANGEMENT TEST GENE

To assess the presence of the Ig gene-specific recombinase, we devised a rearrangement test gene, pHRD,[1] which consists of the *Escherichia coli* xanthine/guanine phosphoribosyltransferase (gpt) gene, whose translation is prevented by the presence of an upstream initiation codon out of frame with respect to the gpt coding sequence. Flanking this barrier initiation codon are the heptamer-spacer-nonamer recognition sequences from a kappa chain variable (V) region and a kappa chain joining (J) region. A correct rearrangement results in the deletion of the translational block and allows expression of the selectable marker. When tested by transfection into fibroblasts, no rearrangement was detected, and the presence of the barrier initiation codon was sufficient to completely abolish gpt expression. When the test gene was transfected into a pre-B cell line, 38B9, 80–100% of the transfectants rearranged the gene. Transfectants with multiple copies of pHRD rearranged from one to all copies. Rearrangement was an ongoing process: transfectants were monitored at various times in culture. Cells with few or no rearrangements early continued to accumulate rearrangements (P.

[a]This work was supported by NIH Grants AI 24780 and HD 23089 to U.S.; NIH Grant HD 17321 to R.B.; a Cancer Research Institute postdoctoral fellowship to K.G.; NIH Training Grant T32 CA 09537 to J.M.; and NIH Training Grants PHS NRSA 5 T32 GM 07270 and T32 CA 09537 to P.E. J.M. also was supported by a stipend from Genetic Systems Corporation, Seattle.

Roth, P. Engler, and U. Storb, unpublished data). Thus, recombinase can access the integrated test gene.

In contrast, when pHRD was transfected into myeloma cells, no rearrangement was detected. Apparently myeloma cells do not have an active recombinase. We are in the process of determining whether this lack is due to the absence of recombinase because of transcriptional or translational inhibition or due to an inhibitor of recombinase activity.

Thus, apparently early in B-cell development, the recombinase is activated. How then is the sequential turning on and off of H- and kappa-gene rearrangement controlled? Studies of Alt *et al.*[2] indicate that accessibility of the V_H genes for rearrangement is evidenced by transcription from these genes. Transcription of V_{kappa} genes presumably determines the start of kappa-gene rearrangement, but no supportive evidence has yet been obtained. The studies reported herein are concerned with the control of rearrangement of all Ig gene classes.

FEEDBACK INHIBITION OF H-GENE REARRANGEMENT

We produced transgenic mice carrying in the germline Ig H genes of several types to observe which genes, if any, would influence H-gene rearrangement. Mice with a complete, functional mu gene containing the VDJ region of the H chain of MOPC-167 (antiphosphoryl choline) (mu mice) and mice with the same gene but whose membrane terminus was deleted (mu-del-mem mice) were obtained.[3] Both transgenic mouse lines expressed the transgenes at a high rate.[3] The mice were mated with kappa-transgenic mice carrying the kappa gene of MOPC-167,[3] and hybridomas were produced to determine the effect, if any, of the transgenes on the rearrangement of endogenous H genes.[4] Hybridomas from the mu mice demonstrated a reduced level of rearrangement of endogenous H genes. Eighteen percent of the cells had no rearrangement of endogenous mu genes, and 62% of the cells had Ig genes in the DJ stage of rearrangement. In contrast, in nontransgenic mice, no B cells without H-gene rearrangement are found in the spleen and only 14% of the H-gene alleles retain a DJ rearrangement.[5] Thus, the presence of the mu transgene apparently influenced the rearrangement of endogenous genes. In contrast, hybridomas from the mu-del-mem mice had no germline H genes, and only 18% of the cells retained a DJ rearrangement. The transmembrane and intracytoplasmic portion of the mu gene apparently must be present for the feedback to occur.

Next, transgenic mice were produced with a complete functional gamma-2b gene.[6] This gene is also expressed at a high rate in transgenic mice. To determine the influence of this gene on endogenous H-gene rearrangement, bone marrow cells were transformed with the Abelson murine leukemia virus (A-MuLV) (K. Denis, R. Brinster, and U. Storb, unpublished data). In these cell lines, endogenous H genes were rearranged to the same degree as were those in A-MuLV cell lines from control mice. The gamma-2b gene therefore exerts no influence on H-gene rearrangement.

Thus, the only H genes that apparently cause feedback inhibition of H-gene rearrangement are the mu gene with a membrane terminus and the delta gene.[5] Secreted mu, or membrane or secreted gamma-2b lack this effect. It is unclear why feedback in transgenic mice is incomplete (see previous discussion and references 4 and 6). Perhaps, in transgenic mice, recombinase precedes the transcriptional competence of the cells. Thus, rearrangement may occur before enough mu protein has been produced to stop the process. Furthermore, feedback on H-gene rearrangement may normally be incomplete. It must be kept in mind that feedback on H-gene rearrangement apparently is an almost superfluous mechanism considering the inaccuracy of the rearrangement process. Only one in three joints is in a correct translational reading frame.[1,7,8] Thus, only about 15% of VDJ rearrangements are functional, and the chance for two correct rearrangements in one cell is about 2%.

Additional questions to be considered are the relative roles of membrane and secreted mu. The latter obviously has no effect as a feedback inhibitor; it may actually compete with membrane mu in the feedback. Results with transgenic mice carrying a human mu gene that only encodes membrane mu seem to indicate that this feedback is complete.[9]

The mechanism of feedback by membrane mu is as yet unknown. Both membrane and secreted mu probably have the same intracellular fate with respect to synthesis in the rough endoplasmic reticulum, transport through the Golgi apparatus to the cell surface, and various steps of addition of carbohydrates in mature B cells. There is some evidence that in pre-B cell lines most of the secreted and membrane mu does not enter the Golgi apparatus, whereas a small proportion of membrane mu, but not secreted mu, does. Thus, the difference presumably lies in the transmembrane or intracytoplasmic portion. Gamma-2b differs in this region from mu, whereas mu and delta are very similar.[10]

FEEDBACK INHIBITION OF KAPPA-GENE REARRANGEMENT

Allelic exclusion of kappa genes appears to be complete.[11] To determine whether kappa would feedback on kappa-gene rearrangement, we produced transgenic mice with a kappa gene from the myeloma MOPC-21.[12] This kappa transgene was expressed at a high rate, specifically in B cells.[13,14] Hybridomas produced from these mice showed clear evidence of feedback inhibition.[15] However, the feedback, that is, the absence of rearrangement of endogenous kappa genes, depended on the production of transgenic kappa together with H chains. Kappa alone, present in B cells whose endogenous H genes were both aberrantly rearranged, was not preventing endogenous kappa-gene rearrangement.

The molecular mechanism of kappa-gene rearrangement feedback is unknown. However, we found that cells containing membrane mu undergo kappa feedback, but B cells from transgenic mice with the mu-del-mem gene do not show kappa-gene rearrangement feedback in the presence of a transgenic kappa gene.[4] Presumably, inhibition of further kappa-gene rearrangement is due to complete shutoff of the recombinase, whereas feedback inhibition of H-gene rearrangement is H-gene specific. After H-gene rearrangement has ceased, recombinase continues to exist and to be engaged in the rearrangement of kappa genes.

LINKAGE MAP OF LAMBDA GENES

For a complete understanding of the control of expression of Ig genes, it is important to know the linkage and distances between the recombining V and JC gene partners. Mouse lambda genes show a strict combination of assortments.[22] V1 has only been found rearranged with C1 or C3, but not with C2. V2 is mostly rearranged with C2 and very rarely with C3/C1. Using unique DNA probes we determined that all lambda-gene rearrangements occur by deletion rather than by gene inversion. The order of the lambda genes was determined to be V2-C2,C4-V1-C3,C1.[23] By pulsed-field gel electrophoresis the distance between the V and C genes was determined. V2 and C2 are approximately 74 kb apart, whereas V1 and C3/C1 are separated by only about 20 kb. V2 and C3/C1 are over 190 kb apart. Thus, the distance between the lambda subloci is inversely proportional to their frequencies of rearrangement (U. Storb, D. Haasch, B. Arp, and J. Miller, unpublished data).

LAMBDA-GENE REARRANGEMENT IN A B-CELL SUBSET THAT LACKS FEEDBACK INHIBITION OF IG GENE REARRANGEMENT

Lambda-producing lymphoid cells lines, as expected, have rearranged at least one of their lambda genes. Surprisingly, however, their kappa genes are also rearranged aberrantly or deleted.[16-18] These findings have been taken to indicate a sequential mode of L-gene rearrangement, in which kappa genes rearrange first and lambda genes only rearrange if the kappa genes have been rearranged aberrantly or deleted.[16-18]

To test the sequential model of kappa/lambda gene rearrangement we produced hybridomas from kappa transgenic mice and analyzed their Ig genes and proteins.[24] Surprisingly, it was found that lambda-producing hybridomas were expressing the transgenic kappa. In addition, most hybridomas had rearranged their endogenous kappa genes. This difference in the behavior of endogenous kappa genes in lambda-producing cells compared with kappa-producing cells, in which feedback was complete, was statistically highly significant. Lambda-producing cells therefore violate kappa allelic exclusion.

To explain these results we proposed a new model for the regulation of lambda-gene rearrangement.[19] The model proposes that a separate B-cell lineage is responsible for lambda rearrangement. Whereas the kappa lineage rearranges kappa genes only, a lambda/kappa lineage rearranges both types of L genes. In contrast to the kappa lineage, the kappa/lambda lineage does not respond to feedback inhibition of L-gene rearrangement at the pre-B cell level. Thus, both kappa and lambda genes can continue to be rearranged. We propose that in many instances kappa genes become deleted in these cells by rearrangement of a recombining sequence (RS)[20,21] downstream of C-kappa with sequences upstream of C-kappa. In this way, the kappa/lambda cell converts into a pure lambda producer. Presumably, there must exist a mechanism different from kappa feedback that at a later time stops the activity or production of the recombinase. This event could conceivably occur after antigen triggering of lambda-producing cells.

Evidence from an analysis of nontransgenic mice also indicates that kappa/lambda-coproducing cells exist. By FACS analysis with monoclonal anti-kappa and anti-lambda antibodies, about 20% of lambda-positive cells were found to coproduce kappa.[24] Furthermore, about one fifth of lambda-producing hybridomas from BALB/c mice coproduce kappa.[24] These results suggest that kappa/lambda-coproducing cells may be a normal transitional stage in the generation of lambda-only B cells.

SUMMARY

Immunoglobulin (Ig) genes are expressed sequentially (first H-, then L-chain genes) during the development of B lymphocytes. These studies, performed with transgenic mice and transfected cells, were aimed at the regulation of turning on and off the rearrangement of Ig genes.

The specific recombinase is active in pre-B cells, but not in plasma cells. Production of membrane mu, but not secreted mu or gamma-2b, turns off rearrangement of H genes. Feedback inhibition of kappa-gene rearrangement requires kappa and membrane mu. Kappa alone or in combination with secreted mu does not stop recombination. Mouse lambda genes were mapped by deletion analysis and pulsed-field gel electrophoresis. The gene order is V2-C2,4-V1-C3,C1. The distance between V2 and C2 is 74 kb, but that between V1 and C3,1 is only 20 kb. V2 and C3,1 are over 190 kb apart. Lambda genes appear to be rearranged in a subset of B cells that do not respond to feedback inhibition at the pre-B cell stage. Lambda and kappa genes are both rearranged and potentially functional in these cells. Kappa genes may then be deleted by recombination of a sequence (described by Selsing and Siminovitch *et al.*) downstream of C-kappa with sequences upstream of C-kappa. Presumably the recombinase is eventually inactivated in kappa-lambda cells by a mechanism that is different from H-kappa feedback.

REFERENCES

1. ENGLER, P. & U. STORB. 1987. High-frequency deletional rearrangement of immunoglobulin kappa gene segments introduced into a pre-B-cell line. Proc. Natl. Acad. Sci. USA **84:** 4949–4953.
2. ALT, F. W., T. K. BLACKWELL, R. A. DEPINHO, M. G. RETH & G. D. YANCOPOULOS. 1986. Regulation of genome rearrangement events during lymphocyte differentiation. Immunol. Rev. **89:** 5–30.
3. STORB, U., C. PINKERT, B. ARP, P. ENGLER, K. GOLLAHON, J. MANZ, W. BRADY & R. L. BRINSTER. 1986. Transgenic mice with μ and κ genes encoding antiphosphorylcholine antibodies. J. Exp. Med. **164:** 627–641.
4. NANZ, J., K. DENIS, O. WITTE, R. BRINSTER & U. STORB. 1988. Feedback inhibition of immunoglobulin gene rearrangement by membrane mu, but not by secreted mu heavy chains. J. Exp. Med., in press.
5. IGLESIAS, A., M. LAMERS & G. KOHLER. 1987. Expression of immunoglobulin delta chain causes allelic exclusion in transgenic mice. Nature **330:** 482–484.
6. TSANG, H., C. PINKERT, J. HAGMAN, M. LOSTRUM, R. BRINSTER & U. STORB. 1988. Cloning of a gamma-2b gene encoding anti *P aeruginosa* H chains and its introduction into the germline of mice. J. Immunol. **141:** 308–314.
7. WEAVER, D., F. COSTANTINI, T. IMANISHI-KARI & D. BALTIMORE. 1985. A transgenic immunoglobulin mu gene prevents rearrangement of endogenous genes. Cell **42:** 117–127.
8. ENGLER, P. & U. STORB. 1988. Immunoglobulin gene rearrangement. *In* Genetic Recombination. R. Kucherlapati & G. R. Smith, Eds. Amer. Soc. Microbiol., in press.
9. NUSSENZWEIG, M. C., A. C. SHAW, E. SINN, D. B. DANNER, K. L. HOLMES, H. C. MORSE & P. LEDER. 1987. Allelic exclusion in transgenic mice that express the membrane form of immunoglobulin mu. Science **236:** 816–819.
10. KABAT, E., T. WU, M. REID-MILLER, H. PERRY & K. GOTTESMAN. 1987. Sequences of proteins of immunological interest. 4th Edition. U. S. Dept. of Health and Human Services, Public Health Service, NIH.
11. COLECLOUGH, C. 1983. Chance, necessity and antibody gene dynamics. Nature **303:** 23–26.
12. BRINSTER, R. L., K. A. RITCHIE, R. E. HAMMER, R. L. O'BRIEN, B. ARP & U. STORB. 1983. Expression of a microinjected immunoglobulin gene in the spleen of transgenic mice. Nature **306:** 332–336.
13. STORB, U., R. L. O'BRIEN, M. D. MCMULLEN, K. A. GOLLAHON & R. L. BRINSTER. 1984. High expression of cloned immunoglobulin κ gene in transgenic mice is restricted to B lymphocytes. Nature **310:** 238–241.
14. STORB, U., K. A. DENIS, R. L. BRINSTER & O. N. WITTE. 1985. Pre-B cells in κ-transgenic mice. Nature **316:** 356–358.

15. RITCHIE, K. A., R. L. BRINSTER & U. STORB. 1984. Allelic exclusion and control of endogenous immunoglobulin gene rearrangement in kappa transgenic mice. Nature 312: 517–520.
16. PERRY, R. P., C. COLECLOUGH & M. WEIGERT. 1981. Reorganization and expression of immunoglobulin genes: Status of allelic elements, pp. 925–933. Cold Spring Harbor Symposia on Quantitative Biology, Vol. 45.
17. HIETER, P. A., S. J. KORSMEYER, T. A. WALDMAN & P. LEDER. 1981. Human immunoglobulin kappa light-chain genes are deleted or rearranged in lambda-producing B cells. Nature 290: 368–372.
18. KORSMEYER, S. J., P. A. HIETER, J. V. RAVETCH, D. G. POPLACK, T. A. WALDMAN & P. LEDER. 1981. Developmental hierarchy of immunoglobulin gene rearrangements in human leukemic pre-B-cells. Proc. Natl. Acad. Sci. USA 78: 7096–7100.
19. STORB, U. 1987. Transgenic mice with immunoglobulin genes. Ann. Rev. Immunol. 5: 151–174.
20. DURDIK, J., M. W. MOORE & E. SELSING. 1984. Novel kappa light-chain gene rearrangements in mouse lambda light chain-producing B lymphocytes. Nature 307: 749–752.
21. SIMINOVITCH, K. A., A. BAKHSHI, P. GOLDMAN & S. J. KORSMEYER. 1985. A uniform deleting element mediates the loss of kappa genes in human B cells. Nature 316: 260–262.
22. EISEN, H. & REILLY, E. B. 1985. Lambda chains and genes in inbred mice. Ann. Rev. Immunol. 3: 337–365.
23. MILLER, J., S. OGDEN, M. MCMULLEN, H. ANDRES & U. STORB. 1988. The order and orientation of mouse λ-genes explain λ-rearrangement patterns. J. Immunol, in press.
24. GALLAHON, K., J. HAGMAN, R. BRINSTER, & U. STORB. 1988. Immunoglobulin λ producing B cells do not show feedback inhibition of gene rearrangement. J. Immunol., in press.

Generation of Antibody Diversity Before and After Immunization[a]

PATRICIA J. GEARHART, ANN M. LAWLER,
NINA S. LEVY, SERGE G. LEBECQUE,
AND URSULA V. MALIPIERO

Department of Biochemistry
The Johns Hopkins University School of Hygiene and Public Health
Baltimore, Maryland 21205

Immunoglobulin variable genes are a large, multigene family whose members rearrange at different times in development. The hallmark of the immune system is diversity, and it is intriguing to observe how B cells, which start out with unrearranged genes or zero diversity, rearrange germline genes to build a repertoire of greater than 10^6 specificities. Which genes rearrange first? Is there a developmental program to rearrangement? How quickly does the repertoire diversify, and does it occur at a molecular level by randomly rearranging genes or at a cellular level after selection by antigen? Analysis of rearranged genes in B cells early in ontogeny has provided striking insights into the formation of the repertoire. Despite over 1,000 variable genes for the heavy chain (V_H) in the germline, only a few, located near the joining (J_H) genes, are rearranged.[1-3] Although less is known about rearrangement of variable genes for the kappa light chain (V_K), preliminary data indicate that genes from many different subfamilies are rearranged. Further analyses of rearranged V_K genes may provide a molecular basis for the phenomenon of the programmed appearance of certain B cells during ontogeny.[4]

Additional diversity is generated in immunoglobulin genes after antigen stimulation by somatic mutation. Much is known about the structural hallmarks of mutation in genes coding for antibodies from secondary responses. Nucleotide substitutions are clustered in a discrete region of DNA surrounding and including the rearranged V gene[5,6]; they occur at a frequency of around 1%; and they are more common in IgG and IgA molecules than in IgM molecules.[7] The elucidation of this unusual mechanism clearly requires studies of a more dynamic character. We have approached this problem by attempting to identify a population of B cells that is actively undergoing somatic mutation. The results indicate that mutation occurs early after B cells are stimulated with a primary injection of antigen. Mutated antibodies then undergo intense selection by antigen to produce those with high affinity. We propose that the major effect of somatic hypermutation is to increase affinity and not to create new specificities that would allow other gene products to participate in an immune response.[8]

ANTIBODY DIVERSITY IN FETAL AND NEONATAL B CELLS

V_H Gene Rearrangements Are Biased Towards Two Genes

To identify the genes that are rearranged in pre-B cells, cells from BALB/c fetal livers were taken in mid-gestation, which is when this early population of cells may be

[a]This work was supported by National Institutes of Health Grant CA34127.

57

in synchronous development. Pre-B cells were transformed with Abelson virus to generate seven cell lines. Seventeen genes were identified by sequencing genomic rearrangements and by Southern blots.[3] Twelve rearrangements contained V genes, and the other five were incomplete $D-J_H$ rearrangements. The data, summarized in TABLE 1, indicate an extraordinary bias for the rearrangement of two genes, $V_H 81X$ of the 7183 subfamily and $V_H Ox2$ of the Q52 subfamily. Five of 12 rearrangements used $V_H 81X$ and 4 of 12 used $V_H Ox2$ in both productive and nonproductive rearrangements. These two genes, therefore, comprise 75% of the rearranged V_H genes out of a potential 1,000 genes, which is highly significant compared with a random distribution ($p < 0.001$). J_H gene segments, with the exception of $J_H 1$, were used equally. It is important to stress that pre-B cells have not rearranged their light chain genes and therefore could not be selected by antigen.

The identification of other rearranged V_H genes indicated that genes in the 7183 subfamily have a very high probability of rearrangement, in accord with previous findings.[1,2] Of 12 genes in the 7183 subfamily, 6 were found rearranged in pre-B cells. In contrast, genes within the other eight subfamilies, with the exception of $V_H Ox2$,

TABLE 1. V_H Genes Rearranged in Fetal Pre-B Cell Lines

Cell Line	V_H Subfamily-Gene	J_H	Type[a]
BFL14	7183–81X	J3	VDJ–
BFL9	7183–81X	J3	VDJ+
BFL23	7183–81X	J4	VDJ+
BFL17	7183–81X	J4	VDJ–
BFL1	7183–81X	J4	VDJ+
BFL1	7183–M21	J4	VDJ–
BFL14	7183–14.29	J3	VDJ–
BFL16	Q52–Ox2	J2	VDJ+
BFL2	Q52–Ox2	J2	VDJ–
BFL14	Q52–Ox2	J3	VDJ–
BFL6	Q52–Ox2	J3	VDJ–
BFL23	3609–23.9	J4	VDJ–

[a]VDJ– indicates the rearrangement is nonproductive, and VDJ+ means the rearrangement is productive and can produce mu heavy chain protein.

have a low probability of rearrangement. This is most evident by the lack of rearrangement in the J558 subfamily, which contains close to 1,000 genes and therefore should have a very high probability of rearrangement. The 7183 subfamily is located proximal to the D and J_H locus, suggesting that the position of unrearranged V_H genes strongly influences rearrangement.[1]

V_K Gene Rearrangements Are Distributed over Many Subfamilies

Hybridoma cell lines from BALB/c fetal liver and day 1 neonatal liver were obtained from John Kearney, and 12 rearranged V_K genes were cloned and sequenced. The genes belong to the following six subfamilies: three genes from $V_K 21$, two genes from $V_K 10$, three genes from $V_K 4$, two genes from $V_K 1$, one gene from $V_K 9$, and one gene from $V_K 12$. Two genes were rearranged twice. The multiple rearrangements from several subfamilies suggest that these V_K rearrangements are not randomly distributed. However, most of the genes are productively rearranged and can form complete antibody molecules with the heavy chain, which means the cells had the potential of being selected by antigen *in vivo*. Analyses of rearrangements from cell lines that have rearranged *in vitro* will indicate if selection has influenced the pattern of V_K usage.

The subfamilies represented in this group are located throughout the V_K locus. According to a map generated using recombinant inbred strains,[9] these subfamilies are positioned in the 5', middle, and 3' regions of the locus. Although the exact position of these genes is not known, it is clear that the pattern is more heterogeneous than is that of the heavy chain and is not directed to the C_K-proximal subfamilies.

Mechanisms of Preferential Rearrangement

Several models, which are not mutually exclusive, have been proposed to explain nonrandom rearrangements of V_H genes. (1) *Tracking:* The recombinase enzyme may track the DNA from the D-J_H complex to the most 3' V_H genes.[10] (2) *Accessibility:* The chromatin of V_H genes may sequentially open up to allow the recombinase enzyme access to V_H substrates.[1] Opening of chromatin may be a critical step for gene activation in any developmental system. (3) *Affinity:* Variable genes may have different affinities for the recombinase enzyme, and at low levels of recombinase, genes with high affinity will preferentially rearrange.[3] Thus, in an open chromatin region where many variable genes are accessible, there may be some genes that rearrange at a higher frequency because of increased affinity for recombinase. The regions that interact with recombinase may include DNA sequences other than the well-defined heptamer-nanomer sites. Indeed, one of the most intriguing aspects of our data is the repeated selection of the V_H81X and V_HOx2 genes at a much higher frequency than that of their closely linked neighbor genes, which are 6 and 9 kb away, respectively.[1,11] V_K gene rearrangements may be more heterogeneous than are V_H genes because of the rapid opening of V_K chromatin and/or increased levels of recombinase in pre-B cells at the time of V_K rearrangement so that it binds to all genes regardless of affinity.

Adult B-Cell Repertoire Is Skewed Towards Two V_H Genes

The high proportion of fetal pre-B cells with V_H81X and V_HOx2 rearrangements suggests that these two genes may be found in high frequency in mature B cells from mice. There is evidence that the frequency of rearrangements involving V_H81X in pre-B cells from adult bone marrow is high, with 4 of 21 alleles using the gene.[1] To determine the frequency of rearrangement of these two genes in B cells from adult spleens, we performed Southern blot analyses on DNA from hybridomas that were stimulated with mitogen, and on nonproductive alleles from hybridomas secreting antibodies to phosphorylcholine (PC).[3] Rearranged genes were identified by size. As shown in TABLE 2, 5 of 36 rearrangements used the V_H81X gene, and 3 of 36 used the V_HOx2 gene. Thus, adult B cells do not use individual V_H genes at random because they are derived from biased pre-B cells. A function for preferential gene rearrangement is not clear. Other investigators have found random use of V_H gene subfamilies in the adult, based on hybridization of RNA.[12] The discrepancy may be due to the lack of discrimination between use of individual genes by the RNA hybridization technique and to a difference between productive and nonproductive alleles due to antigen selection of productive rearrangements.

ANTIBODY DIVERSITY AFTER ANTIGEN STIMULATION

Onset of Somatic Mutation After Primary Immunization

To study the mechanism and enzymes causing somatic mutation of V genes, cells that are undergoing mutation are needed. Mutated genes are evident in the secondary response, so a reasonable time to look for mutating cells is after primary immunization. BALB/c mice were immunized with PC conjugated to keyhold limpet hemocyanin in *Bordetella pertussis* adjuvant. Spleens were removed 7, 9, and 13 days after primary immunization, and cDNA libraries were made from splenic RNA using primers for gamma and kappa constant genes. Genes from several subfamilies were sequenced: genes encoding anti-PC antibodies, including V_H1 from the V_HS107 subfamily, V_KT15 from the V_K22 subfamily, and V_K167 from the V_K24 subfamily; and genes not encoding anti-PC antibodies, including genes from the V_H7183, V_H3660, and V_K21 subfamilies. The latter genes may encode antibodies specific for determinants on hemocyanin or unknown antigens.

The results show mutation in genes from the V_H7183 and V_H3660 subfamilies at day 7, which increases with time by day 13. In contrast, genes encoding anti-PC antibodies and V_K21 genes have a much lower frequency of mutation by day 13. The location of mutations and replacement versus silent amino acid changes in the hypervariable regions suggests that the higher frequency of mutation in V_H7183 and V_H3660 genes may be due to selection for antibodies with increased affinity for their corresponding antigens compared to a small increase in affinity for antibodies against PC. The experiments indicate that mutation occurs early after antigen stimulation, followed by selection of B cells with mutated antibodies.

Major Effect of Somatic Mutation Is To Increase Affinity of Antibodies

Is the major effect of mutation to increase the affinity of antibodies for the immunizing antigen by generating proteins with a better fit, or to create new specificities by making antibodies from gene segments whose germline counterparts do not bind the antigen? We addressed this question by studying a well-defined group of antibodies produced after secondary immunization with the PC hapten.[8] Germline genes were identified, the sequences of mutated antibodies were determined, and the affinity of antibodies was measured.

It was shown that only one V gene from each of the V_HS107, V_K22, V_K24, and V_K8 subfamilies is primarily used to encode the heavy and light chains for anti-PC antibodies. Somatic mutation was found in 20 of 37 heavy and light chains from IgG and IgA antibodies, but in only 1 of 18 chains from IgM antibodies. These data support the hypothesis that mutation is a developmentally activated process that occurs in B cells after antigen stimulation.[7] The results in TABLE 3 indicate that the mutated

TABLE 2. Biased Use of V_H Genes in Adult B Cells[a]

V_H Gene	Pre-B Cells from Fetal Liver	Pre-B Cells from Adult Bone Marrow	B-Cell Hybridomas from Adult Spleen
81X	5/12 (42%)	4/21 (19%)	5/36 (14%)
Ox2	4/12 (33%)	...	3/36 (8%)

[a]Results are expressed as rearrangements per VDJ+ and VDJ− alleles.

TABLE 3. Major Effect of Mutation Is to Increase Affinity of Antibodies

Genes Used by Anti-PC Hybridomas	Mutation	$K_{DPPC} \times 10^5$ $(M^{-1})^a$	Genes Used by Anti-PC Hybridomas	Mutation	$K_{DPPC} \times 10^5$ $(M^{-1})^a$
V_H1-V_KT15			V_H1-V_K167		
M2		4.5	M27		4.7
M5		5.7	G9		3.4
M7		4.2	G28	+	1.6
T15		4.8	G22	+	2.3
G11	+	5.1	G24	+	4.8
G8	+	7.5	G17	?	15.8
G12	+	7.4	G23	+	17.8
G14	+	7.4	G10	+	20.6
G20	+	12.3	G13	+	25.6
G21	+	18.0	G32	+	66.6

^{a}DPPC is N-(2,4-dinitrophenyl)-p-aminophenyl-phosphorylcholine.

antibodies generally have equal or higher affinity for antigen, but not substantially lower affinity. Many investigators have correlated mutations with increased affinity for the immunizing antigen. Conversely, there is little evidence that somatic mutation alters and recruits V genes whose germline antibodies do not bind PC in the PC response. If mutation and recruitment were an important mechanism in generating diversity, one would expect to frequently find the products of different mutated V genes in the primary response. However, in our analysis of the primary response to PC, the products of V genes other than the canonical genes just described were not detected.

Antibody diversity in the primary immune response may be due to the large number of germline genes, the combinatorial joining of gene segments, and the combinatorial association of heavy and light chains. These mechanisms alone can account for perhaps 10^7 unique antibodies; this correlates well with estimates of diversity in primary B cells. Once a B cell is triggered with antigen, somatic mutation introduces random substitutions throughout the V genes. Selection of B cells with higher affinity for the cognate antigen occurs *in vivo*, which serves to fine tune the secondary response. However, somatic mutation rarely appears to create new specificities.

REFERENCES

1. YANCOPOULOS, G. D., S. V. DESIDERIO, M. PASKIND, J. F. KEARNEY, D. BALTIMORE & F. W. ALT. 1984. Preferential utilization of the most J_H-proximal V_H gene segments in pre-B-cell lines. Nature 311: 727–733.
2. PERLMUTTER, R. M., J. F. KEARNEY, S. P. CHANG & L. E. HOOD. 1985. Developmentally controlled expression of immunoglobulin V_H genes. Science 227: 1597–1601.
3. LAWLER, A. M., P. S. LIN & P. J. GEARHART. 1987. Adult B-cell repertoire is biased toward two heavy chain variable region genes that rearrange frequently in fetal pre-B cells. Proc. Natl. Acad. Sci. USA 84: 2454–2458.
4. SIGAL, N. H., P. J. GEARHART, J. L. PRESS & N. R. KLINMAN. 1976. Late acquisition of a germ line antibody specificity. Nature 259: 51–52.
5. KIM, S., M. DAVIS, E. SINN, P. PATTEN & L. WOOD. 1981. Antibody diversity: Somatic hypermutation of rearranged V_H genes. Cell 27: 573–581.

6. GEARHART, P. J. & D. F. BOGENHAGEN. 1983. Clusters of point mutations are found exclusively around rearranged antibody variable genes. Proc. Natl. Acad. Sci. USA **80:** 3439–3443.

7. GEARHART, P. J., N. D. JOHNSON, R. DOUGLAS & L. HOOD. IgG antibodies to phsophoryl-choline exhibit more diversity then their IgM counterparts. Nature **291:** 29–34.

8. GEARHART, P. J., D. M. CARON, R. H. DOUGLAS, U. BRUDERER, M. B. RITTENBERG & L. HOOD. Major effect of somatic hypermutation is to increase affinity of antibodies. Proc. Natl. Acad. Sci. USA, in press.

9. D'HOOSTELAERE, L. A., K. HUPPI, B. MOCK, C. MALLETT & M. POTTER. The Ig_k L chain allelic groups among the Ig_k haplotypes and Ig_k crossover populations suggest a gene order. J. Immunol. **141:** 652–661.

10. WOOD C. & S. TONEGAWA. 1983. Diversity and joining segments of mouse immunoglobu-l-in heavy chain genes are closely linked and in the same orientation: Implications for the joining mechanism. Procl Natl. Acad. Sci. USA **80:** 3030–3034.

11. KATAOKA, T., T. NIKAIDO, T. MIYATA, K. MORIWAKI & T. HONJO. 1982. The nucelotide sequences of rearranged and germline immunoglobulin V_H genes of a mouse myeloma MC101 and evolution of V_H genes in mouse. J. Biol. Chem. **257:** 277–285.

12. DILDROP, R., U. KRAWINKEL, E. WINTER & K. RAJEWSKY. 1985. V_H-gene expression in murine lipopolysaccharide blasts distributes over the nine known V_H-gene groups and may be random. Eur. J. Immunol. **15:** 1154–1156.

Immunochemical and Molecular Properties of Antibodies Exhibiting Binding Properties to Glutamic Acid-Tyrosine Homopolymer and to Self Antigens[a]

NAILA C. BAILEY, MARC MONESTIER, AND
CONSTANTIN A. BONA

Department of Microbiology
Mount Sinai School of Medicine
New York, New York 10029

It was long considered that clones recognizing self antigens were deleted during the ontogenic development of the immune system. However, this concept waned when it was shown that the precursor of self-reactive lymphocytes existed in both B- and T-cell compartments and was present in individuals and animals prone to autoimmune diseases as well as in healthy individuals and animals (not prone to autoimmunity).[1-4]

The development of hybridoma technology allowed extensive analysis of fine specificities of autoantibodies. These studies led to the conclusion that autoantibodies represent a heterogenous population of immunoglobulin molecules composed of pathogenic autoantibodies that, when injected into normal animals, caused symptoms similar to those observed in autoimmune diseases, and also autoantibodies that are associated with diseases without pathogenic properties and, likewise, multispecific autoantibodies.

The synthesis of autoantibodies represents a more complex phenomenon than does the production of antibodies specific for foreign antigen, because the former has to overcome the rule of non-self-reactivity.

Several factors can contribute to non-self-reactivity:

1. Inaccessibility of self antigens. Numerous autoantigens are not found in the circulation because they are sequestered within the cell compartment and organelles; hence, they are not accessible to lymphocytes. However, these sequestered antigens become accessible when they are brought to the surface of the cell by viruses that replicate within the cell or when the aged cells are destroyed. There is no information on the antigenicity of cellular components of destroyed aged cells and the ability of these autoantigens to stimulate an immune response.

2. Lack of class II antigens. Most autoantigens have a complex origin, and the recognition of their epitopes represents a key step in the initiation of the immune response. This recognition process is major histocompatibility complex (MHC) restricted and therefore requires either the processing of the antigens by macrophages and B cells or alternatively the expression of class II antigens by the somatic cells that are the target of the autoimmune phenomenon. Numerous studies clearly indicate that class II antigens can be expressed on the surface of cells that are targets of autoimmune

[a]This work was supported by grant 2092 from the Council for Tobacco Research, USA Inc.

diseases subsequent to stimulation of interferon synthesis by viral infections or other factors (reviewed by Bottazzo et al.[5]).

3. Idiotype suppression can also contribute to non-self-reactivity. The major effect of the interaction between Ab1 and Ab2 in the steady state is the suppression of clones that are stimulated by antigens.[6] Autoreactive B-cell clones, like those reactive to non-self antigen, belong to a unitarian system governed by the same rules concerning the activation, expression, and clonal interaction of lymphocytes. The presence of naturally occurring antiidiotype (anti-Id) antibodies and idiotype-specific suppressor T-cells can contribute to the lack of expansion of the precursors of autoreactive clones.[7,8] Disturbance of this balance by antigen or by anti-Id antibodies produced in response to other stimuli can break the non-self-reactivity. Clearly, this implies a high idiotypic connection between the clones producing autoantibodies and antibodies specific for foreign antigens.

4. Tolerance to autoantigens was considered the major element that contributed to non-self-reactivity.[9] Tolerance to self antigens can represent an intrinsic property of B cells or alternatively can be due to an active phenomenon mediated by suppressor T cells. Limited data indicate that B cells from animals prone to autoimmune diseases are less tolerant to self antigen than are B cells from normal animals.[10] By contrast, there is substantial evidence to indicate an alteration of helper or suppressor subsets of T cells in human autoimmune diseases and in animals prone to autoimmunity (reviewed in reference 11).

There are several mechanisms that may contribute to the breaking of self-tolerance:

a. Self-tolerance can be broken by the release of sequestered antigens into the circulation. This mechanism implies that the initial event that contributes to the activation of self-reactive clones is not of immunologic origin.

b. Activation of self-reactive clones by foreign antigens. This process is very complex and implies cross-reactivity between foreign and self antigens (i.e., shared epitopes) or molecular mimicry (exposure of the same contact residues and its ability to interact with a lymphocytic receptor by unrelated self and foreign antigens) or clones that bear multispecific receptors capable of binding to self and to foreign antigens.

c. Activation of self-reactive clones by anti-Id antibodies produced in response to foreign antigens. This process requires that autoantibodies and antibodies specific for foreign antigens share idiotopes and that these two types of clones are subject to cross-regulatory processes by the same anti-Id antibodies.

During the past 2 years, we conducted studies in our laboratory to investigate the binding specificity of autoantibodies and whether they share idiotopes with foreign antigens.

I. *High frequency of autoantibodies encoded by $V_H J558$ family genes bind to foreign antigens and express the Idx of antibodies specific for foreign antigens.* The binding activity of 20 $V_H J558^+$ autoantibodies with various specificities, obtained from various animals, was tested against a panel of 52 antigens chosen because they interact with antibodies encoded by genes belonging to the $V_H J558$ family.

Our immunochemical studies showed that nine autoantibodies bound to foreign antigens such as glutamic acid-tyrosine (GT), glutamic acid-phenylalanine, phenylarsonate *Escherichia coli,* and *Staphylococcus providencia* polysaccharides.

The binding of autoantibodies to autoantigens was inhibited by foreign antigens. Furthermore, their dissociation constants (Kds) for foreign and autoantigens were very similar.[12]

These data showed that monoclonal autoantibodies produced from animals prone to autoimmune diseases (such as motheaten or MRL/lpr mice) or from animals immunized with autoantigens (SJL strain were immunized with myelin basic protein and CBA/J mice were immunized with thyroglobulin) bound to foreign antigens.

In this study, we also investigated the expression of Idx characteristic of antibodies specific for dextran (J558 Idx), PR8 or X31 influenza viruses (PY211 and PY206 Idx) of anti-glutamic acid-alanine-tyrosine (GAT) antibodies (cGAT Idx) and of antiarsonate antibodies (cross-reactive idiotype [CRI]).

Interestingly, we found that of 20 autoantibodies, 3 shared J558 Idx, 3 were PY211 Idx^+, 2 were cGAT Idx^+, and 3 shared the CRI of antiarsonate antibodies.[12]

These results, taken collectively, suggest that clones producing self-reactive antibodies can be activated by foreign antigen, because the affinity of Ig receptor for foreign and self antigens was very similar. Alternatively, autoreactive clones can be activated by auto-anti-Id antibodies produced during the immune response elicited by conventional antigens or by anti-Id carrying the internal image of foreign antigens.

II. *Immortalization of self-reactive hybridomas from mice immunized with foreign antigens or anti-Id antibodies.* On the basis of our observation that a high fraction of autoantibodies with different specificities bound to GT homopolymer and that they share the idiotype of an anti-GAT antibody, we studied the activation of autoreactive clones by GT and an anti-Id antibody (HP20) that carries the internal image of GT.[13] We found that autoantibodies also bound other more physiologic antigens such as *S. providencia* and *E. coli* polysaccharides and lysozyme. However, we chose GT in this study because we wanted to answer the fundamental question of whether autoreactive clones can be stimulated by foreign antigens.

The GT system has several advantages:

a. It is a well-characterized antigen that elicits an immune response depending on immune response (Ir) gene control.[14]

b. In this system, a monoclonal anti-Id antibody carries the internal image of the antigen (Ab2β) defined by structural criterion, the most faithful criterion to define this category of antibodies. This antibody, designated HP20, bears GTT (glutamic acid-tyrosine-tyrosine) sequences in the CDR III of V_H region.[13]

To study the activation of autoreactive clones by GT or Ab2β, hybridomas were prepared from 1-month-old MRL/lpr mice, a strain prone to develop lupus or an arthritis-like syndrome by 3 to 4 months of age, as well as from C_3H/HeJ mice, a normal strain with the same VHJ haplotype.

The hybridomas were prepared from the following groups of mice:

a. 4-week-old immunized mice with 50 μg of GT in complete Freund's adjuvant (CFA-primary response).

b. 2-week-old mice immunized with 50 μg GT in CFA and 2 weeks later with 50 μg GT in saline solution.

c. 2-week-old mice immunized with CFA (control only).

d. 2-week-old mice immunized three times with 50 μg HP20 in saline solution.

e. 2-week-old mice immunized three times with 50 μg 63-4 monoclonal anti-Id antibody in saline solution. (63-4 recognizes an idiotype borne by a PR8 influenza virus-specific antibody.)

Hybridomas obtained from animals immunized with GT were selected by the ability of antibodies to bind to GT. Positive hybrids were cloned, and the GT binding antibodies were tested for reactivity to three self antigens: Sm, DNA, and IgG2a.

Hybridomas obtained from animals immunized with HP20 or 63-4 were selected for binding to Sm, DNA, and IgG2a, and after cloning, their ability to bind GT was also tested.

The results presented in TABLE 1 illustrate the frequency of hybridomas producing antibodies specific for GT and self antigens or specific for only self antigens obtained from animals immunized with GT or anti-Id antibodies.

TABLE 1. Specificity of Monoclonal Antibodies Obtained from One-Month-Old MRL/lpr and C₃H/HeJ Mice

Origin of Hybridomas	No. of Hybridomas Obtained	Binding Specificity	
		GT + Self Antigens	Self Antigens Only
1-mo-old MRL/lpr injected with CFA	146	None	FM35-4 (DNA)
1-mo-old MRL/lpr GT.CFA (primary)	694	GP138-10, GP99.5, GP88, GP133	GP75-9
1-mo-old MRL/lpr 2 × GT (secondary)	436	GS11-1, GS4-1	GS13-1 "sticky"
1-mo-old MRL/lpr 3 × 50 μg HB20	370	H8-1, H16-5, H4-2, H45-5, H113-1, H164-4, H127-1, H81-16	H17-1 (DNA)
1-mo-old MRL/lpr 3 × 50 μg 63-4	120	None	63-86-7 (DNA), 63-99-7 (DNA)
1-mo-old C₃H 2 × GT (secondary)	192	None	CGS21-7 (DNA, Sm)
1-mo-old C₃H 3 × 50 μg HB20	210	CH154-1, CH113-1	CH24-10 (DNA G2a), CH46-1 (DNA G2a), CH44-7 (DNA), CH558 (G2a)

The hybridomas producing only GT antibodies have not been cloned. These hybridomas have been obtained only in animals immunized with GT.

Our results show that autoreactive clones can be stimulated by GT or by Ab2β antibody, because GT-binding autoantibodies exhibiting self-reactivity were obtained from MRL/lpr mice immunized with GT (primary and secondary response) or HP20 and from C₃H/HeJ immunized with HP20.

A low frequency of multispecific antibodies was observed in the secondary GT response of MRL/lpr mice, and in C₃H/HeJ the lack of these antibodies in secondary response indicates that the clones producing these antibodies belong to preimmune rather than to memory repertoire.

III. *Immunochemical properties of multispecific antibodies.* Antigen-binding specificity of hybridomas obtained from various groups of mice was determined by radioimmunoassay (RIA) in which the microtiter plates were coated with antigens and then incubated with various concentrations of chromatographically purified antibodies. The binding of the antibody to antigen-coated plates was determined by ^{125}I-rat antimurine kappa monoclonal antibody.

The affinity of multispecific antibodies obtained from MRL/lpr mice was determined by both competitive inhibition studies and measuring the Kd, according to previously described methods.[12] These results are shown in TABLE 2. The multispecific antibodies obtained from GT primary response or animals immunized with HP20 have similar Kds for GT and self antigens that vary between 10^{-7} and 10^{-8} g/liter. The binding to GT was inhibited at various degrees by the self antigens with the exception of GP133, GP138-10, GP99-5, and H45-5, in which the DNA failed to inhibit.

These results clearly demonstrate that clones producing multispecific antibodies that bind to foreign and autoantigens with weak or moderate affinity can be expanded by foreign antigens or Ab2β.

IV. *Expression of cGAT Idx.* Studies on the expression of cGAT Idx were investigated by a previously described sensitive sandwich RIA technique.[15] In this assay the microtiter plates were coated with 10 μg/ml of chromatographically purified

HP20 antibody, and various amounts of monoclonal antibodies were added thereafter. Finally, after extensive washing, ^{125}I-labeled HP20 was added. TABLE 3 shows that one of eight antibodies obtained from mice immunized with GT and five of seven antibodies from HP20 immunized mice expressed cGAT Idx.

V. *Utilization of V-gene families by multispecific antibodies.* It is well known that there is a restricted combinatorial association of V_H and V_K or V genes in antibodies specific for various antigens. This restriction is more striking in antibodies specific for polysaccharides, synthetic peptides, and haptens.

With anti-GAT antibodies mainly directed against GT determinants, the specificity is encoded by V_H genes derived from $V_H J558$ in association with V_K derived from

TABLE 2. Antigen Inhibition and Kd of MRL/lpr Multispecific Antibodies

Antibody	Binding to:	% Inhibition at 15 ng by:				Kd
		GT	DNA	Sm	IgG2a	
GP138-10	GT	60	⋯	⋯	⋯	2.7×10^{-6}
	DNA	⋯	11	⋯	⋯	4.3×10^{-7}
	Sm	45	⋯	15	⋯	3.91×10^{-7}
	IgG2a	60	⋯	⋯	15	2.6×10^{-7}
GP99-5	GT	25	60	65	58	6.02×10^{-8}
	DNA	⋯	40	⋯	⋯	3.08×10^{-7}
	Sm	8	⋯	40	⋯	3.0×10^{-8}
	IgG2a	40	⋯	⋯	50	4.65×10^{-7}
GP88	GT	24	53	22	11	3.33×10^{-7}
	DNA	52	18	⋯	⋯	1.11×10^{-6}
	Sm	44	⋯	32	⋯	3.7×10^{-8}
	IgG2a	46	⋯	⋯	13	1.11×10^{-7}
GP133	GT	35	57	31	35	1.47×10^{-8}
	DNA	⋯	37	⋯	⋯	1.0×10^{-8}
	Sm	64	⋯	38	⋯	7.5×10^{-8}
	IgG2a	45	⋯	⋯	49	3.4×10^{-8}
H4-2	GT	50	50	⋯	35	1.02×10^{-8}
	DNA	3	40	⋯	⋯	9.41×10^{-8}
	Sm	65	⋯	15	⋯	6.58×10^{-7}
	IgG2a	50	⋯	⋯	16	4.81×10^{-7}
H8-1	GT	25	36	⋯	⋯	2.24×10^{-8}
	DNA	30	51	⋯	⋯	1.88×10^{-7}
H45-5	GT	60	45	12	⋯	5.65×10^{-8}
	DNA	⋯	38	⋯	⋯	2.14×10^{-7}
	Sm	28	⋯	20	⋯	7.54×10^{-7}
	IgG2a	50	⋯	⋯	37	5.95×10^{-7}
H113-1	GT	45	⋯	70	40	1.05×10^{-7}
	DNA	30	45	⋯	⋯	1.43×10^{-7}
	IgG2a	11	⋯	⋯	25	8.81×10^{-7}
H16-5	GT	30	35	25	⋯	4.05×10^{-8}
	DNA	40	40	⋯	⋯	7.08×10^{-8}
	IgG2a	51	⋯	⋯	75	1.79×10^{-8}

TABLE 3. Expression of G5IDX on Monoclonal Antibodies Produced by MRL/lpr and C_3H/HeJ Hybridomas

Antibody	CPM[a]
BSA	369 ± 100
G5	15,784 ± 1,558
FM35-4	459 ± 101
GP75-9	309 ± 15
GP138-10	321 ± 25
GP99-5	149 ± 15
GP88	1,921 ± 50
GP133	269 ± 53
GS13-1	164 ± 94
GS11-1	277 ± 102
GS4-1	170 ± 26
H16-5	4,070 ± 448
H4-2	471 ± 21
H17-1	240 ± 18
H45-5	1,694 ± 136
H129-1	2,615 ± 409
H113-11	3,452 ± 226
H164-4	2,530 ± 145
63-99-7	197 ± 16
63-86-7	163 ± 9
CH24-10	311 ± 188
CH154-1	248 ± 8
CH113-1	188 ± 11
CH558	181 ± 44
CH46-1	234 ± 71
CH44-7	158 ± 11

[a]Counts per minute average of triplicate ± SD.

V_K1 germline genes.[16] Therefore, it was important to study the use of various V-gene families among the multispecific antibodies obtained from MRL/lpr and C_3H/HeJ mice. This analysis was carried out by Northern blotting; RNA extracted from hybridomas was hybridized with 8 V_H and 11 V_K probes, each a prototype of a given family. TABLE 4 shows the use of V_H and V_K families by this group of multispecific antibodies.

The majority of multispecific autoantibodies are encoded by V_HJ558 and 3' V_H families. In V_K families, we found relatively frequent use of V_K22 and V_K24, both of which are rarely used by monospecific autoantibodies.

The use of V_H and V_K gene families of MRL/lpr and C_3H/HeJ multispecific antibodies is not significantly different from that of multispecific autoantibodies obtained from other normal or autoimmune murine strains, such as motheaten viable, nu/nu, C57BL/6J, BALB/c, and NZB mice (TABLE 5).

DISCUSSION AND CONCLUSION

The results of this study demonstrate that autoreactive clones bearing multispecific receptors and having the ability to bind self and foreign antigens can be activated by GT as well as by a corresponding Ab2β carrying the internal image of GT.

Only a few multispecific antibodies were obtained from animals with a secondary GT response. The difference in the frequency of multispecific antibodies in primary versus secondary responses is probably related to prevalent activation of clones with high affinity during secondary response. These high affinity anti-GT antibodies apparently rarely exhibit any multispecificity.

Clones producing multispecific antibodies were also activated by the administration of HP20 (Ab2β) antibody in both MRL/lpr and C$_3$H/HeJ mice strains.

Interestingly, only a few multispecific antibodies obtained from C$_3$H/HeJ mice immunized three times with HP20 bound to GT. This finding suggests that multispecific autoantibody clones activated by HP20 immunization in C$_3$H/HeJ mice can be related to other nonspecific mechanisms, such as polyclonal activation by lymphokines produced during the activation of B cells by anti-Ig antibodies.[17]

Studies of the idiotypy of multispecific antibodies obtained from animals immunized with GT showed that only one shares the cGAT-dominant Idx of anti-GT antibodies. A higher proportion of cGAT Idx$^+$ multispecific antibodies was observed among MRL/lpr hybridomas obtained from animals immunized with Ab2β. In this case, as predicted, Ab2β induced the activation of two types of clones, namely, Id$^+$Ag$^+$ and Id$^-$Ag$^+$. This pattern of clonal activation corresponds to our previous prediction that an Ab2β by virtue of its idiotypes that mimics the antigen can stimulate antigen-specific Id$^+$ or Id$^-$ clones.[18] This finding is strongly supported by the data originated from the analysis of use of V-gene families by multispecific antibodies.

These antibodies use V genes from various V_H and V_K families, whereas anti-GAT antibodies generally use V genes derived from germline genes belonging to V_HJ558 and V_K1 families.

TABLE 4. V-Gene Families Used by MRL/lpr and C$_3$H/HeJ Hybridomas Producing Autoantibodies

Autoantibody	V_H	V_K
FM35-4	J558	4
GP88	QPC52	19
GP138-10	J558	1
GP99-5	7183	22
GP75-9	J558	8
GP133	J606	NI[a]
GS13-1	S107	1
GS11-1	J606	NI
GS4-1	J558	1
H45-5	J558	1
H16-5	J558	NI
H127-1	QPC52	4
H164-1	QPC52	NI
H17-1	QPC52	22
H4-2	J558	9
H81-16	QPC52	8
H113-1	S107	24
63-99-7	J558	10
63-86-7	J558	NI
CH154-1	7183	10
CH46-1	J558	22
CH55-8	J558	NI
CH24-10	J558	22
CH44-7	QPC52	19
CH113-1	7183	NI
CGS21-17	7183	NI

[a]NI = not identified.

TABLE 5. V_H and V_K Families Used in Multispecific Antibodies Produced by Hybridomas Obtained from Normal and from MRL/lpr Immunized Mice

Origin of Hybridomas	Immunization	V_H								V_K										NI[a]
		X24	36–60	36–09	J606	J558	S107	Q52	7183	1	2	4	8	9	10	19	21	22	24	
C57BL/6	Nil								2						1			1		1
nu C57BL/6	Nil			1	1										1	1				1
BALB/c	Nil		1						3	1	1	1								1
C₃H	GT								1											
C₃H	HB20					3		1	2			1			1		1	2		3
MRL/lpr	FCA					1	1	1	1											
	GT				2	3		4	1	3		1			1			2		2
	HB20					3				1				1				1	1	2
	63-4					2									1					1

[a]NI = not identified.

In conclusion, our findings demonstrate that clones able to produce autoantibodies that bear a receptor that binds with either low or moderate affinity to a foreign antigen can be activated by the corresponding antigen or by an anti-Id antibody carrying the internal image of the foreign antigen.

The specificity of multispecific antibodies produced by such clones is encoded by V_H and V_K genes from various families, indicating that the combinatorial V_H-V_K association is less restricted than is that of antibodies specific for only foreign antigens. This finding is mirrored in the expression of idiotypes of anti-GT antibodies that are expressed only by a fraction of multispecific antibodies.

REFERENCES

1. VAN SNICK, J. L., V. STASSIN, B. DE LESTRE'. 1983 Isotypic and allotypic specificity of mouse Rheumatoid factors. J. Exp. Med. **157:** 1006–1019.
2. BELLON, B., A. MANHEIMER-LORY, M. MONESTIER, T. MORAN, A. DIMITRIU-BONA, F. ALT & C. BONA. 1987. High frequency of autoantibodies bearing cross-reactive idiotypes among hybridomas using V_H7183 genes prepared from normal and autoimmune strains. J. Clin. Invest. **79:** 1044–1053.
3. HOOPER, B., S. WITTINGHAM, J. D. MATHEWS, I. R. MACRAY, D. H. CURNOW. 1972. Autoimmunity in a rural community. Clin. Exp. Immunol. **12:** 79–87.
4. GLIMCHER, L. H., E. M. SHEVACH. 1982. Production of autoreactive I. region restricted T cell hybridomas. J. Exp. Med. **156:** 660.
5. BOTTAZZO, G. F., I. TODD, R. MIRAKIAW, A. BELFIORE, R. PUJOL-BORREL. 1986. Organ specific autoimmunity: A 1986 overview. Immunol. Rev. **94:** 137–169.
6. BONA, C. A., C. VICTOR-KOBRIN, A. J. MANHEIMER, B. BELLON, L. J. RUBINSTEIN. 1984. Regulatory arms of the immune network. Immunol. Rev. **79:** 25–44.
7. ZANETTI, M. 1986. Idiotypic regulation of autoantibody production. Crit. Rev. Immunol. **60:** 151.
8. BONA, C. 1987. Regulatory Idiotopes. Wiley & Sons, New York.
9. BURNET, F. M. 1959. The Clonal Selection Theory of Acquired Immunity. Cambridge University Press, London.
10. BROOKS, M. S. & M. ALDO-BENSON. 1986. Defects in antigen specific immune tolerance in continuous B cell lines from autoimmune mice. J. Clin. Invest. **78:** 784–789.
11. SHOENFELD, Y. & R. S. SCHWARTZ. 1984. Immunologic and genetic factors in autoimmune diseases. N. Engl. J. Med. **311:** 1019–1029.
12. MONSTIER, M., B. BONIN, P. MIGLIORINE, H. DANG, S. DATTA, R. KUPPERS, N. ROSE, P. MAURER, N. TALAL, C. BONA. 1987. Autoantibodies of various specificity encoded by genes from the VH J558 family bind to foreign antigens and share idiotopes of antibodies specific for self and foreign antigens. J. Exp. Med. **166:** 1109–1125.
13. SCHIFF, C. I., M. MILLI, I. HVE, S. RUDIKOFF M. FOUGEREAU. 1986. Genetic basis for expression of the idiotype network. One unique Ig V_H germline gene accounts for the major family of Ab1 and Ab3 (Ab1) antibodies of the GAT system. J. Exp. Med. **163:** 573–587.
14. MOSES, E., H. O. MCDEVITT, J. C. JATON & M. SELA. 1969. The nature of the antigenic determinant in a genetic control of the antibody responses. J. Exp. Med. **130:** 493–504.
15. VICTOR-KOBRIN, C., T. MANSER, T. M. MORAN, T. IMANISHI-KARI, M. GEFTER & C. BONA. 1985. Shared idiotopes among antibodies encoded by V_H genes members of the J558 V_H family as basis for cross-reactivity regulation. Proc. Natl. Acad. Sci. USA **82:** 7696–7700.
16. MAZZA G., V. GUIGOU, D. MOINIER, S. CORBET, P. OLLIER & M. FOUGEREAU. 1987. Molecular interactions in the «GAT», idiotypic network: An approach using synthetic peptides. Ann. Inst. Pasteur/Immunol. **138:** 3–17.
17. MELCHERS, F. 1986. Control of the mitogenic B cell cycle: Facts and speculations. *In* The Molecular Basis of B Cell Differentiation and Function. M. Ferrani & B. Pernis, Eds. Plenum Press, New York & London, Series A: Life Sci. **123:** 49–57.
18. BONA, C. & T. MORAN. 1985. Idiotope vaccines. Ann. Immunol. (Institute Pasteur) **136C:** 229–312.

Structural Characteristics of Peptides Required for Their Interaction with IA^d

HOWARD M. GREY, ALESSANDRO SETTE,
AND SØREN BUUS

Department of Medicine
National Jewish Center for Immunology and Respiratory Medicine
Denver, Colorado 80206

T cells of the helper subset recognize antigen-derived peptides in association with major histocompatibility complex (MHC) class II (Ia) molecules on the cell surface of antigen presenting cells (APC). The nature of the association between antigenic peptides and Ia has been controversial, but recent biochemical evidence supports the concept of a specific receptor-ligand interaction.[1-3] The accumulated data to date strongly suggest that the capacity of peptides derived from a given protein antigen to interact with Ia is a necessary, albeit insufficient, prerequisite for the immunogenicity of the antigen.[4,5] However, it is still not clear how a limited number of Ia molecules can function as receptors for the almost endless variety of potentially immunogenic peptides. Available data on competitive inhibition for Ia binding[4,6] and recent structural delineation of an MHC molecule[7,8] suggest that each Ia possesses a single binding site capable of binding many different peptides.

The studies described herein were performed to understand how a presumably large universe of immunogenic peptides could bind to and be restricted by the very small number of Ia specificities present within an individual. These studies were carried out predominantly with the immunogenic peptide from chicken ovalbumin (Ova) 323–339 and the murine class II MHC restriction element IA^d.

N- AND C-TERMINAL TRUNCATED ANALOGS OF OVA 323–339 DEFINE A CORE REGION CRITICAL FOR IA^d BINDING

To define the IA^d-interacting region within the peptide Ova 323–339, we synthesized a series of N- and C-terminal truncated analogs and tested them for binding to purified IA^d molecules (TABLE 1). Deletions from the C-terminal end of the molecule had no noticeable effect until the seventh (E_{333}) residue was removed; removal led to about a threefold reduction in IA^d binding. Further removal of A_{332} resulted in complete loss of the IA^d interacting capacity. From the N-terminal end of the molecule, the first two residues could be removed without noticeable effects, and removal of the next two residues (Q_{325} and A_{326}) had a marginal but significant effect. A marked (20-fold) decrease was associated with removal of the next residue (V_{327}), and complete loss of binding activity was associated with removal of H_{328}. Thus, the critical residues for interaction with IA^d molecules were contained within the sequence VHAAHA (Ova 327–332) (underlined residues in top row of TABLE 1).

TABLE 1. Truncations of the Ova Peptide 323–339 and Their Binding to IA^d

Ova Peptide	Sequence[a]	Relative IA^d Binding Capacity[b]
323–339	I S Q A V H A A H A E I N E A G R	1.0
323–336	- - - - - - - - - - - - - E	1.1
323–335	- - - - - - - - - - - - N	1.0
323–333	- - - - - - - - - - E	0.6
323–332	- - - - - - - - - A	0.2
323–331	- - - - - - - - H	<0.005
325–339	Q - - - - - - - - - - - - - -	1.1
326–339	A - - - - - - - - - - - - -	0.5
327–339	V - - - - - - - - - - - -	0.3
328–339	H - - - - - - - - - - -	0.014
329–339	A - - - - - - - - - -	<0.005

[a]One-letter code for amino acid sequence is: Ala (A); Arg (R); Asn (N); Asp (D); Cys (C); Gln (Q); Glu (E); Gly (G); His (H); Ile (I); Leu (L); Lys (K); Met (M); Phe (F); Pro (P); Ser (S); Thr (T); Trp (W); Tyr (Y); Val (V).

[b]The IA^d interacting capacity of each peptide is expressed as the amount of unlabeled Ova 323–339 divided by the amount of truncated peptide needed to inhibit the binding of ^{125}I-radiolabeled Ova 323–339 to IA^d by 50% as measured by a gel filtration method.[4] The data represent the average of 2–4 experiments.

STRUCTURAL SIMILARITY BETWEEN OVA 327–333 AND OTHER IA^d BINDING PEPTIDES

We have identified six other peptides from unrelated proteins that also bind strongly to IA^d.[5,9] Because each of these peptides competitively inhibits the IA^d binding of Ova 323–339, they most likely all bind to the same site on IA^d as the Ova peptide, and they therefore should share the critical structural features required for such binding. To estimate the structural relation between two aligned peptide sequences, we adapted the method described by Grantham[10] and Padlan.[11] A dissimilarity value for each pair of corresponding amino acids was obtained from a table that takes into account differences in atomic composition, polarity, and molecular volume. The dissimilarity values were then normalized for mean dissimilarities of random substitutions, and the average (average structural dissimilarity; ASD) was finally calculated for each peptide alignment. Because the experiments with truncated peptides and peptides with single amino acid differences indicated that the sequence VHAAHA encompassed most of the IA^d binding activity, we used this six-residue peptide as a "master" sequence for a pairwise comparison with the six other peptide antigens that have thus far been identified to also bind strongly to IA^d. For each of the six peptides we calculated the ASD values of all the possible linear alignments to Ova 327–332 and chose the alignment that yielded the lowest ASD as the "best fit."

These best fit alignments are shown in TABLE 2A. The common structural motif that emerged from this set of alignments was as follows: Position 1 appeared to be the most similar in the six peptides, being occupied by hydrophobic residues V, I, or L. The next position was occupied by either a basic residue (H, R, or K) or the polar residue threonine. It was followed by two hydrophobic residues in positions 3 and 4. Position 5 was more variable, but tended to be occupied by polar or charged amino acids. Finally, position 6 was occupied either by A or by two other residues with short or no side chain, residues S or G. Although this motif could be discerned in the great majority of good IA^d binding peptides, we recently identified an IA^d binding peptide derived from herpes simplex virus (HSV) gD protein that apparently does not share this motif (TABLE 2B).

To determine experimentally whether the peptide regions shown in TABLE 2A that shared the greatest degree of structural similarity were indeed involved in the IA^d binding capacity of this set of peptides, we synthesized overlapping truncated peptides from two of the strong IA^d binders, influenza virus hemagglutinin (Ha) 130–142 and sperm whale myoglobin (Myo) 106–118.

We previously showed that a synthetic peptide corresponding to residues 130–142 of Ha bound to IA^d molecules with an affinity similar to that of OVA 323–339.[4] As shown in TABLE 2A, residues 135–140 of Ha, VTAACS, possess the greatest structural similarity to the VHAAHA region of the Ova peptide that had been demonstrated to contain the IA^d binding region for Ova 323–339. To determine whether the critical residues for IA^d binding of the Ha peptide involved residues 135–140, we tested a series of 11 residue peptides that spanned through residues 121–146 of Ha for their capacity to bind IA^d. In this series of peptides, because of problems associated with peptide purification, a C → S substitution was made at residue 140. Preliminary data indicated that this substitution had no deleterious effect on the capacity of Ha 130–142 to bind to IA^d (data not shown). As shown in FIGURE 1, the peptides that encompass the N-terminal end of this peptide region did not bind to IA^d. Binding was first observed with peptide 129–139, was maximal with peptides 130–140, 131–141, and 132–142, and decreased thereafter. From these data the C-terminal limit of the region containing the IA^d binding capacity could be localized around residue S_{140}, because its removal from the C-terminus (i.e., peptide 129–139) resulted in a 10-fold decrease in the IA^d binding capacity. Further removal of the residue at position 139 from the C-terminus completely abolished the IA^d binding activity. Similarly, the N-terminal limit of the IA^d binding region could be identified as N_{133}, because its removal completely abolished the IA^d interacting capacity. Thus, the peptide region critical for IA^d binding was Ha 133–140 (NGVTAASS). This peptide contains the sequence, VTAAC/SS, that was predicted to be involved in IA^d binding on the basis of structural similarity to the Ova core binding region.

As a further test of the functional relevancy of the structural similarities between IA^d binding peptides from unrelated proteins, we synthesized a similar series of overlapping undecapeptides spanning through residues 103–125 of sperm whale myoglobin. Myo 112–117 is composed of the sequence IHVLHS (TABLE 2), which is similar to the OVA 327–332 (VHAAHA) sequence. The IA^d binding profile of the

TABLE 2. Structural Similarities Between Unrelated IA^d Binding Peptides

	Residue Number					
	1	2	3	4	5	6
A. Best Fit Alignments of Unrelated Peptides with Good IA^d Binding Capacity						
Ova 327–332	V	H	A	A	H	A
Ha 135–140	V	T	A	A	C	S
Myo 66–71	V	T	V	L	T	A
Myo 112–117	I	H	V	L	H	S
Nase 104–109	V	R	Q	G	L	A
Nase 15–20	I	K	A	I	D	G
Ova 321–326	L	K	I	S	Q	A
B. Sequence of the Peptide HSVgD 245–260						
HSVgD 245–260	A P Y S T L L P P E L S E T P					

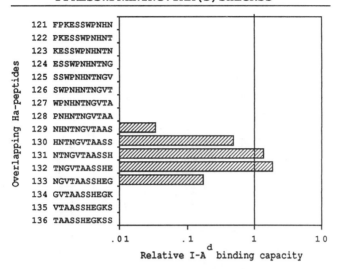

Sequence of Ha 121-146:
FPKESSWPNHNTNGVTAA(S)SHEGKSS

FIGURE 1. IA^d binding profile of Ha 121–146. A series of 11-residue peptides with a 10-residue overlap, spanning through residues 121–146 of Ha, were synthesized. A C → S substitution was introduced at position 140 to avoid cysteine-related problems in the purification of the peptide series. The amount of each peptide necessary to inhibit by 50% the binding of ^{125}I-labeled Ova 323–339 to IA^d was measured by a gel filtration method[4] and normalized to the capacity of unlabeled Ova 323–336 to inhibit binding. The 50% inhibition dose for Ova 323–336 before normalization was 48 μg/ml. The data represent the average of 2–4 experiments.

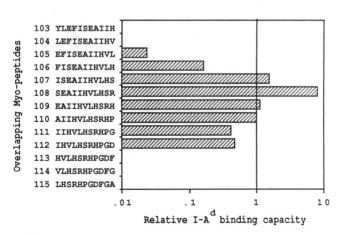

Sequence of Myo 103-125:
YLEFISEAIIHVLHSRHPGDFGA

FIGURE 2. IA^d binding profile of Myo 103–125. A series of 11-residue overlapping peptides spanning through residues 103–125 of Myo was generated and assayed for IA^d binding, as described in FIGURE 1. The data represent the average of 2–4 experiments.

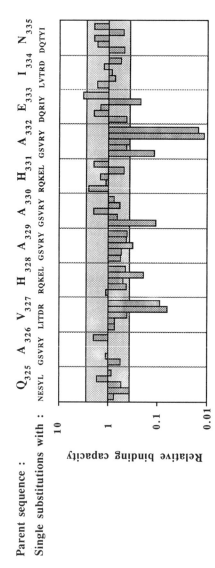

FIGURE 3. IA^d-interacting capacity of single substitution analogs of Ova 323–336. Five different substitutions (two conservative, one semiconservative, and two nonconservative) were introduced into each of the 11 positions, 325–335. These peptides were then tested for IA^d binding. Each *bar* represents the arithmetic mean of 2–4 independent determinations. *Shaded area* represents 99% confidence limits.

overlapping peptides that encompass residues 103–125 of myoglobin is shown in FIGURE 2. From these data it can be concluded that the C-terminal limit of the region containing the IA^d binding site is centered around residues H$_{116}$ and S$_{117}$, because removal of S$_{117}$ resulted in a 10-fold decrease in binding activity, whereas further removal of H$_{116}$ completely abolished the binding activity. The N-terminal limit of the IA^d binding region can be identified as I$_{112}$, because its deletion from the N-terminus completely abolished binding activity. The peptide region thus defined, Myo 112–117 confirms the structural similarity analysis and identifies IHVLHS as the relevant region for IA^d binding.

EFFECT OF SINGLE AMINO ACID SUBSTITUTIONS OF THE IA^d INTERACTING CAPACITY OF OVA 323–336

To further characterize the relative contribution to IA^d binding of individual residues within the Ova peptide, we synthesized a series of 55 single substitution analogs of the peptide 323–336, which is highly stimulatory for certain T cells and binds equally well as Ova 323–339 to IA^d. For each of the 11 positions, 325–335, we synthesized five analogs, each carrying a single amino acid substitution (two conservative, one semiconservative, and two nonconservative). When these analogs were tested for their capacity to bind to IA^d, most of the substitutions had little or no effect on Ia binding. Only 9 of 55 (16%) had a significant (more than threefold reduction, $p < 0.01$) effect, and only 7 (13%) substitutions led to more than a fivefold reduction in IA^d binding capacity (FIG. 3). The most dramatic effects were seen at residues V$_{327}$ and A$_{332}$ (2 and 3, respectively, of 5 substitutions led to greater than a 10-fold reduction in binding). These results are in agreement with those obtained with truncated analogs, and point to V$_{327}$ and A$_{332}$ as being the most critical residues involved in binding to IA^d. A significant but less dramatic effect was detected at H$_{328}$ and E$_{333}$. Although we interpreted the decrease in IA^d binding capacity at these positions as being caused by alterations or deletions in IA^d contact residues, we cannot exclude the possibility that the decreased binding could be secondary to a change in peptide conformation caused by the substitutions. For instance, a 10-fold reduction in binding activity was apparent when A$_{330}$ was replaced by a glycine. Because glycine is known to have a strong influence on peptide conformation,[12] and because it was the only substitution of those tested at this position that showed a significant effect on IA^d binding, we propose that it may be mediated by an alteration in the peptide secondary structure.

DISCUSSION AND CONCLUSIONS

The set of experiments summarized in this report analyze the structure of a previously identified T-cell determinant contained within the IA^d-restricted ovalbumin peptide, Ova 323–339. Using N- and C-terminal truncated analogs we defined a core region of six amino acids as being critical for IA^d binding (Ova 327–332). We also were able to show that a number of peptides from unrelated proteins that are good IA^d binders contain peptide regions structurally similar to the Ova core region. In two instances we were able to demonstrate experimentally that the regions that shared maximum similarity to Ova 327–332 were in fact involved in the binding of peptides to IA^d. We then examined the effect on IA^d binding of a large collection of single substitution analogs of Ova 323–336. The results obtained suggest that as little as two residues may be strongly involved in determining the specific binding to IA^d, whereas two other residues appear to be implicated to a lesser extent. In fact, the interaction between Ia and antigen seems to be very permissive, because more than 85% of the substitutions tested had little or no effect on the binding of Ova 323–336 to IA^d. These findings are in keeping with the determinant selection hypothesis and suggest a possible mechanism by which Ia molecules could bind many unrelated peptides.

It is of interest to compare the IA^d binding regions of the set of proteins just described with the structural pattern associated with generic MHC binding suggested by Rothbard.[13] These investigators sought common structural features of T-cell antigenic peptides, disregarding the animal species in which the peptides were immunogenic and also disregarding the class of MHC or the haplotype to which the peptides were restricted. A feature common to most peptides analyzed was a four-residue peptide region consisting of: polar (or glycine), hydrophobic, hydrophobic, basic (or glycine). In the three IA^d binding peptides that we have analyzed, this region is HAAH for Ova and HVLH for Myo; three of the four residues of Ha (TAA) also share this motif. It is of particular interest that as defined by single amino acid substitutions and the analysis of truncated peptides, the residues that endow the Ova

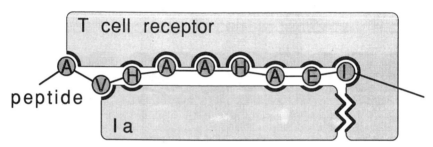

FIGURE 4. Model of the interaction between the Ova peptide, Ia, and the T-cell receptor. Accented concavities in the Ia and T-cell receptor indicate putative contact sites with antigen. The peptide is sandwiched in an extended conformation between IA^d and the T-cell receptor to allow shared recognition of some residues (H_{328}, A_{332}, and E_{333}). All the other residues are shown as either pure T-cell or pure Ia-interaction residues. The T-cell recognition of Ia residues is also indicated.

peptide and most likely the other IA^d binding peptides with the capacity to bind that particular MHC molecule are not contained within this tetrapeptide sequence; rather they are properties of the amino acids flanking the N and C-terminus of the peptide. Thus, it is V_{327} and A_{332} in Ova peptide 327–332 (VHAAHA) that are identified as the IA^d interaction residues of this peptide.[9] On the basis of these observations we suggest that: (1) the central tetrapeptide, HAAH, may not be itself critically involved in determining the binding to a particular MHC molecule, but could be important in determining the capacity of a peptide to interact with MHC molecules in general, perhaps by simply allowing a peptide to assume the appropriate conformation that permits other residues (V_{327} and A_{332} for Ova) to interact with amino acid residues within the IA^d peptide binding site; (2) alternatively, the central peptide may be capable of binding to many different MHC by virtue of its interaction with nonpolymorphic regions of the MHC, whereas the interaction between other residues of the peptide with MHC involves polymorphic residues that endow the overall binding of a peptide with the type of specificity observed experimentally. Depending on the nature of the flanking residues, specificity for different MHC molecules will be displayed. The definition of core binding regions, and the critical MHC interaction residues within such regions, that are associated with MHC molecules other than IA^d will provide a further test of this hypothesis.

Lastly, the data just described can be used to derive a model for the interaction between antigen, Ia molecules, and T-cell receptors. It has been suggested[14] that immunogenic peptides may form amphipathic α-helical structures, one surface of which interacts with Ia and the other surface with the T-cell receptor. This model appears to be inconsistent with our data, because T-cell and Ia residues do not segregate when the peptide is modeled into an α-helix. This lack of segregation also follows from the fact that 9 of the 11 residues studied appeared to be involved in T-cell recognition.[9] We suggest that the most economical model to explain the data consists of a trimolecular complex in which the peptide molecule is "sandwiched" between the Ia molecule and the T-cell receptor in a two-dimensional planar conformation that allows a given residue to interact with either Ia or T-cell receptor, or both (FIG. 4).

REFERENCES

1. BUUS, S., A. SETTE, & H. M. GREY. 1987. The interaction between protein derived immunogenic peptides and Ia. Immunol. Rev. **98:** 116.
2. ALLEN, P. M., B. BABBITT & E. UNANVE. 1987. T cell recognition of lysozyme—the biochemical basis of presentation. Immunol. Rev. **98:** 172.
3. WATTS, T. H. & H. M. McCONNELL. 1986. High-affinity fluorescent peptide binding to IA^d in lipid membranes. Proc. Natl. Acad. Sci. USA **83**(24): 9660–9664.
4. BUUS, S., A. SETTE, S. COLON, C. MILES & H. M. GREY. 1987. The relation between MHC restriction and the capacity of IA to bind immunogenic peptides. Patterns of interaction between 11 peptides and IA^d and Ia^k. Science **235:** 1353.
5. SCHAEFFER, E., A. SETTE, J. SMITH, H. GREY & S. BUUS. The frequency of Ia binding peptides within a protein antigen and the correlation between binding to Ia and T cell immunogenicity. Fed. Proc., in press.
6. GUILLET, J., M. LAI, T. J. BRINER, S. BUUS, A. SETTE, H. GREY, J. SMITH, & M. GEFTER. 1987. Immunological self, nonself discrimination. Science **235:** 1353.
7. BJORKMAN, P. J., M. A. SAPER, B. SAMRAOUI, W. S. BENNETT, J. L. STROMINGER & D. C. WILEY. 1987. Structure of the human class I histocompatibility antigen, HLA-A2. Nature **329:** 506.
8. BJORKMAN, P. J., M. A. SAPER, B. SAMRAOUI, W. S. BENNETT, J. L. STROMINGER & D. C. WILEY. 1987. The foreign antigen binding site and T cell recognition regions of class I histocompatibility antigens. Nature **329:** 512.
9. SETTE, A., S. BUUS, S. COLON, J. A. SMITH, C. MILES & H. M. GREY. 1987. Structural characteristics of an antigen that are required for its interaction with Ia and recognition of T cells. Nature **328:** 395.
10. GRANTHAM, R. 1974. Amino acid formula to help explain protein evolution. Science **185:** 862.
11. PADLAN, E. 1977. Structural implications of sequence variability in immunoglobulins. Proc. Natl. Acad. Sci. USA **24:** 2551.
12. CHOU, P. Y. & G. D. TASMAN. 1978. Empirical predictions of protein conformation. Ann. Rev. Biochem. **47:** 251.
13. ROTHBARD, J. 1986. Pattern recognition among T cell epitopes. Ann. Inst. Past. **137E:** 518.
14. DELISI, C. & J. A. BERZOFSKY. 1985. T cell antigenic sites tend to be amphipathic structures. Proc. Natl. Acad. Sci. USA **82:** 7048.

The Sensitization Phase of
T-Cell-Mediated Immunity[a]

RALPH M. STEINMAN,[b] SUMI KOIDE,[b] MARGIT
WITMER,[b] MARY CROWLEY,[b] NINA BHARDWAJ,[b]
PETER FREUDENTHAL,[b] JAMES YOUNG,[b]
AND KAYO INABA[c]

[b]*The Rockefeller University and
Irvington House Institute for Medical Research
New York, New York 10021*

[c]*Kyoto University
Kyoto 606, Japan*

Major emphasis in research on T-cell-mediated immunity has been placed on the related topics of antigen presentation and T-cell recognition of antigen plus MHC. As summarized in several other reports presented herein (Grey, Gefter), antigen presentation may entail several steps. "Nominal" antigens such as soluble proteins and infectious agents are processed to form peptides 8–18 amino acids in length. The peptides then associate with polymorphic MHC molecules. The secondary and tertiary structures of MHC molecules form a single peptide-binding site that includes most of the polymorphic residues, the latter restricting the type of peptide that can be bound. Finally, the peptide-MHC complex on the presenting cell surface is recognized by the alpha-beta heterodimeric receptor on the T lymphocyte.

Many aspects of antigen presentation and recognition are best studied with monoclonal populations of lymphocytes such as T-cell clones and T-T hybrids. These monoclonal populations are maintained in culture for long periods and do not necessarily correspond to resting lymphocytes. A good example is that many T-cell clones respond vigorously to exogenous growth factors, whereas resting T cells do not. Therefore, the study of antigen presentation to T-cell clones and hybrids does not necessarily provide a complete picture of the requirements for immune responses by resting T cells.

We were attracted to this question because of findings that have emerged from several laboratories on the function of dendritic cells as antigen presenting cells. (See reference 1 for a review.) In tissue culture, the addition of small numbers of dendritic cells to purified lymphocytes—usually in a ratio of 1:30 to 1:100— leads to active mixed leukocyte reactions, antibody production to foreign red cells and hapten-carrier conjugates, proliferation to mitogens, and proliferative and cytotoxic responses to hapten-modified cells. *In situ,* antigens in association with dendritic cells induce graft rejection, contact sensitivity, and antibody formation. In several of these responses, other antigen presenting cells such as macrophages and B lymphocytes have little or no activity.

[a]This work was supported by Grants AI 13013, AI 24501, and K08 CA-00961 from the NIH. Nina Bhardwaj was a Mrs. Arthur Gray fellow of the Irvington House Institute for Medical Research and is a recipient of a grant from the N.Y. Arthritis Association. Peter Freudenthal is a David C. Scott Foundation fellow.

At this time, the only known function of dendritic cells is to *sensitize* T cells, that is, to convert small inactive lymphocytes into large active lymphoblasts. The lymphoblasts release lymphokines and/or kill targets. T blasts interact with other presenting cells such as B lymphocytes and macrophages, leading to effector functions such as antibody formation and microbial killing, which are required for antigen elimination. In contrast to these other antigen presenting cells, dendritic cells are not known to have effector functions. For example, they typically do not phagocytose or clear immune complexes, produce antibodies, or secrete interleukin-1 (IL-1).

In this report, we address recent findings on the mechanisms whereby dendritic cells are specialized to act as accessory cells early, or in the *sensitization* phase, of cell-mediated immunity. Sensitization clearly requires antigen presentation and recognition, but it likely requires other events. Dendritic cell function will be discussed in terms of: the cell's high levels of surface MHC products; molecules required for the formation of dendritic–T-cell contacts; release of lymphocyte-activating factors such as IL-1; and cytokines that may help mobilize active dendritic cells from nonlymphoid organs.

EXPRESSION OF MHC PRODUCTS AND ANTIGEN PRESENTATION

Most studies of dendritic cell function have used populations from lymphoid tissues, blood, and afferent lymph. These "lymphoid" dendritic cells uniformly express high levels of class I and II products of the MHC. In the past, expression of MHC products was monitored by quantitative binding studies with radioiodinated monoclonal antibodies (mAb), autoradiography, and immunofluorescence. It is now feasible to stain and study small numbers of cells by flow cytometry, which provides a rapid and quantitative view of the dendritic cell surface (FIG. 1). This figure illustrates the very high levels of class I (here H-2K; 100 times background) and class II (I-A/E; 600 times background) MHC products on mouse spleen dendritic cells (FIG. 1, left column) and also that dendritic cells react weakly, if at all, to mAb that detect either macrophage- or lymphocyte-restricted epitopes (F4/80, B220, thy-1, CD4; middle column, FIG. 1). The one dendritic cell-specific reagent, 33D1, stains dendritic cells weakly but is cytolytic in the presence of rabbit complement.[2] When a panel of mAb to specific receptors is studied, the 2.4G2 Fc receptor antigen is not detectable, but low levels of other receptors (C3bi and IL-2 receptors, LFA-1; FIG. 1, right) are noted. The surface phenotype of dendritic cells differs markedly from that of macrophages, which typically show lower levels of MHC products and a different constellation of differentiation antigens and receptors. Notably, macrophages from peritoneal cavity (FIG. 2) and spleen (not shown) have relatively high levels of 2.4G2 (Fc receptor) and Mac-1 or M1/70 (C3bi receptor), but little or no 7D4-3C7 antigen (55-kd, low affinity IL-2 receptor).

It is important to point out that the enrichment methods used to prepare dendritic cells do not themselves select for a high content of MHC products. Instead, the procedures select for cells with the unusual shape and surface activity (formation and movement of cell processes) of these leukocytes. These dendritic cells have low levels of Fc receptors and lack many important macrophage and lymphocyte markers, features that are used to develop a variety of purification techniques for dendritic cells in specific tissues. In every case, the enriched populations express high levels of class I and II MHC products. For example, in mouse spleen and thymus (in preparation), dendritic cells are most readily enriched from populations that initially are firmly adherent. After overnight culture, dendritic cells are separated from adherent macrophages by selecting cells that lack abundant Fc receptors and lose the adherence

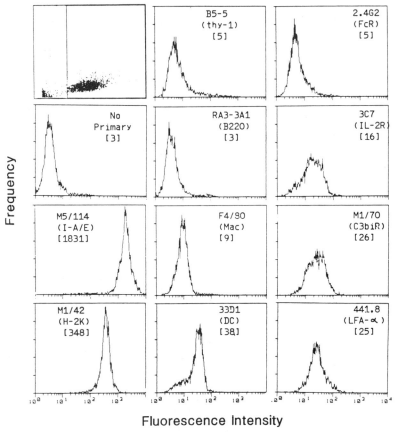

Fluorescence Intensity

FIGURE 1.

FIGURES 1 and 2. Flow cytometric analysis of the cell surface antigens of mouse spleen dendritic cells (FIG. 1) and peritoneal macrophages (FIG. 2). The dendritic cells were Fc receptor negative, spleen-adherent cells,[3] whereas the macrophages were resident cells from the peritoneal cavity. (Similar results are observed with macrophages purified by plastic adherence and/or maintained for a day in culture; not shown.) Side versus forward light scatter dot plots for each population are shown in the *top left panels*. Note that spleen dendritic cells have the light scattering properties of lymphocytes, whereas the macrophages are selected by gating for cells with much larger forward and side scatter. (Most cells with the macrophage-restricted F4/80 and M1/70 antigens fall to the right of the horizontal gate.) Each population was exposed to hybridoma culture supernatants followed by fluorescein-conjugated mouse anti-rat Ig (Boehringer). The monoclonal antibodies[47] (clone name, antigen recognized, median fluorescence) are given on each frequency versus fluorescence tracing. The data and antibodies are arranged in three groups: antibodies to MHC products are on the *left;* antibodies to cell-specific antigens in the *middle;* and antibodies to defined receptors on the *right.* Not shown are several antibodies that did not stain either macrophages or dendritic cells. These included reagents[47] to Lyt-1, Lyt-2, L3T4, interdigitating cell antigen, and KJ/16 T cell receptor antigen.

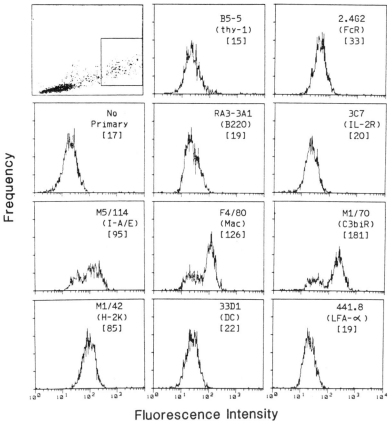

Fluorescence Intensity

FIGURE 2.

property. The nonadherent Fc⁻ cells are almost all dendritic in shape and exhibit the phenotype and high levels of MHC products outlined in FIGURE 1.[3,4] Dendritic cells in suspension from rat lymph or rat lymphoid organs do not adhere to glass or plastic even temporarily. If one depletes lymphocytes, one again enriches for a dendritic population that is rich in transplantation antigen.[5,6] Human blood dendritic cells occupy an intermediate status in terms of adherence. To achieve the best yields, it is best to start the enrichment procedure after 1–2 days in culture when most dendritic cells are nonadherent.[7]

Not only are the levels of MHC products on dendritic cells very high, but also these levels seem to be under distinct controls. This was noted some years ago when it was discovered that MHC products could be upregulated on macrophages, but not on dendritic cells, by T-cell-derived lymphokines.[8] This finding has been verified with recombinant gamma-interferon and quantitative binding studies with ¹²⁵I anti-Ia antibody (TABLE 1).

There are now instances in which immature forms of dendritic cells have been found such as in bone marrow,[9] epidermis,[10,11] and the nonadherent fraction of thymus suspensions.[12] The term "immature" is used, because these populations must be cultured for 1–2 days before optimal levels of surface Ia and accessory function are expressed. In thymus and epidermis, maturation is driven by factors such as IL-1 and GM-CSF.[12,13]

Although lymphoid dendritic cells express high levels of MHC products, more work is needed on their ability to present "nominal" rather than "transplantation" antigens. The processing of various proteins and infectious agents may occur in endocytic vacuoles for class II-restricted antigens and perhaps along the exocytic pathway for class I-restricted antigens such as virus constituents. Lymphoid dendritic cells are not actively endocytic when challenged with a number of soluble tracers and particulates, and have yet to be shown to be permissive for any virus infection. Therefore, how do dendritic cells perform an intracellular processing function to present antigens in association with MHC products? One possibility that we are considering is that most dendritic cells that are isolated from lymph and lymphoid organs have already processed antigens in nonlymphoid tissues *in situ* and have migrated to the lymphoid organs with peptides to be presented to appropriate clones of antigen-specific T cells. In other words, antigen processing and presentation by

TABLE 1. Recombinant Immune Interferon Enhances Expression of Ia Antigens on Splenic Macrophages But Not Dendritic Cells[a]

Spleen Cells	Interferon	Binding Sites/Cells $\times$ 10^{-5}	
		Experiment 1	Experiment 2
Macrophages	−	85	58
	+	180	175
Dendritic cells	−	224	214
	+	231	150

[a]Low density spleen-adherent cells were cultured for 2 days $\pm$ 10 U/ml of recombinant murine gamma-interferon. The cells were then separated into firmly adherent macrophages and nonadherent dendritic cells as described.[4] Each population was exposed to radioiodinated B21-2 mAb to Ia antigens under saturating conditions on ice as described.[8]

dendritic cells may be regulated and may be confined to those intervals in which dendritic cells are exposed to antigens in inflammatory sites.

BINDING TO ANTIGEN-SPECIFIC T LYMPHOCYTES

One of the challenging unknowns in cell-mediated immunity is: how does a receptor in the plasma membrane of one cell, the T lymphocyte, come in contact with antigens displayed on the surface of another cell, the antigen presenting cell? Dendritic cells clearly have solved this challenge. During antibody formation to T-dependent antigens and during the mixed leukocyte reaction, the bulk of the response is carried out in clusters of dendritic cells and lymphocytes.[14–19] Typically the clusters are isolated on day 1 or 2 of the immune response. The response then develops from the aggregates over the next 2–3 days. Clustering with dendritic cells is a feature of both primary and recall ("memory") phases of responses in culture. Similar clusters have been identified *in situ* in delayed type hypersensitivity[20] and allograft rejection.[21]

Several features of the clustering phenomenon have been amenable to study *in vitro*. Clustering is efficient with respect to both the dendritic cell and the antigen-specific T cell. The movement of dendritic cells into clusters is best visualized using fluorescent carbocyanine dyes as a vital label.[19,22] The movement of antigen-specific lymphocytes is monitored by indirect criteria. The response of isolated clusters is observed to be comparable to that of mixtures of clusters and nonclusters, implying that most of the responsive cells are in the aggregates. In a mixed leukocyte reaction, rechallenge experiments performed on nonclustered T cells will demonstrate a depletion of specific or first party reactivity but responsiveness to a donor displaying different or third party MHC products.[15,16]

In primary responses by either CD4+ or CD8+ subsets, T-cell clustering seems specific for dendritic cells. Clusters do not form with macrophages or B lymphocytes,[15,16,23] and there is as yet no direct evidence that resting T cells can establish contacts with these presenting cells in an antigen-specific fashion.

A different situation pertains when lymphoblasts rather than resting T cells are studied. Enriched populations of antigen-specific T lymphoblasts are released from dendritic–T-cell clusters, and these lymphoblasts can bind[23] and activate other antigen presenting cells. In fact, a good criterion for the sensitization process is that the T cell acquires the capacity to bind to other targets so that the efferent limb of the immune response can be carried out. An example is the antibody response to hapten-carrier conjugates.[24] If T cells are primed with dendritic cells and carrier protein *in vitro,* the T blasts apparently activate B cells in a direct, antigen-specific, and MHC-restricted manner. This kind of information supports the view that there are two stages in cell-mediated immunity. During the first or afferent-sensitization stage, contacts are established with dendritic cells, and T-cell growth and function begin. In the second or efferent-effector stage, the T lymphoblast binds and influences the appropriate target to provide effector function. We just exemplified the latter in the context of antibody formation by B cells, but similar findings pertain to the induction of macrophage IL-1 by sensitized T lymphoblasts (Koide; Bhardwaj; in preparation).

The molecular mechanism of dendritic–T-cell clustering is not clear. Both LFA-1 (CD11a) and CD4 are thought to be important accessory molecules for the binding of lymphocytes to presenting cells. However, antibodies to LFA-1 and CD4 do not seem to block the initial binding of dendritic cells to resting or activated T lymphocytes.[25] These antibodies block the subsequent function of the dendritic–T-cell conjugate. Anti-LFA-1 can disassemble the conjugate and make it very susceptible to shear forces, whereas anti-CD4 blocks lymphoblast formation and lymphokine release.

To summarize, we have a situation in which antigen alone does not seem to be the first "signal" for the formation of cell-cell contacts early in the immune response, because antigen on macrophages and B cells does not initiate clustering. Antigen must be available on these presenting cells, given their capacity to interact with T lymphoblasts in a specific way.[15,23] LFA-1 and CD4 also are involved in the communication between presenting cells and lymphocytes, but these molecules do not appear to be the first signals. We are working on the hypothesis that there are novel molecules that mediate an early reversible interaction between dendritic cells and T cells, and that this interaction is followed by antigen recognition and by the function of CD4 and LFA-1.[25] To identify clustering molecules, we are screening antidendritic cell hybridomas for the capacity to block clustering with T cells. This strategy has yet to prove successful. Immunization with dendritic cells primarily leads to the development of anti-MHC antibodies rather than dendritic cell-specific reagents.

RELEASE OF LYMPHOCYTE-ACTIVATING FACTORS

Once dendritic–T-cell contacts have developed, what comes next? Do dendritic cells release a factor that is required for the lymphocyte response, or is the entire process regulated by the interaction between cell surface components? The evidence is now extensive that lymphoid dendritic cells do not produce one specific activating factor, IL-1. Dendritic cells from mouse spleen, human blood, and the exudates of joint effusions of rheumatoid arthritis have been studied.[26,27] In each case, IL-1 production is not detected, whereas mononuclear phagocytes actively make this cytokine. A useful approach involves immunolabeling with a rabbit antiserum to a human IL-1 beta peptide. The antibody stains individual cells with cytoplasmic IL-1[28] and is as sensitive as the D10 bioassay in detecting IL-1 in human monocytes.[27] However, no IL-1 can be detected in dendritic cells when clustered with responding lymphocytes.

Nonetheless, IL-1 amplifies T-dependent proliferative responses in culture as long as the cultures contain dendritic cells. It seems that one of the principal effects of IL-1 is exerted on the dendritic cell.[22] Dendritic cells can be pulsed for 8–18 hours with IL-1, washed, and then added to the mitogenesis assays. In both peripheral and thymocyte proliferative responses, pulsing dendritic cells before use as accessory cells is as effective as adding IL-1 continuously to the cultures.[12,22] The pulsed dendritic cells are not blocked with a neutralizing anti-IL-1 antibody, but the antibody does block the action of IL-1 during the pulsing step.[12]

These results raise two new points with respect to dendritic cell function. The first is that the secretory capacity of dendritic cells and macrophages is different. More products need to be studied. It is not known if dendritic cells make other important effector cytokines that are made by macrophages such as cachectin-tumor necrosis factor and IL-6. A second point is that dendritic cell function can be amplified by cytokines. Interestingly this enhanced function is not associated with an increase in expression of Ia. Instead, the amplifying effect of IL-1 seems to be due to the more efficient clustering of dendritic cells and T lymphocytes before the onset of mitogenesis.[22]

MOBILIZATION, MOVEMENT, AND MATURATION OF TISSUE DENDRITIC CELLS

Antigens are typically deposited in nonlymphoid organs. Where does the T cell learn that antigen is present and begin to respond? Is antigen presented in the periphery and there is an influx of T cells into the inflammatory site, or must antigen move centrally to the lymphoid organ via the afferent lymph to select antigen-specific clones in the T-dependent areas? The latter would seem to be a predominant site for T-cell sensitization for three reasons (see reference 1 for a review): blastogenesis and the production of sensitized T cells are detected early in the draining lymphoid organs; sensitization for contact sensitivity and skin allografts is blocked if the afferent lymphatics are severed; and the continual recirculation of T cells through the T area provides a favorable site for the selection of specific clones by antigen.

If dendritic cells are required for T-cell sensitization, are dendritic cells present at the site of antigen deposition? Because of a lack of mAb that can be used to stain dendritic cells in section, there is a lack of detailed evidence on tissue distribution. However, a combination of criteria—cytologic features by electron microscopy, expression of abundant class II molecules, and absence of certain cytochemical and antigenic markers of macrophages and lymphocytes—indicates that dendritic cells are present in the interstitial tissues of heart,[29,30] lung,[31] and urinary tract[29,32] as well as the T-dependent regions of lymphoid organs.[33,34]

A second feature relates to the migratory properties of dendritic cells. Balfour et al.[35–37] found that dendritic or veiled cells are present in rabbit and pig afferent lymph. Other studies indentified dendritic cells in lymphatics draining contact sensitivity sites in guinea pig[38] and mouse[39,40] and in afferent lymphatics from rat intestine.[6,41] Austyn and colleagues[42,43] labeled mouse spleen dendritic cells and followed their migration *in situ*. Dendritic cells were injected into the bloodstream or foot pads of syngeneic recipients, and migration was monitored using an indium label for quantitation and a DNA-binding fluorochrome for histologic localization. The dendritic cells homed to the T-dependent areas. In spleen, dendritic cells accumulated in the marginal zone by 3 hours and in the T area by 24 hours. Labeled dendritic cells also were applied to frozen sections and noted to bind selectively to the marginal zone region at the periphery of the white pulp.[43]

To assess the functional properties of tissue dendritic cells more directly, Schuler *et al.*[44] undertook a study of mouse epidermal Langerhans cells in culture. Langerhans cells are the principal, if not the only, Ia^+ cell in the epidermis[44] and are responsible for the observed accessory function of epidermal suspensions. (See references 45 and 46 for a review.) Schuler *et al.*[44] found that Langerhans cells had many of the properties of dendritic cells, but only after 1–3 days of co-culture with keratinocytes.[10,11] The cultured Langerhans cells were nonadherent and nonphagocytic, and had low levels of Fc receptors. During culture, the levels of class I and II MHC products increased fivefold,[47] and the accessory function for primary T-dependent responses increased 10- to 30-fold.[10,11]

The development of accessory function in cultured Langerhans cells seems entirely dependent on exogenous cytokines.[13,48] The required cytokines are present in the conditioned medium from cultured keratinocytes and from stimulated macrophages and T cells. The active keratinocyte product has proven to be granulocyte-macrophage colony stimulating factor (GM-CSF). Anti-GM-CSF neutralizes the activity of keratinocyte-conditioned medium, and recombinant GM-CSF is the only purified cytokine that mediates Langerhans cell maturation *in vitro* with half-maximal activity at 0.5 pmol. Once the Langerhans cell has developed in response to GM-CSF, accessory function cannot be blocked by anti-GM-CSF.[13] Heufler *et al.*[48] found that IL-1 enhances the effect of GM-CSF by about twofold, but IL-1 by itself does not influence Langerhans cell viability and function. Several other factors, including macrophage- or M-CSF and IL-3, have no effect.

The observations summarized in this section suggest that an important element in the sensitization phases of the immune response is the influence of cytokines such as GM-CSF on the properties of tissue dendritic cells. GM-CSF is produced by many cell types, not just sensitized T cells, so that it may be released as a very early event in inflammatory sites where antigens are deposited.

SUMMARY

Many cell-mediated immune responses appear to develop in two phases: A *sensitization phase* in which unprimed or memory T cells interact with dendritic cells to become active lymphoblasts, and an *effector phase* in which the T lymphoblasts and other presenting cells interact to eliminate the antigen. Antigen presentation is essential to both phases. Here we review several features that are pertinent to the special sensitization role of dendritic cells. First, dendritic cells from lymphoid tissues, blood, and lymph (lymphoid dendritic cells) express very high levels of class I and II MHC products, and these levels cannot be increased by exposure to cytokines such as immune interferon. Second, dendritic cells efficiently cluster antigen-specific T cells during primary responses. Other presenting cells, like macrophages and B lymphocytes, do not form clusters but do bind to sensitized T lymphoblasts. Dendritic–T-cell binding is not inhibited by mAb to CD4 and LFA-1 antigens. It is suggested that a dendritic-cell-specific molecule is required. Third, it is not yet clear if dendritic cells make a "lymphocyte activating factor." However, IL-1 is not produced, even when dendritic cells are in contact with responding T cells. Fourth, dendritic cells have the capacity to migrate from the tissues and move to T-dependent areas. Epidermal Langerhans cells represent a reservoir of tissue dendritic cells but seem to be immunologically immature. The viability and accessory function of the Langerhans cell greatly depend on a single cytokine, granulocyte-macrophage colony stimulating factor (GM-CSF), leading to the proposal that GM-CSF is critical in mobilizing active dendritic cells at the onset of a cell-mediated immune response.

REFERENCES

1. STEINMAN, R. M., K. INABA, G. SCHULER & M. D. WITMER. 1986. Stimulation of the immune response: Contributions of dendritic cells. *In* Mechanisms of Host Resistance to Infectious Agents, Tumors, and Allografts. R. M. Steinman & R. J. North, Eds. :71–97. The Rockefeller University Press, New York.
2. STEINMAN, R. M., B. GUTCHINOV, M. D. WITMER & M. C. NUSSENZWEIG. 1983. Dendritic cells are the principal stimulators of the primary mixed leukocyte reaction in mice. J. Exp. Med. **157:** 613–627.
3. STEINMAN, R. M., G. KPLAN, M. D. WITMER & Z. A. COHN. 1979. Identification of a novel cell-type in peripheral lymphoid organs of mice. V. Purification of spleen dendritic cells, new surface markers, and maintenance in vitro. J. Exp. Med. **149:** 1–16.
4. NUSSENZWEIG, M. C. & R. M. STEINMAN. 1980. Contributions of dendritic cells to stimulation of the murine syngeneic mixed leukocyte reaction. J. Exp. Med. **151;** 1196–1212.
5. KLINKERT, W. E. F., J. H. LaBADIE & W. E. BOWERS. 1982. Accessory and stimulating properties of dendritic cells and macrophages isolated from various rat tissues. J. Exp. Med. **156:**1–19.
6. PUGH, C. W., G. G. MacPHERSON & H. W. STEER. 1983. Characterization of nonlymphoid cells derived from rat peripheral lymph. J. Exp. Med. **157:** 1758–1779.
7. YOUNG, J. W. & R. M. STEINMAN. 1988. Accessory cell requirements for the mixed leukocyte reaction and polyclonal mitogens, as studied with a new technique for enriching blood dendritic cells. Cell. Immunol. **111:** 167–182.
8. STEINMAN, R. M., N. NOGUEIRA, M. D. WITMER, J. D. TYDINGS & I. S. MELLMAN. 1980. Lymphokine enhances the expression and synthesis of Ia antigen on cultured mouse peritoneal macrophages. J. Exp. Med. **152:** 1248–1261.
9. BOWERS, W. E. & M. R. BERKOWITZ. 1986. Differentiation of dendritic cells in cultures of rat bone marrow cells. J. Exp. Med. **163:** 872–883.
10. SCHULER, G. & R. M. STEINMAN. 1985. Murine epidermal Langerhans cells mature into potent immunostimulatory dendritic cells in vitro. J. Exp. Med. **161:**526–546.
11. INABA, K., G. SCHULER, M. D. WITMER, J. VALINSKY, B. ATASSI & R. M. STEINMAN. 1986. The immunologic properties of purified Langerhans cells: Distinct requirements for the stimulation of unprimed and sensitized T lymphocytes. J. Exp. Med. **164:** 605–613.
12. INABA, K., M. D. WITMER-PACK, M. INABA, S. MURAMATSU & R. M. STEINMAN. 1988. The function of Ia$^+$ dendritic cells, and Ia$^-$ dendritic cell precursors, in thymocyte mitogenesis to lectin and lectin plus IL-1. J. Exp. Med. **167:** 149–163.
13. WITMER-PACK, M. D., W. OLIVIER, J. VALINSKY, G. SCHULER & R. M. STEINMAN. 1987. Granulocyte/macrophage colony-stimulating factor is essential for the viability and function of cultured murine epidermal Langerhans cells. J. Exp. Med. **166:** 1484–1498.
14. INABA, K., M. D. WITMER & R. M. STEINMAN. 1984. Clustering of dendritic cells, helper T lymphocytes, and histocompatible B cells, during primary antibody responses in vitro. J. Exp. Med. **160:** 858–876.
15. INABA, K. & R. M. STEINMAN. 1984. Resting and sensitized T lymphocytes exhibit distinct stimulatory (antigen presenting cell) requirements for growth and lymphokine release. J. Exp. Med. **160:** 1717–1735.
16. FLECHNER, E., P. FREUDENTHAL, G. KAPLAN & R. M. STEINMAN. 1988. Antigen-specific T

lymphocytes efficiently cluster with dendritic cells in the human primary mixed leukocyte reaction. Cell. Immunol. **111:** 167–182.

17. INABA, K. & R. M. STEINMAN. 1987. Dendritic and B cell function during antibody responses in normal and immunodeficient (xid) mouse spleen cultures. *Cell. Immunol.* **105:** 432–442.

18. GREEN, J. & R. JOTTE. 1985. Interactions between T helper cells and dendritic cells during the rat mixed leukocyte reaction. J. Exp. Med. **162:** 1546–1560.

19. INABA, K., J. W. YOUNG & R. M. STEINMAN. 1987. Direct activation of CD8$^+$ cytotoxic T lymphocytes by dendritic cells. J. Exp. Med. **166:** 182–194.

20. KAPLAN, G., A. NUSRAT, M. D. WITMER, I. NATH & Z. A. COHN. 1987. Distribution and turnover of Langerhans cells during delayed immune responses in human skin. J. Exp. Med. **165:** 763–776.

21. FORBES, R. D. C., N. A. PARFREY, M. GOMERSALL, A. G. DARDEN & R. D. GUTTMANN. 1986. Dendritic cell-lymphoid cell aggregation and major histocompatibility antigen expression during rat cardiac allograft rejection. J. Exp. Med. **164:** 1239–1258.

22. KOIDE, S. L., K. INABA & R. M. STEINMAN. 1987. Interleukin-1 enhances T-dependent immune responses by amplifying the function of dendritic cells. J. Exp. Med. **165:** 515–530.

23. INABA, K. & R. M. STEINMAN. 1986. Accessory cell-T lymphocyte interactions: Antigen dependent and independent clustering. J. Exp. Med. **163:** 247–261.

24. INABA, K. & R. M. STEINMAN. 1985. Protein-specific helper T lymphocyte formation initiated by dendritic cells. Science **229:** 475–479.

25. INABA, K. & R. M. STEINMAN. 1987. Monoclonal antibodies to LFA-1 and to CD4 inhibit the mixed leukocyte reaction after the antigen-dependent clustering of dendritic cells and T lymphocytes. J. Exp. Med. **165:** 1403–1417.

26. KOIDE, S. L. & R. M. STEINMAN. 1987. Induction of murine interleukin-1: Stimuli and responsive primary cells. Proc. Natl. Acad. Sci., USA **84:** 3802–3816.

27. BHARDWAJ, N., L. LAU, M. RIVELIS & R. M. STEINMAN. 1988. Interleukin-1 production by mononuclear cells from rheumatoid synovial effusions. Cell. Immunol. **104:** 405–423.

28. BAYNE, E. K., E. A. RUPP, G. LIMJUCO, J. CHIN & J. A. SCHMIDT. 1986. Immunocytochemical detection of interleukin 1 within stimulated human monocytes. J. Exp. Med. **163:** 1267–1280.

29. HART, D. N. J. & J. W. FABRE. 1981. Demonstration and characterization of Ia-positive dendritic cells in the interstitial connective tissues of rat heart and other tissues, but not brain. J. Exp. Med. **154:** 347–361.

30. MCKENZIE, J. L., M. E. J. BEARD & D. N. J. HART. 1984. The effect of donor pretreatment on interstitial dendritic cell content and rat cardiac allograft survival. Transplantation **38:** 371–376.

31. SERTL, K., T. TAKEMURA, E. TSCHACHLER, V. J. FERRANS, M. A. KALINER & E. M. SHEVACH. 1986. Dendritic cells with antigen-presenting capability reside in airway epithelium, lung parenchyma, and visceral pleura. J. Exp. Med. **163:** 436–451.

32. HART, D. N. J. & J. W. FABRE. 1981. Major histocompatibility complex antigens in rat kidney, uterer, and bladder: Localization with monoclonal antibodies and demonstration of Ia-positive dendritic cells. Transplantation **31:** 318–325.

33. WITMER, M. D. & R. M. STEINMAN. 1984. The anatomy of peripheral lymphoid organs with emphasis on accessory cells: Light microscopic, immunocytochemical studies of mouse spleen, lymph node and Peyer's patch. Am. J. Anat. **170:** 465–481.

34. DIJKSTRA, C. D. 1982. Characterization of nonlymphoid cells in rat spleen, with special reference to strongly Ia-positive branched cells in T-cell areas. *J. Reticuloendothel. Soc.* **32:** 167–178.

35. KNIGHT, S. C., B. M. BALFOUR, J. O'BRIEN, L. BUTTIFANT, T. SUMERSKA, & J. CLARK. 1982. Role of veiled cells in lymphocyte activation. Eur. J. Immunol. **12:** 1057–1060.

36. KELLY, R. H., B. M. BALFOUR, J. A. ARMSTRONG & S. GRIFFITHS. 1978. Functional anatomy of lymph nodes. II. Peripheral lymph-borne mononuclear cells. Anat. Rec. **190:** 5–21.

37. DREXHAGE, H. A., H. MULLINK, J. DE GROOT, J. CLARKE & B. M. BALFOUR. 1979. A study of cells present in peripheral lymph of pigs with special reference to a type of cell resembling the Langerhans cells. Cell Tissue Res. **202:** 407–430.

38. SILBERBERG, I. R., L. BAER & S. A. ROSENTHAL. 1976. The role of Langerhans cells in allergic contact hypersensitivity. A review of findings in man and guinea pigs. J. Invest. Dermatol. **66**: 210–217.
39. KNIGHT, S. C., J. KREJCI, M. MALKOVSKY, V. COLIZZI, A. GAUTAM & G. L. ASHERSON. 1985. The role of dendritic cells in the initiation of immune responses to contact sensitizers. I. In vivo exposure to antigen. Cell. Immunol. **94**: 427–434.
40. MACATONIA, S., A. EDWARDS, S. GRIFFITHS, P. FRYER & S. KNIGHT. 1987. Localization of antigen on lymph node dendritic cells after exposure to the contact sensitizer fluorescein isothiocyanate. Functional and morphological studies. J. Exp. Med. **166**: 1654–1667.
41. MAYRHOFER, P., P. G. HOLT & J. M. PAPADIMITRIOU. 1986. Functional characteristics of the veiled cells in afferent lymph from the rat intestine. Immunology **58**: 379–387.
42. KUPIEC-WEGLINSKI, J. W., J. M. AUSTYN & P. J. MORRIS. 1988. Migration patterns of dendritic cells in the mouse. Traffic from the blood, and T cell-dependent and -independent entry to lymphoid tissues. J. Exp. Med. **167**: 632–645.
43. AUSTYN, J. M., J. W. KUPIEC-WEGLINSKI, D. F. HANKINS & P. J. MORRIS. 1988. Migration patterns of dendritic cells in the mouse. Homing to T cell-dependent areas of spleen, and binding within marginal zone. J. Exp. Med. **167**: 646–651.
44. ROMANI, N., G. STINGL, E. TSCHACHLER, M. D. WITMER, R. M. STEINMAN, E. M. SHEVACH & G. SCHULER. 1985. The thy-1 bearing cell line of murine epidermis: A leukocyte distinct from Langerhans cells and perhaps related to NK Cells. J. Exp. Med. **161**: 1368–1383.
45. ROWDEN, G. 1981. The Langerhans cell. CRC Crit. Rev. Immunol. **3**: 95–180.
46. WOLFF, K. & G. STINGL. 1983. The Langerhans cell. J. Invest. Dermatol. **80**: 17s–21s.
47. WITMER-PACK, M. D., J. VALINSKY, W. OLIVIER & R. M. STEINMAN. 1988. Quantitation of surface antigens on cultured murine epidermal Langerhans cells: Rapid and selective increase in the level of surface MHC products. J. Invest., Dermatol. **90**: 387–394.
48. HEUFLER, C., F. KOCH & G. SCHULER. 1987. Granulcoyte-macrophage colony-stimulating factor and interleukin-1 mediate the maturation of murine epidermal langerhans cells into potent immunostimulatory dendritic cells. J. Exp. Med. **167**: 700–705.

Generation and Analysis of a T-Lymphocyte Somatic Mutant for Studying Molecular Aspects of Signal Transduction by the Antigen Receptor[a]

MARK A. GOLDSMITH AND ARTHUR WEISS

Departments of Medicine and of Microbiology and Immunology
School of Medicine
University of California at San Francisco
and
Howard Hughes Medical Institute
San Francisco, California 94143

The T-lymphocyte antigen receptor complex is a multimolecular assembly of integral membrane proteins that mediate antigen-driven cellular responses.[1,2] The Ti-α and -β glycoproteins are disulfide linked,[3] and together constitute the antigen recognition subunit. Each T lymphocyte expresses on its surface a unique Ti heterodimer derived from rearranging genes, which alone accounts for the specificity of the cell for a particular antigen.[4,5] Non-covalently associated with Ti is an array of at least five and possibly seven nonpolymorphic integral membrane proteins collectively referred to as the CD3 (formerly T3) complex (FIG. 1A). That CD3 and Ti are coupled to each other is supported by several lines of evidence: (a) CD3 and Ti proteins may be coimmuno-precipitated under certain conditions[6,7]; (b) CD3 and Ti proteins may be chemically cross-linked to each other[8,9]; (c) CD3 co-internalizes with the Ti dimer following exposure to soluble antireceptor complex antibodies[10]; and (d) CD3 proteins are retained intracellularly in mutants with defective expression of either of the Ti proteins.[11] The biologic role of the CD3 complex remains uncertain; however, it is widely assumed to subserve an "effector" function for the antigen-binding Ti subunit.

The antigen receptor (CD3/Ti complex) converts recognition of a foreign antigen into a cellular response, termed "activation," which can include expression of genes encoding lymphokines and their receptors, as well as initiation of the cytolytic mechanism responsible for target cell destruction. Like many receptors for hormones, the CD3/Ti complex is coupled to the inositolphospholipid second messenger system,[12] in which receptor-induced hydrolysis of the membrane constituent phosphatidylinositol 4,5-bisphosphate (PIP$_2$) releases soluble inositol 1,4,5-trisphosphate (IP$_3$) to promote increases in the concentration of intracellular free Ca^{2+} ([Ca^{2+}]$_i$) and membrane-associated diacylglycerol (DG) to potentiate protein kinase C (pkC) activity.[13] These second messenger events can be mimicked pharmacologically,[2] and they have been linked causally to the distal biologic responses characteristic of the activated T cell (FIG. 1B). Little is known about how the early transmembrane

[a]M.A.G. is an MD/PhD candidate in the NIH Medical Scientist Training Program and is supported by the Rosalind Russell Arthritis Center. A.W. is an Assistant Investigator of the Howard Hughes Medical Institute, and recipient of an Arthritis Investigator Award from the Arthritis Foundation.

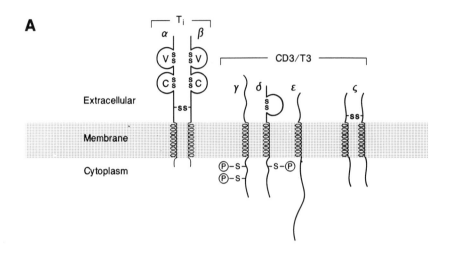

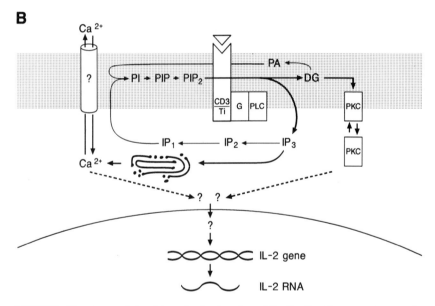

FIGURE 1. Structure and signal transduction function of the T-cell antigen receptor complex. (A) The Ti heterodimer,[1,2] consisting of two disulfide-linked glycoproteins (a relatively acidic α chain and a basic β chain), is the antigen-reactive subunit of the receptor complex. The human CD3 molecular complex[1,2] consists of at least four integral membrane glycoproteins (28-kd γ chain, 20-kd δ, and 16-kd ζ dimer) and at least one nonglycosylated protein (20-kd ϵ chain). An additional 21-kd dimer (p21) has been described in the mouse. Putative sites of phosphorylation of serine residues are indicated (Ⓟ, see Discussion). (B) The CD3/Ti complex is linked to the inositolphospholipid second messenger pathway.[12] A GTP-binding (G) protein is suggested to play a coupling role, communicating between CD3/Ti and the phospholipase C (PLC).[18] The rise in $[Ca^{2+}]_i$ and the activation of pkC are thought to contribute to induction of the IL-2 gene.

signaling activities are able to influence such responses as expression of lymphokine genes.

It is the objective of the studies described herein to develop a more complete molecular picture of the proximal signal transduction events caused by binding of ligand to the receptor. By generating and characterizing somatic T-cell mutants with altered signaling properties, we hope to learn which molecules are required for competence in receptor complex function and how they interact to initiate the intracellular biochemical reactions that lead to activation.

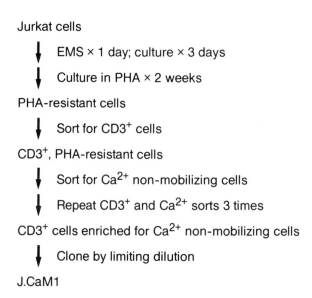

FIGURE 2. Selection protocol for isolating somatic mutants with defective receptor signal transduction function.[14]

RESULTS

Derivation of T-Cell Somatic Mutants

In order to develop a family of mutants with deficient signal transduction function by the antigen receptor, we relied on the availability of a well-characterized human leukemic T-cell line (Jurkat) and of reagents that can serve as agonists to trigger signaling by the antigen receptor. In preliminary studies we noted that the lectin phytohemagglutinin (PHA), which elicits both early signal transduction as well as distal biologic responses in a CD3/Ti-dependent fashion, significantly inhibited the growth of Jurkat cells, a process that also was dependent on surface expression of CD3/Ti.[14] It was reasonable to assume that cells resistant to this growth inhibition might have defective signal transduction responses to PHA. Therefore, Jurkat cells were mutagenized chemically and cultured in the presence of PHA (1 μg/ml). After several weeks, PHA-resistant cells grew out of this culture, many of which failed to express detectable CD3/Ti on the cell surface; receptor-negative cells constitute one class of signaling mutants. We then used fluorescence-activated cell sorting (FACS) to isolate cells still bearing receptors from the PHA-resistant bulk culture, potentially among which were receptor signaling mutants.

To improve the specificity of the selection, we took advantage of the fact that wild-type Jurkat cells respond immediately and substantially to soluble antireceptor antibody by increasing the $[Ca^{2+}]_i$.[15] Using the fluorescent Ca^{2+}-sensitive indicator Indo-1[16] and the FACS, we sorted for cells that failed to mobilize Ca^{2+} in response to the monoclonal antibody (mAb) C305, which is reactive with the Ti expressed on Jurkat.[11] Of the nonresponsive cells obtained from these "Ca^{2+}" sorts, a large proportion were again negative for receptor expression. Therefore, we sorted these cells for receptor-bearing cells. Eventually, after repeated cycles of "receptor-positive" sorts and "Ca^{2+} nonmobilizing" sorts followed by limiting dilution, a line of cells (J.CaM1, for Jurkat-derived Ca^{2+} mutant 1) was obtained that expresses high levels of CD3/Ti on its surface (FIG. 3B), but fails to increase $[Ca^{2+}]_i$ in response to C305 (FIG. 4B). A summary of the selection protocol is shown in FIGURE 2.[14]

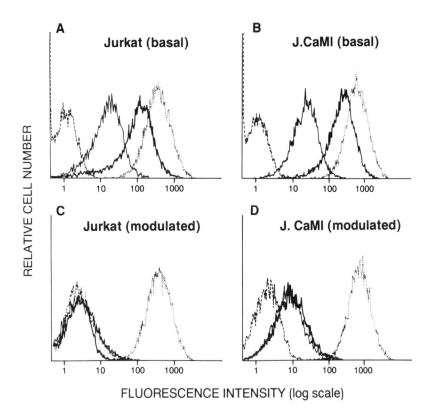

FIGURE 3. Immunofluorescence profiles of Jurkat and J.CaM1 cells before and after receptor internalization. Cells were incubated with various fluoresceinated antibodies (mouse IgG, *dashed line;* anti-β_2-microglobulin, *dotted line;* anti-Leu4, *heavy solid line;* C305, *solid line*) and analyzed by flow cytometry (fluorescent-activated cell sorting, FACS). **(A, B)** Resting Jurkat and J.CaM1 cells. **(C, D)** Jurkat and J.CaM1 cells after a 2.5-hour incubation with C305 (ascites, 1:1000 dilution).

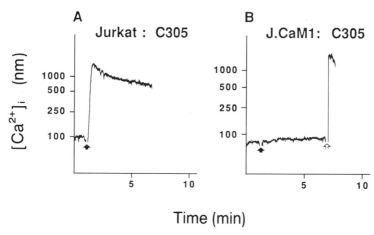

FIGURE 4. Ca^{2+} mobilization responses of Jurkat (**A**) and J.CaM1 (**B**). Cells loaded with Indo-1 were analyzed by conventional fluorimetry as described.[14] Cells were stimulated with C305 (♠, ascites, 1:1000 dilution) followed by ionomycin (⌂, 1 μM, in J.CaM1 only) to demonstrate releasability of intracellular Ca^{2+} stores.

Phenotype of J.CaM1

Calcium Mobilization

The major feature of J.CaM1 is its inability to increase $[Ca^{2+}]_i$ in response to C305. Parental Jurkat cells are extremely sensitive to this mAb, demonstrating large increases in $[Ca^{2+}]_i$ within seconds to minutes following exposure to C305 as demonstrated by Ca^{2+} fluorimetry with Indo-1 (FIG. 4A), and this elevation above basal levels is maintained for at least 2 hours (not shown). Such increases are detectable even with mAb-containing ascites diluted to at least $1/10^6$. In contrast, J.CaM1 is unresponsive to C305 (FIG. 4B), failing to demonstrate significant increases even at a 1/100 dilution of ascites. Therefore, as expected from the selection strategy utilized to obtain J.CaM1, this cell is incapable of mobilizing Ca^{2+} in response to this potent and specific agonist. Importantly, J.CaM1 has not lost the epitope recognized by C305, as demonstrated by the bright fluorescence staining (FIG. 3B) with C305 which is comparable to that of parental Jurkat cells (FIG. 3A).

We next determined the ability of J.CaM1 to mobilize Ca^{2+} in response to other anti-Ti or anti-CD3 reagents. Jurkat cells respond to a wide range of available mAbs (TABLE 1), demonstrating substantial peak levels of $[Ca^{2+}]_i$ upon exposure both to anticlonotypic antibodies and to antibodies against constant determinants on the receptor. Likewise, these wild-type cells respond to many independently derived anti-CD3 mAbs. In contrast, J.CaM1 cells are unresponsive to all the anti-Ti mAbs and several anti-CD3 mAbs. Thus, J.CaM1 cells have a defect that prevents most mAbs directed against a variety of CD3/Ti determinants to elicit transmembrane signaling. Surprisingly, a weak but detectable response is seen with the anti-CD3 mAb anti-Leu4, and a large (comparable to wild-type) increase is observed with the anti-CD3 mAb 235, although this increase is not sustained in J.CaM1 as it is in Jurkat cells.[17] Therefore, the CD3/Ti complex on J.CaM1 is poorly coupled to Ca^{2+}

mobilization as indicated by its lack of responsiveness to many stimuli, but selectively retains responsiveness to some anti-CD3 stimuli.

This residual signaling capacity is evident in several other situations as well. For example, C305 and OKT3, two mAbs that alone are incapable of eliciting a Ca^{2+} response in J.CaM1, together provoke a substantial rise in $[Ca^{2+}]_i$ (TABLE 1). This responsiveness is observed when the antibodies are added to the cells in either order.[14] Additionally, provision of a second antibody (rabbit anti-mouse immunoglobulin) to crosslink the single nonagonist OKT3 restores the agonist property of this mAb for J.CaM1. Therefore, in one sense the sensitivity of the CD3/Ti complex on J.CaM1 appears to have been reduced by the mutation, leaving some capacity to respond to more potent stimuli than is usually required. The usually potent IgM mAb C305 is ineffective in J.CaM1, but it regains its potency even in combination with univalent Fab fragments of anti-Leu4.[14] Thus, cross-linking *per se* does not appear to be necessary to restore agonist potential.

Inositolphospholipid Second Messengers

Calcium mobilization in response to anti-CD3/Ti mAbs is the result of activation of the PIP_2 second messenger pathway.[12] Therefore, it was important to evaluate the generation of these second messengers in J.CaM1, namely, soluble inositol phosphates and a metabolite of DG, phosphatidic acid (PA). Jurkat cells demonstrate substantial increases in the IPs within minutes of receptor stimulation, with a peak near 20 minutes after stimulation (kinetics not shown) and smaller increases still observable at 2 hours. Large increases in IPs and PA are measurable at 20 minutes following stimulation of Jurkat with C305, OKT3, or both mAbs together (FIG. 5A). In J.CaM1, no increases in these second messenger metabolites are detectable at 20 minutes after stimulation with C305 or OKT3 alone (FIG. 5B), but substantial increases are

TABLE 1. Peak $[Ca^{2+}]_i$ (nM) in Jurkat and J.CaM1 after Stimulation by Various Monoclonal Antibodies[a]

Stimulus	mAb	Description	Jurkat	J.CaM1
Anti-Ti				
	C305	Murine anti-idiotype, IgM	1923	82
	WT31	Murine anti-constant, IgG	567	106
	R140	Rat anti-idiotype, IgG	650	73
Anti-CD3				
	OKT3	Murine, IgG	976	70
	UCHT1	Murine, IgG	336	80
	A32.1	Murine, IgG	1117	86
	ANTI-LEU4	Murine, IgG	1322	243
	235	Murine, IgM	831	710
Cross-linked				
	OKT3		(ND)	534
Combination				
	C305 + OKT3		(ND)	1209

[a]The mean basal $[Ca^{2+}]_i$ in these experiments was 87 ± 20 (SD, n = 8) for Jurkat and 92 ± 24 (SD, n = 10) for J.CaM1. Antibodies were used as ascites, 1:1000 dilution. For the cross-linking experiment, purified rabbit anti-mouse immunoglobulin antibody (1 μg/ml final dilution) was added after the OKT3.

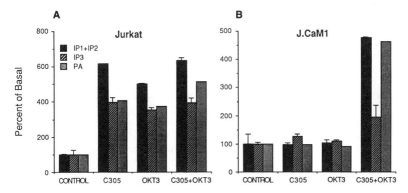

FIGURE 5. Production of second messengers derived from PIP$_2$ in Jurkat (**A**) and J.CaM1 (**B**) cells. Inositol phosphates from cells labeled with ^{3}H-myo-inositol were analyzed as described.[12] Phosphatidic acid (PA) from cells labeled with ^{32}P was extracted and analyzed by thin-layer chromatography essentially as described.[30,31] Cells were cultured either alone or with C305 (ascites, 1:1000), OKT3 (ascites, 1:1000), or both for 20 minutes before extraction. IP$_1$ = inositol 1-monophosphate; IP$_2$ = inositol 1,4-bisphosphate; IP$_3$ = inositol 1,4,5-trisphosphate. Results are the means of triplicate cultures for each condition ± SEM. PA results are single values.

apparent with the combination of both antibodies. Likewise, elevation of IP levels is apparent after stimulation with the anti-CD3 mAb 235 alone,[17] which also elicits mobilization of Ca^{2+} in J.CaM1 (TABLE 1); however, the change in IP levels in J.CaM1 in response to mAb 235 is much smaller than that in Jurkat cells.[17] Therefore, like the Ca^{2+} responses, the production of PIP$_2$-derived second messengers in response to anti-Ti and some anti-CD3 stimuli is dramatically reduced in J.CaM1, but some residual capacity to respond to some stimuli or combinations of stimuli remains in this cell.

Production of PIP$_2$-Derived Second Messengers in Response to AlF$_4^-$

It has been proposed that a GTP-binding protein (G protein) may be involved in coupling the CD3/Ti complex to the hydrolysis of PIP$_2$.[18] This hypothesis has come mainly from the finding that cholera toxin, which covalently modifies some G proteins and alters their behavior, inhibits the ability of the antigen receptor to mediate signal transduction.[18] In addition, we reported that the inorganic anion AlF$_4^-$ is able to elicit production of second messengers derived from PIP$_2$ in Jurkat cells,[19] a property suggestive of the presence of a G protein coupled to the PIP$_2$ pathway.[20] In J.CaM1, the presence of a mutant G protein might account for its signaling phenotype. Therefore, we compared the production of IPs in Jurkat cells and J.CaM1 in response to AlF$_4^-$. Jurkat cells and J.CaM1 both demonstrate large increases in the IP$_1$ and IP$_2$ metabolites (FIG. 6A) and measurable but smaller increases in IP$_3$ (FIG. 6B) during exposure to AlF$_4^-$. The time course and the magnitude of increase in the two cell types are nearly superimposable, with J.CaM1 showing slightly larger increases in IP$_3$ than do Jurkat cells. Thus, a putative direct agonist for G proteins shows no significant difference in biochemical responses between Jurkat cells and J.CaM1, suggesting that the mutation in J.CaM1 may be proximal to the G protein in the signaling pathway.

However, formally it remains possible that the AlF_4^--sensitive G protein coupled to PIP_2 hydrolysis plays no role in CD3/Ti-mediated PIP_2 hydrolysis.

Functional Correlates of Impaired Signal Transduction by CD3/Ti on J.CaM1

The loss in J.CaM1 of much of the signaling capacity of the CD3/Ti complex provides an opportunity to assess the requirement for certain signal transduction events in mediating cellular processes. For example, because it is held that the PIP_2 second messenger pathway is functionally linked to distal activation processes in T cells, it was possible to test this hypothesis with J.CaM1. Indeed, we showed that production of interleukin-2 (IL-2) in response to receptor agonists is virtually ablated in J.CaM1, although the cells retain the ability to produce IL-2 in response to receptor-independent agents such as the combination of a Ca^{2+} ionophore and phorbol ester.[14] This finding supports the notion that the second messengers derived from PIP_2 are indeed necessary for induction of the IL-2 gene,[2] although formally we cannot exclude the possibility that other second messenger(s) are required and are concurrently lost in J.CaM1.

Another cellular process, that of internalization of the receptor from the cell surface following receptor-ligand binding,[10] apparently does not require the PIP_2-derived second messengers. This conclusion is based on the observation that C305 promotes internalization of CD3/Ti by J.CaM1 (FIG. 4D), which is comparable in magnitude to that by Jurkat cells (FIG. 4C), in both cases leaving less than 4% of the basal density of surface CD3/Ti after several hours of exposure to soluble C305. Because C305 fails to trigger detectable PIP_2 metabolism in J.CaM1, it is implied that this signal transduction pathway is not required for internalization caused by perturbation of the receptor.

Many other receptors in and outside of the immune system are coupled to the PIP_2

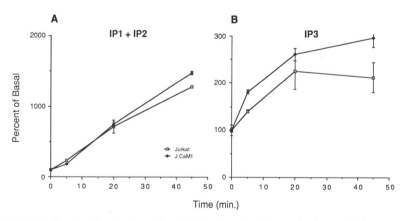

FIGURE 6. Kinetics of production of inositol phosphates in Jurkat and J.CaM1 cells in response to AlF_4^-. Inositol phosphates were quantitated as described[12] in cells cultured with NaF (33 mM) plus $AlCl_3$ (10 μM) for varying lengths of time. (A) IP1 + IP2 = inositol 1-monophosphate + inositol, 1,4-bisphosphate; (B) IP3 = inositol 1,4,5-trisphosphate.

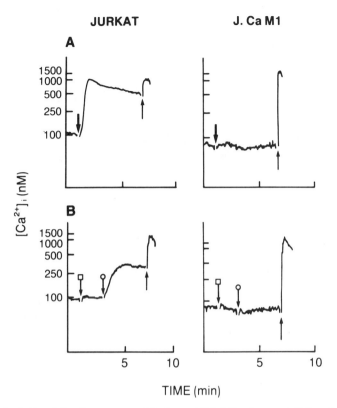

FIGURE 7. Ca^{2+} mobilization responses of Jurkat and J.CaM1 cells to anti-CD3 and anti-CD2 antibodies. Cells loaded with Indo-1 were analyzed by fluorimetry. (**A**) Jurkat and J.CaM1 cells were stimulated with OKT3 (⬇, ascites, 1:1000 dilution), followed by ionomycin (↑, 1 μM). (**B**) Jurkat and J.CaM1 cells were stimulated with purified 9.1 (♀, 1 μg/ml) followed by 9-6 (♀, 1 μg/ml), followed by ionomycin (↑, 1 μM).

pathway. On T cells, the CD2 or "sheep erythrocyte" receptor is able to transduce signals in response to mAbs directed against it,[21] and it has been proposed that signaling via CD2 represents an "alternate pathway of activation" that is distinct from that of CD3/Ti. Recent work by us and by others suggests that CD2 signaling function is dependent on expression of CD3/Ti at the cell surface.[22,23] Because the CD3/Ti complex on J.CaM1 appears to be poorly coupled to PIP_2 hydrolysis, it was of interest to determine whether this phenotype extends to other receptors such as CD2. Parental Jurkat cells demonstrate substantial increases in $[Ca^{2+}]_i$ in response to the anti-CD3 mAb OKT3 (FIG. 7A, left) as well as to the addition of the two mAbs 9.1 and 9-6 (FIG. 7B, left), which are directed against distinct epitopes on CD2; as described by others, the cells do not demonstrate a response to either mAb alone (data not shown). Intriguingly, J.CaM1 shows no appreciable Ca^{2+} mobilization response either to OKT3 (FIG. 7A, right) or to the combination of 9.1 and 9-6 (FIG. 7B, right), although it expresses high levels of 9.1-and 9-6–reactive epitopes (data not shown). Therefore, disruption of the signaling process by CD3/Ti in J.CaM1 concomitantly disrupts that mediated by CD2.

Localization of the Defective Component in J.CaM1

An important step in using somatic mutants to study signal transduction is to identify which component in the signaling pathway is altered from its wild-type form. This localization of the defect can be useful in confirming the role of an already known component or in identifying other proteins not yet linked to the signaling process. In T cells, the only certain components in the signal transduction pathway are the Ti-α and -β chains, which react with the inciting antigen, and a phospholipase C, which hydrolyzes PIP_2. Because expression of the genes encoding the Ti chains is thought to be subject to allelic exclusion, which allows only one allele of each chain to be expressed in a given cell, there appears to be a high probability that one of these chains is the site of the mutation in J.CaM1. Likewise, the observation of some residual signaling capacity with anti-CD3 mAbs suggests that the mutation is in a very proximal component.

To begin to test the hypothesis that one of the Ti chains is mutated in J.CaM1, we turned to conventional somatic hybridization for complementation studies. This laboratory previously described a family of Ti chain expression mutants derived from Jurkat cells,[11] which makes possible specific assessment of the requirement for a given Ti chain for complementation of the mutation in J.CaM1. For example, the cell line J.RT3-T3.5 is a mutant that expresses undetectable levels of mRNA for the expressed Ti-β chain and undetectable levels of CD3/Ti on its cell surface; CD3 proteins can be found intracellularly.[24] An ouabain-resistant and HAT-sensitive variant of J.RT3-T3.5 was fused to J.CaM1 (ouabain-sensitive, HAT-resistant) using polyethylene glycol; selective growth of hybrids was achieved by culturing with ouabain and HAT. After several weeks, a number of colonies grew out of the selection, and these were analyzed further.

As the criterion for complementation, we used restoration of the Ca^{2+} mobilization response to C305, which binds to the Ti-β chain.[24] Because we anticipated the possibility of a heterogeneous response, we used FACS with Indo-1, which can reveal individual responses within a mixed population better than can a fluorimeter. Because the peak emission for Indo-1 varies from a wavelength of 486 nm in the absence of Ca^{2+} to 404 nm in the presence of excess Ca^{2+},[16] a ratio of the fluorescence intensities at 404 nm versus that at 486 nm by intracellular Indo-1 varies directly with the $[Ca^{2+}]_i$ relatively independently of intracellular dye concentration. As expected from the fluorimetry studies, J.CaM1 cells loaded with Indo-1 do not increase the "Indo-1 ratio" appreciably following exposure to C305 (FIG. 8A). However, virtually all hybrids formed by fusion with H.RT3-T3.5 (which alone is nonresponsive to C305 because it does not bind the antibody[24]) respond with a substantial increase in the Indo-1 ratio (FIG. 8B). Thus, fusion between the signaling mutant J.CaM1 and the β-negative mutant J.RT3-T3.5 causes complementation of the signaling defect. This result suggests that (a) the mutation in J.CaM1 is recessive, and (b) it does not lie in the β chain. Parallel experiments with a Ti-α expression mutant demonstrate comparable complementation (data not shown). Therefore, these studies imply that neither the Ti-α nor the Ti-β chain is the site of the mutation in J.CaM1, because neither chain is required for complementation by somatic hybridization. These findings suggest that another molecule(s) is required for competence in signal transduction by the antigen receptor.

DISCUSSION

We have described a process for generating somatic mutants with deficient signal transduction by the T-cell antigen receptor complex, a protocol that may be generalizable to other receptor systems.[14] Using a combination of lectin-mediated growth inhibition, sorting for receptor-bearing cells, and sorting with the Ca^{2+} indicator Indo-1, we obtained a mutant cell line that fails to respond to antireceptor mAbs with the characteristic mobilization of intracellular Ca^{2+}. Usually potent mAbs reactive with either constant or clonotypic determinants fail to elicit this Ca^{2+} response, despite binding to the receptor. This lack of Ca^{2+} response is associated with a lack of PIP_2 metabolism, as indicated by a failure to generate the PIP_2-derived IP and DG second messengers. Therefore, the receptor on J.CaM1 appears to be at least partially dissociated from the PIP_2 second messenger system.

Associated with the loss of signaling via the inositolphospholipid second messenger system in J.CaM1 are selective losses in cellular responses initiated by CD3/Ti. For

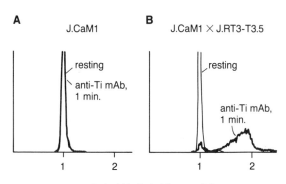

FIGURE 8. Complementation between J.CaM1 and Ti-β^- mutant. J.CaM1 (**A**) and somatic hybrids formed between J.CaM1 and J.RT3-T3.5 (**B**) were loaded with Indo-1 and analyzed by FACS before and 1 minute after exposure to C305 (ascites, 1:1000). For analysis, cells were exposed to a 364-nm exciting beam, and emission was detected at 404 and 486 nm. Shown here is the ratio of fluorescence intensities at 404 versus 486 nm.

example, the CD3/Ti complex has a significantly reduced capacity to mediate the requisite intracellular signals for promoting expression of the IL-2 gene. This finding is expected from the prevailing model that the PIP_2-derived second messengers contribute to induction of the IL-2 gene. In contrast, internalization of the CD3/Ti complex in response to soluble mAb reactive with this complex appears to be independent of these second messengers, because anti-Ti mAb induces essentially complete internalization in J.CaM1 without eliciting PIP_2 metabolism. In some situations, treatment of T cells with phorbol esters[25] or exposure to lectins or antigen[26,27] results in pkC-mediated phosphorylation of CD3 proteins and concomitant internalization of the CD3/Ti complex. However, this internalization does not occur to the same extent as occurs on exposure to antireceptor mAb, and the biologic significance of the phosphorylation as it pertains to internalization has remained undetermined. The findings with J.CaM1 suggest at the least that there must be a pkC-independent mechanism for receptor internalization, because metabolites of the pkC-activator DG are not detectable under conditions in which receptor internalization is normal.

A provocative finding is the failure of the CD2 molecule to transmit signals in J.CaM1. This observation implies that the antigen-driven and alternate pathways of activation may converge at a proximal event or component in the signal transduction pathway. That this common point may be integrally associated with the CD3/Ti complex is suggested by two observations: first, CD2 does not appear to function in mutants lacking surface expression of CD3/Ti[22,23]; and second, the mutation in J.CaM1 appears to reside in a proximal component in the CD3/Ti signaling pathway (see below). This convergence or dependence of one receptor on another is not without precedent, as the murine Thy-1 molecule in transfected human cells appears to require CD3/Ti expression for complete function.[28] There are many plausible explanations for this functional interaction between receptors, including direct receptor-receptor interaction or convergence on a shared coupling protein (e.g., a GTP-binding protein).

It is intriguing that the CD3/Ti complex expressed by J.CaM1 appears to retain some residual capacity to couple to the second messenger system. Combinations of mAbs against Ti and CD3 epitopes, which alone are unable to elicit responses, are in fact able to promote PIP_2 metabolism and Ca^{2+} mobilization. The agonist properties of combinations of stimuli, including multivalent and univalent antibodies as well as cross-linked individual antibodies, suggest that the receptor complex may require a conformational change that is prevented or inhibited in J.CaM1; certain stimuli are able to "force" the conformational shift that results in signal transmission. How it is that some anti-CD3 mAbs alone have not lost their agonist properties for J.CaM1 remains a mystery, but it may depend on the specific CD3/Ti epitope to which a given antibody binds. It thus appears that the signaling pathway in J.CaM1 has not entirely lost a critical element, but instead it contains a defective component that is impaired in its ability to transduce Ti-mediated signals. Obvious candidate molecules include the Ti chains themselves, especially in light of the allelic exclusion phenomenon that makes these cells functionally haploid for the Ti chains.

Surprisingly, the complementation experiments described herein suggest that although the mutation is recessive, neither Ti chain is indeed the site of the mutation. These results must be interpreted with caution, however, because complementation of the mutations in the Ti expression mutant partners cannot be excluded. An additional caution with the Ti-α expression mutant is that it is not completely deficient in α expression, but expresses only low levels of α mRNA.[11] To eschew these complications, we recently developed a novel heterokaryon assay that avoids potential complementation of the transcription defect in the Ti expression mutants.[29] Results with this assay and with DNA-mediated gene transfer experiments demonstrate convincingly that neither Ti chain is the site of the mutation in J.CaM1.

Because the Ti chains do not appear to be the site of the mutation that impairs receptor signaling, it is apparent that there must be at least one additional molecule that contributes to receptor signaling function, and the function of this molecule is impaired in J.CaM1. Based on the single fact that anti-CD3 mAb induces transmembrane signaling that appears comparable to that mediated by the Ti heterodimer, it has been widely assumed that the CD3 proteins contribute to receptor function. However, a plausible alternate explanation for this finding is that the close physical association between CD3 and Ti proteins (an association that serves some other function) permits anti-CD3 stimuli indirectly to cause conformational shifts of the Ti dimer that lead to signal transmission. This possibility seems unlikely now in light of the present results. Because the Ti molecules in J.CaM1 appear normal, it is hard to envision that Ti in J.CaM1 can mediate signals received indirectly through CD3, but not through anti-Ti stimuli themselves. Therefore, a more reasonable model is that the flow of information resulting from antireceptor complex stimuli is from Ti to CD3 and from CD3 to the next component in the pathway. By this reasoning, CD3 proteins do indeed play some role in signal transduction, but precisely what role remains to be elucidated. An attractive hypothesis is that this complex serves as a signal transduction amplifier, increasing either the magnitude of the transmembrane signal or the diversity of second messenger systems to which Ti is coupled. Further studies of J.CaM1 and of other similar mutants may provide some insight into these possibilities.

ACKNOWLEDGMENTS

The authors acknowledge the excellent technical assistance of Paul Dazin, FACS Operator of the Howard Hughes Medical Institute. We also are grateful to Drs. Shu Man Fu and Lewis Lanier for kindly providing antibodies.

REFERENCES

1. ALLISON, J. P. & L. L. LANIER. 1987. Ann. Rev. Immunol. **5:** 503–540.
2. WEISS, A., J. IMBODEN, K. HARDY, B. MANGER, C. TERHORST & J. STOBO. 1986. Ann. Rev. Immunol. **4:** 593–619.
3. ALLISON, J. P., B. W. MCINTYRE & D. BLOCH. 1982. J. Immunol. **129:** 2293–2300.
4. DEMBIC, Z., W. HAAS, S. WEISS et al. 1986. Nature **320:** 232–238.
5. SAITO, T., A. WEISS, J. MILLER et al. 1987. Nature **325:** 125–130.
6. BORST, J., S. ALEXANDER, J. ELDER et al. 1983. J Biol. Chem. **258:** 5135–5141.
7. REINHERZ, E. L., S. C. MEUER, K. A. FITZGERALD et al. 1983. Proc. Natl. Acad. Sci. USA **80:** 4104–4108.
8. ALLISON, J. P. & L. L. LANIER. 1985. Nature **314:** 107–109.
9. BRENNER, M. B., I. S. TROWBRIDGE & J. L. STROMINGER. 1985. Cell **40:** 183–190.
10. MEUER, S. C., K. A. FITZGERALD, R. E. HUSSEY et al. 1983. J. Exp. Med. **157:** 705–719.
11. WEISS, A. & J. D. STOBO. 1984. J. Exp. Med. **160:** 1284–1299.
12. IMBODEN, J. B. & J. D. STOBO. 1985. J. Exp. Med. **161:** 446–456.
13. BERRIDGE, M. J. & R. F. IRVINE. 1984. Nature **312:** 315–321.
14. GOLDSMITH, M. A. & A. WEISS. 1987. Proc. Natl. Acad. Sci. USA **84:** 6879–6883.
15. IMBODEN, J., A. WEISS & J. D. STOBO. J. Immunol. **134:** 663–665.
16. GRYNKIEWICZ, G., M. POENIE & R. Y. TSIEN. 1985. J. Biol. Chem. **260:** 3440–3450.
17. GOLDSMITH, M. A. & A. WEISS. 1988. Science **240:** 1029–1031.
18. IMBODEN, J. B., D. M. SHOBACK, G. PATTISON et al. 1986. Proc. Natl. Acad. Sci. USA **83:** 5673–5677.
19. GOLDSMITH, M. A. & A. WEISS. 1988. In Biology of Growth Factors: Molecular Biology, Oncogenes, Signal Transduction, and Clinical Applications. J. E. Kudlow, D. H. MacClennan, A. Bernstein and A. I. Gottlieb, Eds.: 195–211. Plenum Press, NY.
20. STRYER, L. & H. BOURNE. 1986. Ann. Rev. Cell Biol. **2:** 391–419.
21. JUNE, C. H., J. A. LEDBETTER, P. S. RABINOVITCH et al. 1986. J. Clin. Invest. **77:** 1224–1232.
22. BOCKENSTEDT, L. B., M. A. GOLDSMITH, M. DUSTIN et al. J. Immunol. In press.
23. BREITMEYER, J. B., J. F. DALEY, H. B. LEVINE et al. 1987. J. Immunol. **139:** 2899–2905.
24. OHASHI, P. S., T. W. MAK, P. VAN DEN ELSEN et al. 1985. Nature **315:** 606–609.
25. CANTRELL, D. A., A. DAVIES & M. J. CRUMPTON. 1985. Proc. Natl. Acad. Sci USA **82:** 8158–8162.
26. SAMELSON, L. E., J. HARFORD, R. H. SCHWARTZ et al. 1985. Proc. Natl. Acad. Sci. USA **82:** 1969–1973.
27. CANTRELL, D., A. A. DAVIES, M. LONDEI et al. 1987. Nature **325:** 540–542.
28. GUNTER, K. C., R. N. GERMAIN, R. A. KROCZEK et al. 1987. Nature **326:** 505–507.
29. GOLDSMITH, M. A., P. F. DAZIN & A. WEISS. Proc. Natl. Acad. Sci. USA. In press.
30. SKIPSKI, V. P., M. BARCLAY, E. S. REICHMAN & J. J. GOOD. 1967. Biochim. Biophys. Acta **137:** 80–89.
31. LAPETINA, E. G., J. SILIO & M. RUGGIERRO. 1985. J. Biol. Chem. **260:** 7078–7083.

Developmental Biology of T Lymphocytes

Deletion of Autoreactive T Cells and Impact of the α,β Receptor on the CD4/CD8 Phenotype

HARALD VON BOEHMER,[a,b] HORST BLUETHMANN,[c]
UWE STAERZ,[a] MICHAEL STEINMETZ,[c] AND
PAWEL KISIELOW[a]

[a]Basel Institute for Immunology
CH 4058 Basel, Switzerland

[c]Central Research Units
Hoffmann-LaRoche Co. Ltd.
CH 4002 Basel, Switzerland

Immunology has experienced long-lasting debates on issues that could not be addressed experimentally at the time. For instance the debate over the source of antibody diversity was only closed after several decades by the unforeseen discoveries of Tonegawa[1] and Weigert et al.[2] A similarly long-lasting debate concerns the self-nonself discrimination of the immune system or immunologic tolerance. Hypotheses were put forward at the end of the first half of this century and new ones have been added ever since. Two main streams of thought can be distinguished. One is best described as the deletion model and is associated with the names of Burnet, Lederberg, Cohn, and others. One particular version states that lymphocytes during their differentiation from stem cells pass through a stage in which contact with antigen results in lymphocyte death rather than lymphocyte activation. Other views—perhaps more compatible with Jerne's thinking—propose that autoreactive lymphocytes are not deleted but exist in a suppressed state within the network of the immune system.

In early 1985, we decided to test the clonal deletion hypothesis in T-cell receptor transgenic mice. The idea was to construct mice that, in a large fraction of T cells, expressed a receptor with specificity for self antigens and to chose a receptor that could easily be detected by a monoclonal antiidiotypic antibody. Ideally, this experimental design should allow study of the fate of T cells expressing this receptor in mice lacking or expressing the relevant antigen. We therefore chose to isolate the α,β T-cell receptor genes from a cytotoxic T-cell clone specific for the male antigen in the context of H-D^b and to analyze female and male offspring from α,β T-cell receptor transgenic mice.

EXPRESSION OF α AND β T-CELL RECEPTOR GENES IN TRANSGENIC MICE

Genomic DNA containing the functionally rearranged α and β genes from the male-specific cytotoxic T-cell clone B6.2.16 were injected in fertilized eggs. Initially,

[b]On sabbatical leave at the Massachusetts Institute of Technology, Center of Cancer Research, 40 Ames Street, Cambridge, Massachusetts and the Department of Pathology, University of Florida, Gainesville, Florida 32610.

transgenic mice expressing the β gene only were prepared by Krimpenfort and Berns at the Cancer Institute in Netherland. It was then realized that expression of the introduced β gene required considerable length of 3' flanking sequences containing enhancer motifs.[3] The clone used to construct the mice, COSHY 9-1.14-5, contained 10-kb 5' and 18-kb 3' flanking sequences. Irrespective of whether mice contained 2 or 20 copies of this clone, it was found that the vast majority of T cells expressed the transgene and that the transgene prevented rearrangement of endogenous V_β genes.[4] The B6.2.16 clone was chosen because it expressed the $V\beta8.2$ gene, the product of which can easily be identified by the monoclonal F23.1 antibody.[5] Mice expressing both α and β transgenes were then prepared by coinjecting both clones into fertilized eggs obtained from matings of C57B1/6 × DBA2/J F_1 hybrid mice. It was found that the founder mouse 71 contained four copies of each transgene integrated in tandem. This founder mouse was then backcrossed to C57L mice expressing H-2^b MHC antigens but lacking the $V\beta8$ gene family. This allowed us to estimate the $V\beta8.2$ transgene expression by serology, whereas we do not yet possess an antibody specific for the $V\alpha3$ transgene. On analysis of female offspring we found that the vast majority of T cells expressed the β transgene. Northern blot analysis with the $V\alpha3$ probe indicated that a large proportion of T cells also expressed the α transgene. This was confirmed by analyzing the specificity of CD8$^+$ T cells in α,β transgenic mice under conditions of limiting dilution: one in three CD8$^+$ T cells could be activated to expand clonally by polyclonal activators concanavalin A and interleukin-2. One in six CD8$^+$ T cells responded to activation by male stimulator cells, whereas less than 1 in 5,000 CD8$^+$ T cells from normal female C57L mice were activated by male stimulator cells. This indicated that more than 50% of CD8$^+$ T cells expressed both transgenes in female transgenic mice. The following questions were addressed in subsequent experiments: (1) Is there evidence for deletion of cells with the phenotype of the B6.2.16 clone in male mice? (2) If deletion occurs, at what stage of T-cell differentiation does it occur, and what is the mechanism of the deletion? (3) Does the fact that the α,β transgenes come from a class I MHC-restricted CD8$^+$ clone have any impact on the CD4/CD8 phenotype in female mice?

TRANSGENE-EXPRESSING T CELLS IN MALE MICE CANNOT BE ACTIVATED BY MALE CELLS

As with female transgenic mice, the peripheral lymphoid tissue of male mice contained almost normal numbers of Thy 1.2 positive T cells. Again, the vast majority of them expressed the β transgene as detected by serologic study, and Northern blot analysis revealed no difference in $V\alpha3$ gene expression when compared with that of female mice. In contrast to female mice, however, T cells could not be activated by male stimulator cells. Although 1 in 3 cells responded to concanavalin A, less than 1 in 5,000 cells responded to male stimulators. What then is the reason for this unresponsiveness? Is it suppression, or do the transgene-expressing cells in male mice differ in other aspects of their phenotype from those present in female transgenics or for that matter from the B6.2.16 clone?

TRANSGENE-EXPRESSING T CELLS IN MALE BUT NOT FEMALE MICE HAVE LOW LEVELS OF CD8 ACCESSORY MOLECULES

A more careful comparison of the phenotype of peripheral T cells in male and female transgenic mice revealed that most T cells in male animals expressed much lower levels of CD8 molecules. This fact offered a reasonable explanation for our inability to activate transgene-expressing cells from male mice by male stimulator cells. We know that the B6.2.16 clone exhibits relatively low killing on male targets and is easily inhibited by CD8 antibodies. Therefore, because of the reduced levels of CD8 accessory molecules in transgenic male mice, the avidity of the T cells for male cells is too low for activation. This conclusion is well in line with our earlier experiments showing that CD8 gene transfection into a CD8-negative clone increases its avidity so that its cytolytic activity is augmented at least 100-fold.[6] The important next question then was whether the T-cell phenotype in male transgenic mice reflects down-regulation of the CD8 molecules or deletion of cells expressing high levels of accessory proteins?

IN MALE MICE, NONMATURE THYMOCYTES EXPRESSING α,β TRANSGENES AND HIGH LEVELS OF ACCESSORY MOLECULES ARE DELETED

The first obvious difference in the thymus of female and male transgenic mice was the size. The female thymus contained on average 10 times more lymphocytes than did the male thymus. Staining revealed that about 80% of lymphocytes in the female thymus expressed the transgenes as well as high levels of CD4 and CD8 accessory molecules. This population is virtually absent in the male thymus. All cells in the male thymus, whether single or double positive, express low levels of CD8 proteins. We conclude from these data that nonmature, double positive cells expressing α,β transgenes as well as high levels of CD8 molecules are deleted in male mice, leaving behind a population of single and double positive cells with low avidity for male cells.

THE α,β T-CELL RECEPTOR DETERMINES THE CD4/CD8 RATIO

The fairly strict correlation of CD4/CD8 phenotype and the specificity of T cells for class II and class I MHC antigen, respectively, has been a mystery since we learned that both subsets of T cells use the same gene segments to make up their α,β receptors. It might be argued that this correlation is only an apparent one in that there are, in fact, many CD4$^+$ T cells with class I and many CD8$^+$ T cells with class II MHC antigen-restricted α,β receptors. It has been argued that such a constellation does not allow T-cell activation, because the most important signal in T-cell triggering is the cross-linking of the CD4 and CD8 molecules, on the one hand, with the α,β receptor, and on the other hand, by the same MHC molecule.[7] (This, of course, assumes that CD4 and CD8 proteins bind to class II and class I MHC antigens, respectively.) The alternative, not mutually exclusive, view, which avoids the accumulation of noninducible T cells in the periphery, is that the specificity of the heterodimer determines the CD4/CD8 phenotype.[8] This view would require that the specificity of the α,β heterodimer for MHC antigen is monitored during development in the absence of the nominal antigen, in our case the male antigen. It is obvious that the latter proposal can be tested in α,β female transgenic mice expressing an α,β receptor derived from a class I MHC-restricted T-cell clone. We therefore compared the CD4/CD8 ratio of T cells from female α,β transgenic and female transgenic mice expressing the β gene only.[4] Although we detected no difference in the periphery of these mice when the ratio was 1:1, we noted clear differences in the thymus: in the β transgenic mice the ratio was 2:1 or 3:1, but it was 1:3 or even 1:10 in the thymus of α,β transgenic mice. Thus, there is a clear influence of the α,β heterodimer on the CD4/CD8 ratio in the thymus. We have prepared bone marrow chimeras by injecting α,β transgenic stem cells into lethally x-irradiated C57L and B10.BR recipients. The reversed CD4/CD8 ratio is seen in the former but not in the latter recipient mice.

DISCUSSION

Our experiments are in principal agreement with recent conclusions by Kappler and colleagues[9] suggesting that tolerance to MHC antigens may involve deletion of T cells. Because of the different experimental design, our results allow us to draw definitive and novel conclusions. First, we can be confident that the apparent deletion cannot be explained by internalization of receptors or even masking of idiotypes, because we observe a drastic reduction in cells expressing the transgenes and high levels of accessory molecules. Conversely, T cells with low levels of accessory molecules, but normal levels of α,β transgene expression, clearly can accumulate in the peripheral lymphoid tissue of transgenic mice. This tends to rule out antiidiotypic suppression as the mechanism of deletion, because that mechanism should allow no accumulation of idiotype-expressing cells. The most important conclusion is that deletion occurs among nonmature thymocytes before they acquire functional competence. Recent experiments support the view that double positive thymocytes can act as precursors for single positive T cells.[10,11] Our experiments further indicate that the CD4 and CD8 accessory molecules do play a critical role not only in T-cell activation, but also in the deletion process, resulting in tolerance to self.

The fact that Kappler *et al.*[9] did not notice that the target of deletion was a nonmature double positive T cell requires some comment. It may well be that the double positive population of thymocytes expressing relatively high levels of α,β receptors that we are seeing in female α,β transgenic mice is a major population because of positive selection and represents only a minor population in normal mice. This would explain why we see an enormous deficit in cells of this phenotype in male mice, whereas Kappler *et al.* do not report a deficit of idiotype-expressing thymocytes with immature phenotype in their experiments. Another difference is that in contrast to Kappler *et al.*, we clearly see a role of accessory molecules in the deletion process, which may be explained by the assumption that their α,β receptor has a high affinity for self. Another explanation is that the role of accessory molecules is not seen, because the cells expressing low levels of accessory molecules would represent a minor population in their system.

Finally, we also know that expression of α,β transgenes but not the β transgene alone reverses the CD4/CD8 ratio of single positive thymocytes. This finding is compatible with models arguing that the specificity of α,β T-cell receptors is monitored in the thymus in the absence of nominal antigen, in our case the male antigen. Our experiments in chimeras indicate that this effect is dependent on MHC antigens expressed by the host. These experiments constitute the first direct evidence that the interaction of α,β receptors with thymic MHC antigens in the absence of nominal antigen directs the phenotype and specificity of peripheral T cells.

REFERENCES

1. TONEGAWA, S. 1983. Nature **302:** 575.
2. CLARKE, S. H., K. HUPPI, D. RUEZINSKY, L. STAUDT, W. GERHARD & M. WEIGERT. 1985. J. Exp. Med. **161:** 687.

3. KRIMPENFORT, P., R. DE JONG, Y. UEMATSU, Z. DEMBIC, S. RYSER, H. VON BOEHMER, M. STEINMETZ & A. BERNS. EMBO J., in press.
4. UEMATSU, Y., S. RYSER, Z. DEMBIC, P. BORGUELYA, P. KRIMPENFORT, A. BERNS, H. VON BOEHMER & M. STEINMETZ. Cell, in press.
5. STAERZ, U. D., H. G. RAMMENSEE, J. D. BENEDETTO & M. J. BEVAN. 1985. J. Immunol. 134: 3994.
6. DEMBIC, Z., W. HAAS, R. ZAMOYSKA, J. PARNES, M. STEINMETZ & H. VON BOEHMER. 1987. Nature 326: 510.
7. EMMRICH, F., V. STRITTMATTER & K. EICHMANN. 1986. Proc. Natl. Acad. Sci. USA 83: 8298.
8. VON BOEHMER, H. 1986. Immunology Today 7: 333.
9. KAPPLER, J. W., N. ROEHM & P. MARRACK. 1987. Cell 47: 273.
10. SMITH, L. 1987. Nature 326: 798.
11. VON BOEHMER, H., K. KARJALAINEN, J. PELKONEN, P. BORGULYA & H. G. RAMMENSEE. 1988. Immunol. Rev. 101: 16.

Genes Encoding T-Cell Antigens[a]

JANE R. PARNES

Division of Immunology S-021
Department of Medicine
Stanford University Medical Center
Stanford, California 94305

CD8 is a cell surface glycoprotein expressed by most thymocytes and by mature T lymphocytes that recognize class I major histocompatibility complex (MHC) molecules. Most CD8 cells are cytotoxic or suppressor in function. It has been postulated that the function of this molecule is to increase the avidity of the interaction between T cells and target cells or antigen-presenting cells.[1-3] Recent evidence provides strong support for this notion.[4-6] The presumed ligand for CD8 is a nonpolymorphic region of class I MHC molecules,[1-3] but there has been no direct demonstration of such binding to date. To explain data in which monoclonal antibodies (mAbs) specific for CD8 inhibit T-cell activation induced by lectins or anti-CD3 mAbs, it has alternatively been suggested that the function of CD8 might be to deliver a negative signal to the T cell.[7,8] However, there are currently no data to indicate transmission of such a signal. In this report I will review some of our recent studies of the molecular structure, expression, and function of CD8.

CD8 STRUCTURE

In humans the CD8 molecule is thought to consist of disulfide-linked homodimers of a single glycosylated (O-linked) polypeptide chain of 34 kd.[9-12] Higher multimers are found on both peripheral T cells and thymocytes, but only on thymocytes are the higher multimers disulfide linked to the class I molecule CD1.[9-14] In contrast, the subunit structure of mouse CD8 is distinct. The mouse CD8 molecular complex (Ly-2, 3) consists of disulfide-linked heterodimers of one polypeptide chain bearing the Ly-2 determinant (α: 38 kd or α': 34 kd) and a second chain bearing the Ly-3 determinant (β: 28–30 kd).[15,16] Each of these chains contains asparagine-linked carbohydrate.[17,18] No association with a CD1-like protein has been described in mouse thymocytes. We and others have shown that the mouse gene homologous to human CD8 encodes Ly-2 and not Ly-3.[19,20] The encoded protein has the typical features of a cell surface molecule, including a signal peptide that is cleaved off to yield the mature polypeptide structure, an external portion, a hydrophobic transmembrane domain, and a highly basic cytoplasmic tail. The sequence indicates that Ly-2, like human CD8, is a member of the immunoglobulin (Ig) gene superfamily by virtue of an aminoterminal external domain that is homologous to Ig variable regions. We have further shown that the α and α' chains are both encoded by a single Ly-2 gene, but that the two distinct polypeptide chains arise by alternative patterns of mRNA splicing.[19,21] Exon 4 sequence, consisting of 31 nucleotides and encoding the beginning of the cytoplasmic tail, is either retained to yield α mRNA or spliced out to yield α' mRNA (FIG. 1).

[a]This work was supported by NIH Grants GM34991 and AI19512. J. R. P. is the recipient of an Established Investigator award from the American Heart Association.

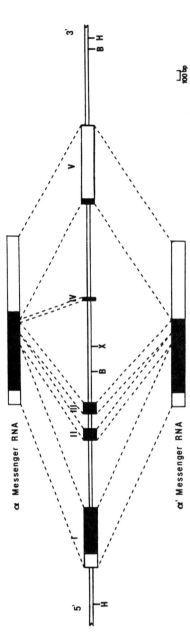

FIGURE 1. Structure and alternative splicing patterns of the Ly-2 gene. The structure of the Ly-2 gene is shown in the center of the figure. The exons are shown as boxes and are given Roman numerals. The *shaded boxes* represent the protein coding regions and the *open boxes* represent the 5' and 3' untranslated regions. The HindIII (H), BamHI (B), and XbaI (X) recognition sites are also indicated. The two forms of mRNA encoded by this gene are shown above (α) and below (α') the gene. *Dotted lines* indicate where genomic exons are represented in the two forms of mRNA. (Reprinted from reference 21 with permission of the publisher.)

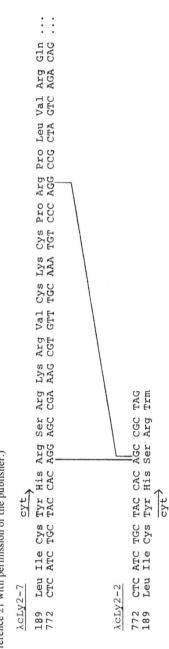

FIGURE 2. Comparison of the 3' nucleotide and amino acid sequence of the alternative forms of cDNA encoding Ly-2. The 3' ends of the coding regions of cDNA clones λcLy2-7 and λcLy2-2 are shown, and the 31-bp deletion in clone λcLy2-2 is indicated. As this deletion changes the reading frame, only two additional amino acids are specified before a termination codon is reached. The 3' untranslated sequence of clone λcLy2-2 matches exactly the remaining 3' sequence of clone λcLy2-10 (not shown). (Reprinted from reference 19 with permission of the publisher, Copyright Cell Press.)

Exclusion of these 31 nucleotides results in a frameshift and early termination of the α' protein. The result is a polypeptide that is identical to α in its external and transmembrane regions but has a distinct and foreshortened cytoplasmic tail of 4 instead of 29 amino acids[19,21] (FIG. 2). Although mouse CD8 consists primarily of heterodimeric structures on mouse thymocytes and peripheral T cells, the α and α' chains of Ly-2 can each be expressed as homodimers on transfection of the respective cDNA clones into tissue culture cells.[22,23]

We recently cloned the gene and cDNA encoding mouse Ly-3 (β) and found that this gene is located 36 kb to the 5' side of Ly-2.[24] As shown for the rat homolog,[25] Ly-3 is also a member of the Ig gene superfamily, but its sequence shows no significant similarity to that of Ly-2 beyond the features common to most members of this extended gene family.[24,26,27] In contrast to our results with Ly-2, we found that cell surface expression of Ly-3 requires the presence of Ly-2, at least in transfectants.[24] Although no human protein homologous to mouse Ly-3 has been described, a human homolog of the Ly-3 gene has been isolated and is transcribed.[28,29] We are currently investigating whether a protein product is produced from these transcripts and whether human CD8, at least under some circumstances, is a heterodimer.

EXPRESSION OF CD8

CD8 protein has only been described on T-lineage cells. In accord with these findings, we have not detected mRNA corresponding to the chains of mouse CD8 in other cell types.[19,24] However, studies of the structure of mouse CD8 in thymus versus peripheral T cells indicate a difference in the structural composition of the molecule. Although there are close to equal amounts of the α and α' chains on the surface of mouse thymocytes, peripheral T cells almost exclusively express α chains.[22,23,30] We found no difference in the relative amounts of the two mRNA species in thymus versus the periphery; rather, the difference in cell surface expression is the result of a posttranslational regulatory process that distinguishes between the α and α' chains in mature T cells.[23] The possibility of functional differences between these two polypeptide chains is being examined.

FUNCTIONAL STUDIES

We explored the function of mouse CD8 in a series of collaborative studies involving gene transfer into functional T-cell hybridomas.[4,5] Dembić et al.[31] had previously transferred the genes encoding the α and β chains of the T-cell receptor (Tcr) from Ly-2$^+$ cytotoxic T-cell clone BDFL1.1.3, specific for D^d plus the hapten fluorescein (FL), into the Ly-2$^-$ cytotoxic T-cell hybridoma SPH1.3, specific for K^k plus the hapten p-sulfophenyldiazo-4-hydroxyphenyl acetic acid (SP). While killing by the donor cell, BDFL1.1.3, could be blocked by anti-Ly-2 mAb, killing by the nontransfected recipient, SPH1.3, could not. After gene transfer they found that the transfectant, BD7-S17, could not kill targets expressing normal amounts of D^d + FL (i.e., fluoresceinated D^d-expressing lipopolysaccharide [LPS]-induced lymphoblasts), but it could kill fluoresceinated L-cell targets that had been selected for overexpression of a transfected D^d gene. These results suggested that the affinity of the transferred Tcr for D^d + FL was low and that the absence of Ly-2 in the recipient cells might explain the failure to kill target cells expressing normal levels of D^d + FL. We therefore transfected the gene encoding Ly-2 into the recipient hybridoma cells and

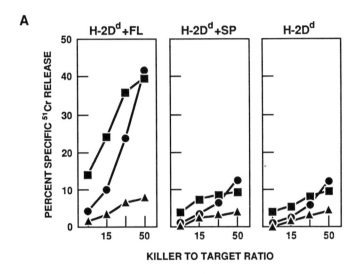

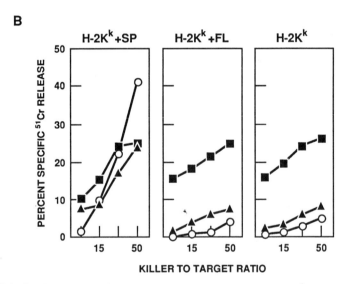

FIGURE 3. Cytolytic activity of cytolytic T-cell clones on (a) DBA/2 H-2^d) and (b) CBA/J (H-2^k) ^{51}Cr-labeled LPS-induced lymphoblasts. The cytolytic assay was conducted as previously described.[32] Effectors were: (**A**) ● BDFL1.13 (donor T-cell hybridoma); ▲ BD7-S17 (recipient hybridoma expressing transfected Tcr from the donor); ■ BD7-S17-Ly2(2) (recipient hybridoma expressing Tcr genes and Ly-2 gene); (**B**) ○ SPH/1.3 (nontransfected recipient hybridoma); ▲ BD7-S17; ■ BD7-S17-Ly2(2). (Reprinted by permission from Nature **326:** 510–511. Copyright 1987, Macmillan Journals Limited.)

TABLE 1. IL-2 Secretion of Cells Transfected with the Lyt-2 and/or T-Cell Receptor Genes in Response to Stimulation by H-2Kᵇ-Transfected L Cells, Irradiated Spleen Cells, or Anticlonotypic Antibodies[a]

Transfected Responder Cells			IL-2 Secreted (U/ml) in Response to:						
Name	Parental Cell	Gene(s) Transfected	Ltk⁻	CA60.6.4 (Kᵇ-positive L-cell transformant)	CBA/J Splenocytes ($H-2^k$)[a]	B10.MBR Splenocytes (K^b, I^k, D^q)[a]	F23.1-Sepharose[b]	Désiré-1-Sepharose[b]	Leukoagglutinin
DO-11.10	—	None	<7.5	<7.5	<7.5	<7.5	>135	<7.5	>135
DC25.11	DO-11.10	Ly-2	<7.5	<7.5	<7.5	<7.5	>135	<7.5	>135
DC27.15	DO-11.10	KB5-C20 Tcr	9	<7.5	9.5	<7.5	18	>135	>135
DC41.8	DC25.11	Ly-2 KB5-C20 Tcr	<7.5	48	9.5	122	21	>135	>135
DC43.12	DC27.10	Ly-2 KB5-C20 Tcr	14	>135	<7.5	>135	41	>135	>135

NOTE: The amounts of IL-2 produced by the T-cell hybridomas were assessed after 24 hours. Results were expressed as units of IL-2 per milliliter of undiluted supernatant. The minimum detectable in this assay was 7.5 U/ml.
[a]Irradiated, T-depleted spleen cells.
[b]mAb coupled to Sepharose beads at 3 mg/ml of beads.
Reprinted from reference 5 with permission of the publisher (Copyright Cell Press).

found that the ability to kill LPS lymphoblast targets was indeed restored by expression of surface Ly-2 protein[4] (FIG. 3). Furthermore, this killing could be blocked by mAb specific for Ly-2 to the same extent as could killing by the original donor cell.[4] These findings demonstrate that the product of the transferred Ly-2 gene can increase the avidity of the interaction between a cytotoxic T-cell hybridoma and its target, so that killing can be accomplished with a lower concentration of cell surface antigen.

These conclusions have been extended to a helper hybridoma system in a collaboration with Gabert et al.[5] In this instance the α and β chain genes of the Tcr from a CTL clone (KB5-C20) specific for allogeneic class I MHC molecule K^b were transfected into a $CD4^+$ T-cell hybridoma (DO-11.10) specific for Ia^d plus ovalbumin. As in the experiment just described, the donor CTL clone, KB5-C20, was $Ly-2^+$ and its cytotoxic function was blockable by mAb specific for Ly-2, whereas the recipient hybridoma, DO11.10, was $Ly-2^-$, and its normal function (as measured by interleukin-2 [IL-2] release) was not blocked by anti-Ly-2 mAb. As shown in TABLE 1, transfer of the KB5-C20 Tcr genes alone (transfectant DC27.15) did not result in transfer of the ability to respond to the antigen K^b as presented by either spleen cells or L cells expressing a transfected K^b gene.[5] However, the transfected Tcr genes were expressed in a functionally relevant manner in that an antiidiotypic mAb, Désiré-1, specific for the transfected Tcr, could stimulate release of IL-2 by the transfectants when bound to Sepharose beads. In contrast, when in addition to the Tcr genes (transfectants DC41.8 and DC43.12) the gene encoding Ly-2 was transfected into the recipient cells, the resulting cloned transfectants could respond to K^b presented on either spleen cells or transfected L cells by releasing IL-2 (TABLE 1). Furthermore, this response could be blocked by mAb specific for Ly-2, but not by mAb specific for either Thy-1 or mouse CD4. These results extend the previous study by showing that the functional requirement by Ly-2 is independent of the particular type of T cell, but rather is dependent on the specific Tcr (and the antigen being recognized by this Tcr). In this instance the KB5-C20 Tcr could not functionally respond to antigen (K^b) in the absence of Ly-2 or when Ly-2 was blocked by mAb, independent of whether it was in a CTL or a helper hybridoma. The most likely explanation is that the affinity of this Tcr is too low for it to be stimulated by its specific antigen in the absence of an interaction between Ly-2 and its ligand (presumably class I MHC).

Notably, the findings in both sets of experiments indicate a positive function for Ly-2; expression of the gene allows responses that do not occur in its absence under the conditions tested. Although it cannot be concluded that a positive signal is being transmitted through the Ly-2 molecule, it can be concluded that in these systems the function is clearly not to transmit a negative signal and turn off a response. Finally, the functional activity in both systems is being measured in the absence of the Ly-3 chain. It remains to be determined whether the physiologically more relevant heterodimers between the Ly-2 and Ly-3 polypeptide chains might function either better or differently than do Ly-2 homodimers.

REFERENCES

1. SWAIN, S. L. 1983. Immunol. Rev. **74:** 129–142.
2. MACDONALD, H. R., A. L. GLASEBROOKE, C. BRON, A. KELSO & J.-C. CEROTTINI, Immunol. Rev. **68:** 89–115.
3. REINHERZ, E. L., S. C. MEUER & S. F. SCHLOSSMAN. 1983. Immunol. Rev. **74:** 83–112.
4. DEMBIĆ, Z., W. HAAS, R. ZAMOYSKA, J. PARNES, M. STEINMETZ & H. VON BOEHMER. 1987. Nature **326:** 510–511.
5. GABERT, J. C., LANGLET, R., ZAMOYSKA, J. R. PARNES, A.-M. SCHMITT-VERHULST & B. MALISSEN. 1987. Cell **50:** 545–554.

6. RATNOFSKY, S. E., N. PETERSON, J. GREENSTEIN & S. J. BURAKOFF. 1987. J. Exp. Med. **166:** 1747–1757.
7. HUNIG, T. 1984. J. Exp. Med. **159:** 551–558.
8. SCHREZENMEIER, H., R. KURRIE, H. WAGNER & B. FLEICHER. 1985. Eur. J. Immunol. **15:** 1019–1024.
9   LEDBETTER, J. A., R. L. EVANS, M. LIPINSKI, C. CUNNINGHAM-RUNDLES, R. A. GOOD & L. A. HERZENBERG. 1981. J. Exp. Med. **153:** 310–323.
10. SNOW, P., H. SPITS, J. DEVRIES & C. TERHORST. 1983. Hybridoma **2:** 187–199.
11. SNOW, P. M. & C. TERHORST. 1983. J. Biol. Chem. **258:** 14675–14681.
12. SNOW, P. M., G. KEIZER, J. E. COLIGAN & C. TERHORST. 1984. J. Immunol. **133:** 2058–2066.
13. LEDBETTER, J. A., T. TSO & E. A. CLARK. 1985. J. Immunol. **134:** 4250–4254.
14. SNOW, P. M., M. VAN DE RIJN & C. TERHORST. 1985. Eur. J. Immunol. **15:** 529–532.
15. LEDBETTER, J. A., W. E. SEAMAN, T. T. TSU & L. A. HERZENBERG. 1981. J. Exp. Med. **153:** 1503–1516.
16. WALKER, I. D., B. J. MURARY, P. M. HOGARTH, A. KELSO & I. F. MCKENZIE. 1984. Eur. J. Immunol. **14:** 906–910.
17. ROTHENBERG, E. & TRIGLIA, D. 1983. J. Exp. Med. **157:** 365–370.
18. LUESCHER, B., M. ROUSSEQUX-SCHMID, H. Y. NAIN, H. R. MACDONALD & C. BRON. 1985. J. Immunol. **135:** 1937–1944.
19. ZAMOYSKA, R., A. C. VOLLMER, K. C. SIZER, C. W. LIAW & J. R. PARNES. 1985. Cell **43:** 153–163.
20. NAKAUCHI, H. G. P. NOLAN, C. HSU, H. S. HUANG, P. KAVATHAS & L. A. HERZENBERG. 1985. Proc. Natl. Acad. Sci. USA **82:** 5126–5130.
21. LIAW, C. W., R. ZAMOYSKA & J. R. PARNES. 1986. J. Immunol. **137:** 1037–1043.
22. TAGAWA, M., H. NAKAUCHI, L. A. HERZENBERG & G. P. NOLAN. 1986. Proc. Natl. Acad. Sci. USA **83:** 3422–3426.
23. ZAMOYSKA, R. & J. R. PARNES. 1988. EMBO J. **7:** 2359–2367.
24. GORMAN, S. D., Y. H. SUN, R. ZAMOYSKA & J. R. PARNES. 1988. J. Immunol. **140:** 3646–3653.
25. JOHNSON, P. & A. F. WILLIAMS. 1986. Nature **323:** 74–76.
26. NAKAUCHI, H., Y. SHINKAI & K. OKUMURA. 1987. Proc. Natl. Acad. Sci. USA **84:** 4210–4214.
27. PANACCIO, M., M. T. GILLESPIE, I. D. WALKER, L. KIRSZBAUM, J. A. SHARPE, G. H. TOBIAS, I. F. C. MCKENZIE & N. J. DEACON. 1987. Proc. Natl. Acad. Sci. USA **84:** 6874–6878.
28. JOHNSON, P. 1987. Immunogenetics **26:** 174–177.
29. SHIUE, L., S. D. GORMAN & J. R. PARNES. In preparation.
30. WALKER I. D., B. J. MURRARY, P. M. HOGARTH, A. KELSO & I. F. C. MCKENZIE. 1984. Eur. Immunol. **14:** 906–910.
31. DEMBIĆ, Z., W. HAAS, S. WEISS, J. MCCUBREY, H. KIEFER, H. VON BOEHMER & M. STEINMETZ. 1986. Nature **320:** 232–238.
32. HAAS, W., H. POHLIT & H. VON BOEHMER. 1979. Eur. J. Immun. **9:** 868–874.

The Human Interleukin-2 Receptor

Recent Studies of Structure and Regulation

WARNER C. GREENE,[a] ERNST BÖHNLEIN,[a]
MIRIAM SIEKEVITZ,[b] B. ROBERT FRANZA,[c]
AND JOHN LOWENTHAL[a]

[a]Howard Hughes Medical Institute
Duke University Medical Center
Durham, North Carolina 27710

[c]Cold Spring Harbor Laboratory
Bung Town Road
Cold Spring Harbor, New York 11724

In its simplest terms, the growth of human T lymphocytes can be viewed as a biologic response comprised of two separate stages. In the first stage, the binding of antigen or mitogen to specific receptors present on the surface of resting T cells triggers the transduction of intracellular signals, leading to lymphocyte activation.[1,2] These activation signals promote the *de novo* expression of genes regulating T-cell growth including interleukin-2 (IL-2) and interleukin-2 receptors (IL-2R).[3–5] The subsequent interaction of IL-2, with its high affinity receptor, promotes cell cycle progression and clonal expansion of the cells that originally reacted with antigen.

Recent studies have permitted identification of three different affinity forms of the IL-2R. The high affinity IL-2R apparently corresponds to a membrane receptor complex composed of at least two subunits including the 55-kd Tac antigen (p55, IL-2Rα)[6,7] and the recently recognized 70–75-kd protein (p70, IL-2Rβ),[8–12] each of which independently binds IL-2. The IL-2Rβ protein alone can be expressed in the absence of IL-2Rα and corresponds to a second class of IL-2R that binds ligand with intermediate affinity (K_d of 0.5–1.0 nM).[10–12] Similarly, the IL-2Rα subunit can be expressed at the cell surface in the absence of the IL-2Rβ subunit[9,12,13] and corresponds to the low affinity (K_d of 10–20 nM) form of IL-2R.[7,13] Recent evidence suggests that the IL-2Rα and IL-2Rβ chains of the high affinity IL-2R interact with different epitopes on the IL-2 molecule,[11] thus providing a rational explanation for high affinity binding to the complex. Furthermore, the kinetics of ligand binding to these individual subunits is strikingly different.[14,15] Specifically, the IL-2Rα protein rapidly binds IL-2 with a $t_{1/2}$ of about 5 seconds; however, the ligand dissociates with a $t_{1/2}$ of 5–10 seconds.[13] In sharp contrast, IL-2 associates with the IL-2Rβ protein remarkably slowly with a $t_{1/2}$ of 40–50 minutes,[14,15] suggesting that this process may not be limited solely by diffusion of ligand. However, once bound to the IL-2Rβ protein, IL-2 dissociates very slowly with a $t_{1/2}$ of 4–5 hours.[13] The calculated binding coefficients of these individual chains measured in Scatchard plots closely agree with the affinities determined by the kinetics of association and dissociation. Interestingly, the high affinity receptor displays a composite of these binding kinetics, reflecting properties of each subunit.[14,15] The on rate of IL-2 binding to the high affinity receptor occurs with a

[b]Present address: Mt. Sinai Medical Center, One Gustave Levy Place, Annenberg Bldg., Room 1664, New York, New York 10029.

$t_{1/2}$ of approximately 30 seconds, which is similar to the rapid association rate of the IL-2Rα chain.[14] The off rate, however, is slow, occurring with a $t_{1/2}$ of about 4 hours, which is similar to the slow dissociation rate characteristic of the IL-2Rβ chain.[14] These findings underscore the important contributions of each subunit to the assembly of a receptor complex uniquely able to rapidly bind and retain IL-2.

Recent studies also have shown that the IL-2Rβ protein alone can mediate rapid endocytosis of ligand in a manner identical to that of the high affinity receptor.[16] In contrast, the IL-2Rα protein alone does not internalize IL-2. As the intracytoplasmic domains of proteins largely regulate endocytotic properties, these results suggest that the cytoplasmic protein of IL-2Rβ may be larger than the 13 residues present in the IL-2Rα chain.[17]

Constitutive expression of the IL-2Rβ protein was recently detected on the surface of resting T cells[18] and natural killer cells.[19-21] In the presence of large quantities of IL-2, the interaction of ligand with these intermediate affinity IL-2Rβ appears to transduce signals, leading to activation in resting T cells[18] and increased cytolytic activity in natural killer cells.[21] Interestingly, with both cell types, IL-2 binding to the IL-2Rβ protein activates IL-2Rα gene expression, ultimately leading to the assembly of high affinity IL-2R.[18,21] At present, it is unknown whether the IL-2Rβ protein corresponds to a tyrosine kinase. Notwithstanding, this subunit likely plays a central role in signal transduction mediated by the high affinity receptor.

Our investigations recently focused on the regulation of IL-2Rα gene expression, because its rapid induction plays a pivotal role in the assembly of high affinity IL-2R. The 5' flanking region of the IL-2Rα gene was analyzed both for critical cis-acting sequences required for mitogen activation[22-25] and for its interaction with trans-acting nuclear factors.[25] To define sequences required for mitogen activation, a series of Bal 31 deletion mutants of the IL-2Rα promoter were prepared and cloned in correct orientation immediately upstream of the chloramphenicol acetyltransferase (CAT) reporter gene. These expression plasmids were then used for transfection assays in various lymphoid cell lines, followed by activation of the transfected cells with different mitogens.[25] In Jurkat T cells, we found that only sequences 3' of nucleotide -317 (numbered relative to the major 3' cap site) are required for phytohemagglutinin (PHA) and phorbol 12-myristic 13-acetate (PMA) activation of the IL-2Rα promoter.[25] In sharp contrast, only sequences 3' of base -271 were required for PMA activation of this promoter in the immature YT-1 leukemic T-cell line. In addition, IL-2Rα gene expression induced by the transactivator (tax) gene product of HTLV-1 in Jurkat T cells only required sequences downstream of -271.[25] Thus, the requisite upstream sequences apparently differ, depending on the nature of the activation signal and perhaps the state of cellular maturation.

Two imperfect direct repeats (IDRs) occur within the IL-2Rα promoter sequence immediately flanking either side of base -271. Because repetitive elements may be involved in the binding of transcriptional factors, we investigated whether the IDRs within the IL-2Rα promoter were capable of interacting with proteins.[25] Three different double-stranded oligonucleotides were synthesized. The IL-2R I oligonucleotide contained sequences within and around the upstream IDR region; IL-2R II contains sequences associated with the downstream IDR region, whereas the IL-2R III oligonucleotide contained sequences spanning both of these IDRs. Using the IL-2R III probe, we demonstrated that nuclear proteins isolated from Jurkat T cells stimulated with PHA and PMA formed two specifically retarded complexes in gel-shift mobility assays.[25] In contrast, neither of these retarded species was observed with nuclear proteins prepared from unstimulated Jurkat cells. These findings suggest that the proteins involved were inducible. These DNA-protein complexes proved specific, as unlabeled IL-2R III blocked their formation, whereas a size-matched oligonucleotide from the ampicillin resistance gene did not. These two retarded complexes were also demonstrable with nuclear extracts from Jurkat cells induced with PMA, PHA, or combinations of these agents and YT cells stimulated with PMA alone, or PMA in combination with forskolin. Furthermore, nuclear extracts from two HTLV-1 infected cell lines, HUT 102B2 and MT-1 cells, which constitutively display high levels of surface IL-2Rα, also produced these two DNA-protein complexes.[25]

Competition studies with different oligonucleotides were performed at the binding site of these proteins.[25] The IL-2R II oligonucleotide, which contains sequences corresponding to the downstream IDR, completely blocked the binding of both proteins to IL-2R III. In contrast, IL-2R I, which contains sequences from the upstream IDR region, failed to compete. In direct binding assays, the IL-2R II probe formed one complex with induced Jurkat nuclear extracts, but two complexes with induced YT nuclear extracts. This finding was intriguing in view of the observation that IL-2Rα promoter sequences upstream of -271 were required for mitogen activation in Jurkat cells but not in YT-1 cells. Studies are presently underway to determine if same or different proteins are involved in Jurkat and YT-1 cells.

To specifically map the binding site of the downstream transcriptional factor(s), a series of mutations of the IL-2R II oligonucleotide were prepared and tested for competitive effects and direct binding activity.[26] With this approach, a 12-bp region located between nucleotides -267 and -256 was defined as a binding site for at least one of these transcription factors. Comparison of the sequence of this putative IL-2Rα promoter region with other known binding sites revealed a striking similarity to the enhancer element of the type I human immunodeficiency virus (HIV-1).[27] This sequence homology proved functionally significant, as unlabeled HIV-1 enhancer oligonucleotides completely blocked the binding of proteins to the IL-2Rα promoter.[24] Conversely, IL-2Rα promoter oligonucleotides also inhibited the formation of at least two inducible DNA-protein complexes with the HIV-1 enhancer. Direct evidence for the binding of an identical transcriptional factor to both the IL-2Rα promoter and the HIV enhancer was obtained using a microscale DNA affinity precipitation assay.[26,28] Nuclear proteins from induced or uninduced Jurkat cells were labeled with ^{35}S-methionine and then incubated with either biotinylated wild-type or mutant oligonucleotide probes from the IL-2Rα promoter and the HIV-I enhancer.[26] DNA-protein complexes were precipitated with avidin-agarose and the eluted proteins analyzed on high resolution two-dimensional polyacrylamide gels. Both the wild-type HIV-1 enhancer and IL-2Rα promoter wild-type oligonucleotides specifically complexed to an 86-kd inducible protein termed HIVEN86A.[26] In contrast, an IL-2Rα promoter oligonucleotide mutated in the 12-bp binding site failed to interact with this inducible DNA binding factor. These findings confirmed that both the HIV-1 enhancer and the IL-2Rα promoter shared the binding of at least one common nuclear factor.

In previous studies, we and others found that the HIV-1 LTR is activated by a variety of mitogens including such agents as ionomycin, PHA, PMA, and tax.[27,29-31] These same agents also activate the IL-2Rα promoter.[22-25,32] These mitogen-induced responses of the HIV-1 LTR importantly depend on the enhancer element, although additional upstream regulatory elements contribute in both a positive and a negative manner to the overall level of the response. However, the HIV-1 enhancer alone is sufficient to impart mitogen inducibility to the mitogen-insensitive thymidine kinase promoter.[29,31] Nabel and Baltimore[27] reported that the nuclear factor NF-κB binds to the HIV-1 enhancer. Although NF-κB presently corresponds to an activity defined primarily by its sequence specificity, it is possible that HIVEN86A[28] and NF-κB correspond to the same protein or that HIVEN86A is a member of the NF-κB family of proteins. Alternatively, these proteins may be different, but they share a common DNA binding specificity.

NF-κB activity has been described in nonlymphoid HeLa cells after PMA stimulation[27]; therefore, we tested whether the IL-2Rα promoter and the HIV-1 enhancer could be activated in PMA-induced HeLa cells.[26] Transfection studies revealed no mitogen-induced changes in the IL-2Rα promoter expression in these nonlymphoid cells or a significant PMA-induced response of the HIV-1 LTR, although considerable basal activity was present.[26] These findings raise the possibility that either a second lymphoid-specific factor or a lymphoid-specific modification of NF-κB is required for mitogen-induced IL-2Rα gene expression and HIV-1 enhancer activation. Additional studies are clearly required to determine the relation of NF-κB to HIVEN86A and to dissect the possible involvement of yet other proteins in the activation of these transcription units.

In summary, although activation of IL-2Rα gene expression is involved in the promotion of T-cell growth, and activation of HIV gene replication is commonly associated with T-cell death, these diverse responses apparently are initially regulated by the same inducible nuclear transcription factors. Activation of the HIV LTR may play an important role in controlling the state of viral replication. The design of therapeutic agents that would interfere with enhancer-dependent LTR activation might inhibit the conversion from latent to lytic forms of productive viral infection and the attendant cell death. However, these drugs must also be carefully evaluated for their potential effects on the activation of a variety of genes involved in normal T-cell growth including the IL-2Rα gene.

REFERENCES

1. WEISS, A., J. IMBODEN, D. SCHOBACK & J. STOBO. 1984. Role of T3 surface molecules in the activation of human T cells: T3 dependent activation results in a rise in cytoplasmic free calcium. Proc. Natl. Acad. Sci. USA **81:** 4169–4173.
2. WEISS, A. & J. B. IMBODEN. 1987. Cell surface molecules and early events involved in human T lymphocyte activation. Adv. Immunol. **41:** 1–38.
3. TANIGUCHI, T., H. MATSUI, T. FUJITA, M. HATAKEYAMA, N. KASHIMA, A. FUSE, J. HAMURO, C. NISHI-TAKAOKA & G. YAMADA. 1986. Molecular analysis of the interleukin-2 system. Immunol. Rev. **92:** 121–133.
4. GREENE, W. C., W. J. LEONARD & J. M. DEPPER. 1986. Growth of human T lymphocytes: An analysis of interleukin-2 and its cellular receptor. Prog. Hematol. **14:** 283–301.
5. SMITH, K. A. 1984. Interleukin 2. Ann. Rev. Immunol. **2:** 319–333.
7. LEONARD, W. J., J. M. DEPPER, R. J. ROBB, T. A. WALDMANN & W. C. GREENE. 1982. A monoclonal antibody that appears to recognize the receptor for human T-cell growth factor. Nature **300:** 267–269.
6. ROBB, R. J., A. MUNCK & K. A. SMITH. 1981. T cell growth factor receptors. Quantitation, specificity, and biological relevance. J. Exp. Med. **154(5):** 1455–1474.
8. SHARON, M., R. D. KLAUSNER, B. R. CULLEN, R. CHIZZONITE & W. J. LEONARD. 1986. Novel interleukin-2 receptor subunit detected by cross-linking under high-affinity conditions. Science **234:** 859–863.
9. TSUDO, M., R. W. KOZAK, C. K. GOLDMAN, & T. A. WALDMANN. 1986. Demonstration of a non-Tac peptide that binds interleukin 2: A potential participant in a multichain interleukin 2 receptor complex. Proc. Natl. Acad. Sci. USA **83:** 9694–9698.
10. TESHIGAWARA, K., H. M. WANG, K. KATO & K. A. SMITH. 1987. Interleukin 2 high-affinity receptor expression requires two distinct binding proteins. J Exp. Med. **165:** 223–238.
11. ROBB, R. J., C. M. RUSK, J. YODOI & W. C. GREENE. 1987. Interleukin 2 binding molecule distinct from the Tac protein: Analysis of its role in formation of high-affinity receptors. Proc. Natl. Acad. Sci. USA **84:** 2002–2006.
12. DUKOVICH, M., Y. WANO, L. THUY, P. KATZ, B. R. CULLEN, J. H. KEHRL & W. C. GREENE. 1987. A second human interleukin-2 binding protein that may be a component of high-affinity interleukin-2 receptors. Nature **327:** 518–522.

13. FUJII, M., K. SUGAMURA, K. SANO, M. NAKAI, K. SUGITA & Y. HINUMA. 1986. High-affinity receptor mediated internalization and degradation of interleukin 2 in human T cells. J. Exp. Med. **163**: 550–555.
14. LOWENTHAL, J. W. & W. C. GREENE. 1987. Contrasting interleukin 2 binding properties of the α (p55) and β (p70) protein subunits of the human high affinity interleukin 2 receptor. J. Exp. Med. **166**: 1156–1161.
15. WANG, H.-M. & K. A. SMITH. 1987. The interleukin 2 receptor: Functional consequences of its bimolecular structure. J. Exp. Med. **166**: 1055–1069.
16. ROBB, R. J. & W. C. GREENE. 1987. Internalization of interleukin 2 is mediated by the β chain of the high affinity interleukin 2 receptor. J. Exp. Med. **165**: 1202–1212.
17. LEONARD, W. J., J. M. DEPPER, G. R. CRABTREE, S. RUDIKOFF, J. PUMPHREY, R. ROBB, M. KRÖNKE, P. B. SVETLIK, N. J. PEFFER, T. A. WALDMANN & W. C. GREENE. 1984. Molecular cloning and expression of cDNAs for the human interleukin-2 receptor. Nature **311**: 626–631.
18. LE THI BICH-THUY, M. DUKOVICH, N. J. PEFFER, A. S. FAUCI, J. H. KEHRL & W. C. GREENE. 1987. Direct activation of human resting T cells by IL-2: the role of an IL-2 receptor distinct from the Tac protein. J. Immunol. **139(5)**: 1550–1556.
19. TSUDO, M., C. K. GOLDMAN, K. F. BONGIOVANNI, W. C. CHAN, E. F. WINTON, M. YAGITA, E. A. GRIMM & T. A. WALDMANN. 1987. The p75 peptide is the receptor for interleukin 2 expressed on large granular lymphocytes and is responsible for the interleukin 2 activation of these cells. Proc. Natl. Acad. Sci. USA **84(15)**: 5394–5398.
20. SIEGEL, J. P., M. SHARON, P. L. SMITH & W. J. LEONARD. 1987. The IL-2 receptor beta chain (p70): Role in mediating signals for LAK, NK, and proliferative activities. Science **238(4823)**: 75–78.
21. KEHRL, J. H., M. DUKOVICH, G. WHALEN, P. KATZ, A. S. FAUCI & W. C. GREENE. 1988. Novel interleukin-2 (IL-2) receptor appears to mediate IL-2 induced activation of natural killer cells. J. Clin. Invest. **81**: 200–205.
22. MARUYAMA, M., H. SHIBUYA, H. HARADA, M. HATAKEYAMA, M. SEIKI, T. FUJITA, J. INOUE, M. YOSHIDA & T. TANIGUCHI. 1987. Evidence for aberrant activation of the interleukin-2 autocrine loop by HTLV-I-encoded p40^x and T3/Ti complex triggering. Cell **48**: 343–350.
23. CROSS, S. L., M. B. FEINBERG, J. B. WOLF, N. J. HOLBROOK, F. WONG-STAAL & W. J. LEONARD. 1987. Regulation of the human interleukin-2 receptor α chain promoter: Activation of a nonfunctional promoter by the transactivator gene of HTLV I. Cell **49**: 47–56.
24. SUZUKI, N., N. MATSUNAMI, H. KANAMORI, N. ISHIDA, A. SHIMIZU, Y. YAOITA, T. NIKAIDO & T. HONJO. 1987. The human IL-2 receptor gene contains a positive regulatory element that functions uncultured cells and cell-free extracts. J. Biol. Chem. **262**: 5079–5086-5.
25. LOWENTHAL, J. W., E. BÖHNLEIN & W. C. GREENE. 1988. Regulation of IL-2 receptor (Tac) gene expression: Binding of inducible nuclear proteins to discrete promoter sequences correlates with transcriptional activation. Proc. Natl. Acad. Sci. USA **85**: 4468–4472.
26. BÖHNLEIN, E., J. W. LOWENTHAL, M. SIEKEVITZ, B. R. FRANZA & W. C. GREENE. 1988. The same inducible transcription factor regulates mitogen induced activation of the interleukin-2 receptor alpha gene and type 1 human immunodeficiency virus. Cell **53**: 827–836.
27. NABEL, G. & D. BALTIMORE. 1987. An inducible transcription factor activates expression of human immunodeficiency virus in T cells. Nature **326**: 711–783.
28. FRANZA, R. B., S. F. JOSEPHS, M. Z. GILMAN, W. RYAN & B. CLARKSON. 1987. Characterization of cellular proteins recognizing the HIV enhancer using a microscale DNA-affinity precipitation assay. Nature **330**: 391–395.
29. SIEKEVITZ, M., S. F. JOSEPHS, M. DUKOVICH, N. PEFFER, F. WONG-STAAL & W. C. GREENE. 1987b. Activation of the HIV LTR by T-cell mitogens and the *tat*-I protein of HTLV-I. Science **238**: 1575–1578.
30. KAUFMAN, J. D., G. VALANDRA, G. RODRIGUEZ, G. BUSHAR, C. GIRI & M. D. NORCROSS. 1987. Phorbol ester enhances human immunodeficiency virus-promoted gene expression

and acts on a repeated 10-base-pair functional enhancer element. Mol. Cell Biol. **7:** 3759–3766.

31. TONG-STARKSEN, S. E., P. A. LUCIW & B. M. PETERLIN. Human immunodeficiency virus long terminal repeat responds to T-cell activation signals. Proc. Natl. Acad. Sci. USA **84:** 6845–6849.

32. SIEKEVITZ, M., M. B. FEINBERG, N. HOLBROOK, J. YODOI, F. WONG-STAAL & W. C. GREENE. 1987a. Activation of interleukin-2 and interleukin-2 receptor (Tac) promoter expression by the trans-activator (tat) gene product of human T-cell leukemia virus, type I. Proc. Natl. Acad. Sci. USA **84:** 5389–5393.

Interleukin-1[a]

CHARLES A. DINARELLO

Department of Medicine
Tufts University and New England Medical Center Hospitals
Boston, Massachusetts 02111

The polypeptide hormone interleukin-1 (IL-1) is one of the key mediators of a host's response to microbial invasion, inflammation, tissue injury, or immunologic reactions. IL-1 is a prominent member of a group of polypeptide mediators now called "cytokines." In the first hours after infection or injury, the biologic effects of IL-1 are manifested in nearly every tissue and organ. Historically, IL-1 was first described in the 1940s as a fever-producing substance released by activated leukocytes. At that time it was called "pyrexin" or "endogenous pyrogen." Atkins[1] characterized the production of endogenous pyrogen during experimental fevers and established that endogenous pyrogen was a polypeptide distinct from the lipopolysaccharide endotoxin. Purified endogenous pyrogen,[2,3] however, did more than cause fever. It co-purified with a substance called "leukocytic endogenous mediator"[4] which induced hepatic acute-phase protein synthesis, decreased plasma iron and zinc levels, and produced neutrophilia. "Lymphocyte activating factor" was a protein described by Gery and Waksman[5] that augmented T-lymphocyte responses to mitogens and antigens, but was indistinguishable from endogenous pyrogen (reviewed in reference 6). After the molecular cloning of IL-1, the term IL-1 now includes the originally described endogenous pyrogen, leukocytic endogenous mediator, lymphocyte activating factor, as well as mononuclear cell factor,[7] catabolin,[8] osteoclast activating factor, and hemopoietin-1.

TWO GENES CODE FOR IL-1

Two biochemically distinct but structurally related IL-1 cDNAs have been cloned: IL-1-beta was first cloned from human blood monocytes[9] and IL-1-alpha was cloned from a mouse macrophage line.[10] Subsequently, the two IL-1 forms were reported in several species. The two IL-1 forms in each species share only small stretches of amino acid homology (26% for human IL-1-beta versus human IL-1-alpha). However, between the species, the IL-1 forms are more closely related; for example, nearly 88% amino acid homology exists between human and mouse IL-1-beta. Therefore, it is not surprising that human IL-1 is active on murine cells. The homologies between the species of IL-1-alpha forms are approximately 70%.

Each form of IL-1 is coded by a separate gene,[11,12] both genes are located on chromosome 2,[13] and each gene contains seven exons. IL-1-beta mRNA predominates over that of IL-1-alpha in mouse as well as human cells. In some cases such as human endothelial and smooth muscle cells, transcription IL-1-alpha is not observed unless cycloheximide is included in the medium during stimulation.[14] One explanation for the dominance of IL-1-beta is that it contains a second promoter-like sequence that is

[a]These studies are supported by NIH Grant AI15614.

missing in IL-1-alpha. Circulating blood monocytes and resident peritoneal macrophages do not contain mRNA coding for either IL-1-beta or IL-1-alpha. However, attachment to surfaces such as glass or polystyrene provides a signal for spreading and transcription. Agents such as endotoxin, inflammatory substances such as C5a, or phagocytosis stimulates considerably more IL-1 transcription. Substances that inhibit cyclooxygenase do not affect IL-1 transcription, but corticosteroids added before cells are stimulated prevent mRNA synthesis. Inhibitors of the lipoxygenase pathway block IL-1 production, but it is unclear if this occurs at the transcriptional level. Activators of protein kinases such as phorbol esters are potent inducers of IL-1 gene expression.

TRANSLATION AND PROCESSING OF IL-1

IL-1 is synthesized by a wide variety of cells including synovial fibroblasts; keratinocytes and Langerhans cells of the skin; mesangial cells of the kidney; B lymphocytes; natural killer cells; astrocytes and microglial cells of the brain; vascular endothelial and smooth muscle cells; corneal, gingival, and thymic epithelial cells; and some T-lymphocyte cell lines. Circulating blood monocytes begin transcribing IL-1 mRNA within 15 minutes after adherence to plastic or glass surfaces. Transcription for IL-1 can be initiated without there being much translation into the IL-1 protein, and in some mice with the HeJ genetic defect, there is a high level of transcription with very low levels of translated protein.[15] IL-1 is initially translated as a 31-kd precursor protein that requires limited proteolysis for processing into more active mature peptides. Stimulating cells with agents such as endotoxin or with phagocytosis not only increases transcription, but also has a major effect on translation and processing of the IL-1 precursor. There is a period of short-lived transcription that can be increased by suppressing the synthesis of a repressor protein.[16] Translation is reduced by prostaglandin-induced cyclic AMP production. A positive signal is provided by calcium ionophores and products of arachidonate lipoxygenase (leukotrienes). The monocyte/macrophage remains an important source of IL-1 because of its strategic locations, its ability to synthesize large amounts of IL-1 (100 fg/cell per 24 hours of IL-1-beta), and its ability to process the IL-1 precursor more effectively than other cells, perhaps because of its high levels of elastase and other serine proteases.

Because IL-1 lacks a distinct cleavage sequence, a considerable amount of it remains cell associated, either intracellularly[17] or as part of the cell membrane. The 31,000-Da IL-1 precursor and a 22,000-Da form are associated with the cell, and either size can comprise "membrane-bound IL-1."[18,19] Processing of IL-1 is accomplished through the action of serine proteases, particularly elastase and plasmin,[18,20] and in the cell, IL-1 is associated with lysosomes, not the endoplasmic reticulum.[21] Membrane-bound IL-1, first described by Unanue and associates,[22] is biologically active; in fact, membrane-bound IL-1 may account for a significant part of the immunostimulatory effects of IL-1 in local tissues such as lymph nodes, joints, and skin. Membrane-bound IL-1 participates in antigen presentation and is also active on nonlymphoid cells such as chondrocytes. Evidence suggests that most of the membrane-bound IL-1 is the alpha form and that the beta form is secreted into the extracellular fluid. The concept of membrane-bound IL-1 explains the ability of IL-1 to participate in autocrine and paracrine events without inducing the systemic effects that occur when IL-1 is processed into its mature peptide, is released from cells, and gains access to the circulation. FIGURE 1 illustrates key events in the activation, transcription, translation, and processing of IL-1.

STRUCTURE OF IL-1

Initially translated as precursor polypeptides, the generation of the N-terminus of the 17.5-kd "mature" peptides of IL-1-beta and alpha as well as smaller peptides occurs by the action of serine proteases. Some of the smaller (<17.5 kd) IL-1 peptides are biologically active.[23] FIGURE 2 illustrates the structure of human IL-1-beta with regions of amino acid homology to IL-1-alpha and the exons coding for the different regions of the molecule. Likely cleavage sites by serine proteases are also shown. The amino acid homologies between the beta and alpha forms have been identified and labeled in alphabetic order.[24] Of considerable interest is the homologous region termed "C-D" which is entirely coded by the VIth exon. Studies employing synthetic peptides[25] and translated cDNA mutants[26] suggest that this region may contain the

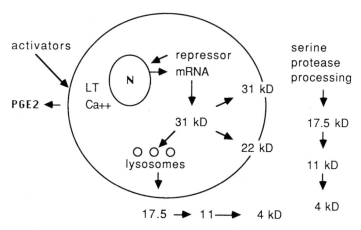

FIGURE 1. Events during the production of IL-1. Activators include a large number of both endogenous and exogenous substances that stimulate gene expression for IL-1. (See reference 6.) PGE_2 (prostaglandin E_2) is usually produced during cell activation and has via cAMP a suppressive effect on translation, not transcription. Leukotrienes (LT) and calcium act as positive signals of gene expression. The pro-IL-1 precursor molecule (31 kD) is translated and processed by serine proteases; some of the pro-IL-1 is trapped in the plasma membrane where it is biologically active. Extracellular serine proteases cleave IL-1 into its mature 17.5-kD peptide as well as smaller, biologically active subunits. (Derived from references 16–23.)

minimal recognition site for IL-1 receptors. However, to date there are no data that reveal that synthetic peptides to the alpha/beta homologous regions of IL-1 interfere with native IL-1 binding to its putative receptor. Receptors for IL-1 equally recognize the beta and alpha forms, both forms possess the same spectrum of biologic properties, and molecular modeling studies reveal that the two IL-1s are comprised of beta-folded sheets (F. Cohen, personal communication).

MULTIPLE BIOLOGIC PROPERTIES OF IL-1

The use of recombinant IL-1 has confirmed most, but not all, of the multiple biologic properties of IL-1. For example, recombinant IL-1 produces endogenous

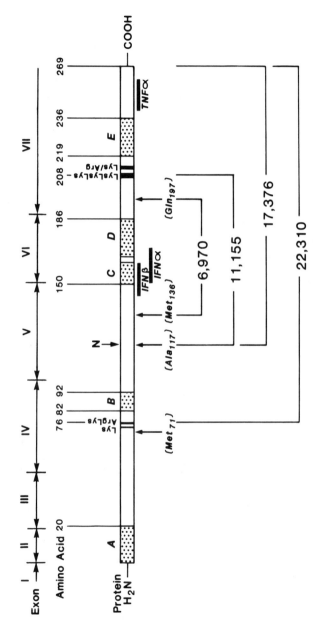

FIGURE 2. Organization of IL-1 genomic exons and protein sequence homology between IL-1-beta and IL-1-alpha. The numbers indicate the amino acid numbers of the IL-1-beta protein, and the shaded areas show the sequence homologies with IL-1-alpha. (Derived from data in references 9–12, 18, and 24.)

pyrogen fever, stimulates prostaglandin (PG) E_2, and induces the proliferation of fibroblasts and T lymphocytes. The list of some *in vitro* effects of recombinant IL-1 (either beta or alpha) is given in TABLE 1. The effective concentration of IL-1 that induces these effects ranges from 1 nmol to 1 pmol (in some cases less); unlike interferons and bone marrow growth factors, IL-1 has no species specificity.

IL-1 specifically binds to a variety of cells, but the precise nature of the IL-1 receptor(s) and the nature of the receptor-ligand interaction remain unclear. For example, human neutrophils express specific receptors for IL-1, but intracellular calcium levels and oxidative metabolism are unaffected by IL-1. Similar discrepancies between specific IL-1 binding and biologic responses have been observed in endothelial cells. Studies using T-lymphocytes and fibroblasts suggest the existence of a single class of high affinity receptor with a dissociation constant (kD) that varies from 5–50 pmol with 100–4,000 binding sites per cell. Most studies of IL-1 receptor binding have used the EL4 mouse thymoma cells line. Recently we studied the murine helper T-cell

TABLE 1. *In Vitro* Effects of Recombinant Interleukin-1

Fibroblast, Keratinocyte, Mesangial and Glial Cell Proliferation
Increased Collagen and Procollagenase Synthesis Chrondrocyte Protease and Proteoglycan Release Increased Chondrocyte Plasminogen Activator Bone Resorption (Osteoclast Activating Factor) PGE$_2$ Synthesis in Dermal and Synovial Fibroblasts
Chemotaxis of T and B Lymphocytes Neutrophil and Monocyte Thromboxane Synthesis Basophil Histamine Release Eosinophil Degranulation
Cytotoxic for Tumor Cells, Beta Islet Cells, and Thyrocytes
Vascular Smooth Muscle Cell Proliferation Synthesis of Interferon Beta-1 and Beta-2 (IL-6) Increased Endothelial Plasminogen Activator Inhibitor Expression of Endothelial Cell Leukocyte Adherence Receptors
Increased Intestinal Mucus Production Decreased Synthesis of Adipocyte Lipoprotein Lipase Decreased Hepatic Albumin Transcription Increased Hepatic Metallothionen Transcription

line, D10.G4.1, and found evidence that both a high as well as a low affinity receptor exists. The kD of the low affinity receptor is 250–300 pmol and 15,000 sites per cell.[27] The high affinity receptors are rapidly internalized, they bind to nuclear structures, and responsiveness to IL-1 is down-regulated.[28-31] The rapid down-regulation of the IL-1 receptor is specific and may account, in part, for modulating IL-1 effects in several cells. To date, the amino acid sequence of a putative IL-1 receptor is unknown. In cells stimulated with IL-1, cytosolic calcium increases, sodium/potassium ion fluxes occur, and increased protein kinase activity has been observed. Many effects of IL-1 *in vitro* are mimicked by agents such as phorbol esters that directly activate protein kinases.

The ability of IL-1 to initiate PG synthesis is perhaps one of its most important biologic properties, accounting for many local and systemic effects. Like the febrile response to IL-1, increased slow wave sleep can be observed within minutes after an intravenous injection. IL-1 also induces the release of several hypothalamic and pituitary peptides including endorphins, corticotropin releasing factor, ACTH, and somatostatin. Some of these peptides exert considerable effects on the immune system. Although IL-1 raises the level of circulating corticosterone by the release of ACTH,[32] IL-1 also acts directly on the adrenal gland to augment steroid synthesis.[33] One possibility is that the net effect of IL-1 is one of immunosuppression due to its ability to stimulate the production of corticosteroids. In isolated hepatocytes, IL-1 leads to decreased transcription of albumin but increased transcription of factor B, metallothionen, and amyloid A. IL-1 also stimulates the biosynthesis of complement protein C3, alpha$_1$-antichymotrypsin, alpha$_1$-acid glycoprotein, and inter-alpha$_1$-trypsin inhibitor.[34] The ability of IL-1 to induce anorexia[35] is probably due to its effects on the liver.

IL-1 AS AN INDUCER OF CYTOKINES

With the exception of hepatic albumin and adiopocyte lipoprotein lipase transcription, exposure of a wide variety of cells to IL-1 increases gene expression. IL-1 stimulates synthesis of insulin, collagen, collagenases, procoagulant proteins, proteoglycans, and several growth factors (TABLE 1). Cells that themselves produce IL-1 will, in turn, respond to IL-1 and produce more of it.[36] IL-1 stimulates the production of IL-2, the interferons, IL-3 and other bone marrow colony stimulating factors, and B-cell-stimulating factor-2.[37] This latter cytokine is identical to interferon-beta-2 and is now termed IL-6. Although IL-1 has no direct effect on marrow precursors, it acts synergistically with bone marrow growth factors during the reconstitution of antimetabolite-suppressed hematopoiesis. This recently described property of IL-1 identifies it as a previously described molecule called hemopoietin-1. It is clear that IL-1 participates in what could be described as a network of cytokine-induced cytokines. Such a network may be important for the augmentation or suppression of various biologic properties during host responses to infection or inflammation. For immunologic responses, IL-1-induced production of itself, IL-2 and B-lymphocyte growth factors augment the immune response to antigens, whereas IL-1-induced gamma-interferon production results in an antiproliferative and antiinflammatory effect.

IL-1 AND INFLAMMATION

IL-1 is found in the joint fluid of individuals with inflammatory and destructive arthritis where it is thought to contribute to pain, leukocyte activation, and tissue remodeling. *In vitro*, IL-1 induces synovial cell and chondrocyte PGE$_2$, collagenase, and phospholipase A$_2$ production. In addition to attracting leukocytes into inflamed tissues, IL-1 also causes degranulation of basophils and eosinophils, stimulates thromboxane synthesis in macrophages and neutrophils, and potentiates the activation of neutrophils by chemoattractant peptides. Osteoclast activation is also a property of IL-1. In contrast to its catabolic activities, IL-1 participates in the reparative process by increasing fibroblast proliferation and the synthesis of collagens and glucosaminoglycans. IL-1 is mitogenic for mesangial cells in the kidney, glial cells in the brain, and keratinocytes. In fibroblasts, IL-1 directly increases the transcription of Type 1, Type III, and Type IV (basement membrane) collagen. Fibrosis and deposition of abnormal proteins in tissues appear to be mediated in part by IL-1, and in rheumatoid joint disease, this contributes to thickening of the scar tissue that restricts joint movement.

ROLE OF IL-1 IN IMMUNE RESPONSES

IL-1 stimulates the immune system by (1) participating in the direct activation of lymphocytes and (2) indirectly by inducing the synthesis of molecules that in turn activate lymphocytes. In fibroblasts, endothelial cells, macrophages, and lymphocytes, IL-1 induces the production of interferons, hemopoietic colony stimulating factors, and T- and B-lymphocyte growth and differentiation factors. Although the tumor necrosis factor also induces these immunostimulatory cytokines, IL-1 also participates in the direct activation of lymphocytes. For example, in the presence of IL-1, proliferation of resting T- and B-lymphocytes to growth factors is enhanced, differentiation and antibody production are augmented, and the binding of natural killer lymphocytes to their tumor targets is increased. IL-1 is also a chemoattractant for lymphocytes. A pattern has emerged that suggests that IL-1, like phorbol esters, up-regulates the functional responses of immunocompetent cells. This property of IL-1 supports the notion that the molecule is one of the body's natural adjuvants, and like all adjuvants, IL-1 nonspecifically increases the immune response to antigens and malignant cells.

Particular attention has focused on the role of IL-1 in T-lymphocyte-dependent immune responses. To proliferate, T lymphocytes require the growth hormone IL-2 and the expression of IL-2 receptors. Studies on IL-1 receptor-bearing T-lymphocyte cell lines show that 1–10 pM concentrations of IL-1 induce the transcription, synthesis, and secretion of IL-2 as well as the expression of IL-2 receptors. These responses to IL-1, however, are greatly enhanced (10–100-fold) by the presence of agents that raise cytosolic calcium levels and activate protein kinase C. There is no lack of data to demonstrate that IL-1 lowers the threshold for mitogen- or antigen-induced T-lymphocyte proliferation, and that this decrease is due to increased IL-2 production and IL-2 receptor expression. This co-stimulation is a well-described phenomenon for IL-1-induced T-lymphocyte activation. However, an *absolute* requirement for IL-1 during T-lymphocyte responses to antigen is unclear, particularly in the strict absence of macrophages.

During the immune response, specific antigen is presented on the surface of an antigen-presenting cell together with the class II major histocompatibility complex; in addition, a second, antigen-nonspecific signal is required for T lymphocytes to proliferate. The first signal can be substituted by direct activation of the antigen receptor on the surface of the T lymphocyte, but in the absence of macrophages, cell division does not take place. In some studies, the addition of soluble IL-1 replaces the requirement for the macrophage to proliferate, but in other experiments, soluble IL-1 cannot restore the immune response to antigen without macrophages. An absolute requirement for soluble IL-1 seems variable, depending on the state of activation of the T lymphocyte. Because fixed macrophage membranes can restore the response, it is possible that membrane-bound IL-1 participates in providing the second signal.[22] TABLE 2 depicts the immunologic activities of IL-1.

MODULATION OF IL-1

The production of biologic activities of IL-1 are important considerations in some pathologic processes. Circulating levels of IL-1 increase in a variety of diseases but also in physiologic states, such as ovulation, and after strenuous exercise and exposure to ultraviolet light, In some infectious and inflammatory diseases, IL-1 production *in vitro* from blood leukocytes is elevated, whereas decreased production has been observed in humans and animals with metastatic tumors and certain nutritional deficiencies. Because IL-1 is highly inflammatory and stimulates catabolic processes in bone and cartilage, attention has focused on how to down-regulate IL-1 production or inhibit its activity. To date, only corticosteroids block IL-1 transcription and reduce its production. Because IL-1 induces ACTH release, this effect may be a built-in negative feedback loop.[32] Cyclooxygenase inhibitors are useful for reducing IL-1-induced synthesis of PG and thromboxane, which are potent immunosuppressive agents. Substances that inhibit the biologic activity of IL-1 by either binding the molecule[38] or interfering with the IL-1 receptor[39] are only considerations for immunosuppression in some diseases. Uromodulin[38] is urinary glycosylated Tamm-Horstfall protein that binds via its glycosylated portion to IL-1, and this is thought to be part of the mechanism by which uromodulin acts as an immunosuppressive agent.

It is presently unclear if these naturally produced inhibitors will be useful in treating clinical disease, but it is important to recognize from a biologic point of view

TABLE 2. Immunologic Effects of Interleukin-1

T Lymphocytes:
  Co-stimulator Activity; IL-2 Production; Increased IL-2 Receptor Number or Binding; Growth Factor for T cells; Induction of Gamma-Interferon, IL-3, and Other Lymphokine Synthesis

B Lymphocytes:
  Growth Factor for Transformed B cells; Synergism with B-cell Growth and Differentiation Factors (IL-4 and IL-6)

Natural Killer Cells:
  Synergism with IL-2 and Interferons for Tumor Lysis; Increased Binding to Tumor Cells; Induction of Cytokine Synthesis

Macrophages:
  Synthesis of PGE_2, Induction of Cytotoxicity, Increased Migration; Synthesis of IL-I, Colony Stimulating Factors, and Other Cytokines

Bone Marrow Cells:
  Increased Synthesis of Colony Stimulating Factors; Synergism with Colony Stimulating Factors (Hemopoietin-1 Activity) on Immature Precursors

---

that these counterregulatory molecules exist and that an imbalance between IL-1 and its natural inhibitors may underlie certain disease states, particularly immunosuppressive disease. Another aspect of modulating IL-1's effects is its ability to down-regulate its own receptor, which may explain the protective role of IL-1 to lethal challenge by radiation,[40] hyperoxia,[41] or infection.[42] In these examples, IL-1 is only effective when given to animals 24 hours before the lethal challenge. A functional immune system is necessary for the elimination of microbial invaders and neoplastic cells, and IL-1's ability to activate T and B lymphocytes, natural killer cells, and macrophages may also contribute to this process. However, IL-1-induced changes take place at a considerable cost to the host, and when the production and activity of IL-1 persist and escape regulation, IL-1 itself contributes to pathologic processes and perhaps the death of the host. It is consistent with the biology of IL-1 to consider that the molecule is of vital importance to the host as long as its production and activity are appropriately modulated.

SUMMARY

Interleukin-1 (IL-1) is a polypeptide that is produced following infection, injury, or antigenic challenge. Although the macrophage is a primary source of IL-1, epidermal, epithelial, lymphoid, and vascular tissues synthesize IL-1. When IL-1 gains access to the circulation, it induces a broad spectrum of systemic changes in neurologic, metabolic, hematologic, and endocrinologic systems. However, because IL-1 lacks a signal peptide, a considerable amount of the IL-1 that is synthesized may remain associated with the cell, particularly as part of the plasma membrane; moreover, membrane-associated IL-1 is biologically active, especially in its ability to participate in lymphocyte activation and mesenchymal tissue remodeling. There are two gene products coding for IL-1: IL-1-beta and IL-1-alpha. The spectrum of biologic activities of IL-1 are induced by both forms. IL-1 activates lymphocytes and plays an important role in the initiation of the immune response. Receptors for IL-1 recognize both forms, but receptors are scarce and their affinities often do not match the potency of the biologic response. The most consistent property of IL-1 is up-regulation of cellular metabolism and increased expression of several genes coding for biologically active molecules. IL-1 is a highly inflammatory molecule and stimulates the production of arachidonic acid metabolites. IL-1 also acts synergistically with other cytokines, particularly tumor necrosis factor. The multitude of biologic responses to IL-1 is an example of the rapid adaptive changes that take place to increase the host's defensive mechanisms.

ACKNOWLEDGMENTS

The author thanks Drs. J. G. Cannon, F. Cohen, S. Endres, J. A. Gelfand, T. Ikejima, P. Libby, G. Lonnemann, J. W. M. van der Meer, N. Savage, S. J. C. Warner, and S. M. Wolff for their contributions.

REFERENCES

1. ATKINS, E. 1960. The pathogenesis of fever. Physiol. Rev. **40:** 580–646.
2. MURPHY, P. A., J. CHESNEY & W. B. WOOD, JR. 1974. Further purification of rabbit leukocyte pyrogen. J. Lab. Clin. Med. **83:** 310–319.
3. DINARELLO, C. A., L. RENFER & S. M. WOLFF. 1977. Human leukocytic pyrogen: Purification and development of a radioimmunoassay. Proc. Natl. Acad. Sci. USA **74:** 4624–4627.
4. MERRIMAN, C. R., L. A. PULLIAM & R. F. KAMPSCHMIDT. 1977. Comparison of leukocytic pyrogen and leukocytic endogenous mediator. Proc. Soc. Exp. Biol. Med. **154:** 224–227.
5. GERY, I. & B. H. WAKSMAN. 1972. Potentiation of the T-lymphocyte response to mitogens. II. The cellular source of potentiating mediator(s). J. Exp. Med. **136:** 143–155.
6. DINARELLO, C. A. 1984. Interleukin-1. Rev. Infect. Dis. **6:** 51–95.
7. KRANE, S. M., J.-M. DAYER, L. S. SIMON & S. BYRNE. 1985. Mononuclear cell-conditioned medium containing mononuclear cell factor (MCF), homologous with interleukin-1, stimulates collagen and fibronectin synthesis by adherent rheumatoid synovial cells: Effects of prostaglandin E_2 and indomethacin. Collagen Rel. Res. **5:** 99–117.
8. SAKLATVALA, J., S. J. SARSFIELD & Y. TOWNSEND. 1984. Pig interleukin-1. Purification of two immunologically different leukocyte proteins that cause cartilage resorption, lymphocyte activation, and fever. J. Exp. Med. **162:** 1208–1222.
9. AURON, P. E., A. C. WEBB & L. J. ROSENWASSER, S. F. MUCCI, A. RICH, S. M. WOLFF & C. A. DINARELLO. 1984. Nucleotide sequence of human monocyte interleukin-1 precursor cDNA. Proc. Natl. Acad. Sci. USA **81:** 7907–7911.

10. LOMEDICO, P. T., U. GUBLER, C. P. HELLMAN, M. DUKOVICH, J. G. GIRI, Y. E. PAN, K. COLLIER, R. SEMIONOW, A. O. CHUA & S. B. MIZEL. 1984. Cloning and expression of murine interleukin-1 in *Escherichia coli*. Nature 312: 458–462.
11. CLARK, B. D., K. L. COLLINS, M. S. GANDY, A. C. WEBB & P. E. AURON. 1986. Genomic sequence for human prointerleukin-1 beta: Possible evolution from a reverse transcribed prointerleukin-1 alpha gene. Nucl. Acids Res. 14: 7897–7905.
12. FURUTANI, Y., M. NOTAKE, T. FUKI, M. OHUE, H. NOMURA, M. YAMADA & S. NAKAMURA. 1986. Complete nucleotide sequence of the gene from human interleukin-1-alpha. Nucleic Acids Res. 14: 3167–3179.
13. WEBB, A. C., K. L. COLLINS, P. E. AURON, R. L. EDDY, H. NAKAI, M. G. BYERS, L. L. HALEY, W. M. HENRY & T. B. SHOWS. 1986. Interleukin-1 gene (IL-1) assigned to long arm of human chromosome 2. Lymphokine Res. 5: 77–85.
14. LIBBY, P., J. M. ORDOVAS, L. K. BIRINYI, K. R. AUGER & C. A. DINARELLO. 1986. Inducible interleukin-1 gene expression in human vascular smooth muscle cells. J. Clin. Invest. 78: 1432–1438.
15. IKEJIMA, T., S. F. ORENCOLE, S. J. C. WARNER & C. A. DINARELLO. 1987. TSST-1 resistance in mice is related to interleukin-1 production. J. Leukocyte Biol. 42: 561.
16. FENTON, M. T., B. D. CLARK, K. L. COLLINS, A. C. WEBB, A. RICH & P. E. AURON. 1987. Transcriptional regulation of the human prointerleukin-1-beta gene. J. Immunol. 138: 3972–3979.
17. LEPE-ZUNIGA, B. & I. GERY. 1984. Production of intracellular and extracellular interleukin-1 (IL-1) by human monocytes. Clin. Immunol. Immunopathol. 31: 222–230.
18. AURON, P. E., S. J. C. WARNER, A. C. WEBB, J. G. CANNON, H. A. BERNHEIM, K. J. P. W. MCADAM, L. J. ROSENWASSER, G. LOPRESTE, S. F. MUCCI & C. A. DINARELLO. 1987. Studies on the molecular nature of human interleukin-1. J. Immunol. 138: 3403–3407.
19. BEUSCHER, H. U., R. J. FALLON & H. R. COLTEN. 1987. Macrophage membrane interleukin-1 regulates the expression of acute phase proteins in human hepatoma 3B cells. J. Immunol. 139: 1896–1901.
20. MATSUSHIMA, K., M. TAGUCHI, E. J. KOVACS, H. A. YOUNG & J. J. OPPENHEIM. 1987. Intracellular localization of human monocyte associated interleukin 1 (IL-1) activity and release of biologically active IL-1 from monocytes by trypsin and plasmin. J. Immunol. 136: 2883–2891.
21. BAKOUCHE, O., D. C. BROWN & L. B. LACHMAN. 1987. Subcellular localization of human monocyte interleukin-1: Evidence for an inactive precursor molecule and a possible mechanism for IL-1 release. J. Immunol. 138: 4249–4253.
22. KURT-JONES, E. A., J. M. KIELY & E. R. UNANUE. 1985. Conditions required for expression of membrane IL-1 on B-cells. J. Immunol. 135: 1548–1550.
23. DINARELLO, C. A., G. H. A. CLOWES, JR., A. H. GORDON, C. A. SARAVIS & S. M. WOLFF. 1984. Cleavage of human interleukin-1: Isolation of a peptide fragment from plasma of febrile humans and activated monocytes. 1984. J. Immunol. 133: 1332–1338.
24. AURON, P. E., L. J. ROSENWASSER, K. MATSUSHIMA, T. COPELAND, C. A. DINARELLO, J. J. OPPENHEIM & A. C. WEBB. 1985. Human and murine interleukin-1 share sequence similarities. J. Mol. Immunol. 2: 231–239.
25. ANTONI, G., R. PRESENTINI, F. PERIN, A. TAGLIABUE, P. GHIARA, S. CENSINI, G. VOLPINI, L. VILLA & D. BORASCHI. 1987. A short synthetic peptide fragment of human interleukin-1 with immunostimmulatory but not inflammatory activity. J. Immunol. 137: 3201–3215.
25. ROSENWASSER, L. J., A. C. WEBB, B. D. CLARK, S. IRIE, L. CHANG, C. A. DINARELLO, L. GEHRKE S. M. WOLFF, A. RICH & P. E. AURON. 1986. Expression of biologically active human interleukin-1 subpeptides by transfected simian COS cells. Proc. Natl. Acad. Sci. USA 83: 1–4.
26. DINARELLO, C. A., G. H. A. CLOWES, JR., A. H. GORDON, C. A. SARAVIS & S. M. WOLFF. 1984. Cleavage of human interleukin-1: Isolation of a peptide fragment from plasma of febrile humans and activated monocytes. J. Immunol. 133: 1332–1338.
27. SAVAGE, N., S. F. ORENCOLE, G. LONNEMANN & C. A. DINARELLO. 1987. Characterization of interleukin-1 (IL-1) receptors on a subclone of D10.G4.1 T cells which proliferates in response to IL-1 in the absence of mitogen. J. Leukocyte Biol. 42: 593.
28. LOWENTHAL, J. W. & H. R. MACDONALD. 1987. Binding and internalization of interleu-

kin-1 by T cells. Direct evidence for high- and low-affinity classes of interleukin-1 receptor. J. Exp. Med. **164:** 1060–1074.

29. MATSUSHIMA, K., J. YODOI, Y. TAGAYA & J. J. OPPENHEIM. 1986. Down regulation of interleukin-1 receptor expression by IL-1 and fate of internalized 125-I-labeled IL-1-beta in a human large granular lymphocyte cell line. J. Immunol. **137:** 3183–3188.

30. MIZEL, S. B., P. L. KILIAN, J. C. LEWIS, K. A. PAGANELLI, & R. A. CHIZZONITE. 1987. The interleukin 1 receptor. Dynamics of interleukin 1 binding and internalization in T cells and fibroblasts. J. Immunol. **138:** 2906–2912.

31. BIRD, T. A. & J. SAKLATVALA. 1987. Studies on the fate of receptor-bound 125-I-interleukin 1 beta in porcine synovial fibroblasts. J. Immunol. **139:** 92–97.

32. BESEDOVSKY, H., A. DEL REY, E. SORKIN & C. A. DINARELLO. 1986. Immunoregulatory feedback between interleukin-1 and glucocorticoid hormones. Science **233:** 652–654.

33. ROH, M. S., K. A. DRAZENOVICH, B. S. JEFFREY, J. J. BARBOSE, C. A. DINARELLO & C. F. COBB. 1987. Direct stimulation of the adrenal cortex by interleukin-1. Surgery **102:** 147–154.

34. PERLMUTTER, D. H., C. A. DINARELLO, P. PUNSAL & H. R. COLTEN. 1986. Cachectin/tumor necrosis factor regulates hepatic acute phase gene expression. J. Clin. Invest. **78:** 1349–1345.

35. MCCARTHY, D. O., M. J. KLUGER & A. J. VANDER. 1987. Suppression of food intake during infection: Is interleukin-1 involved? Am. J. Clin. Nutr. **42:** 1179–1182.

36. DINARELLO, C. A., T. IKEJIMA, S. J. C. WARNER, S. F. ORENCOLE, G. LONNEMANN, J. G. CANNON & P. LIBBY. 1987. Interleukin-1 in rabbits *in vivo* and in human mononuclear cells *in vitro*. J. Immunol. **139:** 1902–1910.

37. VAN DAMME, J. & A. BILLIAU. 1987. Identification of the human 26-kD protein, interferon Beta-2, as a B cell hybridoma/plasmacytoma growth factor induced by interleukin-1 and tumor necorsis factor. J. Exp. Med. **165:** 914–919.

38. BROWN, K., A. V. MUCHMORE & D. L. ROSENSTREICH. 1987. Uromodulin, an immunosuppressive protein derived from pregnancy urine, is an inhibitor of interleukin 1. Proc. Natl. Acad. Sci. USA **83:** 9119–9123.

39. BALAVOINE, J. F., B. DEROCHEMONTEIX, K. WILLIAMSON, P. SECKINGER, A. CRUCHAUD & J.-M. DAYER. 1987. Prostaglandin E2 and collagenase production by fibroblasts and synovial cells is regulated by urine-derived human interleukin-1 and inhibitor(s). J. Clin. Invest. **78:** 1120–1124.

40. NETA, R., S. DOUCHES & J. J. OPPENHEIM. 1987. Interleukin 1 is a radioprotector. J. Immunol. **136:** 2483–2488.

41. WHITE, C. W., P. GHEZZI, C. A. DINARELLO, S. A. CALDWELL, I. J. MCMURTRY & J. E. REPINE. 1987. Recombinant tumor necrosis factor/cachectin and interleukin-1 pretreatment decreases lung oxidized glutathione accumulation, lung injury and mortality in rats exposed to hyperoxia. J. Clin. Invest. **79:** 1863–1873.

42. VAN DER MEER, J. W. M., M. BARZA, S. M. WOLFF & C. A. DINARELLO. 1988. Low dose recombinant interleukin-1 protects granulocytopenic mice from lethal Gram-negative infection. Proc. Natl. Acad. Sci. USA **85:** 1620–1623.

Polymorphisms of Immunologically Relevant Loci in Human Disease

Autoimmunity and Human Heavy Chain Variable Regions[a]

INAKI SANZ,[b] LARN-YUAN HWANG,[b]
CHARLES HASEMANN,[c] JAMES THOMAS,[b]
RICHARD WASSERMAN,[d] PHILIP TUCKER,[b]
AND J. DONALD CAPRA[b]

[b]Department of Microbiology
and
[c]Graduate Program in Immunology
University of Texas Southwestern Medical Center
Dallas, Texas 75235

In higher vertebrates there are three major groups of polymorphic molecules that are central to immunologic specificity. The genes of the major histocompatibility complex were demonstrated to be polymorphic and associated with a number of human diseases over two decades ago, and "HLA typing" is now routinely performed for several human diseases.[1,2] Polymorphisms of the human T-cell receptor complex were more recently documented, and as of this writing allelic variants of T alpha, T beta, and T gamma have been described.[3-6] In several instances these variations have been associated with human disease.[7-9]

Immunoglobulins are composed of heavy and light polypeptide chains; in man, allotypic forms are known within the kappa (Km) and heavy (Gm) chain families, the multiple forms of lambda being isotypic. The Gm and Km allotypes were first detected serologically, and over the years evidence has accumulated that these allotypic forms are associated with certain human diseases.[10-12] As data from other species (particularly rabbit and mouse) accumulated in which serologic markers for the variable regions could be followed in pedigree analyses with allotypes in the constant region, a paradox emerged. Although there were certain preferences for certain V regions to be associated with certain C regions, by and large there was no evidence of significant linkage disequilibrium between the variable and constant region genes.[13,14] The hypothesis developed that the described disease associations were largely related to limited amino acid variations in the constant regions of immunoglobulin molecules that somehow affected immunoglobulin function (for example, complement fixation or opsonizing capabilities). Because serologic markers in the variable region have been difficult to define in man, several investigators have turned to molecular genetic studies.

Historically, human immunoglobulin V_H structures have been divided into three

[a]This research was supported by the National Institutes of Health (1-R03-DK39800-01), the North Texas Chapter of the Arthritis Foundation, and the Robert Welch Foundation.

[d]Current address: Baylor University Medical Center, 3500 Gaston Ave., Dallas, Texas 75246.

133

and only three "families," "subgroups," and the like.[15] Therefore, of the first 100 human V_H proteins sequenced, there was relatively little disagreement that they fell into the V_HI, V_HII, and V_HIII families. Genes for these three families were isolated in several laboratories about 5 years ago, and Southern filter hybridization analyses revealed 10 (V_HII) to 30–50 (V_HI and V_HIII) restriction fragments.[16,17] Some investigators furthur noted that relatively little difference exists between the restriction fragment pattern in unrelated individuals.[18] More recently, a gene was isolated from a genomic library[19] adjacent to a V_HII gene that had been identified by screening the library with a human V_HII probe. This gene was shown by Southern filter analysis to hybridize to a unique set of restriction fragments in human DNA; therefore, it was made the prototype of the V_HIV family. V_HIV is distantly related to human V_HII, and in retrospect (FIG. 1), some of the previously defined V_HII proteins probably should be reclassified as V_HIV. More recently, a family of genes that seems to be preferentially rearranged in human lymphatic leukemias has been identified.[20,21] The sequence of this molecule, like the sequence of the aforementioned V_HIV gene, was distinct and fulfilled the criteria that had been established in the murine V_H families for representing a new human V_H family. The V_HV family is relatively small, consisting of only three genes, two of which are pseudogenes. The functioning V_HV gene is modestly polymorphic and located relatively close to D.[20,21] Work from several laboratories indicates that unlike the usual situation in the mouse in which the nine V_H families are arranged in clusters, the human V_H genes are interspersed.[22]

Schroeder *et al.*[23] isolated, from a fetal liver cDNA library, clones that represent each of the previously defined V_H families (with the exception of V_HV). Furthermore, they identified a new family that has been called V_HVI.[23] Berman *et al.*[24] have also identified a V_HVI gene. Like V_HV, V_HVI is a small family with only 1–3 members.

```
                                                CDR1                 CDR2               CDR4
VH4-CON     QVQLQESGPGLVKPSETLSLTCTVSGGSISSXSXXWSWIRQPPGKGLEWIGYIY   YSGSTNYNPSLKSRVTISVDTSKNQFSLKLSSVTAADTAVYYCAR

WU-VH2-CON  --T-R----A----T---T-------F-L-TXGMXVG--------A---LAR-NX  WDDDKY-XT--R--L---K------VV-XMXNMDPV---T-----
VH2 CE1 *   --N-R----A---ATH--T----F--L-VNTRGMSV---------A---LAR-D   WDDDK--GT--ET-L---K------VV-IVTNMDP----T-----
    COR *   --T-R----A----TQ--T----F--F-L--TGMCVG-----------LAR-D   WDDDKY--T--ET-L---K---R--VV-TM   DPV---T-----
    DAW *   --T-R----A--R-TQ--T----F--F-L-GETMCVA-------EA---LAWDI   LNDDKY-GA--ET-LAV-K------VV-SMNT-GPG---T-----
    OU  *   --T-T----A----KQP-T----F--F-L-TSRMRV----R----A---LAR-D   DDDKFYWST--RT-LS--KND----VV-IMIN-NPV---T-----
    MCE'*   -IT-K----T----T---T----F--F-L-TSGVGVG----R---A---LAF-N   WDDDNR-S---R--L-GTKN--R--VV-TITNMDPV-SGT-F--H
    HE  *   --T-K-N--T----T---T----L--L-LTTDGVAVG----G--RA---LAWLLY  WDDDKRFS------L-VTR------VV-TMTNMDPV---T---VH

VH4 71-2    ---------------------------V--G-YY------------------     ----------------------------------------------
    v58     -----QW-A--L----------A-Y---V -G YY------------------     ------N-------A-------------N-----------C---
    V2-1    -L---------------------------S-YY-G-------------S--      ---D-Y-----------------H--------------------
   58P2 +   ----------------------------   YY------------------     ----------------------------------------------
 SUP-T1 *   -------------------------Y----GYYWG -------------S--H     ----Y-----------------------------------------
   NEWM *   ------------R--Q----------STF-NDYYT  -V-----R-------VF    -H-TSDDTTP-R----ML----------R---------------
    WAH *   RL-------------------I----P-RRTGYY-G--------------GV-     -T--IY-----RG---------R-----N-R-MS-----M-----
   HIG1 *   -----QW-A-------------A-F---F-GYY  ---------R------E-N    H------KT---------L-----L--------------------

        * = Currently listed as VH2 in Wu.
        + = Currently listed as VH2 by Perlmutter.
```

FIGURE 1. Relationship between human V_HII and V_HIV protein sequences. A V_HIV consensus has been generated on the basis of the genomic clone sequenced by Honjo's group.[19] In retrospect, 6 of the 10 proteins previously sequenced and classified as V_HII appear to fall into a clear clustering. The newly described V_HIV sequences, along with the previously probed sequenced proteins WAH and H1G1, clearly define a new subgroup or family presently referred to as V_HIV. The 58P2 sequence of Schroeder *et al.*[23] can also be reclassified as a V_HIV.

TABLE 1. Relationship of Human V_H Families

	VH1		VH2		VH3		VH4		VH5		VH6
	20p3	51p1	CE1	COR	30p1	56p1	71-2	v58	251	32	15p1
VH1 20p3	—	80	33	36	53	55	46	44	64	64	37
51p1		—	32	35	57	58	48	44	63	65	41
VH2 CE1			—	82	43	46	57	50	37	39	49
COR				—	48	51	59	49	41	41	52
VH3 30p1					—	88	56	51	53	56	50
56p1						—	54	50	54	55	51
VH4 71–2							—	86	49	51	68
v58								—	47	49	62
VH5 251									—	91	39
32										—	41
VH6 15p1											—

TABLE 1 displays the protein sequence homologies of several V_H sequences, pointing out the degree of variation in the human V_H families.

THE HUMAN V_H COMPLEX CONSISTS OF A MINIMUM OF SIX V_H FAMILIES

We obtained probes for each of these human V_H families (kindly provided by T. Honjo, R. Perlmutter, and S. Korsmeyer). In addition, within our own laboratory we constructed cDNAs from human autoantibodies, including those that are multiple organ reactive (obtained from Abner Notkins and Paolo Casali), anti-Sm (obtained from Norman Talal and Howard Dang), antiinsulin, and antithyroglobulin. The mRNAs and later the cDNAs of these cell lines were analyzed and found to largely consist of members of the V_HIII, V_HIV, and V_HV families. No member of the V_HI, V_HII, or V_HVI families was detected.

Southern filter hybridization of the same filter stripped and reprobed with the six human V_H probes is illustrated in FIGURE 2. Each V_H family contains unique restriction fragments, ranging from 2 (V_HVI) to over 50 (V_HI and V_HIII). This analysis has been repeated with several restriction enzymes including *Eco*RI, *Hind*III, and *Bam*HI and has provided essentially the same result.

EACH HUMAN V_H FAMILY CONTAINS POLYMORPHIC GENES, ALTHOUGH POLYMORPHISM SEEMS TO BE CONSIDERABLY LOWER THAN THAT IN THE INBRED MOUSE

Brodeur and Riblet[25] described polymorphisms in murine V_H genes and documented the ease with which the various murine strains can be distinguished by the pattern of restriction fragments that hybridize with the nine murine V_H probes. The striking difference between the murine and human systems is illustrated in FIGURE 3. *Eco*RI-digested DNA from 10 unrelated normal Caucasians was hybridized with probes representing the V_HI and V_HIII families. The pattern of hybridization with the two probes was quite different. However, strikingly, with only a few exceptions, all individuals contained the same restriction fragments with both the V_HI and the V_HIII

HUMAN V$_H$ FAMILIES

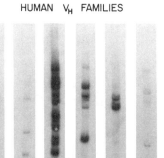

I   II   III   IV   V   VI

FIGURE 2. Southern filter hybridization of the same strip of DNA from a single individual probed, stripped, and reprobed with the six human V$_H$ probes described in the text. Identical hybridization and washing conditions were used for each filter.

probes. The same analysis was performed with the other four V$_H$ family probes with similar results. There are indeed some restriction fragments that clearly distinguish individuals; however, their number is remarkably small. More recently we probed filters of DNA from individuals of different racial backgrounds with similar results. Thus, in contrast to the mouse in which it is unusual to detect identity between two strains in the V$_H$ complex, this seems to be the rule in humans. It is surprising that the level of polymorphism for these genes is lower in an outbred population such as humans than in inbred strains of mice. In this regard, it would be helpful to know the situation in wild mice. However, the presence of little polymorphism in the light chain locus among most inbred strains suggests that extensive inbreeding may not be the only explanation for this discrepancy.

HUMAN V$_H$ GENES ARE INHERITED AS A LINKED COMPLEX

The conclusion that human V$_H$ genes are linked is perhaps obvious from evidence that all human V$_H$ genes are on the 14th chromosome. There is mounting evidence that the V$_H$ genes are found within a 1–2 megabase region of the 14th chromosome. Thus, it would not be surprising if the genes in this complex were not inherited as a cluster. FIGURE 4 illustrates the method of analysis in which, within a single pedigree, the restriction fragment (noted with an arrow) is seen to be segregating. This kind of analysis has been done with all six probes, using the same filter from the family, and immunoglobulin V_H haplotypes can easily be generated. Although at the time of this writing we have only analyzed four families (each pedigree being analyzed with *Eco*RI, *Tac*I, *Bgl*II, and *Bam*HI), in each instance the whole V_H complex seems to be inherited as a block. This "haplotyping" of the human V_H complex is important in disease association studies that will follow, as in "two proband" families we should be able to identify the inheritance of the V_H genes within a family with relative ease.

THERE IS AN APPARENT DISCREPANCY BETWEEN V_H GENES IDENTIFIED BY EPSTEIN-BARR VIRUS (EBV) OR MALIGNANT TRANSFORMATION OF PBLs AND THOSE FROM MYELOMAS

As just mentioned, human myeloma proteins can easily be grouped into three V_H families on the basis of the amino acid sequence of their N-terminal 100 amino acids. Although a few exceptions are evident in retrospect (FIG. 1), the vast bulk of human V_H proteins can still be classified as $V_H I$, $V_H II$, and $V_H III$. However, by EBV transformation of human peripheral blood lymphocytes and further selection for autoantibody specificity, no expressed $V_H II$ genes were identified and only one $V_H I$ family member was identified. This could be explained by (1) bias in our selection for autoantibodies; (2) selection bias by EBV transformation; or (3) selection bias in the choice of tissue (peripheral blood versus bone marrow). We therefore analyzed 10 randomly generated EBV-transformed lines selected by *transformation* and *not by antibody specificity.*

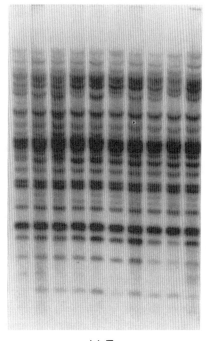

FIGURE 3. Remarkable similarity in the restriction fragment pattern of 10 unrelated normal Caucasians probed with $V_H I$ and $V_H III$ probes. Same conditions as those in FIGURE 2.

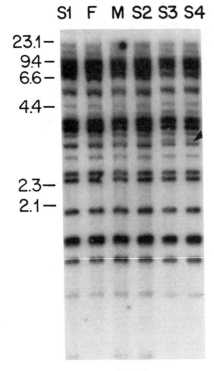

FIGURE 4. Segregation analysis of RFLP patterns within a single family. The fragment noted with an *arrow* can be seen to be segregating.

Additionally, 10 EBV-transformed tonsillar cell lines were generated, with no selection for antibody specificity. The results of slot blot analyses using six human V_H probes are shown in TABLE 2. These results parallel our results with the autoantibodies and demonstrate a dramatic shift away from the V_HI and V_HII families to the V_HIII, V_HIV, and V_HV families. These studies have been extended by analyzing bone marrow from a single normal human. Although the data are incomplete and preliminary, they parallel the observations shown in TABLE 2, that is, a significant distortion exists between these results and traditional myeloma data.

Taken together, these findings suggest that expression of particular immunoglobulin V_H genes may be related to the maturation stage of the B cell, microenvironmental factors, or other unknown factors. Bone marrow, tonsil, and peripheral blood lympho-

TABLE 2. Distribution of V_H Families in 20 Randomly Generated EBV-Transformed Cells

	Mu	Gamma	Alpha	V_HI	V_HII	V_HIII	V_HIV	V_HV	V_HVI
Tonsil	7	3	0	0	0	6	3	0	1
PBL	6	4	0	2	0	6	1	1	0
Total	13	7	0	2	0	12	4	1	1

cytes are less differentiated than are the plasma cells that give rise to the myelomas. Studies are in progress to address this maturation stage issue by analyzing plasma cells separated from lymphocytes, and peripheral blood lymphocytes separated into CD5-positive and CD5-negative populations.

THE PRIMARY STRUCTURE OF CERTAIN AUTOANTIBODIES APPEARS TO BE GERMLINE ENCODED

A large body of experimental evidence has developed concerning the almost exclusive use of V kappa IIIb and V_HI germline genes in human rheumatoid factors.[26-39] At the protein level it is notable that light chains isolated from unrelated individuals are so similar (the average Wa-positive rheumatoid factor light chain differs from the "prototype" by only two amino acids in the V_L region). We recently demonstrated that one of the autoantibodies sequenced in our laboratory (4B4, an anti-Sm antibody) has a nucleotide sequence identical to the V_H gene segment of a cDNA clone isolated from fetal liver by Perlmutter's group. Similarly, an antiinsulin antibody has, at most, six nucleotide differences from the functional germline V_HV gene isolated from an unrelated individual. Similar identities have been noted among some of the V_HIII genes from the multiple-organ-reactive antibodies. These results, together with data from other laboratories, suggest that autoantibodies may be direct copies of germline genes. It is noteworthy that the V_HIV genes sequenced in our laboratory are the first expressed V_HIV genes found whose specificity is known, and they constitute about 50% of the human multireactive autoantibodies sequenced in our laboratory. In much the same way we found the first V_HV gene expressed in an antibody of known specificity, and again it is an autoantibody (antiinsulin).

CONCLUDING REMARKS

Why then do autoantibodies in patients with autoimmune disease appear "aggressive," whereas "normal" autoantibodies appear relatively benign? Two main structural explanations come to mind: (1) The D segments of these two groups of antibodies appear significantly different and have no known germline counterparts. This suggests either that there are additional germline D segments or that novel mechanisms are involved in the generation of D segments in autoantibodies, a notion that has been described in detail by Meek et al.[40] (2) The pathogenic autoantibodies still remain largely unknown, and few have been subjected to structural analysis. It may well be that somatic events operate on physiologic autoantibodies and alter them either by increasing their affinity or by changing the idiotype. This in turn may allow them to escape idiotypic control.

If the genetic origin of autoantibodies is no different in normal subjects and in patients with autoimmune disease, we are left with the relatively uninspiring conclusion that autoimmunity has no genetic component among the immunoglobulin genes. This would fly in the face of a large body of data suggesting that idiotypes of both rheumatoid factors and anti-DNA antibodies are heritable as well as considerable statistical evidence suggesting that a second or third genetic system in addition to the MHC is involved in human autoimmunity. One way to reconcile the information is to postulate that the difference lies in complex regulatory pathways of the immune system (timing of expression in ontogeny, selection for or against a certain T-cell repertoire, and so forth). All those factors, along with MHC products and environmental agents, could interact in autoimmune patients to expand clones that in normal subjects are also present but are down-regulated.

ACKNOWLEDGMENTS

We would like to thank Margaret Wright for her assistance with the preparation of this manuscript, and Howard Dang, Norman Talal, Abner Notkins, and Paolo Casali for allowing us to quote unpublished work. Carol Williams provided superb technical assistance.

REFERENCES

1. McDevitt, H. O. & W. F. Bodmer. 1974. HL-A, immune response genes and disease. Lancet I: 1269.
2. Brewerton, D. A. 1976. HLA-B27 and the inheritance of susceptibility to rheumatic disease. Arth. Rheumat. 19: 1976.
3. Hoover, M. L., J. Marks, J. Chipman, E. Palmer, P. Stastny & J. D. Capra. 1985. Restriction fragment length polymorphism of the gene encoding the alpha chain of the human T cell receptor. J. Exp. Med. 162: 1087.
4. Robinson, M. A. & T. J. Kindt. 1985. Segregation of polymorphic T cell receptor genes in human families. Proc. Natl. Acad. Sci. USA 82: 3804.
5. Li, Y., P. Szabo & D. N. Posnett. 1988. Molecular genotypes of the human T cell receptor gamma-chain. J. Immunol. 140: 1.
6. Concannon, P., R. A. Gatti & L. E. Hood. 1987. Human T cell receptor V beta gene polymorphism. J. Exp. Med. 165: 1130.
7. Hoover, M. L. & J. D. Capra. 1987. The T cell receptor and autoimmune disease. Mol. Biol. Med. 4: 123.
8. Hoover, M. L., G. Angelini, E. Ball, P. Stastny, J. Marks, J. Rosenstock, P. Raskin, G. B. Ferrara, R. Tosi & J. D. Capra. 1986. HLA-DQ and T cell receptor genes in insulin dependent diabetes mellitus. Cold Spring Harbor Symp. Quant. Biol. 51: 803.
9. Millward, B. A., K. I. Welsh, R. D. G. Leslie, D. A. Pyke & A. G. Demaine. 1987. T cell receptor beta chain polymorphisms are associated with insulin dependent diabetes. Clin. Exp. Immunol. 70: 242.
10. Ambrosino, D. M., G. Schiffman, E. C. Gotschlich, P. H. Schur, G. A. Rosenberg, G. G. DeLange, E. van Loghem & G. R. Siber. 1985. Correlation between G2m(n) immunoglobulin allotype and human antibody response and susceptibility to polysaccharide encapsulated bacteria. J. Clin. Invest. 75: 1935.
11. Tait, B. D., D. N. Propert, L. Harrison, T. Mandel & F. I. R. Martin. 1986. Interaction between HLA antigens and immunoglobulin (Gm) allotypes in susceptibility to type I diabetes. Tissue Antigens 27: 249.
12. Salier, J.-P., R. Sesboüé, C. Martin-Mondière, M. Daveau, P. Cesaro, B. Cavelier, A. Coquerel, L. Legrand, J. M. Goust & J. D. Degos. 1986. J. Clin. Invest. 78: 533.
13. Kindt, T. J., W. J. Mandy & C. W. Todd. 1970. Association of allotypic specificities of group a with allotypic specificities A11 and A12 in rabbit immunoglobulin. Biochemistry 9: 2028.
14. Weigert, M. & M. Potter. 1977. Antibody variable region genetics. Immunogenetics 4: 401.
15. Capra, J. D. & J. M. Kehoe. 1975. Hypervariable regions, idiotypy and the antibody combining site. Adv. Immunol. 30: 1.
16. Ben-Neria, Y., J. B. Cohen, G. Rechavi, R. Zakut & D. Givol. 1981. Polymorphism of germ-line immunoglobulin V_H genes correlates with allotype and idiotype markers. Eur. J. Immunol. 11: 1017.

17. RECHAVI, G., D. RAM, L. GLAZER, R. ZAKUT & D. GIVOL. 1983. Evolutionary aspects of immunoglobulin heavy chain variable region (V_H) gene subgroups. Proc. Natl. Acad. Sci. USA **80:** 855–859.

18. KODAIRA, M., T. KINASHI, I. UMEMURA, F. MATSUDA, T. NOMA, Y. ONO & T. HONJO. 1986. Organization and evolution of variable region genes of the human immunoglobulin heavy chain. *In* P. Chambon, Ed. Academic Press, London.

19. LEE, K. H., F. MATSUDA, T. KINASHI, M. KODAIRA & T. HONJO. 1987. A novel family of variable region genes of the human immunoglobulin heavy chain. J. Mol. Biol **195:** 1.

20. SHEN, A., C. HUMPHRIES, P. TUCKER & F. BLATTNER. 1987. Human heavy-chain variable region gene family nonrandomly rearranged in familial chronic lymphocytic leukemia. Proc. Natl. Acad. Sci. USA **84:** 1987.

21. HUMPHRIES, C. G., A. SHEN, W. A. KUZIEL, J. D. CAPRA, F. R. BLATTNER & P. W. TUCKER. 1988. Characterization of a new human immunoglobulin V_H family that shows preferential rearrangement in immature B cell tumors. Nature **331:** 446.

22. RATHBUN, G. A., J. D. CAPRA & P. W. TUCKER. 1987. Organization of the murine immunoglobulin V_H complex in the inbred strains. EMBO J. **6:** 2931–2937.

23. SCHROEDER, H. W., J. L. HILLSON & R. M. PERLMUTTER. 1987. Early restriction of the human antibody repertoire. Science **238:** 791.

24. BERMAN, J. E., S. J. MELLIS, R. POLLOCK, C. SMITH, H. Y. SUH, B. HEINKE, C. KOWAL, U. SURTI, L. CHESS, C. CANTOR & F. W. ALT. 1988. Content and organization of the human Ig V_H locus: Definition of three new V_H families and linkage to the Ig C_H locus. EMBO J. **7:** 727.

25. BRODEUR, P. H. & R. RIBLET. 1984. Eur. J. Immunol. **14:** 922–930.

26. KUNKEL, H. G., V. AGNELLO, F. G. JOSLIN, R. J. WINCHESTER & J. D. CAPRA. 1973. Cross-idiotypic specificity among monoclonal IgM proteins with anti-gamma-globulin activity. J. Exp. Med **137:** 331.

27. KUNKEL, H. G., R. J. WINCHESTER, F. G. JOSLIN & J. D. CAPRA. 1974. Similarities in the light chains of anti-gamma-globulins showing cross-idiotypic specificities. J. Exp. Med. **139:** 128.

28. ALT, F. W., T. K. BLACKWELL & G. D. YANCOPOULOS. 1987. Development of the primary antibody repertoire. Science **238:** 1079.

29. CAPRA, J. D. & J. M. KEHOE. 1974. Structure of antibodies with shared idiotypy: The complete sequence of the heavy chain variable regions of two IgM antigamma globulins. Proc. Natl. Acad. Sci. USA **71:** 4032.

30. CAPRA, J. D. & D. G. KLAPPER. 1976. Complete amino acid sequence of the variable domains of two human IgM anti-gamma globulins (Lay/Pom) with shared idiotypic specificities. Scand. J. Immunol. **5:** 677.

31. ANDREWS, D. W. & J. D. CAPRA. 1981. Complete amino acid sequence of variable domains from two monoclonal human anti-gamma globulins of the Wa cross-idiotypic group: Suggestion that the J segments are involved in the structural correlate of the idiotype. Proc. Natl. Acad. Sci. USA **78:** 3799.

32. ANDREWS, D. W. & J. D. CAPRA. 1981. Amino acid sequence of the variable regions of light chains from two idiotypically cross-reactive human IgM anti-gamma-globulins of the Wa group. Biochemistry **20:** 5816.

33. ANDREWS, D. W. & J. D. CAPRA. 1981. Amino acid sequence of the variable regions of heavy chains from two idiotypically cross-reactive human IgM anti-gamma-globulins of the Wa group. Biochemistry **20:** 5822.

34. CROWLEY, J. J., R. D. GOLDFIEN, R. E. SCHROHENLOHER, H. L. SPIEGELBERG, G. J. SILVERMAN, R. A. MAGEED, R. JEFFERIS, W. J. KOOPMAN, D. A. CARSON & S. FONG. 1988. Incidence of three cross-reactive idiotypes on human rheumatoid factor paraproteins. J. Immunol. **140:** 3411.

35. KIPPS, T. J., S. FONG, E. TOMHAVE, P. P. CHEN, R. D. GOLDFIEN & D. A. CARSON. 1987. High-frequency expression of a conserved K light-chain variable-region gene in chronic lymphocytic leukemia. Proc. Natl. Acad. Sci. USA **84:** 2916.

36. CHEN, P. P., D. L. ROBBINS, F. R. JIRIK, T. J. KIPPS & D. A. CARSON. 1987. Isolation and characterization of a light chain variable region gene for human rheumatoid factors. J. Exp. Med. **166:** 1900.

37. CHEN, P. P., K. ALBRANDT, T. J. KIPPS, V. RADOUX, F.-T. LIU & D. A. CARSON. 1987. Isolation and characterization of human $V_K III$ germline genes: Implications for the molecular basis of human $V_K III$ light chain diversity. J Immunol. **139:** 1727.
38. SILVERMAN, G. J., R. D. GOLDFIEN, P. CHEN, R. A. MAGEED, R. JEFFERIS, F. GONI, B. FRANGIONE, S. FONG & D. A. CARSON. 1988. Idiotypic and subgroup analysis of human monoclonal rheumatoid factors: Implications for structural and genetic basis of autoantibodies in humans. J. Clin. Invest. **82:** 469.
39. GOLDFIEN, R. D., P. CHEN, T. J. KIPPS, G. STARKEBAUM, J. G. HEITZMANN, V. RADOUX, S. FONG & D. A. CARSON. 1987. Genetic analysis of human B cell hybridomas expressing a cross-reactive idiotype. J. Immunol. **138:** 940.
40. MEEK, K., D. JESKE, S. ALKAN, J. URBAIN & J. D. CAPRA. 1987. Structural characterization of syngeneic and allogeneic anti-idiotypic antibodies in the anti-arsonate system. *In* Idiotypes and Disease. M. Zanetti, C.A. Bona, & F. Celada, Eds.: 109. Karger AG, Basel.

Polymorphism of HLA Class II Genes in Various Diseases

ERNA MÖLLER, B. CARLSSON, O. OLERUP,
AND J. WALLIN

Department of Clinical Immunology and Center for Biotechnology
Huddinge Hospital
Karolinska Institute Medical School
Stockholm, Sweden

Many diseases are associated with genes of the HLA region. Several disease associations were described before class II genes were known, such as ankylosing spondylitis to HLA-B27 and psoriasis vulgaris to HLA-B13, 17, and 37. Knowledge of the B27 association is now almost complete. In our material as well as in the data of the 1980 Histocompatibility Workshop, all patients with ankylosing spondylitis or pelvospondylitis ossificans are B27 positive. B27-negative patients with pelvospondylitis seem to have a different disease as the basis for their spondylitis. In contrast, psoriasis vulgaris is now more closely associated with Cw6 and DR7, alleles that are in linkage disequilibrium with B13, 17, and 37. Similarly, insulin-dependent diabetes mellitus (IDDM) was first associated with HLA-B8 and 15 and later more closely asssociated with the cellular specificities Dw3 and w4 and the corresponding serologic specificities DR3 and 4.[1]

With the possibilities of also determining variation within the DQ locus using RFLP analysis and cDNA probes, the association with IDDM was found to be secondary to particular alleles of the DQ locus, referred to as DQβIV[2] and DQw3.2 by Nepom *et al.*[3] Todd *et al.*[4] recently reported amino acid sequence analyses of DQ alleles known to be positively and negatively associated with IDDM and identified residue 57 in the DQβ chain as a candidate responsible for IDDM susceptibility or resistance or both.

To define the genes responsible for disease susceptibility, it is imperative to have methods of resolving the relevant level of genomic variability of genes that determine T-cell repertoire and serve as restricting elements for T-cell recognition. Genes of the HLA-D region were first detected by cellular methods and typing in MLR using homozygous typing cells. Later, when class II products were shown to be present only on some lymphoid cells, serologic reagents that recognized class II antigens were selected. Names for such specificities, such as D Related-DR, were adopted to fit reactivities of these antibodies with HLA-D typed cell panels. At this time, D was thought to represent only one locus. Some DR specificities fit well with the adopted D terminology, such as Dw1 and DR1 in Caucasoids, whereas others did not. As many as five distinct D specificities were all associated with serologic specificity DR4, named Dw4, 10, 13, 14, and 15. The DR7 group comprised cellular specificities Dw7, 11, and 17, and DR2 could be subdivided into Dw2, Dw12, MN2 (= AZH) as well as cells with unknown D type (Dwx).

When the polymorphic characters of the DQ locus were defined using biochemical, serologic, and molecular approaches, it became apparent that earlier defined D specificities were the total product of class II antigens expressed by the DR and the DQ locus.[5] Therefore, the D "alleles" were not true alleles of one locus, and the means of defining the biologically relevant level of class II gene polymorphism had to be elaborated and correlated with earlier definitions.

In this communication we shall describe briefly our efforts to identify genomic variability using various kinds of cDNA probes for DRβ and DQα and β chains and to correlate this level of variability with serologic definitions of class II antigen polymorphism. The findings indicate that the exonic and intronic parts of class II genes are extremely well preserved in different DR-DQ haplotypes, that the total number of different DR-DQ haplotypes is limited within the Caucasoid population, that a combination of DR and DQ antigens constitutes the majority of earlier defined D specificities, and that a new level of polymorphism has been described that has greatly elucidated the genetic basis for HLA and disease associations.

We have employed full-length cDNA probes to elucidate class II gene polymorphism using DNA digested with various restriction enzymes, Southern blotting, and visualization of hybridized ^{32}P-labeled cDNA probes by autoradiography. Typing can indeed be performed using cDNA probes, RFLP patterns segregate with the HLA haplotypes in families, and different cells from unrelated type D individuals identically give identical or very similar RFLP patterns.[6,7] We also found that DQα and β genes were more polymorphic than had been described earlier using serologic tools.[2,8] Only three specificities had been identified serologically. The DQw1 "antigen" was usually present in cells typed DR1, 2, w6, or w10; DQw2 was present in cells typed DR3, 5, w6, or w8, and DQw3 was present in DR4 or 5 cells. In the DR molecule only the β chain is variable, whereas in DQ molecules both α and β chains vary. Spielman et al.[9] first identified RFLP using the DQα probe that correlated well with DQw serologic typing. DQw1, 2, and 3 probably are determinants present on different DQβ chains.[8] Several RFLP patterns were visualized with the DQβ probe, and we suggested a local nomenclature for this polymorphism.[2] We also found that different DR-DQ haplotypes contained a varying number of DRβ genes, whereas the number of DQα and β genes was always constant. There are two DQα and β genes in all haplotypes; the use of exon-specific DRβ probes revealed that DRw8-positive haplotypes only had one DRβ gene, whereas DR4 and DR7-positive haplotypes contained up to four genes. Of these, two were pseudogenes.[10] Many haplotypes express two distinct DR molecules, with one identical and invariable α chain. DRw52 and DRw53 are determinants on molecules containing, respectively, the βIII and βIV chains, whereas the βI gene harbors the variability encoding the conventional DR1, 2, and 3 specificities and so forth.[11] One exception is probably DRw8, which could be a determinant encoded by a DRw52 allele on a distinct β gene nonallelic to DR1, 2, and 3.[12]

TABLE 1 shows the present degree of variability that we have identified using cDNA probes and its correlation with DR serology. All individuals typed DR1 in our panel have identical DRβ and DQα and β patterns. The data presented in this table are based on digestion with Taq1, which gives the highest resolution and best identifies polymorphic patterns that correlate with serology. This finding is consistent with the fact that almost all DR1-positive individuals are also Dw1 positive, that is, all DR1-positive cells carry identical DQ alleles on the same haplotype. DR2-positive individuals have at least two distinct patterns for DRβ and two distinct patterns for DQβ. These splits correlate perfectly with earlier definitions using D-typing methods. DRβII-DQβII corresponds to Dw2, DRβII-DQβI is Dwx, DQβII*-DQβI is MN2, and DRβII with a new DQβ type is most probably Dw12 (references 8 and 13 and unpublished data). For DR3, there are rare splits at the DRβ locus, but all HLA-B8-positive individuals are DR3 with the DRβIV pattern. Interesting data were obtained in studies of DR4-positive individuals. Similar patterns for DRβ were accompanied by three distinct DQβ patterns, which we have called IV, V, and VII. The DQβIV pattern also occurs in cells that are DR7 and DRw8 positive. Later studies showed that this DQ split of DR4 corresponds to the reactivity with a DQ-specific monoclonal reagent, TA10.[14,15] Haplotypes that are TA10 positive are DQβV positive, whereas TA10 negative haplotypes are DQβIV. This is the split that has also been referred to as DQw3.1 and DQw3.2 by Kim *et al*.[16] and correlates with susceptibility to IDDM (to be discussed). DRw6 was recently serologically split into DRw13 and DRw14. We have found that this group contains many different DR-DQ subgroups according to RFLP analysis. However, these splits also seem to be biologically relevant, because cells that are DRw13 with DQβII are Dw18 positive and cells with DRw13 and DQβI are Dw19. In addition, the DQβI and DQβII-related determinants can now be recognized by monoclonal antibodies (Histocompatibility Testing, 1987).

Finally, we would like to emphasize that not all relevant, cellularly defined specificities can be visualized directly using this method, because the Dw splits of DR4,

TABLE 1. Definition of DR-DQ Haplotypes by Combination of Linked Patterns

Serologic DR Types	DR and DQ Allelic Patterns			Taq I Haplotype	Haplotype Frequency
	DRβ	DQ α	DQβ		
DR1	I	I	I	T-1	26/26
DR2	II	II	II	T-2.1	47/50
	II	II	I	T-2.2	2/50
	XVI	II	I	T-2.3	1/50
DR3	IV	IV	III	T-3.1	24/25
	VIII	IV	III	T-3.2	1/25
DR4	XII	V	IV	T-4.1	33/50
	XII	V	V	T-4.2	16/50
	XII	V	VII	T-4.3	1/50
DR7	XIII	V	IV	T-7.1	14/25
	XIII	V	VI	T-7.2	5/25
	XIV	V	VI	T-7.3	6/25
DRw8	V	II	IV	T-8.1	17/18
	V	II	VII	T-8.2	1/18
DRw9	XIII	V	VII	T-9	2/2
DRw10	III	I	I	T-10	7/7
DRw11	VI	IV	V	T-11	13/13
DRw12	VII	IV	V	T-12	6/6
DRw13	VIII	III	II	T-13.1	10/35
	IX	III	II	T-13.2	12/35
	X	II	I	T-13.3	12/35
	XV	IV	V	T-13.4	1/35
DRw14	XI	I	I	T-14	7/7

corresponding to DW4, w10, w13, w14, and w15, depend on minor differences in sequences of the DRβ chain[17] that seem to have arisen by gene conversion events using other DRβ chain genes as donors[10] and that can actually be visualized with selected oligonucleotide probes.[18]

Our findings indicate that the Caucasoid population contains a limited set of DR-DQ haplotypes, which all demonstrate marked linkage disequilibria.

We recently studied DR-DQ haplotypes in individuals from Liberia in West Africa who have natural resistance to malaria infection. Data show several different DR-DQ haplotypes that are not present in the Caucasoid population and also that these patients share one particular DR-DQ haplotype in a high frequency (Olerup and Troye-Blomberg, unpublished data).

A sound basis for further analysis of HLA and disease association demands not only good resolution of HLA gene polymorphism but also adequate clinical evaluations of patients included in these studies. Rheumatoid arthritis is a good example. About 50% of patients with classical or definite rheumatoid arthritis are DR4 positive. However, this proportion increases significantly when only patients with seropositive and erosive disease are included. Patients with Felty's syndrome are all DR4 positive.

We have used the RFLP method to better define the locus and the polymorphism that are associated with different diseases, earlier known to be class II dependent, and will present studies on rheumatoid arthritis (RA), insulin-dependent diabetes mellitus (IDDM), multiple sclerosis (MS), myasthenia gravis (MG), and psoriasis vulgaris. Patients with IDDM have an increased frequency of DR3 and/or DR4 and a significantly increased proportion of heterozygotes, implying that transcomplementation could give rise to a distinct DR3/4 hybrid molecule associated with the risk of disease.[1] If true, the likelihood of a primary association with the DQ locus rather than the DR locus would be high, because both α and β genes vary among DQ alleles. We did not find that DR3-positive diabetic patients differed from healthy controls, but we did find a particular DR-DQ haplotype that was typical of patients with IDDM. All patients with IDDM in our study who were DR4 carried the DQβIV pattern, whereas only approximately two thirds of healthy controls did.[19] Similar data were reported independently by Nepom et al. and Schreuder et al.[3,14,15,20] and indicate that the DR4-positive haplotype carrying DQβV is associated with resistance to the development of diabetes. In addition, we found that the DR2 haplotype, which is significantly reduced in patients with IDDM, is different in patients and healthy controls. All DR2-positive patients with IDDM were DQβI positive, a rare variant in healthy controls. Therefore, the common DR2-DRβII-DQβII haplotype protects from IDDM. Other studies showed that patients with IDDM who are DR2 positive carry the MN2 HLA-D specificity.[13] In addition, we recently found that this particular haplotype also differs from normal DR2 in RFLP typing using DRβ probes. We have indicated this DR2-correlated RFLP as XVI in TABLE 1.

Patients with MS were also studied using the new level of DR and DQ polymorphism. The two different forms of MS, known as chronic progressive disease and relapsing/remitting MS, were found to have distinct genetic bases. Whereas it was earlier known that MS is associated with DR2, we have now demonstrated that only its chronic progressive (CP) form is HLA associated; no significant association was found for relapsing/remitting disease. Furthermore, CP-MS is associated with two different DQβ genotypes: DQβII and DQβIV. TABLE 2 shows these data, which will be

TABLE 2. HLA-DR and HLA-DQ Associations in Patients with Multiple Sclerosis Revealed by RFLP Analysis

	RR[a]
All MS patients	
DRβII	3.5**
DQβII	2.7*
Chronic progressive MS	
DRβII	4.2*
DQβII	6.0**
DQβIV	2.7*
DQβII/βIV	7.2**

[a]Relapsing/remitting MS, no significant association.

TABLE 3. Different DR4-Positive Haplotypes in Various Diseases

	DQβIV (= DQw3.2)	DQβV (= DQw3.1)
CP MS	10	0
Controls	19	6
RA	32	3
Controls	15	10
IDDM	19	0
Controls	34	14

important for further characterization of the genetic basis for MS. In addition, it may help determine which patients have a poor prognosis and might be candidates for therapeutic approaches (references 21 and 22 and unpublished data).

The DQβIV/V split of DR4-positive individuals has been studied also in patients with RA. Only patients with seropositive erosive disease were included in this study. We found a significantly increased frequency of DR4-DQβIV haplotypes in these patients compared with the controls.[23] Recently, similar studies were carried out by Singal et al.[24] and Sansom et al.,[25] but they found completely opposite results, namely, a dominant proportion of patients were DR4-DQV (or DQw3.1) positive. The reason for this discrepancy is not known.

In TABLE 3 we have summarized our findings on the prevalence of DQβIV and V genotypes in DR4-positive patients and controls. It should be stressed that different control materials were used in different studies, but the higher frequency of DR4-positive individuals being DQβIV is the same in all control materials.

Several DQ genotypes are found in DR7-positive haplotypes (TABLE 1). Recently, Carlsson (unpublished data) studied whether these subdivisions correlate with the HLA-Dw splits referred to as Dw7, w11, and w17, but with negative findings. Psoriasis vulgaris is associated with DR7, and in a pilot study Olerup et al.[26] found that patients with psoriasis did not differ from controls in any of these DQβ subtypes. Possibly, psoriasis is primarily associated with the products of either of the two different DR beta chains expressed in DR7-positive haplotypes. The methods that we have employed have not given the degree of resolution needed to clarify this issue.

Myasthenia gravis is known to be associated with HLA B8 and DR3. There are two different clinical entities of MG that demonstrate distinct HLA associations. MG occurring in young, predominantly female, patients who do not develop thymoma is associated with B8 and DR3. Patients with MG and thymoma do not have an increased frequency of B8 and/or DR3. We investigated 61 patients with MG, 51 without and 10 with thymoma. Of the 51 patients without thymoma 36 were both B8 and DR3 positive. Only 1 of 10 patients with thymoma had B8 and/or DR3. However, there was a high frequency of DR2-positive haplotypes in these 10 patients, and 3 of the 10 were DR2 homozygous. These patients were all positive for the DRβII-DQβII conventional haplotype. We could not confirm the high prevalence of a specific HindII band in patients with MG reported by Bell et al.[27] In our material this corresponds to the DR7-linked DQβI genotype.[8]

However, there was another clear genetic distinction between patients with and those without thymoma. In the patients with MG without thymoma, the DRβXVI-DQβI haplotype was relatively frequent, having been observed earlier only in DR2-positive diabetic patients and in only 1 of 130 healthy controls. Three of eight DR2-positive haplotypes in this group of patients with MG had this rare haplotype, compared with none of the patients with MG with thymoma (Carlsson *et al.,* unpublished data). In addition, we found this rare haplotype in two patients with nickel allergy, studied in a separate investigation (Olerup, unpublished data). The identification of specific DR-DQ haplotypes, frequently or never present in patients with different diseases, will be the only valid basis for future analysis of definite sequences in expressed molecules to identify disease susceptibility structure. In addition, it is possible that HLA-associated diseases depend on dysregulation of class II expression; therefore, it will be important also to study sequences involved in the control of regulation.

In summary, we have identified particular DR-DQ genotypes positively or negatively associated with different diseases. This information can form the basis for a genetic definition of specific sequences, involved in disease susceptibility and resistance as performed by Todd *et al.*[4] Furthermore, our new data indicate that the two clinically distinct forms of MS, known as chronic progressive and relapsing/remitting disease, have a completely different genetic basis and most probably are two distinct disease entities. Similar data have emerged from studies of patients with MG in whom the disease in those with thymoma shows an HLA association that is clearly different from

TABLE 4. Distribution of Two Distinct DR2 Genotypes in Patients and Controls

	Genomic DR2 Split	
Patients	DRβXVI	DRβII
MG-thymoma	0	9
IDDM	4	0
MG-no thymoma	3	5
Panel	1	92

that in patients with MG in the absence of thymoma and that DR2-positive patients with MG without thymoma frequently have a DR2-positive haplotype, which also occurs in patients with IDDM and only very rarely in healthy controls (TABLE 4).

REFERENCES

1. SVEJGAARD, A., P. PLATZ, L. P. RYDER, L. STAUB NIELSEN & M. THOMSEN. 1975. HL-A and disease associations—A survey. Immunol. Rev. **22:** 3.
2. BÖHME, J., M. ANDERSSON, G. ANDERSSON, E. MÖLLER, P. A. PETERSON & L. RASK. 1985. HLA-DRβ genes vary in number between different DR specificities whereas the number of DQβ genes is constant. J. Immunol. **135:** 2149.
3. NEPOM, B. S., J. PALMER, S. J. KIM, J. A. HANSEN, S. L. HOLBECK & G. T. NEPOM. 1986. Specific genomic markers for the HL-DQ subregion discriminate between DR4+ insulin-dependent diabetes mellitus and DR4+ seropositive juvenile rheumatoid arthritis. J. Exp. Med. **164:** 345.
4. TODD, J. A., J. I. BELL & H. O. MCDEVITT. 1987. HLA-DQβ gene contributes to susceptibility and resistance to insulin-dependent diabetes mellitus. Nature (Lond.) **329:** 599.
5. REINSMOEN, N. L. & F. H. BACH. 1986. Clonal analysis of HL-DR and -DQ associated determinants—their contribution to Dw specificities. Hum. Immunol. **16:** 329.
6. WAKE, C. T., E. O. LONG & B. MACH. 1982. Allelic polymorphism and complexity of the genes for HLA-DRβ chains—direct analysis by DNA-DNA hybridization. Nature (Lond.) **310:** 372.

7. ANDERSSON, M., J. BÖHME, G. ANDERSSON, E. MÖLLER, E. THORSBY, L. RASK & P. A. PETERSON. 1984. Genomic hybridization with class II transplantation antigen cDNA provides a complementary technique in tissue typing. Hum. Immunol. 11: 57.
8. CARLSSON, B., J. WALLIN, J. BÖHME & E. MÖLLER. 1987. HLA-DR-DQ haplotypes defined by restriction fragment analysis. Correlation to serology. Hum. Immunol. 20: 95.
9. SPIELMAN, R. S., J. LEE, W. F. BODMER, J. G. BODMER & J. TROWSDALE. 1984. Six HLA-D region α-chain genes on human chromosome 6: Polymorphisms and associations of DCα-related sequences with DR types. Proc. Natl. Acad. Sci. USA 81: 3461.
10. ANDERSSON, G., D. LARHAMMAR, E. WIDMARK, B. SERVENIUS, P. A. PETERSON & L. RASK. 1987. Class II genes of the human major histocompatibility complex. Organization and evolutionary relationship of the DRβ genes. J. Biol. Chem. 262: 274B.
11. HURLEY, C. K., R. C. GILES, G. NUNEZ, R. DEMARS, L. NADLER, R. WINCHESTER, P. STASTNY & D. CAPRA. 1984. Molecular localization of human class II MT2 and MT3 determinants. J. Exp. Med. 160: 472.
12. ANDERSSON, G., B. LINDBLOM, L. ANDERSSON, B. MACH & L. RASK. The single DRβ gene of the DR8 haplotype is related to the DRw52β gene. Submitted.
13. SEGALL, M., H. NOREEN, L. SCHLUENDER, M. SWENSON, J. BARBOSA & F. H. BACH. 1986. DR2+ haplotypes in insulin-dependent diabetes: Analysis of DNA restriction fragment length polymorphisms. Hum. Immunol. 17: 61.
14. SCHREUDER, G. M. Th., H. MAEDA, F. KONING & J. D'AMARO. 1986. TA10 and 2B3, two new alleles in the HLA-DQ region recognized by monoclonal antibodies. Hum. Immunol. 16: 127.
15. SCHREUDER, G. M. Th., M. G. J. TILANUS, R. E. BONTROP, G. J. BRUINING, M. J. GIPHART, J. J. VAN ROOD & R. P. DE VRIES. 1986. HLA-DQ polymorphism associated with resistance to type I diabetes detected with monoclonal antibodies, isoelectric point differences, and restriction fragment length polymorphism. J. Exp. Med. 164: 938.
16. KIM, S. J., S. L. HOLBECK, B. NISPEROS, J. A. HANSEN, H. MAEDA & G. T. NEPOM. 1986. Identification of a polymorphic variant associated with HL-DQw3 and characterized by specific restriction sites within the DQβ chain gene. Proc. Natl. Acad. Sci. USA 83: 3361.
17. GREGERSON, P. K., M. SHEN, Q. SONG, P. MERRYMAN, T. SEKI, J. MACCARI, D. GOLDBERG, H. MURPHY, J. SCHWENZER, C. Y. WANG, R. J. WINCHESTER, G. T. NEPOM & J. SILVER. 1986. Molecular diversity of HLA-DR4 haplotypes. Proc. Natl. Acad. Sci. USA 83: 2642.
18. FREEMAN, S. M., H. J. NOREEN, C. A. DAHL, P. J. NELSON, N. L. REINSMOEN & F. H. BACH. 1987. Determination of DRβ1 alleles of DR4/Dw subtypes by oligonucleotide probing. Hum. Immunol. 20: 1.
19. BÖHME, J., B. CARLSSON, J. WALLIN, E. MÖLLER, B. PERSSON, P. A. PETERSON & L. RASK. 1986. Only one restriction fragment pattern of each DR specificity is associated with insulin-dependent diabetes. J. Immunol. 137: 941.
20. TAIT, B. D. & A. J. BOYLE. 1986. DR4 and susceptibility to type I diabetes mellitus: Discrimination of high risk and low risk DR4 haplotypes on the basis of TA10 typing. Tissue Antigens 28: 65.
21. OLERUP, O., S. FREDRIKSSON, T. OLSSON & S. KAM-HANSEN. 1987. HLA class II genes in chronic progressive and in relapsing/remitting multiple sclerosis. Lancet ii: 327.
22. OLERUP, O., B. CARLSSON, J. WALLIN, T. OLSSON, S. FREDRIKSON, J. ERNERUDH & E. MÖLLER. 1987. Genomic HLA-typing by RFLP-analysis using DR and DQ cDNA probes reveals normal DR-DQ linkages in patients with multiple sclerosis. Tissue Antigens 30: 135.
23. WALLIN, J., B. CARLSSON, H. STRÖM & E. MÖLLER. 1987. A DR4-associated DR-DQ haplotype is significantly associated with rheumatoid arthritis. Arth. Rheumat. 30: xxxx.
24. SINGAL, D. P., M. D'SOUZA, B. REID, W. G. BENSEN, Y. B. KASSAM & J. D. ADACHI. 1987. HLA-DQβ-chain polymorphism in HLA-DR4 haplotypes associated with rheumatoid arthritis. Lancet ii: 1118.
25. SANSOM, D. M., J. L. BIDWELL, P. J. MADDISON, G. CAMPION, P. T. KLOUDA & B. A.

BRADLEY. 1987. HLA DQα and DQβ restriction fragment length polymorphisms associated with Felty's syndrome and DR4-positive rheumatoid arthritis. Hum. Immunol. **19:** 269.

26. OLERUP, O., J. WALLIN, B. CARLSSON, J. MARCUSSON, L. EMTESTAM, E. BJÖRNELIUS & E. MÖLLER. 1987. Genomic HLA-typing by RFLP analysis using DRβ and DQβ cDNA probes reveals normal DR-DQ linkages in patients with psoriasis vulgaris. Tissue Antigens **30:** 139.

27. BELL, J., S. SMOOT, C. NEWLY, K. TOYKA, L. RASSENTI, K. SMITH, R. MOHLFELD, H. MCDEVITT & L. STEINMAN. 1986. HLA-DQβ chain polymorphism linked to myasthenia gravis. Lancet **i:** 1058.

Role of MHC Class II Antigen Expression in Thyroid Autoimmunity[a]

TERRY F. DAVIES, LINDA A. PICCININI,
SHEILA H. ROMAN, WATARU HIROSE,
AND DAVID S. NEUFELD

Department of Medicine
Mount Sinai School of Medicine
New York, New York

Major histocompatibility complex (MHC) class II antigens are represented in man by the HLA-D region gene family which is composed of polymorphic genetic loci (DR, DP, and DQ) mapping to the short arm of chromosome 6, in mice by the Ia gene family on chromosome 17 (IA and IE), and in the rat by RT1.B, D, and H gene regions (FIG. 1).[1] The typical MHC class II antigen molecule is a heterodimer, consisting of an alpha (34-kd) and a beta (28-kd) glycopeptide chain that is linked noncovalently within the plasma membrane and is associated intracellularly with an invariant (33-kd) glycopeptide.[2] The genetic variation both within the human population and within different animal species at the MHC class II region is largely attributable to the amino acid sequence differences within the first external domain of the polymorphic beta chain.

Many studies have demonstrated the association between MHC genes, particularly those of class II, and autoimmune thyroid disease in animals and humans[3] (TABLE 1). The relative risk of autoimmune thyroid disease attached to any of these antigens (principally HLA-DR3 and DR5) in humans is low, and 30–50% of patients with disease do not express an associated HLA antigen. However, studies of HLA haplotypes within individual multiplex families of patients with autoimmune thyroid disease indicate that unique familial associations may be of primary importance,[4] a fact that improved methods of HLA typing may detect in the general population. Similarly, particular murine and rat strains are known to be high or low immunoresponders to thyroid antigens, and this responsiveness has been linked to the MHC class II gene complex.[5,6] In addition to these disease-specific relationships, particular HLA haplotypes have been associated with abnormal immune responsiveness of a nonantigen-specific nature. For example, normal HLA-DR3 individuals have less effective T-cell suppressor function than do non-DR3 normals.[7]

ROLE OF MHC CLASS II ANTIGENS

A major function of class II antigens on the cell surface of monocyte/macrophages is their role in antigen presentation to the immune system. Large protein antigens are "processed" by monocyte/macrophages and related cells (such as dendritic, Kuppfer, and Langhans cells), acting as antigen presenting cells (APC) that possess surface class II molecules.[8] This processing results in an association between the class II molecule and a part of the processed antigen on the cell surface, in which the antigen

[a]This work was supported in part by Grants DK28242 and DK35764 from NIDDKD.

151

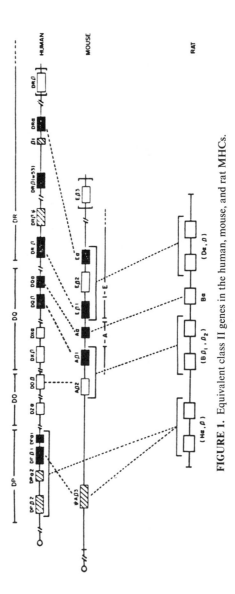

FIGURE 1. Equivalent class II genes in the human, mouse, and rat MHCs.

sits within an antigen-binding pocket.[9] The mechanism by which the T helper/inducer cell recognizes the class II/antigen combination is the specific polymorphic T-cell receptors on their cell surface. T-cell receptors exhibit nonantigen-specific polymorphisms associated with autoimmune disease.[10]

The MHC class II antigens have also been shown to facilitate mixed lymphocyte reactions (MLR). These much studied reactions consist of T-cell proliferation in response to foreign or self lymphocytes with which they are co-cultured. The MLR, including autologous MLR, are inhibited by antibodies to MHC class II antigens in animals and humans.[11] Some controversy exists over whether recognition of the MHC class II/foreign or autoantigen complex is also involved in autologous MLR, the T cells responding to self MHC class II antigens combined unintentionally with an *in vitro* antigen from, for example, fetal calf serum.[12] Nevertheless, most carefully obtained evidence suggests that *in vivo* MHC class II expression is associated with local T-cell amplification phenomena such as *in vivo* MLR.

TABLE 1. MHC and Thyroid Autoimmunity

Disease	MHC	Subjects	Pts	Controls	RR[a]
			Typical Frequency		
1. Human					
Graves' disease	B8, DR3	Caucasians	68%	28%	3–6
	B35, DRw12	Japanese	57%	21%	4–5
Autoimmune thyroiditis					
Atrophic	DR3		55%	26%	3–6
Goitrous (Hashimoto's)	DR5		49%	23%	3–4
Postpartum thyroiditis	DR3		44%	23%	2.5
	DR5		60%	27%	3–4
	?DR4		58%	33%	2.5–4.5
2. Mouse					
Good responders	H-2k & H-2s	*e.g.,* CBA/J			
Poor responders	H-2b & H-2d	*e.g.,* BALB/c, CBA			
3. Rat					
Good responders	RT1.B/Db	*e.g.,* Buffalo			
Poor responders	RT1.B/Dc	*e.g.,* Fisher			

[a]RR = relative risk = (No. of patients with the HLA antigen) × (No. of controls without the antigen)/(No. of controls with the antigen) × (No. of patients without the antigen).

EXPRESSION OF MHC CLASS II ANTIGENS IN THE THYROID GLAND

MHC class II antigens may be expressed in a variety of tissues that are not normally considered part of the immune system. These tissues usually contain lymphocytic infiltrates in areas adjacent to class II antigen expression. (For reviews see references 2 and 13.) Immunohistochemical examination of thyroid glands removed from patients with autoimmune thyroid disease indicates widespread expression of HLA-DR and DP, and less often DQ, by thyroid epithelial cells, particularly in areas where lymphocytic infiltration is most pronounced[14] (FIG. 2). MHC class II antigen expression is not observed in normal thyroid. Laboratory animals immunized with thyroid antigens, such as thyroglobulin, show widespread MHC class II antigen expression by thyroid epithelial cells as well as classical lymphoid infiltration.[15,16] In parallel studies we examined intrathyroidal HLA-DR alpha chain specific mRNA by *in situ* hybridization[17] (FIG. 3). High grain counts were localized to similar areas of the glands as observed for antigen expression, with a marked induction of alpha-chain-specific mRNA in areas of gross lymphocytic infiltration in patients with Graves' disease and Hashimoto's thyroiditis (FIG. 4). Interestingly, HLA-DR alpha-chain-specific mRNA expression was consistently greater in thyroid tissue from glands affected by Graves' disease rather than thyroiditis, even in areas of thyroiditis with minimal destruction of follicles. These data suggest that such MHC class II expression may be accentuated by the thyroid-stimulating hormone (TSH) receptor agonism of thyroid-stimulating antibodies or is secondary to a different T-cell population involved within the thyroid in these two different diseases (see below).

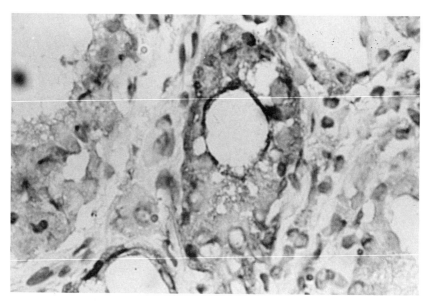

FIGURE 2. Localization of HLA-DR expression in Graves' disease thyroid tissue. The *arrow* indicates the most extensively stained areas of thyroid follicles. (Original magnification × 100.)

MOLECULAR CHARACTERIZATION OF THYROID CELL MHC CLASS II GENE TRANSCRIPTION

Using Northern blot analysis of human thyroid, we found single HLA-DR, DP, and DQ alpha-chain-specific mRNA species of 1.3–1.4 kb in size in total cellular RNA prepared from thyroid tissue of patients with autoimmune thyroid disease, with the highest concentrations again being found in cellular RNA prepared from tissue of those with Graves' disease, far in excess of any possible contribution from DR-positive lymphocytic infiltration[18] (FIG. 5). Only low levels of class II transcripts were found in normal thyroid tissue. These observations are consistent with the histologic data just discussed, and the mRNA species are typical of lymphoid cell HLA-D transcripts indicating a lack of tissue-specific polymorphism. Nevertheless, the question of low levels of constitutive expression of MHC class II antigens remained unresolved using these techniques in human tissue.

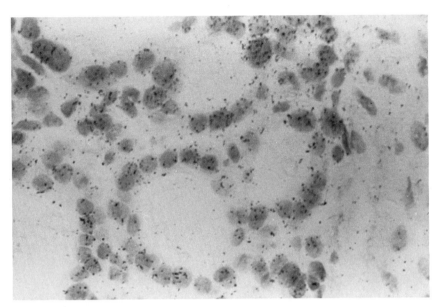

FIGURE 3. *In situ* hybridization using HLA-DR alpha-chain sense probes. This figure illustrates a representative field in a 10-μ section of Graves' disease thyroid tissue hybridized with [3H]-DR alpha-chain-specific sense RNA transcripts generated using SP6 RNA polymerase.[17] Slides were exposed for 4 weeks, developed, and counterstained with hematoxylin and eosin before microscopic examination using bright-field illumination. (Original magnification × 200.)

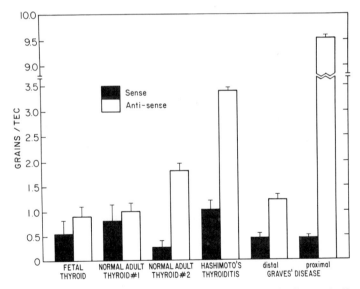

FIGURE 4. Quantitative *in situ* hybridization. This figure illustrates the silver grain distribution over a variety of human thyroid tissue sections hybridized with either HLA-DR alpha-chain sense or antisense RNA probes. Counts represent the mean number of grains over 10 thyroid follicles selected at random within each tissue section, and results are expressed as grains per thyroid epithelial cell (TEC).

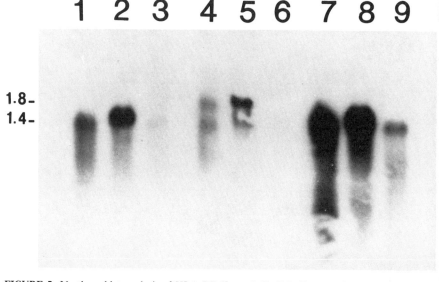

FIGURE 5. Northern blot analysis of HLA-DP (*lanes 1–3*), DQ (*lanes 4–6*), and DR (*lanes 7–9*) alpha-chain gene expression in thyroid tissue. *Lanes* 1, 4, and 7 show Raji B-cell positive control, *lanes* 2, 5, and 8 Graves' thyroid cellular RNA, and *lanes* 3, 6, and 9 normal thyroid. (From reference 22.)

LACK OF THYROID CELL CONSTITUTIVE MHC CLASS II GENE EXPRESSION

The problem of constitutivity initially was most easily answered by turning to an animal model. We had earlier developed a useful Fisher rat thyroid cell clone named 1B-6, derived from the FRTL-5 line.[19] Using a newly developed probe to the RT1.D region, which was 100-fold more sensitive than the human DR alpha-specific probe under low stringency,[20] we were unable to detect constitutive MHC class II transcripts, just as we were unable to detect surface antigen. Subsequent to these studies we had immortalized human fetal thyroid cells with a retrovirus vector incorporating the 12S E1a gene. One clone of these cells, named 12S, remained sensitive to TSH stimulation as measured by induction of cyclic AMP accumulation and has been fully character-ized.[21] Human thyroid clone 12S also demonstrates a lack of basal HLA class II transcripts, using the human alpha-chain-specific probe, and class II antigen expres-sion.

INDUCTION OF MHC CLASS II ANTIGEN EXPRESSION IN AUTOIMMUNE THYROID DISEASE

Although Graves' and Hashimoto's thyroid tissues have thyroid epithelial cells with easily detectable MHC class II antigens, this antigen expression is lost after transfer of thyroid tissue to nude mice.[13] Similarly, fresh preparations of Graves' thyroid cells exhibit class II antigen expression that is lost during *in vitro* culture.

These observations indicate that MHC class II antigen expression in autoimmune thyroid disease is secondary to *in vivo* extracellular stimulation. When normal thyroid cells, either human or rat, are exposed *in vitro* to appropriate recombinant gamma-interferon (IFN-γ) preparations, class II alpha-chain-specific mRNA and antigen are induced (FIG. 6). After withdrawal of IFN-γ there is a gradual loss of detectable class II antigen.[2] These data confirm that the expression of MHC class II antigens on normal and diseased thyroid cells can be secondary to an external stimulus and that IFN-γ is one such potential initiator.

As discussed earlier, expression of class II antigen genes in normal thyroid epithelium has not been detected at the translational (i.e., protein) level using currently available techniques. However, low levels of alpha-chain gene transcripts are measurable by Northern blot analysis and *in situ* hybridization, depending on the source of the thyroid tissue[17,18] (FIG. 4). Often these experiments use histologically normal tissue from thyroid lobes removed because of benign adenomas. However, these tumors also may have a local peripheral inflammatory reaction that may induce low levels of MHC class II gene transcription.[18] Hence, the question of constitutive expression can only be answered by experiments with fetal thyroid (which was found to be class II negative) and the human and rat thyroid cell lines outlined earlier (also constitutively class II negative).

HLA-DP AND DQ ANTIGEN EXPRESSION

In all studies of human thyroid tissue performed to date at both the transcriptional and translational level, there has been a consistent parallel induction of all three MHC class II antigen genes in the order of DR > DP > DQ.[22] Hence, in many tissues we have not observed DQ antigen expression. However, we have never seen DP antigens without being able to detect DR antigens (FIG. 7). Human thyroid cell clone 12S shows only HLA-DR and DP, not HLA-DQ, inducible class II genes.

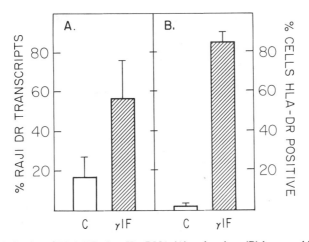

FIGURE 6. Induction of HLA-DR class II mRNA (**A**) and antigen (**B**) by recombinant human gamma-interferon (100 U/ml) in normal human thyroid monolayer cells. Data are expressed as % HLA-DR positive Raji lymphoblast control RNA using densitometry.

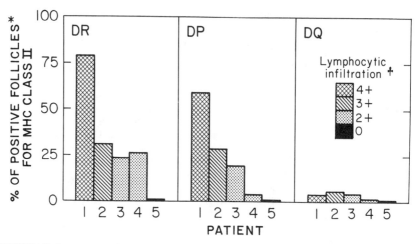

FIGURE 7. Immunocytochemical quantitation of HLA-D antigen expression in thyroid tissue from Graves' thyroid (patients 1–4) and a representative normal thyroid (patient 5). Lymphocytic infiltration was evaluated by counting T cells per 10 high power (40×) fields: 4+ = >500, 2+ = 100–300.

MODULATORS OF THYROID CELL MHC CLASS II ANTIGEN EXPRESSION

It remains unclear whether IFN-γ is the most important regulator of class II expression *in vivo*, because a variety of other lymphokines and cytokines may be involved. This is particularly apparent by the expression of class II antigens in papillary thyroid carcinoma in the absence of profuse lymphocytic infiltration[14] (FIG. 8). In addition, many data suggest that TSH and thyroid-stimulating antibodies are also able to modulate the action of IFN-γ on the induction of MHC class II antigens.[23] This is most striking in the IB-6 rat thyroid cell model in which no MHC class II induction takes place in the absence of TSH (FIG. 9).

HAPLOTYPIC EXPRESSION OF THYROID CELL MHC CLASS II ANTIGENS

The monoclonal antibodies used to detect HLA-D antigen expression are broadly specific and involve sites on both alpha and beta chains of the molecules. Therefore, they fail to recognize the polymorphic determinants of human HLA-D. For this reason we subjected IFN-γ-treated human thyroid cells to HLA-DR antigen typing using over 55 polyclonal antisera of known DR specificity.[24] These studies showed that in four of five cultures there was complete agreement between B-cell and thyroid cell HLA-DR designations. In addition, using two-color fluorescence we performed complement-mediated cytotoxicity studies with IFN-γ-treated thyroid cells and showed that a monoclonal anti-DR3 was able to lyse the thyroid cells from an HLA-DR3 individual. Hence, all evidence to date indicates that the HLA-DR molecule expressed on thyroid cells is similar to that expressed on B cells.

FUNCTION OF THYROID CELL MHC CLASS II ANTIGENS

When we co-incubated Graves' thyroid cells with autologous peripheral blood T cells, we observed T-cell activation of uncertain etiology. Later, we observed that if HLA-DR antigen-positive normal thyroid cells were used, autologous co-cultures of normal individuals also revealed T-cell activation.[25] These data suggest that class II antigen expression on the human thyroid cell results in a phenomenon similar to an autologous mixed lymphocyte reaction (AMLR).[11] This amplification of lymphocytic infiltration *in vivo* would itself then induce IFN-γ secretion from the participating T cells and further stimulate thyroid cell HLA-D antigen expression. We recently reanalyzed this phenomenon in greater detail using the Fisher rat model.[23] In these experiments we used rat thyroid cell clone 1B-6 with syngeneic T cells of splenic origin. We observed that MHC class II positive 1B-6 cells induced rat helper (CD4+) T-cell proliferation but had no influence on rat suppressor/cytotoxic (CD8+) T cells (FIG. 10). In contrast, MHC class II negative 1B-6 cells had no such effect. This type of immune amplification is nonspecific with respect to the thyroid, but in man and susceptible animals it may be aided by the mild nonspecific T-cell defect often seen with autoimmune thyroid disease.[2] Additional support for this "nonspecific" hypothesis has come from intrathyroidal T-cell lines and cloning studies that reveal the high prevalence of nonspecific T cells within the thyroid glands of patients with autoimmune thyroid disease.[26]

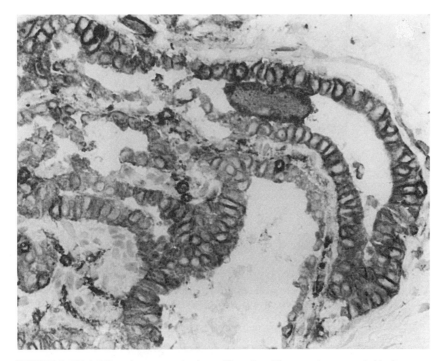

FIGURE 8. HLA-DR antigen expression in papillary thyroid cancer tissue revealed by immunocytochemistry using L243 monoclonal antibody. Note the lack of lymphocytic infiltration.

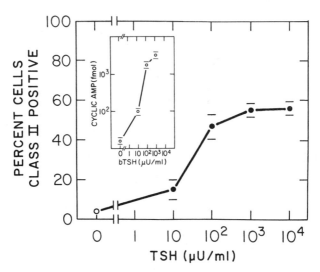

FIGURE 9. Thyroid-stimulating hormone (TSH)-dependent induction of rat MHC class II antigen expression in the 1B-6 clone of FRTL-5 rat thyroid cells stimulated with 100 U/ml of recombinant rat gamma-interferon. The *inset* shows the sensitivity of this clone to TSH as measured by the generation of extracellular cyclic AMP.

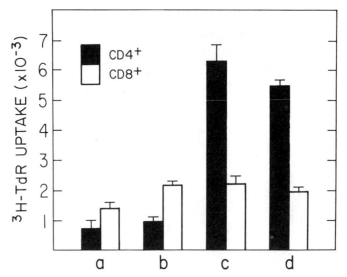

FIGURE 10. Induction of CD4+ rat T-cell proliferation by MHC class II positive syngeneic thyroid cells (1B-6). CD4+ T cells and CD8+ T cells from normal Fisher rat spleens were incubated (*a*) alone, (*b*) stimulated with irradiated MHC class II negative thyroid cells, (*c*) stimulated with class II positive thyroid cells, or (*d*) syngeneic thymocytes. Results are expressed as mean cpm ± SD of triplicate determinations.

PRESENTATION OF THYROID ANTIGEN TO HELPER T CELLS

Within the immune system the presence of HLA-DR antigen has usually implied that the cell has the ability to present specific antigen to the helper T cell. Human thyroid cells have been shown able to present already processed viral antigen to responsive T cells.[27] In addition, the derivation of thyroid-specific T-cell clones that proliferate only in the presence of autologous thyroid cells[26] implies direct presentation of thyroid antigen to the appropriate T cell. We examined 57 clones of activated T cells from thyroid tissue of patients with autoimmune thyroid disease. All of these clones were successfully expanded and tested for reactivity, cytotoxicity, helper/suppressor

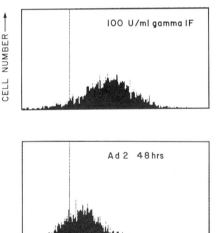

FIGURE 11. Adenoviral induction of MHC class II antigen expression in rat thyroid cells. Data were obtained by flow cytometry and demonstrate the control background (*top*), the 3-day response to 100 U/ml gamma-interferon (*middle*), and the response at 3 days to a 2-hour adenoviral type 2 infection (*bottom*).

function, and phenotype. In the reactivity assays, clones were tested for responses to autologous and allogeneic PMC and thyroid cells as well as human thyroglobulin (hTg) and microsomal antigen (M-Ag). Two distinct patterns of functional T-cell clones emerged from these characterization studies. Seventy-five percent of T-cell clones recovered from Graves' disease thyroid tissue ($n = 21$) were of helper-inducer (CD4+/4B4+) phenotype and most were effective IgG helper clones. Fifty percent of Graves' disease T-cell clones responded to autologous PMC, and 33% had a proliferative response to autologous thyroid cells. No cytotoxic clones were derived from Graves' thyroid tissue. By contrast, intrathyroidal T-cell clones from patients with autoimmune thyroiditis ($n = 36$) were of the suppressor/cytotoxic (CD8+) phenotype in 59%, 17% suppressed IgG secretion, and 55% were cytotoxic to allogeneic blast cells. Fifty-five percent of clones also responded to autologous PMC, and one clone was nonspecifically autocytotoxic. In thyroid antigen proliferation assays, 11% of thyroiditis clones reacted to hTg, but none responded to microsomal antigen. Two clones were cytotoxic to autologous but not allogeneic thyroid cells. These data demonstrate that the majority of intrathyroidal T cells in autoimmune thyroid disease are autoreactive when examined under these T-cell cloning conditions. However, a small number are thyroid specific and are principally helper-inducer T cells in Graves' disease of the thyroid and cytotoxic T cells in autoimmune thyroiditis. We have characterized a thyroid-specific cytotoxic T-cell clone in further detail.[28]

VIRAL INITIATION OF MHC CLASS II ANTIGEN EXPRESSION

Although the consequences of thyroid cell MHC class II antigen expression have become clearer, with evidence of local immune cell amplification and the potential for presentation of thyroid antigen to thyroid-specific T cells, the initiating insult that causes the human thyroid cell to vigorously express class II antigens is unknown. It has been postulated that MHC class II antigen expression may be spontaneous,[29] but the weight of data already reviewed herein suggests that such expression is usually a secondary phenomenon. Could a viral infection of thyroid cells initiate this expression, as recently observed with rodent neuronal cells?[30] Recent experiments in our laboratory have indicated that both adenovirus and reovirus infection of rat thyroid cells can induce MHC class II gene induction and that MHC class II antigen may be expressed in over 40% of cultured cells[31] (FIG. 11). How these viruses can induce MHC class II gene transcription is currently under investigation. Furthermore, whether this observation has any relation to the initiation of thyroid autoimmunity in "at risk" individuals with the appropriate HLA genes remains to be further explored.

REFERENCES

1. WATTERS, J. W. F., J. D. LOCKER, H. W. KUNZ & T. J. GILL. 1987. Polymorphism and mapping of the class II genes in the rat: RT1.B, RT1.D and RT1.H, a new DP-like region. Immunogenetics 26: 220–229.
2. DAVIES, T. F. & L. A. PICCININI. 1987. HLA class II antigens and the human thyroid cell—an overview. Endocrinol. Metab. Clin. N. Am. 16: 247–268.
3. FARID, N. R., & J. C. BEAR. 1983. Autoimmune endocrine disorders and the major histocompatibility complex. In Autoimmune Endocrine Disease. T. F. Davies, Ed.: 59–92. Wiley, New York.
4. UNO, H., T. SASAZUKI, H. TAMIA & H. MATSUMOTO. 1981. Two major genes, linked to HLA and Gm, control susceptibility to Graves' disease. Nature 292: 768–770.
5. VLADUTIU, A. O. & N. R. ROSE. 1975. Cellular basis of the genetic control of immune responsiveness to thyroglobulin in mice. Cell. Immunol. 17: 106–113.
6. PENHALE, W. J., A. FARMER, S. J. URBANIAK, & W. J. IRVINE. 1975. Susceptibility of inbred rat strains to experimental thyroiditis. Clin. and Exp. Immunol. 19: 179–187.
7. KALENBERG, C. G. M., R. J. L. KLAASSEN, J. M. BEELEN & T. H. THE. 1985. HLA-B8/DR3 phenotype and the primary immune response. Clin. Immunol. Immunopathol. 34: 135–140.
8. MARRACK, P. & J. KAPPLER. 1986. The T cell and its receptor. Sci. Am. 254: 36–45.
9. BJORKMAN, P. J., M. A. SAPER, B. SAMRAOUI, W. S. BENNET, J. L. STROMINGER & D. C. WILEY. 1987. The foreign antigen binding site and T cell recognition regions of class I histocompatibility. Nature 329: 512–518.

10. DEMAINE, A., K. I. WELSH, B. S. HAWE & N. R. FARID. 1987. Polymorphism of the T cell receptor beta chain in Graves' disease. J. Clin. Endocrinol. and Metab. **65:** 643–646.
11. WEKSLER, M. E., C. E. MOODY & R. W. KOZAK. 1981. The autologous mixed lymphocyte reaction. Adv. Immunol. **31:** 271–312.
12. STEINBERG, A. D. 1984. Autologous mixed lymphocyte reactions—a commentary. J. Mol. Cell. Immunol. **1:** 101.
13. PICCININI, L. A., S. H. ROMAN & T. F. DAVIES. 1987. Thyroid cell MHC class II antigens—a perspective on the etiology of autoimmune thyroid disease. Clin. Endocrinol. **26:** 253–272.
14. GOLDSMITH, N. K., S. DIKMAN, B. BERMAS, T. F. DAVIES & S. H. ROMAN. 1988. HLA class II antigen expression and the autoimmune thyroid response in patients with benign and malignant thyroid tumors. Clin. Immunol. Immunopathol. **48:** 161–173.
15. COHEN, S. B. & A. P. WEETMAN. 1987. Characterization of different types of experimental autoimmune thyroiditis in the Buffalo strain rat. Clin. Exp. Immunol. **69:** 25–32.
16. SALAMERO, J., M. MICHEL-BECHET & J. CHARREIRE. 1981. Differences de rapartition des antigenes de class I and II du complexe majeur d'histocompatibilité (CMH) à la surface des cellules epitheliales de thyroide (CET) murines en culture. C. R. Acad. Sc. Paris **293:** 745.
17. PICCININI, L. A., N. K. GOLDSMITH, B. S. SCHACHTER & T. F. DAVIES. 1988. Localization of HLA-DR alpha chain mRNA in normal and autoimmune human thyroid using in situ hybridization. J. Clin. Endocrinol. Metab. **66:** 1307–1308.
18. PICCININI, L. A., W. A. MACKENZIE, M. PLATZER & T. F. DAVIES. 1987. Lymphokine sensitivity of HLA-DR antigen gene expression in human thyroid cell cultures. J. Clin. Endocrinol. Metab. **64:** 543–548.
19. DAVIES, T. F., C. YANG & M. PLATZER. 1987. Cloning the FRTL-5 cell: Variability in clonal growth and cyclic AMP response to TSH. Endocrinology **121:** 78–83.
20. NEUFFELD, D. & T. F. DAVIES. 1988. Detection and regulation of rat thyroid MHC class II transcripts. Mol. Endocrinol. **2:** 507–511.
21. CONE, R. D., M. PLATZER, L. A. PICCININI, M. JARAMILLO, Y. GLUZMAN & T. F. DAVIES. 1988. HLA-DR gene expression in a proliferating, TSH sensitive, human thyroid cell clone (12S). Endocrinology, in press.
22. PICCININI, L. A., N. K. GOLDSMITH, S. H. ROMAN & T. F. DAVIES. 1987. HLA-DP, DQ and DR gene expression in Graves' disease and normal thyroid epithelium. Tissue Antigens **30:** 145–154.
23. PLATZER, M., D. S. NEUFELD & T. F. DAVIES. 1987. MHC class II gene induction in rat thyroid cells by TSH and gamma interferon. Endocrinology **121:** 2087–2092.
24. DOWER, S. M., L. A. PICCININI, S. H. ROMAN, R. SAFIRSTEIN & T. F. DAVIES. 1988. Allospecific DR gene expression on the human thyroid cell—evidence for thyroid cell involvement in disease susceptibility. Autoimmunity **1:** 37–44.
25. DAVIES, T. F. 1985. Co-cultures of human thyroid monolayer cells and autologous T cells—impact of HLA class II antigen expression. J. Clin. Endocrinol. Metab. **61:** 418–422.
26. MACKENZIE, W. A., A. E. SCHWARTZ, E. W. FRIEDMAN & T. F. DAVIES. 1987. Intrathyroidal T cell clones from patients with autoimmune thyroid disease. J. Clin. Endocrinol. Metab. **64:** 818–824.
27. LONDEI, M., J. R. LAMB, G. F. BOTTAZZO & M. FELDMAN. 1984. Epithelial cells expressing aberrant MHC class II determinants can present antigen to cloned human T cells. Nature **312:** 639–641.
28. MACKENZIE, W. A. & T. F. DAVIES. 1987. An intrathyroidal T cell clone specifically cytotoxic for human thyroid cells. Immunology **61:** 101–103.
29. BOTTAZZO, G. F., R. PUJOL-BORRELL, T. HANAFUSA & F. FELDMAN. 1983. Role of aberrant HLA-DR expression and antigen presentation in induction of endocrine autoimmunity. Lancet **2:** 1115–1118.
30. MASSA, P. T., R. DORRIES & V. TER MEULEN. 1986. Viral particles induce Ia antigen expression on astrocytes. Nature **320:** 543–546.
31. NEUFELD, D. S. & T. F. DAVIES. 1987. Viral induction of rat thyroid MHC class II gene expression. American Thyroid Association, Washington DC, September. Abstract #34.

Immunopathogenic Mechanisms in Human Immunodeficiency Virus (HIV) Infections

ZEDA F. ROSENBERG AND ANTHONY S. FAUCI

National Institute of Allergy and Infectious Diseases
National Institutes of Health
Bethesda, Maryland

It has been widely documented that infection with human immunodeficiency virus (HIV) ultimately leads to a significant quantitative depletion of T4 lymphocytes.[1-3] Because of the central role that T4 lymphocytes play in the functioning of the immune system, HIV-induced depletion of these cells results in a profound immunosuppression that leaves the infected individual susceptible to opportunistic infections and neoplasms. Although HIV can be rapidly cytopathic for T4 lymphocytes *in vitro*,[4,5] it is apparent from the long and variable latent period between initial HIV infection and the development of symptomatic disease, that the virus can remain in a low-level or latent state *in vivo* for many years. During this time, low-level HIV expression may cause functional impairment of otherwise viable cells. Alternatively, the virus may lay dormant within cells until some event causes activation of virus expression, virus replication, cell death, and spread of virus to other susceptible cells.

This report briefly reviews the immunopathogenic mechanisms of T4-cell destruction by HIV and focuses specifically on the early and selective effects of HIV on antigen-responsive T cells and on the mechanisms of conversion from a latent or chronic HIV infection to a productive infection. The potential role of the monocyte/macrophage as a major reservoir of HIV infection in the body is also discussed.

IMMUNOPATHOGENIC MECHANISMS

Virus-Cell Interactions

The broad scope of immunologic defects seen in patients with AIDS is the result of the depletion and/or functional impairment of lymphocytes bearing the CD4 phenotypic marker (the T4 cell).[1-3] It has been convincingly demonstrated that the CD4 molecule is a high affinity receptor for the HIV envelope glycoprotein (gp120).[4-7] Because the initial step in viral infection is the binding of the virus to a cellular receptor, it is clear that the T4 cell, with its abundance of CD4 molecules on the surface, represents a principal target for HIV infection. However, virtually any cell in the body that expresses CD4 is capable of binding to and becoming infected with HIV, such as cells of monocyte/macrophage lineage.[8-13]

After binding to the CD4+ cell, HIV fuses with the cellular membrane, is internalized, and is uncoated. Once in the cell, the viral reverse transcriptase transcribes the virion RNA into DNA, which can exist either in an unintegrated form or as a provirus that is integrated into cellular DNA. At this point, the provirus may remain latent in the host cell until cellular activation results in proviral DNA transcription into virion RNA and messenger RNA. After protein synthesis, processing, and viral assembly, the mature HIV particle buds from the surface of the cell.[14]

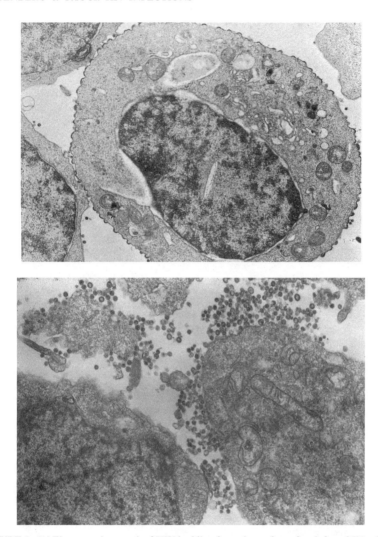

FIGURE 1. (A) Electron micrograph of HIV budding from the surface of an infected T4 cell. (B) On stimulation with PHA, the T4 cell virtually explodes with mature virions.

Cytopathic Effect of HIV

The exact manner by which HIV induces a quantitative loss of T4 cells is unknown. The depletion of T4 cells may be the result of a direct cytopathic effect of the virus *in vivo*, because it was shown early that HIV infection of T cells *in vitro* can result in cell death.[4,5] The question arises whether the profound quantitative deficiency of T4 cells can be explained entirely by the direct destruction of each T4 cell by HIV or whether other more indirect mechanisms contribute to the ultimate depletion of these cells.

Although several proposed mechanisms of cytopathicity, including rupture of the cell membrane as a result of massive budding of viral particles (R. C. Gallo, personal communication) (FIG. 1A and B) and the accumulation of large amounts of uninte-grated viral DNA,[15] can result in direct T4-cell death, the low frequency of detectable HIV-infected cells in the blood[16] suggests that other pathogenic mechanisms are at play. It is possible that a T4-cell precursor or stem cell is infected with HIV, leading to a lack of production of mature cells. Alternatively, HIV may infect and kill a subset of T4 cells or even CD4+ nonlymphoid cells that are critical to the growth of the entire T-cell pool. Another potential mechanism for T4-cell depletion is HIV-induced secretion of soluble substances with toxic effects on T4 cells.[17]

There is increasing evidence to suggest that both the CD4 molecule and the virus

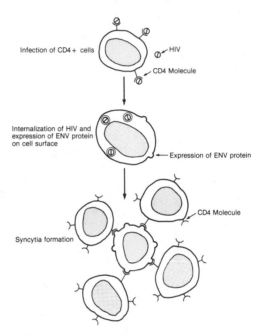

FIGURE 2. Schematic diagram of the formation of syncytia with HIV-infected and HIV-uninfected CD4+ cells.

envelope glycoprotein play a role in cell killing. The interaction of the envelope glycoprotein that is expressed on the surface of HIV-infected cells with the CD4 molecule on the surface of uninfected T4 cells leads to fusion of the cell membranes and formation of multinucleated giant cells (syncytia) (FIG. 2).[18-21] After approxi-mately 48 hours, the syncytia usually undergo cytolysis and death. It is also possible that the CD4 molecule and envelope glycoproteins form intracellular complexes that are subsequently involved in the destruction of the cell.[22]

The interaction of the CD4 molecule with HIV envelope proteins may also result in the induction of autoimmune phenomena. The binding of free envelope proteins to the CD4 molecule on uninfected cells may result in the immune system's recognition and elimination of these cells as non-self.[23] A second autoimmune theory involves immune system clearance of cells bearing the class II major histocompatibility complex (MHC) molecule.[24] Because the HIV envelope and class II MHC molecules both bind to the CD4 molecule, it is thought that an immune response directed against the envelope proteins can potentially cross-react with class II MHC.

The importance of the role of the CD4 molecule in pathogenesis is suggested in the observation that although virtually all CD4-bearing cells can be infected with HIV, a wide range of degree of cytopathicity is observed among different CD4+ cells. For example, T4 lymphocytes are remarkably sensitive to killing by HIV. However, cells of the monocyte/macrophage lineage appear to be more refractory. This phenomenon may be due to differences in the relative levels of CD4 expression, because the level of expression of CD4 on monocytes/macrophages is considerably lower than that on T4 cells.[10,25] Additional evidence for the role of CD4 in cytopathicity is suggested by the fact that no cytopathic effect was observed on superinfection of HTLV-1-infected T8 clones with HIV, although a productive infection and accumulation of unintegrated HIV DNA were present. This finding is in contrast to the cytopathic effect seen in HIV superinfected HTLV-1-infected T4 clones.[26]

Functional Impairment of T4 Lymphocytes

In addition to the quantitative depletion of T4 lymphocytes, there is growing evidence that HIV can functionally impair T4 cells in the absence of a cytopathic effect. Early experiments demonstrated that antigen-responsive T cells are selectively deficient in patients with AIDS and that this deficiency occurs early in the course of the disease.[27] Unfractionated peripheral blood mononuclear cells (PBMNC) from patients with AIDS exhibit a diminished response to mitogens such as pokeweed, phytohemagglutinin (PHA), or concanavalin A, and to the soluble antigen tetanus toxoid (TT). Whereas the PBMNC response to mitogens could be augmented by enriching the cultures for T4 cells (i.e., depleting T8 cells), the markedly diminished response of unfractionated PBMNC from patients with AIDS to TT could not be augmented by enrichment for T4 cells.[27] These results suggest that although the decreased response to mitogens was due to a disproportionate number of non-T4+ cells in cultures from patients with AIDS, the diminished response to soluble antigen was due to a selective depletion or functional impairment of the antigen-responsive T4 cell.

Because the decreased response to soluble antigen occurred early in the disease even in patients with total lymphocyte counts above 1,000 cells/mm³,[27] functional impairment of T4 cells may represent an initial critical immune defect in HIV infection. Such an early defect was seen in a cohort of totally asymptomatic, seropositive individuals with normal numbers of CD4+ cells who displayed a lack of response to TT (H. C. Lane, and A. S. Fauci, unpublished observations) (FIG. 3). The defective response to TT and other test antigens[28] is likely the result of a functional impairment of antigen-responsive cells, because a depletion of antigen-responsive cells encompassing the entire scope of the antigen-specific T-cell repertoire would result in a cumulative loss of most of the CD4+ cells.

Studies of identical twins, in which one sibling has AIDS and the other is seronegative and healthy, have generated further evidence for a selective defect in antigen-responsive T4 cells.[29] In these experiments, the addition of monocytes from the HIV-negative twin to his own autologous T cells resulted in good response to TT. However, monocytes from the seronegative twin failed in co-culture to augment the defective TT response of the T4 cells from the twin with AIDS.

Further support for the presence of functional impairment of T4 cells during HIV infection comes from a series of experiments that measured the proliferative responses of normal PBMNC to antigen after exposure to low, noncytopathic concentrations of HIV.[30] PBMNC were stimulated *in vitro* with a soluble antigen such as TT or keyhole limpet hemocyanin (KLH), briefly exposed to HIV, and subsequently challenged with antigen or mitogen. The exposed but not infected (reverse transcriptase-negative) PBMNC showed marked inhibition of response to soluble antigen and less inhibition of response to mitogen. It has also been demonstrated that purified HIV proteins, such as the gp120 envelope protein, that are exposed to lymphocytes could block antigen-specific responses.[31,32]

There are two possible mechanisms that explain how exposure to HIV without actual infection can functionally impair antigen-specific T cells. HIV or its envelope protein may block antigen-specific responses by binding to the CD4 molecule on the T cell and interfering with the normal interaction of the CD4 molecule with the class II

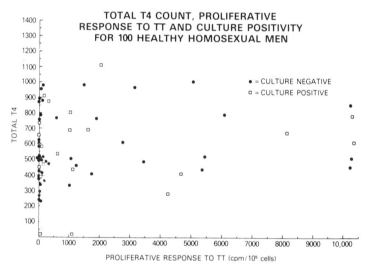

FIGURE 3. Reduction in the TT-specific response in asymptomatic HIV-infected individuals with normal numbers of CD4+ T cells (600–1,200 T4 cells/mm^3).

MHC molecule on the monocyte during antigen presentation.[33,34] Because the responses of T4 cells to mitogens are not critically dependent on CD4-MHC interaction, the cellular activation pathway of mitogen stimulation could bypass this step and induce a normal proliferative response in cells that were rendered refractory to antigenic stimulation.

Another hypothesis is that exposure of T cells to HIV or its products could cause a desensitizing or tolerogenic signal, resulting in a postreceptor signal transduction defect that mitogen, but not soluble antigen, can partially override. Because soluble antigens and mitogens can activate T cells through different pathways,[35] it is possible that the virus-induced block in T-cell function occurs after the binding of ligand to the antigen receptor and that this block is partially bypassed by mitogens.

A noncytopathic infection of T4 cells could also explain the functional abnormalities seen in this cell population. For example, HIV-infected T4 cells no longer express

CD4 molecules on their surfaces.[22] This lack of CD4 molecules would impair the ability of the T4 cell to interact with the MHC complex on antigen-presenting cells.

Role of the Monocyte/Macrophage in HIV Infection

It was noted early that monocyte function in HIV-infected individuals is impaired. Monocytes from patients with AIDS exhibit decreased chemotaxis and cytotoxic function.[36–38] Subsequent studies demonstrated that HIV, like other lentiviruses, can be isolated from cells of the monocyte/macrophage lineage, including those found in the brain[11,13,39] and in the blood,[12] and can infect monocyte/macrophage cell lines *in vitro*.[8–10,40] Because of the low frequency of infection of circulating monocytes and the observation that T4-cell-produced gamma-interferon can reconstitute certain defective monocyte functions,[41] monocyte abnormalities will likely result from a deficiency of inductive signals from the T4 cell.

Although monocyte/macrophages can engulf the virus, certain subsets of monocytes express CD4 molecules and can be infected through binding of the virus envelope glycoprotein to the CD4 molecule. The major difference in HIV infection of monocytes versus T4 lymphocytes is that the cytopathic effect in monocytes is much smaller. This finding raises the possibility that the monocyte can act as a reservoir of HIV and transport the virus to various organs in the body. In support of this hypothesis, we recently showed that a promonocyte cell line, U937, can be chronically infected with HIV. Virus can be induced from a nonproducer, latently infected U937 clone, U1, by certain cytokines.[42,43] In addition, it was recently demonstrated that under certain circumstances, monocytes can serve as a source of virus production *in vitro*.[44]

Activation of Latent HIV Infections

As mentioned previously, the development of immunologic abnormalities after infection with HIV *in vivo* occurs after a long and variable period of latency. During the years that an HIV-infected individual remains asymptomatic, the virus likely exists in a latent (integration without virus expression) or chronic (low-level virus expression) form in infected cells. Understanding how an asymptomatic HIV infection develops into full-blown AIDS is essential to understanding the immunopathogenesis of HIV, and it may generate insights into methods to interfere with the development of disease. Therefore, we have approached the problem of indentifying the mechanisms of conversion from a latent to an active infection *in vivo* by examining how latently or chronically infected cells can be induced *in vitro* to produce virus.

In initial attempts to isolate HIV from the lymphocytes of patients with AIDS, it had been observed that mitogen stimulation of latently infected PBMNC resulted in virus replication. In addition, treatment with PHA is necessary for infection of cells *in vitro* with HIV.[45,46] The HIV-infected individual, however, would probably not be exposed to potent mitogen stimulation but would more likely be exposed to a wide range of antigenic stimuli. Therefore, it was important to discern whether physiologically relevant activation signals, rather than the more powerful mitogen stimulation, could induce latently or chronically infected cells to produce virus. To address this question, we preincubated PBMNC with potential cellular activator such as the soluble antigens TT and KLH prior to exposure to HIV. PBMNC that had been activated by antigen before HIV exposure were 10 to 100 times more susceptible to viral replication than were PBMNC that had been preincubated without antigen.[30]

Heterologous viruses are one group of antigens that HIV-infected individuals may be exposed to during the course of their infection, and it has been postulated that infection with these viruses could induce HIV expression.[29] A series of experiments were performed to determine whether coinfection with heterologous viruses such as cytomegalovirus, Epstein-Barr virus, hepatitis B virus, and herpes simplex virus could activate latent HIV infection.[47] SW480 human colon carcinoma cells were cotransfected with a recombinant plasmid containing the HIV long terminal repeat (LTR) linked to the chloramphenicol acetyltransferase (CAT) gene, as well as plasmids containing the HIV *tat* gene and/or the immediate early genes from a variety of heterologous DNA viruses. These cotransfection experiments and others[48,49] demonstrated that heterologous viral DNAs can stimulate CAT enzyme synthesis when under the control of the HIV promoter, suggesting that these viruses could up-regulate HIV gene expression and affect the clinical course of HIV infection *in vivo*. In fact, it

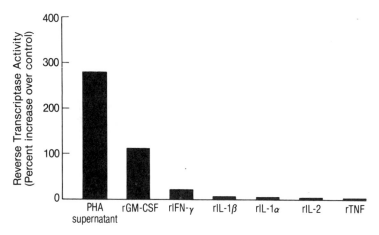

FIGURE 4. Effect of recombinant cytokines on HIV-1 expression in U1 cells. Chronically HIV-infected U1 cells were incubated with various cytokines for 48 hours at 37°C. Culture supernatants were stored at −70°C and later assayed together for reverse transcriptase activity. (Reproduced, with permission, from Folks *et al.*[42])

was recently shown that HIV reverse transcriptase activity increases when a full-length infectious HIV clone is cotransfected with heterologous viral DNAs.[50]

In addition to mitogens, antigens, and coinfecting viruses, cells normally are exposed to a variety of physiologic cellular inductive signals, commonly referred to as cytokines. To address the question of the importance of these signals in the activation of HIV expression, we used an HIV-infected, nonproducing U1 cell clone derived from promonocyte cell line U937 (see above) that can be induced to express virus on stimulation with phorbol myristic acetate (PMA).[43] This particular cell line was chosen because of our belief that the monocyte may serve as a major reservoir of HIV infection in the body.

We initially found that exposure of U1 cells to cytokine-containing delectinized supernatants of PHA-stimulated human mononuclear cells resulted in the induction of significant reverse transcriptase activity.[42] We then exposed U1 cells to a variety of recombinant cytokines including granulocyte/macrophage-colony stimulating factor

(GM-CSF), interleukin (IL)-1 alpha, IL-1 beta, gamma-interferon (IFN-γ), and tumor necrosis factor (TNF)-alpha (FIG. 4). It was found that GM-CSF was able to induce HIV expression. Preliminary data suggest that the up-regulation of HIV expression by cytokines is due to the induction of the promoter of HIV by transactivation via a DNA binding protein (T. M. Folks, et al., manuscript in preparation).

These studies indicate that physiologic cellular inductive signals that are elaborated on stimulation of immunocompetent cells can lead to up-regulation of HIV infection in chronically infected cells. These findings are important in understanding how latent or chronic HIV infections in asymptomatic HIV carriers can be activated and develop into a profound immunodeficiency.

It was also of interest to determine if the presence of integrated HIV proviral DNA in the U1 clone would affect the induction of cellular genes. In this regard, we treated U1 cells with PHA supernatants and measured the surface expression of IL-1 beta, a membrane bound cytokine that is expressed on the surface of monocytes after cellular activation.[42] Treatment of U1 cells with PHA supernatants resulted in the up-regulation of membrane-bound IL-1 beta, whereas treatment of the uninfected parent cell line, U937, did not increase IL-1 beta expression. Because monocytes can activate T cells via IL-1 beta, enhanced expression of IL-1 beta by infected monocytes might result in an increased susceptibility of T cells to infection with HIV by inducing or maintaining their state of activation. In addition, through an autocrine function, enhanced monocyte production of IL-1 beta may enable the monocyte to remain activated and support viral replication.[51]

SUMMARY

Infection with HIV can result in a complex array of immunopathogenic effects. HIV infection involves both a direct quantitative depletion of T4 lymphocytes as well as an indirect qualitative effect on the function of several types of immune effector cells. The combination of T4-cell destruction and functional abnormalities contributes to the broad scope of immunologic aberrations and opportunistic diseases seen in HIV-infected individuals. In addition, HIV infection of monocyte/macrophages may play an important role as a reservoir or sanctuary of infection in the host and contribute to the characteristically long incubation period between HIV infection and disease. The activation of HIV from latent or chronically infected cells in vitro by mitogens, antigens, heterologous viruses, and cytokines represents a potential mechanism whereby HIV infection in individuals progresses from an asymptomatic carrier state to clinical AIDS. The release of virus from activated cells can lead to the spread of the virus to other target cells and result in both a qualitative or quantitative defect in immunocompetent cells and subsequent immunosuppression. It is also clear that HIV infection can result in the modulation of expression of certain cellular genes, thereby potentially compounding immunoregulatory abnormalities. Further knowledge of the complex relation between HIV and its target cells will be essential to our understanding of the myriad of potential pathogenic mechanisms of HIV infection and may lead to ways of interrupting the progression of HIV-induced disease.

REFERENCES

1. FAUCI, A. S. 1985. Immunological abnormalities in the acquired immunodeficiency syndrome (AIDS). Clin. Res. 32: 491–499.
2. BOWEN, D. L., H. C. LANE & A. S. FAUCI. 1985. Immunopathogenesis of the acquired immunodeficiency syndrome. Ann. Intern. Med. 103: 704–709.

3. Ho, D. D., R. J. Pomerantz & J. C. Kaplan. 1987. Pathogenesis of infection with human immunodeficiency virus. N. Engl. J. Med. **317:** 278–286.
4. Klatzmann, D., F. Barre-Sinoussi, M. T. Nugeyre, C. Dauguet, E. Vilmer, C. Griscelli, F. Vezinet-Brun, J. C. Gluckman, J.-C. Chermann & L. Montagnier. 1984. Selective tropism of lymphadenopathy associated virus (LAV) for helper-inducer T lymphocytes. Science **225:** 59–64.
5. Dalgleish, A. G., P. C. L. Beverley, P. R. Clapham, D. H. Crawford, M. F. Greaves & R. A. Weiss. 1984. The CD4 (T4) antigen is an essential component of the receptor for the AIDS virus. Nature **312:** 763–767.
6. McDougal, J. S., M. S. Kennedy, J. M. Sligh, S. P. Cort, A. Mawle & J. K. A. Nicholson. 1986. Binding of HTLV-III/LAV to T4+ T cells by a complex of the 110K viral protein and the T4 molecule. Science **231:** 382–385.
7. Maddon, P. J., A. G. Dalgleish, J. S. McDougal, P. R. Clapham, R. A. Weiss & R. Axel. 1986. The T4 gene encodes the AIDS virus receptor and is expressed in the immune system and the brain. Cell **47:** 333–348.
8. Levy, J. A., J. Shimabukuro, T. McHugh, C. Casavant, D. Stites & L. Oshiro. 1985. AIDS-associated retroviruses (ARV) can productively infect other cells besides human T helper cells. Virology **147:** 441–448.
9. Ho, D. D., T. R. Rota & M. S. Hirsch. 1986. Infection of monocyte/macrophages by human T lymphotropic virus type III. J. Clin. Invest. **77:** 1712–1715.
10. Nicholson, J. K. A., G. D. Cross, C. S. Callaway & S. J. McDougal. 1986. In vitro infection of human monocytes with human T lymphotropic virus type III/lymphadenopathy-associated virus (HTLV-III/LAV). J. Immunol. **137:** 323–329.
11. Koenig, S., H. E. Gendelman, J. M. Orenstein, M. C. Dal Canto, G. H. Pezeshkpour, M. Yungbluth, F. Janotta, A. Aksamit, M. A. Martin & A. S. Fauci. 1986. Detection of AIDS virus in macrophages in brain tissue from AIDS patients with encephalopathy. Science **233:** 1089–1093.
12. Gartner, S., P. Markovits, D. M. Markovitz, M. H. Kaplan, R. C. Gallo & M. Popovic. 1986. The role of mononuclear phagocytes in HTLV-III-/LAV infection. Science **233:** 215–219.
13. Wiley, C. A., R. D. Schrier, J. A. Nelson, P. W. Lampert & M. A. Oldstone. 1986. Cellular localization of human immunodeficiency virus infection within the brains of AIDS patients. Proc. Natl. Acad. Sci. USA **83:** 7089–7093.
14. Rabson, A. B. The molecular biology of HIV infection: Clues for possible therapy. In AIDS Pathogenesis and Treatment. J. A. Levy, Ed. Marcel Dekker, New York. In press.
15. Shaw, G. M., B. H. Hahn, S. K. Arya, J. E. Groopman, R. C. Gallo & F. Wong-Staal. 1984. Molecular characterization of human T-cell leukemia (lymphotropic) virus type III in the acquired immunodeficiency syndrome. Science **226:** 1165–1171.
16. Harper, M. E., L. M. Marselle, R. C. Gallo & F. Wong-Staal. 1986. Detection of lymphocytes expressing human T-lymphotropic virus type III in lymph nodes and peripheral blood from infected individuals by in situ hybridization. Proc. Natl. Acad. Sci. USA **83:** 772–776.
17. Laurence, J. & L. Mayer. 1984. Immunoregulatory lymphokines of T hybridomas from AIDS patients: Constitutive and inducible suppressor factors. Science **225:** 66–69.
18. Sodroski, J., W. C. Goh, C. Rosen, K. Campbell & W. A. Haseltine. 1986. Role of the HTLV-III/LAV envelope in syncytium formation and cytopathicity. Nature **322:** 470–474.
19. Lifson, J. D., G. R. Reyes, M. S. McGrath, B. S. Stein & E. G. Engleman. 1986. AIDS retrovirus induced cytopathology: Giant cell formation and involvement of CD4 antigen. Science **232:** 1123–1127.
20. Lifson, J. D., M. B. Feinberg, G. R. Reyes, L. Rabin, B. Babapour, S. Chakrabarti, B. Moss, F. Wong-Staal, K. S. Steimer & E. G. Engleman. 1986. Induction of CD4-dependent cell fusion by the HTLV-III/LAV envelope glycoprotein. Nature **323:** 725–728.
21. Yoffe, B., D. E. Lewis, B. L. Petrie, C. A. Noonan, J. L. Melnick & F. B. Hollinger. 1987. Fusion as a mediator of cytolysis in mixtures of uninfected CD4+ lymphocytes and cells infected by human immunodeficiency virus. Proc. Natl. Acad. Sci. USA **84:** 1429–1433.

22. HOXIE, J. A., J. D. ALPERS, J. L. RACKOWSKI, K. HUEBNER, B. S. HAGGARTY, A. J. CEDARBAUM & J. C. REED. 1986. Alterations in T4 (CD4) protein and mRNA synthesis in cells infected with HIV. Science **234:** 1123–1127.
23. KLATZMANN, D. & J. C. GLUCKMAN. 1986. HIV infection: Facts and hypotheses. Immunol. Today **7:** 291–296.
24. ZIEGLER, J. L. & D. P. STITES. 1986. Hypothesis: AIDS is an autoimmune disease directed at the immune system and triggered by a lymphotropic retrovirus. Clin. Immunol. Immunopathol. **41:** 305–313.
25. ASJO, B., I. IVHED, M. GIDLUND, S. FUERSTENBERG, E. M. FENYO, K. NILSSON & H. WIGZELL. 1987. Susceptibility to infection by the human immunodeficiency virus (HIV) correlates with T4 expression in a parental monocytoid cell line and its subclones. Virology **157:** 359–365.
26. DE ROSSI, A., G. FRANCHINI, A. ALDOVINI, A. DEL MISTRO, L. CHIECO-BIANCHI, R. C. GALLO & F. WONG-STAAL. 1986. Differential response to the cytopathic effects of human T-cell lymphotropic virus type III (HTLV-III) superinfection in T4+ (helper) and T8+ (suppressor) T-cell clones transformed by HTLV-1. Proc. Natl. Acad. Sci. USA **83:** 4297–4301.
27. LANE, H. C., J. M. DEPPER, W. C. GREENE, G. WHALEN, T. A. WALDMANN & A. S. FAUCI. 1985. Qualitative analysis of immune function in patients with the acquired immunodeficiency syndrome. N. Engl. J. Med. **313:** 79–84.
28. GIORGI, J. V., J. L. FAHEY, D. C. SMITH, L. E. HULTIN, H. CHENG, R. T. MITSUYASU & R. DETELS. 1987. Early effects of HIV on CD4 lymphocytes in vivo. J. Immunol. **138:** 3725–3730.
29. FAUCI, A. S. 1987. AIDS: Immunopathogenic mechanisms and research strategies. Clin. Res. **35:** 503–510.
30. MARGOLICK, J. B., D. J. VOLKMAN, T. M. FOLKS & A. S. FAUCI. 1987. Amplification of HTLV-III/LAV infection by antigen-induced activation of T cells and direct suppression by virus of lymphocyte blastogenic responses. J. Immunol. **138:** 1719–1723.
31. PAHWA, S., R. PAHWA, C. SAXINGER, R. C. GALLO & R. A. GOOD. 1985. Influence of the human T-lymphotropic virus/lymphadenopathy-associated virus on functions of human lymphocytes: Evidence of immunosuppressive effects and polyclonal B cell activation by banded viral preparations. Proc. Natl. Acad. Sci. USA **82:** 8198–8202.
32. SHALABY, M. R., J. F. KROWKA, T. J. GREGORY, S. E. HIRABAYASHI, S. M. MCCABE, D. S. KAUFMAN, D. P. STITES & A. J. AMMANN. 1987. The effects of human immunodeficiency virus recombinant envelope glycoprotein on immune cell functions in vitro. Cell. Immunol. **110:** 140–148.
33. GAY, D., P. MADDON, R. SEKALY, M. A. TALLE, M. GODFREY, E. LONG, G. GOLDSTEIN, L. CHESS, R. AXEL, J. KAPPLER & P. MARRACK. 1987. Functional interaction between human T-cell protein CD4 and the major histocompatibility complex HLA-DR antigen. Nature **328:** 626–629.
34. DOYLE, C. & J. L. STROMINGER. 1987. Interaction between CD4 and class II MHC molecules mediates cell adhesion. Nature **330:** 256–259.
35. ALCOVER, A., D. RAMARLI, N. E. RICHARDSON, H.-C. CHANG & E. L. REINHERZ. 1987. Functional and molecular aspects of human T lymphocyte activation via T3-Ti and T11 pathways. Immunol. Rev. **95:** 5–36.
36. SMITH, P. D., K. OHURA, H. MASUR, H. C. LANE, A. S. FAUCI & S. M. WAHL. 1984. Monocyte function in the acquired immune deficiency syndrome. J. Clin. Invest. **74:** 2121–2128.
37. PRINCE, H. E., D. J. MOODY, B. I. SHUBIN & J. L. FAHEY. 1985. Defective monocyte function in acquired immune deficiency syndrome (AIDS): Evidence from a monocyte-dependent T-cell proliferative system. J. Clin. Immunol. **5:** 21–25.
38. POLI, G., B. BOTTAZZI, R. ACERO, L. BERSANI, V. ROSSI, M. INTRONA, A. LAZZARIN, M. GALLI & A. MANTOVANI. 1985. Monocyte function in intravenous drug abusers with lymphadenopathy syndrome and in patients with acquired immunodeficiency syndrome: Selective impairment of chemotaxis. Clin. Exp. Immunol. **62:** 136–142.
39. GABUZDA, D. H., D. D. HO, S. M. DE LA MONTE, M. S. HIRSCH, T. R. ROTA & R. A. SOBEL. 1986. Immunohistochemical identification of HTLV-III antigen in brains of patients with AIDS. Ann. Neurol. **20:** 289–295.

40. SALAHUDDIN, S. Z., R. M. ROSE, J. E. GROOPMAN, P. D. MARKHAM & R. C. GALLO. 1986. Human T lymphotropic virus type III infection of human alveolar macrophages. Blood **68:** 281–284.

41. MURRAY, H. W., B. Y. RUBIN, H. MASUR & R. B. ROBERTS. 1984. Impaired production of lymphokines and immune (gamma) interferon in the acquired immunodeficiency syndrome. N. Engl. J. Med. **310:** 883–889.

42. FOLKS, T. M., J. JUSTEMENT, A. KINTER, C. A. DINARELLO & A. S. FAUCI. 1987. Cytokine-induced expression of HIV in a chronically infected promonocyte cell line. Science **238:** 800–802.

43. FOLKS, T. M., J. JUSTEMENT, A. KINTER, S. SCHNITTMAN, J. ORENSTEIN, G. POLI & A. S. FAUCI. 1988. Characterization of a promonocyte clone chronically infected with HIV and inducible by 13-phorbol-12-myristate acetate. J. Immunol. **140:** 1117–1122.

44. GENDELMAN, H. E., J. M. ORENSTEIN, M. A. MARTIN, C. FERRUA, R. MITRA, T. PHIPPS, L. A. WAHL, H. C. LANE, A. S. FAUCI, D. E. BURKE & M. S. MELTZER. 1988. Efficient isolation and propagation of human immunodeficiency virus on recombinant colony-stimulating factor 1-treated monocytes. J. Exp. Med. **167:** 1428–1441.

45. MCDOUGAL, J. S., A. MAWLE, S. P. CORT, J. K. A. NICHOLSON, G. D. CROSS, J. A. SCHEPPLER-CAMPBELL, D. HICKS & J. SLIGH. 1985. Cellular tropism of the human retrovirus HTLV-III/LAV. I. Role of T cell activation and expression of the T4 antigen. J. Immunol. **135:** 3151–3162.

46. FOLKS, T. M., J. KELLY, S. BENN, A. KINTER, J. JUSTEMENT, J. GOLD, R. REDFIELD, K. W. SELL & A. S. FAUCI. 1986. Susceptibility of normal human lymphocytes to infection with HTLV-III/LAV. J. Immunol. **136:** 4049–4053.

47. GENDELMAN, H. E., W. PHELPS, L. FEIGENBAUM, J. M. OSTROVE, A. ADACHI, P. M. HOWLEY, G. KHOURY, H. S. GINSBERG & M. A. MARTIN. 1986. Transactivation of the human immunodeficiency virus long terminal repeat sequence by DNA viruses. Proc. Natl. Acad. Sci. USA **83:** 9759–9763.

48. MOSCA, J. D., D. P. BEDNARIK, N. B. K. RAJ, C. A. ROSEN, J. G. SODROWSKI, W. A. HASELTINE & P. M. PITHA. 1987. Herpes simplex virus type-1 can reactivate transcription of latent human immunodeficiency virus. Nature **325:** 67–70.

49. DAVIS, M. G., S. C. KENNEY, J. KAMINE, J. S. PAGANO & E.-S. HUANG. 1987. Immediate-early gene region of human cytomegalovirus trans-activates the promotor of human immunodeficiency virus. Proc. Natl. Acad. Sci USA **84:** 8642–8646.

50. OSTROVE, J. M., J. LEONARD, K. E. WECK, A. B. RABSON & H. E. GENDELMAN. 1987. Activation of the human immunodeficiency virus by herpes simplex virus type 1. J. Virol. **61:** 3726–3732.

51. DINARELLO, C. A., T. IKEJIMA, S. J. C. WARNER, S. F. ORENCOLE, G. LONNEMANN, J. G. CANNON & P. LIBBY. Interleukin-1 induces interleukin-1. I. Induction of circulating interleukin-1 in rabbits in vivo and in human mononuclear cells in vitro. J. Immunol. In press.

Ontogeny of the Clonal Selection Theory of Antibody Formation[a]

Reflections on Darwin and Ehrlich

JOSHUA LEDERBERG

The Rockefeller University
New York, New York 10021

This is an idiosyncratically personal account of the origins, about 30 years ago, of the clonal selection theory, a no longer controversial integrating theme of immunological research. As an interested participant, the perspectives I can offer are those within my own ken, inevitably an egocentric one. This will unfortunately understate the independent roles played by a host of others, including several in these proceedings. Other historical accounts[1,2] may give a more objective view. However, some parts of my story have not been told before. It will be of particular interest to students of the philosophy and sociology of science to analyze the processes of resistance and acceptance of clonal selection theory after 1957, until its general acceptance around 1967.[3-5]

My personal mise-en-scène begins in 1955. I had been at the University of Wisconsin since 1947, having gone there directly from my work in Ed Tatum's lab at Yale and Francis Ryan's at Columbia. If I needed any reinforcement about the interest antigens and antibodies would have for general biological theory, I would have received this amply from M. R. Irwin. Ray Owen had left Wisconsin for Caltech just before I arrived, but his intellectual trace was everywhere. However, my own work was strictly confined to the genetics of *Escherichia coli* and of salmonella. The diversity of serotypes in salmonella had been one of the conceptual clues to genetic recombination in bacteria, and I had at least one experimental contact with immunology, namely, serology of flagellar and somatic antigens.[6]

The principal antecedental threads of clonal selection, at least for this microbiologist, were: (1) physicochemical concepts of serological specificity, spanning from Paul Ehrlich to Karl Landsteiner and Linus Pauling; (2) the revalidation of Darwinian models (namely, prior spontaneous mutation and natural selection) in their application to adaptation in microorganisms, such as the development of specific resistance to antibiotics; (3) an emerging understanding of gene expression in protein synthesis, particularly in substrate-induced enzyme synthesis in bacteria; and (4) a developing conception of a genetics of somatic cells by analogy with the genetics of bacteria (Mendelian models).

Karl Landsteiner's "The Specificity of Serological Reactions" focused attention on antigen-antibody reaction as a prototype of biological specificity. Pauling's chapter in the 1945 edition[7] showed how "specificity can arise in the interaction of large molecules as a result of the spatial configuration of the molecules." The seminal value of this stereochemical axiom was unfortunately not matched by well-founded speculations on the mechanism of antibody synthesis. In the early 1950s, there was notably little serious discussion of the mechanism of antibody formation. The most prevalent

[a]Dedicated to the memory of Frank Macfarlane Burnet (1899–1985) and Peter Medawar (1915–1987).

notions were those elaborated by Haurowitz,[8] that the antigen itself acted as a template on which the antibody globulin was molded. Pauling and Campbell[9] had even published experiments in 1942 claiming the synthesis of antibody *in vitro* by the renaturation of globulin in the presence of antigen. One minor variant challenged the need for the continuous presence of the antigen and supposed that an intermediate mold was generated, perhaps in many copies, from the initial antigen conformation. Another gave homage to the central role of RNA and DNA in protein synthesis, but supposed that antigen could be attached to or modify the nucleic acid in directing the course of protein synthesis. These models, which I later classified as "instructive," reflected a miscomprehension of the most basic feature of the genetic coding theory: the linear correspondence of the nucleotide sequence in the DNA/RNA to the amino sequence of a protein.[10]

My own research, starting in 1946, had made extensive use of artificial selection to discover rare recombinant or mutant genotypes in large microbial populations.[11] Francis J. Ryan introduced me to this at Columbia in an investigation on a leucine-dependent mutant of Neurospora. Placed on nutritionally deficient media, this mutant would "adapt" to that constraint on its growth. We established that this adaptation was a genetic reverse-mutation with crossing studies. We presumed that it occurred spontaneously, the deficient medium selecting for the mutants, but we could adduce no compelling evidence. Our thinking was of course influenced by Luria and Delbruck's demonstration in 1943[12] that the statistics of phage resistance in bacteria also agreed with the Darwinian paradigm. Shortly after the Neurospora experiments, a similar method of selection enabled the discovery of genetic recombination in *E. coli* K-12, which achieved a certain reinforcement to "think selection" for a variety of experimental purposes and as a pervasive strategy in natural process.

Many of the aforementioned findings went against contemporary traditions. For example, many bacteriologists still held that drug resistance was evoked by some chemical reaction of the drug with the bacterial protoplasm—a view that continued for many years to be nourished by the authority of Sir Cyril Hinshelwood, President of the Royal Society of London. Several never unraveled the difference between genetic changes in individual cells, changes in the proportion of genotypes in populations, and the reversible regulation of enzyme synthesis by inducing substrates. To others, it was congenial as a last stronghold of Lysenkoism: a direct effect of environment on hereditary traits. Francis Ryan continued to devote much of his energy to studying adaptive mutation in bacteria.[13]

The development of the replica-plating technique in 1952[14] was similarly motivated: it allowed indirect selection of resistant mutants in a fashion that assured their presence among cells that had never been exposed to the drug. As a constructive demonstration it did finally quiet that controversy. It was also a further reinforcement of "think selection."

The study of enzyme induction, and of the genetic control of B-galactosidase, was one of the first tasks I addressed with the use of genetic recombination analysis in *E. coli*. With the help of Karl Paul Link and Martin Seidman, *o*-nitrophenyl galactoside[b] became available as a chromogenic substrate for assay of the enzyme.[15] I was soon struck by the fact that "uninduced" cells, grown in the absence of galactosides, nevertheless showed an unmistakable basal level of the enzyme. Subsequently, I found that neolactose, altrose-β-D-galactoside, was a noninducing substrate that could be

___

[b]It is curious to recall that W. Goebel and O. T. Avery had synthesized nitrophenyl glycosides in 1929 as intermediates in the synthesis of artificial conjugated haptens.[17]

used to select constitutive mutants that produced full-blown levels of the enzyme without specific induction. These findings supported the view that enzyme specificity was inherent in the bacterial genome; the inducer was a quantitative regulator of gene expression.[16]

Finally, under the stimulus of conversations with G. Klein and H. Koprowski, in 1955 I started to beat the drums for a research strategy of "a genetics of somatic and tumor cells."[18,19] Bacteria had also been thought to be intractable; it seemed certain to me that mammalian cells could be made to fuse, and at least chromosome reassortment could be readily studied.

My first published thoughts about antibodies[20] were a brief statement of possible analogy to induced enzyme formation. The complexity of the animal system seemed to defeat experimental analysis. Then, in November 1955, at a symposium on Enzymes in Detroit, Jacques Monod again posed the question of whether the inducer provided the information needed to mold the enzyme. In my discussion, I responded in the negative, citing the aforementioned evidence. The role of the inducer was to regulate the expression of that genetic information, as we would now all agree. In a spectacularly unprescient fashion, my impromptu discussion went on to contrast the induction of enzymes with the antibody response:

> "The immune response has provoked a similar discussion. Ehrlich had proposed that specific antibodies were normal products, subject to quantitative variation under the influence of the antigen. Pauling and others believe that the antigen plays a direct role in molding the antibody protein. Enzymes are generally less specific than antibodies in their range of complex formation, but more so in their catalytic action. Furthermore, antibodies are constructed from a common gamma globulin, whereas enzymatic specificity can call on a more fundamental variety in structure. We need not assume, therefore, that both syntheses follow the same plan."[21]

Calling on the prevailing common wisdom, that was not my most insightful moment. The only other comment about antibody synthesis at that meeting was Pauling's reiteration of his 1940 model.

When I returned home, I found the November issue of the PNAS and therein Nils Jerne's paper on: "The Natural-Selection Theory of Antibody Formation."[22] I wrote him promptly to apologize for not having cited his paper, and to express my approbation of approaches that avoided an instructional role for the antigen. He responded that I was the only one to date to express any interest in his proposals. Felix Haurowitz had criticized him, on the one hand, for neglecting to mention Ehrlich's precedent in proposing the spontaneous formation of antibodies. On the other, it was just not possible for an animal to be preadapted to form antibodies to artificial haptenes like Landsteiner's azophenyl arsonate. Jerne responded that a million specificities randomly chosen would be far less than the "million million million" globulin molecules in the blood, the supposed targets of selection according to his model. At that point, I was sure that some Darwinian model would handle the problem of antibody formation; I was a bit skeptical of the self-replication of circulating antigen-selected globulin molecules that he was proposing. More plausible targets of selection would have been diversified protein-synthesizing units (in the cell), still bound to their antibody product. It still did not occur to me that the cell itself satisfied that criterion. In fact, not working directly in immunology, it was only at conferences that offered the stimulus of dialectic with people actively working in the field, that I would put much attention into scientific speculation. What perils meetings like this may have for the unwary!

In August 1957, however, I found myself in Macfarlane Burnet's laboratory in

Melbourne, on a trimester's Fulbright fellowship.[c] I had gone there to learn about the influenza virus, and its recombinational processes,[26] and was dismayed to hear that Mac had just closed down his research on flu; he had decided to go full blast into the mechanism of antibody synthesis. We began earnest discussions about the new wrinkle that Mac had placed on Jerne's proposal: it had to be the *cells* that varied and were subject to selection.[25] But, I expostulated, there must be far many more species of antibody than there are cells available! "Mac, how do you know that? How do you know as a matter of experimental fact that there are more than a few thousand species?" I realized instantly how I had taken for granted a spurious "fact" that had misled the entire field. (A complete history would trace the ultimate origin of that ikon, of the infinity of antibodies. Today we would use information-theoretic criteria to measure specificity, and might avoid such pitfalls.)

Our discussion became intense, although somewhat clouded by Burnet's tendency to resist the "simplistic" mechanisms of DNA-based molecular genetics that are today's foundation stone. I would receive his exciting ideas, and then have to translate them into a contemporary idiom to get the full benefit of his marvelous biological intuition.

There was also an opportunity to construct some experiments to test the hypothesis, as difficult as this was in the absence of any reliable procedure to clone antibody-forming cells. Working with Burnet was a young, audacious, postdoctoral fellow: Gus Nossal. He was more than eager to attack the theory. Could we at least study the phenotype of individual cells in animals stimulated with two or more antigens. The Pauling model made no particular exclusion; on a clonal selection model, cells making two kinds of antibodies would be vanishingly rare, barring second order complexities.

I had been doing serological microassays with motile salmonella strains, in this case to study the genetics of the flagellar antigens in single-cell pedigrees of the bacteria.[27] I suggested that we characterize the antibody released by single lymphoid cells by immobilization of the bacteria in microdroplets in paraffin oil. The feasibility of the assay was proven during the brief months I still had in Melbourne, and Nossal continued thereafter until 62 reactive cells had been tested: 33 immobilized *Salmonella adelaide,* 29 *S. typhi,* none both.[28] This was only one step toward proof of clonal selection. Propagable clones would be needed for that. The paper made a few mumbles of alternative possibilities, like an analogy to mutual exclusion of viruses. This was my first and last experimental involvement. I need hardly tell you about Nossal's further career. When I went to Stanford in 1959, I persuaded him to join me for an interval, but his roots in Australia ran very deep and he returned, eventually to succeed Burnet as director of the Hall Institute.

Returning to Wisconsin in November 1957, I had a number of other matters in mind besides antibody synthesis. Sputnik had opened up the exploration of space in ways that were dramatized by an encounter with J. B. S. Haldane in Calcutta, en route[29]; and I saw little evidence that scientific objectives were to be honored in the development of the nation's space programs. It seemed an urgent task to move the National Academy of Sciences to take leadership for this objective and to include biological questions on its agenda. What was later termed "exobiology" was initiated the spring of 1958. I also became engaged in the negotiations that would lead to my going to Stanford. But during 1958, Burnet's ideas came up on a number of occasions

[c]Burnet's memoirs[23,24] have a small factual error—he had me in Melbourne November and December, after he had published his paper on clonal selection theory[25]; in fact, it was August through October 1957. Briefly visiting Melbourne at that time was Carlton Gajdusek, just on his way to New Guinea to study kuru among the Fore—and to discover the slow viruses.

where I felt they would receive greater due after being retranslated into DNA language.[19]

When Bernard Davis invited me to give the Howard J. Mueller memorial lecture at Harvard that November, I decided to use the occasion to frame a critical reformulation of the clonal selection theory. Burnet's uncanny biological intuition was not matched by his resonance with molecular biology or a detailed familiarity with its chemical precepts. At one point he refers to himself as "positively schizophrenic about molecular biology"—his main grievance "the arrogance which defines biology as the chemistry of the nucleic acids." By 1958, I had long since consolidated the philosophical position he had repudiated. Meanwhile, David Talmage, at the University of Chicago, had reached a substantially similar posture. Quite independently of Burnet's revelation of how to read Jerne, he had published a succinct statement of the same theory of clonal selection of cells.[30] In October, I asked him if he would meet in Madison. The upshot was an exchange of manuscripts and an agreement that we would submit papers to *Science*, for publication back to back.[31,32] Meanwhile, I had still other diversions: a surprise invitation to revisit Stockholm once again (I had attended the International Congress of Microbiology in August), this time in December on Alfred Nobel's birthday. I was far too busy to prepare still another paper that would do credit to the occasion; quite literally, I was packing to move my home and my lab to Stanford, targeted for end January. But I did manage to present the Mueller lecture, and was gratified by the interested, if mostly skeptical, discussion it aroused. The talk I finally did present in Stockholm, the next May, was in a similar mood. So much had happened in the 12 years since my initial work on genetics in bacteria that I decided to devote my address[33] not primarily to my own work, but precisely to the extent to which biology had become the chemistry of the nucleic acids, as coding agents for proteins.

Our papers appeared in *Science*, June 1959. Talmage focused on experimental data, including his own important contributions, on the overlapping diversity of antibodies—an essential point in the argument that antibodies are normal globulins. Mine focused on the theoretical framework of the cell selection theory. It is reprinted here (at the end of this article), the more substantial part of this presentation. It generally followed Burnet's reasoning. One deviation was my proposal that clonal diversification was a life-long process; he would have confined that to the perinatal period as part of his model of induced tolerance.

The sharp delineation of "instructive" from "elective models" is now a matter of common understanding. Nevertheless, a reminder is needed to distinguish "elective" from "selective." Purification of a globulin preparation on an affinity column is an elective process. If it permitted replication of the elected units, it would also be selective. Likewise, inducers play an elective role in enzyme synthesis in bacteria, by derepressing the expression of preexisting genes. They are not *ipso facto* selective; substrates may be so when they encourage the differential reproduction of specified genotypes. Thus, the hypothesis analogizing immunogenesis to enzyme induction was an elective one; it did not yet embrace genotypic diversification and selection therefrom. These distinctions are important in efforts to apply these concepts to further domains such as neurobiology.

For some time, many immunologists' reaction was that they could not see what experimental basis there was to support the selection theory. This was entirely legitimate, but the alternatives to be sorted out were not always logically coherent, such as efforts to distinguish our selection theory from one based on "cellular differentiation."[34,35] Even today, to describe a phenomenon as epigenetic rather than genetic[19] is hardly to explain it. The restriction of antibody potentialities that Nossal and I had reported (no more than one antibody species per cell) came under sharp experimental attack, especially by Attardi *et al.*[36] At one point, Nossal and Makela themselves[37] found a few cells that, depending on the assay method used, seemed to be bipotent. This was not a mortal wound to selection theory: we were, after all, working with diploid cells; but I was acutely uncomfortable with the kinetics of the model needed to accommodate two sequential mutations, one on each chromosome. Of course, other compromises were available—and one has emerged as fact: substantial reduplication of genes for immunoglobulins. Without experimental necessity, I was loathe to multiply entities. But it appears as if immunobiology falls outside the domain of Occam's razor. After 1959, I did not lose interest in immunogenetics, but my medium was an administrative one: the new department of genetics at Stanford. Gus Nossal, Av Mitchison, Walter Bodmer, and Leonard Herzenberg having occupied chairs there, I could confidently direct my own experimental interests elsewhere.

Meanwhile, chemistry was marching ahead. Brenner, Jacob, and Meselson had given us the messenger RNA, and the role of DNA in protein coding began to be shaped in its contemporary form.[10] And in 1962–1964, a number of studies made it clear that the specificity of antibodies was related to their primary structure, an amino acid sequence whose determination could hardly have any other provenience than the DNA. Ollie Makela also stuck to his guns and clarified some of the methodological problems that may have given bipotent cells as artefacts[38]; Benacerraf's group also gave a strong affirmation of unipotency of cells.[39] It appears that Nossal and Lederberg were probably correct in 1958, but in view of the methodological problems, that has to be put down to sheer luck. The experiment had the undeniable virtue of providing a target of skeptical investigation more pointed than the generalities of the theory that was its background.

By the 1967 Cold Spring Harbor Symposium, the clonal selection theory was an undeniable fundament for almost every investigation of the chemistry of antibodies or the biology of immunocytes. It was also clear that further progress would depend on the propagation of antibody-forming cells as clones. We do not have a detailed intellectual biography of the precursors to Kohler and Milstein's famous experiment.[40] Some of the precedent ideas about fusing immunocytes with neoplastic cells to produce such clones have been reviewed by Bodmer.[41] In a *popular* piece I wrote in 1972: "Many products of differentiated cells, such as specific enzymes and antibodies, could become important in medicine if we could produce them in larger, predictable quantities. Cell fusion should enable scientists to increase the rate at which these substances are produced by cells in culture."[42] This remark was inspired by Henry Harris's observation that the dormant nucleus of the chick erythrocyte could be reactivated by fusion with mouse cells. Into the ears of babes . . .?

The immune response stands today as the first epigenetic phenomenon for which a chemical structural interpretation can be given. Nature often returns to the same handbook of tricks; it surely will not be the last to violate the dogma of somatic cell constancy of DNA, the apparent reversibility of cell differentiation notwithstanding.[43,44]

RETROSPECTION: THIRTY YEARS LATER

1. The greatest weakness in reference 32 is its economy of cell types. What sane person would have postulated today's menagerie in 1959?

2. The interpretation of immunological tolerance needs be far more complex, although within the same general conceptual framework as offered there.[45]

3. We would have gotten to a modern theoretical perspective as a direct yield of structural chemical studies of immunoglobulins. Doubtless, these labors get some motivational push and focus from the theoretical context. For example, I would rather

see intensive comparison of DNA sequences of selected sites in samples from differentiated tissues: muscle, neurones, fibroblasts versus gonia, than a mindless traverse of one complete genome. The latter would have told us nothing about immunogenesis.

4. Don't let conflicting and awkward "facts" stand in the way of an esthetically satisfying theory whose fundamentals are consistent with the world model and with one another! And be suspicious of "facts" that seem in the way of any coherent theory. In some measure, the uniformity of the genome among somatic cells may be one of these.

Note added in proof: The last word on the clonal selection mechanism is: TONEGAWA, S. 1988. Somatic generation of immune diversity. Prix Nobel 1987; pp. 203–227. Also appeared in In Vitro Cell. Dev. Biol. **24**(4): 253–265.

REFERENCES

1. SCHAFFNER, K. F. 1974. Logic of discovery and justification in regulatory genetics. Studies in History and Philosophy of Science **4**: 397–433; 1980. Discovery in the biomedical sciences: logic or irrational intuition? *In* Scientific Discovery: Case Studies. T. Nickles, Ed.: 171–205. D. Reidel Publ. Co., Boston, MA.
2. SILVERSTEIN, A. M. 1985. History of immunology. A history of theories of antibody formation. Cell. Immunol. **91**: 263–283.
3. ADA, G. L. & G. NOSSAL. 1987. The clonal-selection theory. Sci. Amer. **257**(2): 62–69.
4. TALMAGE, D. 1986. The acceptance and rejection of immunological concepts. Ann. Rev. Immunol. **4**: 1–11.
5. FENNER, F. 1987. Frank Macfarlane Burnet (3 September 1899–31 August 1985). Biographical Memoirs of Fellows of the Royal Society **33**: 101–162.
6. LEDERBERG, J. & P. R. EDWARDS. 1953. Serotypic recombination in Salmonella. J. Immunol. **71**: 232–240.
7. PAULING, L. 1945. Molecular structure and intermolecular forces. *In* The Specificity of Serological Reactions. K. Landsteiner, Ed.: 275–293. Harvard University Press, Cambridge, MA.
8. HAUROWITZ, F. 1960. Immunochemistry. Ann. Rev. Biochem. **29**: 609–634.
9. PAULING, L. 1940. A theory of the structure and process of formation of antibodies. J. Am. Chem. Soc. **62**: 2643–2657; PAULING, L. & D. H. CAMPBELL. 1942. The manufacture of antibodies in vitro. J. Exp. Med. **76**: 211–220.
   The history of this fiasco has been studied by Kay, L. E. 1987. Cooperative individualism and the growth of molecular biology at the California Institute of Technology, 1928–1953. Ph.D. Dissertation, Johns Hopkins University. Ann Arbor, MI. University Microfilms Intl.
10. JUDSON, H. F. 1979. The Eighth Day of Creation. Simon & Schuster. New York, NY.
11. LEDERBERG, J. 1987. Genetic recombination in bacteria: A discovery account. Ann. Rev. Genet. **21**: 23–46.
12. LURIA, S. E. & M. DELBRUCK. 1943. Mutations of bacteria from virus sensitivity to virus resistance. Genetics **28**: 491–511.
13. RAVIN, A. W. 1976. Francis Joseph Ryan (1916–1963). Genetics **84**: 1–15.
14. LEDERBERG, J. & E. M. LEDERBERG. 1952. Replica plating and indirect selection of bacterial mutants. J. Bacteriol. **63**: 399–406.
15. LEDERBERG, J. 1950. The beta-D-galactosidase of Escherichia coli, strain K-12. J. Bacteriol. **60**: 381–392.
16. LEDERBERG, J., E. M. LEDERBERG, N. D. ZINDER & E. R. LIVELY. 1951. Recombination analysis of bacterial heredity. Cold Spring Harbor Symposium on Quantitative Biology **16**: 413–443.
17. GOEBEL, W. F. & O. T. AVERY. 1929. Chemo-immunological studies on conjugated carbohydrate-proteins. I. The synthesis of *p*-aminophenol *β*-glucoside, *p*-aminophenol *β*-galactoside, and their coupling with serum globulin. J. Exp. Med. 521–531.

18. LEDERBERG, J. 1956. Prospects for the genetics of somatic and tumor cells. Ann. N. Y. Acad. Sci. 63: 662–665.
19. LEDERBERG, J. 1958. Genetic approaches to somatic cell variation: Summary comment. J. Cell. Comp. Physiol. 52(suppl. 1): 383–402.
20. LEDERBERG, J. 1948. Problems in microbial genetics. Heredity 2: 145–198.
21. LEDERBERG, J. 1956. Comments on gene-enzyme relationship. In Enzymes: Units of Biological Structure and Function. O. H. Gaebler, Ed. Ford Hospital International Symposium. Academic Press. New York, NY.
22. JERNE, N. K. 1955. The natural-selection theory of antibody formation. Proc. Natl. Acad. Sci. 41: 849–859; 1969. The natural selection theory of antibody formation; ten years later. 301–313. In Phage and the Origins of Molecular Biology. J. Cairns, G. S. Stent, & J. D. Watson, Eds. Laboratory of Quantitative Biology, Cold Spring Harbor.
23. BURNET, F. M. 1967. The impact of ideas on immunology. Cold Spring Harbor Symposium on Quantitative Biology 32: 1–8.
24. BURNET, F. M. 1969. Changing Patterns: An Atypical Autobiography. American Elsevier, New York, NY.
25. BURNET, F. M. 1957–58. A modification of Jerne's theory of antibody production, using the concept of clonal selection. Aust. J. Sci. 20: 67–69.
26. BURNET, F. M. & P. E. LIND. 1953. Influenza virus recombination: Experiments using the de-embryonated egg technique. Cold Spring Harbor Symposium on Quantitative Biology 18: 21–24.
27. LEDERBERG, J. 1956. Linear inheritance in transductional clones. Genetics 41: 845–871.
28. NOSSAL, G. J. V. & J. LEDERBERG. 1958. Antibody production by single cells. Nature 181: 1419–1420.
29. LEDERBERG, J. 1987. Sputnik +30. J. Genet. 66: 217–220.
30. TALMAGE, D. W. 1957. Allergy and immunology. Ann. Rev. Med. 8: 239–256.
31. TALMAGE, D. W. 1959. Immunological specificity. Unique combinations of selected natural globulins provide an alternative to the classical concept. Science 129: 1643–1648.
32. LEDERBERG, J. 1959. Genes and antibodies. Science 129: 1649–1653.
33. LEDERBERG, J. 1959. A view of genetics. Les Prix Nobel en 1958. 170–189.
34. MEDAWAR, P. B. 1960. Theories of immunological tolerance. In Cellular Aspects of Immunity. Ciba Foundation Symposium 134–149. J. A. Churchill Ltd., London.
35. MEDAWAR, P. B. 1961. Immunological tolerance. Les Prix Nobel en 1960. 125–134.
36. ATTARDI, G., M. COHN, K. HORIBATA & E. S. LENNOX. 1964. Antibody formation by rabbit lymph node cells, I, II, and III. J. Immunol. 92: 335–371.
37. NOSSEL, G. J. & O. MAKELA. 1962. Kinetic studies on the incidence of cells appearing to form two antibodies. J. Immunol. 88: 604–612.
38. MAKELA, O. 1967. The specificities of antibodies produced by single cells. Cold Spring Harbor Symposium Quantitative Biology 32: 423–430; MAKELA, O. & A. M. CROSS. 1970. The diversity and specialization of immunocytes. Progr. Allergy 14: 145–207.
39. GREEN, I., P. VASSALLI, V. NUSSENZWEIG & B. BENACERRAF. 1967. Specificity of the antibodies produced by single cells following immunization with antigens bearing two types of antigenic determinants. J. Exp. Med. 125: 511–536.
40. KOHLER, G. & C. MILSTEIN. 1975. Continuous cultures of fused cells secreting antibody of predefined specificity. Nature 256: 495.
41. BODMER, W. 1982. Monoclonal antibodies: Their role in human genetics. Sixth International Congress of Human Genetics, 1981. Bonne-Tamir, B., Ed.: 125–140. Part A. Human Genetics: The Unfolding Genome. Alan R. Liss, NY.
42. LEDERBERG, J. 1972. Cell fusion and the new genetics. In 1972 Science Year of the World Book Encyclopedia.: 191–203.
43. BORST, P. & D. R. GREAVES. 1987. Programmed gene rearrangements altering gene expression. Science 235: 658–667.
44. LEDERBERG, J. & T. IINO. 1956. Phase variation in Salmonella. Genetics 41: 743–757.
45. NOSSAL, G. J. 1987. How tolerance is generated. Ciba Foundation Symposium 129: 59–72.

The following article is reprinted from *Science,* June 19, 1959, vol. 129, pages 1649–1653. Copyright 1959 by the AAAS.

CURRENT PROBLEMS IN RESEARCH

Genes and Antibodies

Do antigens bear instructions for antibody specificity
or do they select cell lines that arise by mutation?

Joshua Lederberg

An antibody is a specific globulin which appears in the serum of an animal after the introduction of a foreign substance, an antigen (*1*). Each of the many globulins is specified by its reaction with a particular antigen (*2*). Our present concern is to formulate a plausible mechanism for the role of the antigen in evoking large amounts of a specific complementary globulin. An important element of any theory of antibody formation is its interpretation of self-recognition, the means by which an organism discriminates its own constituents from the foreign substances which are valid stimuli of the immune response.

Recent speculation about antibody formation (*3–8*) has been dominated by instructive theories which suppose that the antigen conveys the instructions for the specificity of the globulin synthesized under its governance. Elective theories date from Ehrlich (*9*) and have been revived principally by Jerne (*10*), Talmage (*2, 11*), and Burnet (*12*). These postulate that the information required to synthesize a given antibody is already inherent in the organism before the antigenic stimulus is received, and the stimulus then functions to stimulate that mechanism electively. Jerne had proposed an elective transport of antibody-forming templates to functioning sites; Talmage and Burnet have explicitly proposed an elective function based on cellular selection. The details which distinguish the various proposals are pointed out in the following discussion.

Immunology does not suffer from a lack of experimental data, but still some of the most elementary questions are

The author is professor of genetics at the Stanford University Medical School, Stanford, Calif. This paper was delivered as the second J. Howard Mueller memorial lecture at Harvard Medical School, 13 Nov. 1958.

undecided, and it is not yet possible to choose between instructive and elective theories. However, the latter have had so little expression in the past few decades that a detailed exposition may serve a useful function, if only as a target for experimental attack. This article is an attempt to formulate an elective theory on the basis of genetic doctrines developed in studies of microbial populations.

Of the nine propositions given here, only number 5 is central to the elective theory. The first four are special postulates chosen as an extreme but self-consistent set; however, they might well be subject to denial or modification without impairing the validity of the elective approach. The last four propositions are stated to account for the general features of antibody formation in cellular terms and may be equally applicable to instructive and elective theories. If this theory can be defended, and I know of no fatal refutation of it, then clearly elective theories of antibody formation perhaps less doctrinaire in detail should have a place in further experimental design, each proposition being evaluated on its own merits. I am particularly indebted to Burnet (*13*) for this formulation, but Burnet should not be held responsible for some elaborations on his original proposal, especially in propositions 1 through 4. A connected statement of the nine propositions is given in Table 1, and each one is discussed in detail in the following sections.

Antibody Globulin

A1. *The stereospecific segment of each antibody globulin is determined by a unique sequence of amino acids.*

This assertion contradicts the more popular notion, and the usual basis of instructive hypotheses, of a uniform se-

quence subject to differential folding. The chemical evidence is far from decisive. For example, Karush (*14*) rejects this proposition not on analytical evidence but on the cogent argument that miscellaneous antigenic compounds can scarcely convey instructions for sequence. But if instructive-sequence is implausible, this perhaps argues against instruction rather than differential sequence. Karush has also demonstrated the remarkable stability of antibody through cycles of exposure to denaturing concentrations of urea. He attributes the structural continuity to stabilizing disulfide linkages, but determinant amino acid sequences may also be involved.

Elective antibody formation is of course equally compatible with sequence or folding. In such a theory, the mechanism of assembly does not have to be specified, so long as the product (the prospective antibody) recognizes—that is, reacts with—the antigen. Differential sequence is proposed (i) to stress the ambiguity of present evidence and (ii) as being more closely analogous to current conceptions of genically controlled specificity of other proteins (*15*).

The direct analysis of antibody structure by physicochemical methods has been equivocal. The fractionation of globulins by partition chromatography (*16*) might be interpreted as differential exposure of phenolic, amino, and carboxyl groups rather than differences in essential composition. Characterization of amino acid composition has given sharply different results with rabbit globulins, on the one hand, and equine and human globulins, on the other. Rabbit globulins, including various antibodies, apparently have a uniform N-terminal sequence, so far identified for five residues as (*17*):

Alanine-leucine-valine-aspartic-glutamyl

Various antibodies were, furthermore, indistinguishable in over-all composition (*18*). Any chemical differences would then have to attach to a central, differential segment. This possibility is made more tangible by Porter's recent finding (*19*) that rabbit antibody globulin could be split by crystalline papain into three fragments. One of these was crystallizable (and presumably homogeneous), devoid of *antibody* activity, but equivalent as an *antigen* to the intact globulin. The remaining fractions were more heterogeneous and retained the antigen-combining specificity of the intact antibody. As these fractions may well correspond to the differential segments, their

Table 1. Nine propositions.

A1. The stereospecific segment of each antibody globulin is determined by a unique sequence of amino acids.
A2. The cell making a given antibody has a correspondingly unique sequence of nucleotides in a segment of its chromosomal DNA: its "gene for globulin synthesis."
A3. The genic diversity of the precursors of antibody-forming cells arises from a high rate of spontaneous mutation during their lifelong proliferation.
A4. This hypermutability consists of the random assembly of the DNA of the globulin gene during certain stages of cellular proliferation.
A5. Each cell, as it begins to mature, spontaneously produces small amounts of the antibody corresponding to its own genotype.
A6. The immature antibody-forming cell is hypersensitive to an antigen-antibody combination: it will be suppressed if it encounters the homologous antigen at this time.
A7. The mature antibody-forming cell is reactive to an antigen-antibody combination: it will be stimulated if it first encounters the homologous antigen at this time. The stimulation comprises the acceleration of protein synthesis and the cytological maturation which mark a "plasma cell."
A8. Mature cells proliferate extensively under antigenic stimulation but are genetically stable and therefore generate large clones genotypically preadapted to produce the homologous antibody.
A9. These clones tend to persist after the disappearance of the antigen, retaining their capacity to react promptly to its later reintroduction.

ing either the original or a copy of the antigenic message. On the other hand, a powerful elective theory is generated by substituting the term *microsomal RNA* for the terms *chromosomal DNA* and *gene* in the various propositions. Since a single cell may have millions of microsomes, this theory would allow for any imaginable multiplicity of antibody-forming information in a single cell. If the potential variety of this information approaches that of the total antibody response, further instructions in an antigenic input would become moot. In addition, the complexities of selection of cellular populations would be compounded by those of microsomal populations within each cell. These degrees of freedom which blur the distinction between microsomal instruction and election favor the utility of the chromosomal hypothesis as a more accessible target for experimental attack.

further immunological and chemical analysis will be of extraordinary interest.

In contrast to the uniformity of rabbit globulins, normal and antibody globulins of horse serum proved to be grossly heterogeneous but equally so, a wide variety of N-terminal groups being found in all preparations (20). This merely confirms the concept of the plurality of antibodies evoked by a given antigen, which have in common only the general properties of normal gamma globulins and the capacity of reacting with the evoking antigen. The globulins of man, and in particular the characteristic globulins produced by different patients suffering from multiple myeloma, are likewise recognizably different, inter se, in amino acid composition (21).

Gene for Globulin Synthesis

A2. The cell making a given antibody has a correspondingly unique sequence of nucleotides in a segment of its chromosomal DNA: its "gene for globulin synthesis."

This postulate follows plausibly from proposition A1, and would trace antibody-forming specificity to the same source as is imputed to other specific proteins. As the most deterministic of genetic hypotheses, it should be the most vulnerable to experimental test. For example, a single diploid cell should be capable of *at most* two potentialities for antibody formation, one for each chromosome.

In tests of single antibody-forming

cells from rats *simultaneously* immunized against two *Salmonella* serotypes, Nossal and I (22) could find only monospecific cells producing one or the other antiflagellin. Coons (23) and White (24) have reached a similar conclusion in applications of fluorescent labeling technique. However, Cohn and Lennox (25) have convincing evidence for some bispecific antibody-forming cells in rabbits *serially* immunized against two bacteriophages. Experiments pertinent to the possibility of a single cell's carrying more than two antibody-forming specificities remain to be done (26).

The chromosomal localization of antibody-forming specificity is uncoupled from its elective origin in proposals (7, 8, 27) that an antigen induces a mutation in a gene for globulin synthesis, though not necessarily involving a new nucleotide sequence.

Multiple specificity would stand against a simple chromosomal basis for antibody formation (28), leaving two alternative possibilities: (i) replicate chromosomal genes or (ii) extrachromosomal particles such as microsomes. These might best be disentangled by some technique of genetic recombination.

The differentiation of microsomes must be implicit in any current statement of a theory of antibody formation that recognizes their central role in protein synthesis. The main issue is whether or not their specificity is dependent on that of the chromosomal DNA. Autonomy of microsomes, in contradiction to proposition A2, is implicit in most instructive theories, the microsome carry-

Genic Diversity of Precursor Cells

A3. The genic diversity of the precursors of antibody-forming cells arises from a high rate of spontaneous mutation during their lifelong proliferation.

Three elements of this statement should be emphasized: (i) that antibody-forming cells are specialized, (ii) that their diversity arises from some random process, and (iii) that the diversification of these cells continues, in company with their proliferation, throughout the life of the animal.

Item (i) and its justification by various experiments have already been discussed as an aspect of proposition A2. Talmage (2) also stresses the specialization of antibody-forming cells by referring to their progressive *differentiation*. This is entirely consistent with propositions A3 and A4, which then postulate a specific mechanism of cellular differentiation, in this case, gene mutation. If, on Talmage's model, fully differentiated cells are ultimately left with no more than one antibody-forming specificity per chromosome, the general consequences will be the same whether this final state represents the unique activation of one among innumerable chromosomal loci (see 27) or the evolution of one among innumerable specific alleles at a given locus. Once again, the final resort for decision may have to be a recombinational technique.

If the discrepancy between the experiments of Nossal and Lederberg (22) and those of Cohn and Lennox (25), as discussed under proposition A2, is real and depends on the timing of immunization, it may furnish strong support for (ii), the random origin of antibody-forming specificity. If antibody-forming cells can have two (or any small number of) specificities randomly derived, only a negligible proportion will have just the two being tested for. This would correspond to the case of simultaneous immunization with the two test antigens. If, however, a population of cells carrying one specificity is selected for, followed by selection for a second specificity among all available cells, this is the case of serial immunization and is precisely the method one would predict to obtain a clone "heterozygous" for two mutant alleles. Simultaneous versus serial immunization would be analogous to the suppression versus selection of bacterial mutants resistant to two antibiotics (29). Further experiments are needed to exclude more trivial reasons for the scarcity of bispecific antiflagellin-forming cells.

Item (iii) diverges from Burnet's proposal that the "randomization" of antibody-forming cells is confined to *perinatal* life, thereby generating a set of then stable clones corresponding to the antibody-forming potentiality of the animal. These clones would then be irreplaceable if lost either by random drift or as a consequence of premature exposure to the corresponding antigen. The arguments against Burnet's proposal are by no means decisive; however, the correspondence between cells and antibodies is made more difficult by having to maintain each clone at a sufficient population size to compensate for loss by random drift. Further, the recurrence of antibody-forming specificity is supported by experiments showing the decay of immune tolerance in the absence of the corresponding antigen (30; see comment on proposition A6). Since immune reactivity in these experiments may return during adult life, susceptibility to the induction and maintenance of tolerance by the timely introduction of the antigen may have only a coincidental relationship to the immunological incompetence of the newborn animal.

Hypermutability

A4. *This hypermutability consists of the random assembly of the DNA of the "globulin gene" during certain stages of cellular proliferation.*

This *ad hoc* proposal is doubtless the least defensible of the propositions, and certainly the furthest removed from experimental observation. It is stated to illustrate that accurate replication rather than mutability is the more remarkable phenomenon, whatever the detailed mechanism for the variation. If, as has been suggested, many nucleotide triplets are *nonsensical* (31), the triplets rather than single nucleotides would have to be posed as the unit of assembly in this case.

To carry this speculation one step further, *heterochromatin* has been proposed to be, on the one hand, a random sequence, and, on the other hand, a dissynchronously assembled segment of the genome (32). If both views are correct, proposition A4 might be restated: "the globulin gene is heterochromatic during certain stages of cellular proliferation" (becoming by implication, euchromatic in the mature stages of propositions A8 and A9).

For the theory of microsomal election it might be postulated that globulinogenic microsomes are initially fabricated as faulty replicas of the globulin gene, but are then capable of exact, autonomous replication.

Pending more exact knowledge and agreement of opinion on the morphogenetic relationships of antibody-forming cells, the term *certain stages* cannot be improved upon. On the other hand, as is shown under proposition A8, a model might be constructed even on the basis of a constant but high mutation rate of all antibody-forming cells.

Further insight into the mechanism of cellular diversity in antibody formation may be won by studies on the genetic control of reactivity to various antigens in inbred animals (33); two cautions, however, must be stated: (i) for effects on the transport of particles of different size, and (ii) for effects from cross-reactions with gene-controlled constituents evoking autotolerance.

Spontaneous Production of Antibody

A5. *Each cell, as it begins to mature, spontaneously produces small amounts of the antibody corresponding to its own genotype.*

Note the implication that antibody is formed prior to the introduction of the antigen into the antibody-forming cell. The function of spontaneous antibody is to mark those cells preadapted to react with a given antigen, either to suppress these cells for the induction of immune tolerance (proposition A6) or to excite them to massive antibody formation (proposition A7). Therefore, the antigen need participate in no type of specific reaction with cell constituents other than antibody itself, the one type of reaction available to chemically diverse antigens that requires no further special pleading. There is no agreement whether the reactive globulins found in the serum of untreated animals are produced spontaneously or by casual exposure to cross-reacting antigens (see 2). Accordingly, the spontaneous antibody postulated in proposition A5 may or may not be produced in the quantity and form needed for it to be liberated and detected in the serum. The nonspecific fragment of antibody-globulin described by Porter raises the possibility that the same *determinant* segment may be coupled either to a diffusible or to a cell-bound residue, the latter corresponding to various aspects of cellular immunity, including the suppression or excitation of antibody-forming cells by reactions with the corresponding antigen.

Induction of Immune Tolerance

A6. *The immature antibody-forming cell is hypersensitive to an antigen-antibody combination: it will be suppressed if it encounters the homologous antigen at this time.*

This is the first of four propositions which bear less on the source of antibody-forming specificity than on its subsequent expression in terms of cellular behavior. These propositions are therefore equally applicable to instructive theories.

The duality of reactions of antigens with antibody-forming cells is simply a restatement of the experimental observations of tolerance versus immunity (34). It seems plain that every cell of the antibody-forming system must be marked to inhibit its reactivity both to the autologous antigens of the same animal and extraneous antigens introduced and maintained from a suitably early time of development. In the light of current evidence for the persistence of antigenic molecules (5, 6) and for the loss of tolerance when a given antigen has dissipated (30) there are no more plausible candidates for the self-markers then the antigens themselves. The distinction between the function of an antigen as inhibitor (self-marker) or as inducer of antibody formation is then the time when the antigen is introduced into the potential antibody forming cell. We may profitably define maturity in terms of the progression of the cell from sensitivity towards reactivity.

The suppression of this process of maturation is a sufficient attribute to account for tolerance, and this need not involve so drastic an event as the destruction of the cell. However, the elective hypothesis proposes that only a limited number of cells will spontaneously react with a given antigen, so that their destruction by premature reaction can safely be invoked as the means of their suppression. It may be hoped that presently documented phenomena of cellular hypersensitivity may furnish a precedent for cellular destruction by such reactions. The cytotoxicity of the antigen to hypersensitive cells is still controversial even in the historical case of tuberculin sensitivity (35). However, the destruction of invading lymphocytes of the host in the course of rejection of a sensitizing homograft (36) supports the speculation of some role of cellular destruction of immature antibody-forming cells in the induction of tolerance.

The nature of immaturity remains open to question. It might reflect the morphogenetic status of the antibody-forming cell—for example, sensitive lymphocyte → reactive plasma cell (37), some particular composition of immature sensitizing antibody, or merely a very low level of antibody so that complexes are formed in which antigen is in excess.

Finally, one additional hint of an implication of hypersensitivity in the early stages of the antibody response: the transient skin sensitivity of delayed type (and transferable by cells) appearing in the course of immunization, as observed by several workers (38). If these skin reactions reflect the destruction of some antibody-forming cells, it would speak for some overlapping or reversibility of the two stages of maturation.

The implications of proposition A6 in the elective theory may be summarized as follows: If an antigen is introduced prior to the maturation of any antibody-forming cell, the hypersensitivity of such cells, while still immature, to an antigen-antibody reaction will eliminate specific cell types as they arise by mutation, thereby inducing apparent tolerance to that antigen. After the dissipation of the antigen, reactivity should return as soon as one new mutant cell has arisen and matured. As a further hopeful prediction, it should be possible to induce tolerance in clones of antibody-forming cells from adult animals by exposing a sufficiently small number of initials to a given antigen.

Excitation of Massive Antibody Formation

A7. *The mature antibody-forming cell is reactive to an antigen-antibody combination: it will be stimulated if it first encounters the homologous antigen at this time. The stimulation comprises an acceleration of protein synthesis and the cytological maturation which mark a "plasma cell."*

These principles of the cellular response to *secondary* antigenic stimulation are widely accepted and are readily transposed to the *primary* response on the elective hypothesis whereby some cells have spontaneously initiated antibody formation according to proposition A5.

Proliferation of Mature Cells

A8. *Mature cells proliferate extensively under antigenic stimulation but are genetically stable and therefore generate large clones genotypically preadapted to produce the homologous antibody.*

This proposition takes explicit account of the secondary response, the magnitude of which is a measure of the increase in number of reactive cells (26). However, the antigen *need* play no direct part in the stabilization of antibody-forming genotype which might accompany the determinate maturation of the cell whether or not it is stimulated. In fact, it may be suggested to dispense with the postulate that mature cells are less mutable by adopting a mutation rate which is an effective compromise: to furnish a variety of genotypes for the primary response while selected genotypes may still expand for the secondary response. For example, by mutation of one daughter chromosome per ten cell divisions, on the average, after ten generations about 600 chromosomes of the same type would have been produced, together with 100 new genotypes distributed among the other 400 or so cells. Selection must then compensate for the mutational drift if a given clone is to be maintained.

Persistence of Clones

A9. *These clones tend to persist after the disappearance of the antigen, retaining their capacity to react promptly to its later reintroduction.*

This is a restatement of the possibly controversial phenomenon of lifelong

immunity to viruses (4, 5). A substantial reservoir of immunological memory should be inherent from one cycle of expansion of a given clone. Its ultimate decay might be mitigated either by continued selection (that is, persistence of the antigen) stabilization of genotypes, or dormancy (to cell division or remutation, or both) on the part of a fraction of the clone.

Discussion

Each element of the theory just presented has some precedent in biological fact, but this is testimony of plausibility, not reality. As has already been pointed out, the most questionable proposition is A4, and it may be needlessly fanciful to forward a too explicit hypothesis of mutability for antibody formation when so little is known of its material basis anywhere.

Theories of antibody formation have, in the past, been deeply influenced by the physiology of inducible enzyme synthesis in bacteria. In particular, instructive theories for the role of the substrate in enzyme induction have encouraged the same speculation about antibody formation. This interpretation of enzyme induction, however, is weakened by the preadaptive occurrence of the enzymes, at a lower level, in uninduced bacteria (39).

One of the most attractive features of the elective theory is that it proposes no novel reactions: the only ones invoked here are (i) mutability of DNA; (ii) the role of DNA, presumably through RNA, as a code for amino acid sequence and (iii) the reaction between antibody and antigen, already known to have weighty consequences for cells in its proximity. The conceptual picture of enzyme induction would be equally simplified if the enzyme itself were the substrate-receptor. Clearly, susceptibility to enzymic action is not a necessary condition for a compound to be an inducer —for example, neolactose and thiomethylgalactoside for the β-D-galactosidase of *Escherichia coli* (39, 40), but formation of complexes with the enzyme may be. The picture is somewhat complicated by the intervention of specific transport systems for bringing the substrate into the cell (40).

Antibody formation is the one form of cellular differentiation which inherently requires the utmost plasticity, a problem for which the hypermutability of a patch of DNA may be a specially evolved solution. Other aspects of differentiation may be more explicitly canalized under genotypic control. Nucleotide substitution might still play a role here by modifying the level of activity rather than the specificity of neighboring loci, and elective recognition of transient states spontaneously derived then remains as a formal, if farfetched, possibility for other morphogenetic inductions.

References and Notes

1. This definition excludes antibody-like substances such as the hemagglutinins found in normal human sera. These reagents do not, however, pose the problem of the mechanism of specific response which is the burden of this discussion.
2. Talmage, in this issue of *Science*, discusses various aspects of antibody specificity, including the number of antibodies, which may be exaggerated in current immunological thought. For the present discussion, however, this number is left open for experimental determination, for it would embarrass a theory of cellular selection only if it is large compared with the number of potential antibody-forming cells in the organism. To anticipate proposition A1, as few as five determinant amino acids would allow for $20^5 = 3,200,000$ types of antibody.
3. L. Pauling, *J. Am. Chem. Soc.* 62, 2640 (1940).
4. F. M. Burnet and F. Fenner, *Heredity* 2, 289 (1948).
5. F. Haurowitz, *Biol. Revs. Cambridge Phil. Soc.* 27, 247 (1952).
6. D. H. Campbell, *Blood* 12, 589 (1957).
7. A. H. Coons, *J. Cellular Comp. Physiol.* 52, Suppl. 1, 55 (1958).
8. R. S. Schweet and R. D. Owen, *ibid.* 50, Suppl. 1, 199 (1957).
9. P. Ehrlich, *Studies in Immunity* (Wiley, New York, 1910).
10. N. K. Jerne, *Proc. Natl. Acad. Sci. U.S.* 41, 849 (1955).
11. D. W. Talmage, *Ann. Rev. Med.* 8, 239 (1957).
12. F. M Burnet, *Australian J. Sci.* 20, 67 (1957).
13. I am also indebted to the Fulbright Educational Exchange Program for furnishing the opportunity of visiting Burnet's laboratory in Melbourne.
14. F. Karush, in *Serological and Biochemical Comparisons of Proteins*, W. H. Cole, Ed. (Rutgers Univ. Press, New Brunswick, N.J., 1958), chap. 3.
15. V. M. Ingram, *Scientific American* 198, No. 1, 68 (1958).
16. R. R. Porter, *Biochem. J.* 59, 405 (1955).
17. ———, *ibid.* 46, 473 (1950); M. L. McFadden and E. L. Smith, *J. Biol. Chem.* 214, 185 (1955).
18. E. L. Smith, M. L. McFadden, A. Stockell, V. Buettner-Janusch, *J. Biol. Chem.* 214, 197 (1955).
19. R. R. Porter, *Nature* 182, 670 (1958).
20. M. L. McFadden and E. L. Smith, *J. Biol. Chem.* 216, 621 (1955).
21. E. L. Smith, D. M. Brown, M. L. McFadden, V. Buettner-Janusch, B. V. Jager, *ibid.* 216, 601 (1955); F. W. Putnam, *Science* 122, 275 (1955).
22. G. J. V. Nossal and J. Lederberg, *Nature* 181, 1419 (1958); G. J. V. Nossal, *Brit. J. Exptl. Pathol.* 39, 544 (1958).
23. A. H. Coons, *J. Cellular Comp. Physiol.* 50, Suppl. 1, 242 (1957).
24. R. G. White, *Nature* 182, 1383 (1958).
25. M. Cohn and E. S. Lennox, private communication.
26. An indirect measure of polyspecificity would be the total number of antibodies multiplied by the proportion of competent cells *initially* recruited to yield a particular species. Coons (7) has not attempted to count the antibody-forming cells in primary response, but his statements are compatible with an incidence of 10^{-5} to 10^{-8} of cells forming antialbumin in lymph nodes 4 days after inoculation. Nossal (*Brit. J. Exptl. Pathol.*, in press) found about 2 percent of yielding cells in a primary response after 7 days. These figures are subject to an unknown correction for the extent of proliferation in the interval after inoculation. They perhaps also raise the question whether all the yielding cells are indigenous to the lymph node, or whether circulating cells of appropriate type can be filtered by a node which locally administered antigen has accumulated.
27. J. Schultz, *Science* 129, 937 (1959). Schultz makes an analogy between antibody formation and serotype determination in *Paramecium*, stressing the role of cytoplasmic feedback mechanisms in the *maintenance* of specificity.
28. A diploid cell should be heterozygous for at most two alleles at one locus, but strictly speaking, this is a restriction of genotype, not phenotype. A cell whose proximate ancestors had mutated through a series of different states might carry a phenotypic residue of information no longer represented in its reduction clones: B. A. D. Stocker, *J. Gen. Microbiol.* 15, 575 (1956); J. Lederberg, *Genetics* 41, 845 (1956)]. Pending tests on clones from single cells, bi- or polyspecificity of antibody-forming phenotype remains subject to this qualification.
29. V. Bryson and M. Demerec, *Am. J. Med.* 18, 723 (1955).
30. C. H. Tempelis, H. R. Wolfe, A. Mueller, *Brit. J. Exptl. Pathol.* 39, 323 (1958); R. T. Smith and R. A. Bridges, *J. Exptl. Med.* 108, 227 (1958); P. B. Medawar and M. F. A. Woodruff, *Immunology* 1, 27 (1958); G. J. V. Nossal, *Nature* 180, 1427 (1957).
31. F. H. C. Crick, J. S. Griffith, L. E. Orgel, *Proc. Natl. Acad. Sci. U.S.* 43, 416 (1957).
32. C. D. Darlington and K. Mather, *Nature* 149, 66 (1942); J. Schultz, *Cold Spring Harbor Symposia Quant. Biol.* 12, 179 (1947); A. Ficq and C. Pavan, *Nature* 180, 983 (1957).
33. J. H. Sang and W. R. Sobey, *J. Immunol.* 72, 52 (1954); M. A. Fink and V. A. Quinn, *ibid.* 70, 61 (1953).
34. M. Cohn, *Ann. N.Y. Acad. Sci.* 64, 859 (1957).
35. C. B. Favour, *Intern. Arch. Allergy* 10, 193 (1957); B. H. Waksman and M. Matoltsy, *J. Immunol.* 81, 220 (1958).
36. J. M. Weaver, G. H. Algire, R. T. Prehn, *J. Natl. Cancer Inst.* 15, 1737 (1955).
37. J. W. Rebuck, R. W. Monto, E. A. Monaghan, J. M. Riddle, *Ann. N.Y. Acad. Sci.* 73, 8 (1958).
38. L. Dienes and T. B. Mallory, *Am. J. Pathol.* 8, 689 (1932); M. Tremaine, *J. Immunol.* 79, 467 (1957); J. W. Uhr, S. B. Salvin, A. M. Pappenheimer, Jr., *J. Exptl. Med.* 105, 11 (1957); S. Raffel and J. M. Newel, *ibid.* 108, 823 (1958).
39. J. Lederberg, in *Enzymes: Units of Biological Structure and Function*, O. H. Gaebler, Ed. (Academic Press, New York, 1956), p. 161. A feeble attempt in this paper to homologize antibody formation with elective enzyme induction was hindered by an uncritical rejection of proposition A1 and by the want of a tangible cellular model such as Burnet and Talmage have since furnished.
40. J. Monod, *ibid.*, p. 7.

Somatic Diversification of Anti-DNA Antibodies

SAMUEL M. BEHAR AND MATTHEW D. SCHARFF

Albert Einstein College of Medicine
Bronx, New York 10461

We chose to study autoantibodies encoded by the $V_H S107$ family because we had previously shown *in vitro* that somatic mutation of the S107 $V_H 1$ germline gene can convert a protective antibody that binds phosphorylcholine (PC) on bacterial cell walls into an autoantibody that binds dsDNA. The $V_H S107$ family is known to encode anti-DNA antibodies in both MRL/lpr and NZB × NZW F1 (NZBWF1) autoimmune mice, and some human anti-DNA antibodies appear to be encoded by $V_H 26$, the human homolog of $V_H S107$. To definitively demonstrate somatic diversification of anti-DNA antibodies, the rearranged and expressed variable region gene must be compared to its germline sequence from the relevant stain of mouse. The $V_H S107$ family lends itself to this type of analysis, because it consists of only four germline genes and has been well characterized in BALB/c and C57BL/10 mice.

We generated hybridomas from NZBWF1 autoimmune mice that had been immunized with PC-KLH. These monoclonal anti-dsDNA antibodies bind dsDNA in a solid phase ELISA and may be inhibited from binding to a DNA-coated plate by dsDNA, demonstrating that it is truly binding dsDNA. These antibodies bind PC-BSA poorly, if at all.

The sequencing of five NZBWF1 anti-dsDNA antibodies encoded by the $V_H S107$ family, and the cloning of the germline genes of this heavy chain variable region family from both parental strains of mice have allowed us to demonstrate conclusively the somatic diversification of autoantibodies. It was determined that the relevant germline gene for the five anti-dsDNA antibodies is $V_H 11$. The $V_H 11$ germline gene was cloned from both NZB and NZW mice, and the coding and immediate flanking sequence is identical in the two strains of mice. The five anti-dsDNA antibodies are similar in that they all use the same $V_H D J_H$ combination with identical N sequences and junctional diversity. There is extensive somatic hypermutation in the heavy chain variable region (6–16 changes). A single V_K gene appears to be used in all five hybridomas, and it is 87% homologous with the V_K of S107B, an unusual light chain first identified in the S107 myeloma cell line. The light chains all use the $V_K J_K$ combination, and there are multiple mutations when compared to a consensus sequence derived from nine hybridomas. Although these monoclonal antibodies appear to be derived from a single B-cell precursor, it has been impossible to construct a satisfactory genealogy using shared base changes, and Southern analysis of the nonproductive rearrangements has not yet clarified the situation. One criterion of antigen selection for antibodies is the ratio of the number of DNA substitutions producing amino acid replacement (R) versus the number of silent (S) mutations (R/S ratio). A ratio of greater than 2.9 (expected for random mutation) indicates positive selection such as the selective amplification of higher affinity antibodies. Such an analysis of NZBWF1 anti-DNA antibodies shows that antigen selection may be acting on the light chain, although the high R/S ratio in the framework (FW) regions suggests that other interactions, possibly involving an idiotypic network, are involved. Two questions remain unanswered: (1) Is somatic mutation required for these antibodies to bind DNA, and (2) what is the role of PC in the production of anti-dsDNA antibodies encoded by $V_H 11$?

Inhibition of IFN-γ-Induced Transcriptional Activation of HLA-DRα by Cycloheximide

M. A. BLANAR, E. C. BÖTTGER, AND R. A. FLAVELL

Biogen Research Corporation
Cambridge, Massachusetts 02142

The human major histocompatibility (MHC) class II complex consists of three class II antigens: HLA-DR, DP, and DQ. These molecules are expressed primarily in cells of lymphoid lineage, namely, B cells, macrophages/monocytes, and some activated T cells. In addition, many nonlymphoid cell types are able to express class II antigens.[1] Certain reports have indicated that these cells, once induced, are capable of presenting antigen to T helper cells.[2]

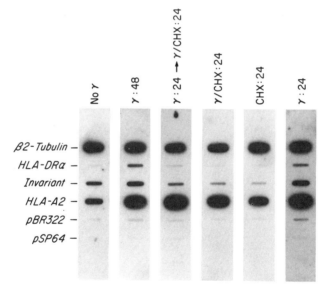

FIGURE 1. Effect of IFN-γ on HLA-DRα, HLA-A2, and invariant chain gene transcription. Runoff assays were performed on nuclei isolated from HeLa cells with no treatment, with IFN-γ alone for 48 hours, with IFN-γ for 24 hours followed by IFN-γ and CHX for an additional 24 hours, with IFN-γ and CHX for 24 hours, with CHX alone for 24 hours, or with IFN-γ alone for 24 hours. As a control, the transcription rate of β_2-tubulin was also determined.

Treatment of cells with gamma-interferon (IFN-γ) has been shown to increase the steady-state levels of class II mRNA, which leads to the increase observed in cell-surface expression of protein.[1] Protein factors have been described that bind at or near various human class II promoters.[3,4] As yet, no direct evidence exists to show that class II genes respond to IFN-γ by increasing their rate of transcription or whether induction requires production of a new protein or merely modification of a preexisting factor. We have sought to characterize the induction of DRα in a genetically and biochemically well-defined cell line, HeLa, that would facilitate isolation of the factor responsible for IFN-γ induction of MHC class II gene expression.

Stimulation of the human epithelial-like cell line, HeLa, with IFN-γ induces steady-state levels of HLA-DRα mRNA. Using a sensitive RNase-mapping procedure, we can detect induced DRα mRNA as early as 8 hours after treatment with IFN-γ; maximal accumulation occurs by 48 hours. Treatment with the protein

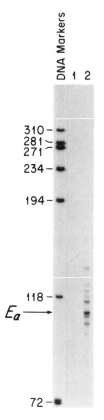

FIGURE 2. The murine E_α gene transiently transfected into HeLa cells responds to human IFN-γ. *Lane 1:* HeLa cells transfected with E_α, no treatment; *Lane 2:* HeLa cells transfected with E_α, 30 hours of human IFN-γ treatment.

synthesis inhibitor cycloheximide abolishes the IFN-γ-induced accumulation of DRα mRNA, indicating that *de novo* synthesis of a transacting protein factor is required for MHC class II gene induction. Nuclear runoff transcription assays (FIG. 1) demonstrate that treatment with IFN-γ for 24 or 48 hours increases the amount of DRα gene transcription from the undetectable levels of transcription observed in untreated HeLa cells. These findings indicate that IFN-γ-induced DRα mRNA accumulation acts directly through the activation of HLA-DRα gene transcription. Transcription of the invariant chain gene, although present in the uninduced state, was induced three- to fivefold by IFN-γ and the rate of HLA-A2 transcription increased 10- to 20-fold over that of untreated HeLa nuclei. IFN-γ-induced transcription of HLA-DRα and of the invariant chain gene was blocked by treatment with cycloheximide, whereas the interferon-induced transcription of HLA-A2 was unaffected. Surprisingly, cycloheximide by itself significantly induced HLA-A2 transcription. Our findings indicate that transcriptional induction of HLA-DRα and the invariant chain gene by IFN-γ requires the action of a novel transacting protein.

Finally, when transfecting a genomic clone of the murine E_α gene into HeLa cells, human IFN-γ induces mRNA expression of the transfected xenogenic MHC class II gene (FIG. 2). Thus, the mechanisms that mediate IFN-γ action with respect to MHC class II expression in HeLa cells apparently operates across species barriers.

REFERENCES

1. COLLINS, T. *et al.* 1984. Proc. Natl. Acad. Sci. USA **81:** 4917.
2. POBER, J. S. *et al.* 1983. Nature (London) **305:** 726.
3. SHERMAN, P. A. *et al.* 1987. Proc. Natl. Acad. Sci. USA **84:** 4254.
4. MIWA, K. *et al.* 1987. Proc. Natl. Acad. Sci. USA **89:** 4939.

Content and Organization of the Immunoglobulin Heavy Chain Variable Gene Locus in the Mouse

T. BLANKENSTEIN,[a] G. LEHLE,[b] R. SCHÜPPEL,[b]
C. KOLB,[b] C. KAPPEN,[a] E. WEILER,[b]
AND U. KRAWINKEL[a]

[a]Institut für Genetik der Universität zu Köln
Weyertal 121
D-5000 Köln 41, FRG

[b]Lehrstuhl für Immunbiologie
Fachbereich Biologie der Universität Konstanz
Postfach 7733
D-7750 Konstanz, FRG

The Igh-locus of the mouse contains multiple diverse V_H-, D_H-, and J_H-gene segments that after somatic rearrangement in a B lymphocyte encode the variable region of immunoglobulin heavy chains.[1] V_H-gene segments are distributed over nine families

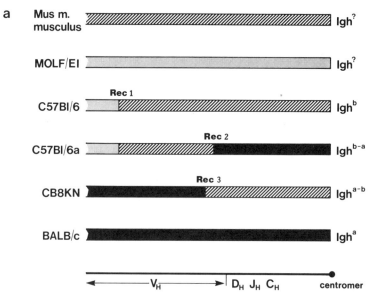

FIGURE 1a. Schematic map of breakpoints of recombination in the Igh[a] and the Igh[b] locus. The Igh[b] locus in C57BL/6 is the result of a recombination between Igh loci derived from a Mus m. musculus and a Mus m. molossinus (inbred strain MOLF/EI). The Igh V^bC^a locus in C57BL/6a and the Igh V^aC^b locus in CB8KN (BALB/c genetic background) have been generated by recombinations between Igh[a] and Igh[b].

192

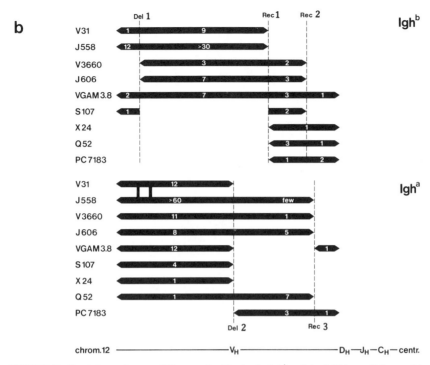

FIGURE 1b. Partial genetic map of V_H-gene families in the Igh^b and the Igh^a locus. Polymorphic restriction fragments carrying V_H genes are ordered with respect to breakpoints of recombination (Rec), to end points of deletion (Del), associated with VDJ rearrangement and the centromer (centr.). Numbers indicate the number of mapped V_H bands. Bars connecting families V31 and J558 in Igh^a indicate physical linkage. The X24 family could not be mapped with respect to Rec 2.

that are defined by sequence homology between their members.[2,3] The complexity of some V_H families, in particular the J588 family, varies considerably among Igh haplotypes.[4] The total number of V_H genes in the mouse, therefore, differs from strain to strain. In the Igh^a locus, as represented by the BALB/c strain, estimates of the V_H-gene content in the J558 family vary between ~ 100[2,4] and $\sim 1,000$[5] copies, depending on the method of counting.

A complete physical map of the murine Igh locus is currently not available. Although D_H-, J_H-, and C_H-gene segments have been linked physically by chromosomal walking,[6,7] little information is available pertaining to the organization and spatial extension of V_H-gene families. We here present a summary of our attempts to order V_H-gene families in the Igh^a and the Igh^b haplotype with respect to breakpoints of recombination in the V_H-gene cluster and end points of deletion associated with VDJ rearrangement. The Igh^b locus, represented by strain C57BL/6, very likely has been generated by a recombination between Igh loci derived from a Mus m. musculus and an M. m. molossinus, the latter represented by the inbred strain MOLF/EI.[8] V_H genes on restriction fragments showing length polymorphism in liver DNA of C57BL/6 and MOLF/EI mice are ordered with respect to recombination breakpoint 1 (Rec 1, Fig. 1). The recombinant Igh locus identified in the C57BL/6 IghV^{b}C^a (C57BL6/a) mouse results from a recombination between the Igh^b and the Igh^a locus.[13] V_H genes on polymorphic restriction fragments in C57BL/6 and BALB/c mice were ordered with respect to recombination breakpoint 2 (Rec 2, FIG. 1). In addition, we counted V_H genes that had been deleted from the Igh^b locus on rearrangement of a gene from the J558 family (Del 1, FIG. 1b) in hybridoma S24.63.63.[8]

In the Igh^a locus, V_H-gene families were mapped with respect to the breakpoint of recombination 3 (Rec 3, FIG. 1) in the Igh locus of the CB8KN mouse.[9,10,13] The latter locus was generated by a recombination between Igh haplotypes a and b. As a point of reference for deletion mapping we used the position of the J558-related V_H gene (Del 2, FIG. 1) that had been rearranged in hybridoma $20.2\text{-}267\delta$.[8] Our mapping studies indicate that V_H genes in the Igh locus are neither completely dispersed nor organized in separate clusters, as suggested elsewhere.[11] They seem rather to be ordered in overlapping clusters.[8,12] Physical linkage of V_H genes from families J558 and V31[8] confirms the notion that members of different V_H gene families are interspersed.

REFERENCES

1. TONEGAWA, S. 1983. Nature 307: 575.
2. BRODEUR, P. & R. RIBLET. 1984. Eur. J. Immunol. 14: 922.
3. WINTER et al. 1985. EMBO J. 4: 2861.
4. BLANKENSTEIN et al. 1987. Immunogenetics 26: 237.
5. LIVANT, D. et al. 1986. Cell 47: 461.
6. SHIMIZU, A. et al. 1982. Cell 28: 499.
7. WOOD C. & S. TONEGAWA. 1983. Proc. Natl. Acad. Sci. USA 80: 3030.
8. BLANKENSTEIN, T. & U. KRAWINKEL. 1987. Eur. J. Immunol. 17: 1351.
9. KOLB, C. et al. 1979. Immunogenetics 9: 455.
10. SCHÜPPEL et al. 1987. Eur. J. Immunol. 17: 739.
11. BRODEUR, P. 1987. In New Comprehensive Biochemistry, 17: 81. Elsevier, Amsterdam.
12. RATHBUN et al. 1987. EMBO J. 6: 2931.
13. LEHLE et al. 1988. Eur. J. Immunol. 18: 1275.

Regulation of Ia Gene Expression in Murine Macrophages

E. C. BÖTTGER, M. A. BLANAR, AND R. A. FLAVELL

Biogen Research Corporation
Cambridge, Massachusetts 02142

The murine Ia antigens, encoded by a family of genes (E_α, E_β, A_α, and A_β) that reside in the major histocompatibility complex (MHC), regulate the immune response through their role as restriction elements in antigen presentation.[1] In antigen-presenting cells, such as macrophages, the expression of Ia is not constitutive, but is regulated by gamma-interferon (IFN-γ).[1] Thus, treatment with IFN-γ has been

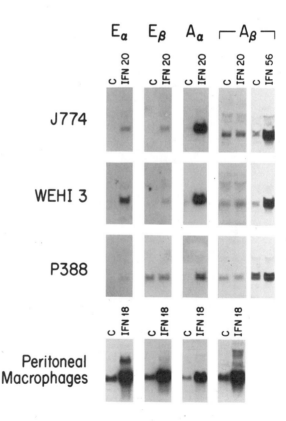

FIGURE 1. Effect of IFN-γ (250 U/ml) on accumulation of E_α, E_β, A_α, and A_β mRNA in J774 A.1, WEHI-3, P388 D.1, and peritoneal macrophages. J774 A.1, WEHI-3, and P388 D.1 were exposed to IFN-γ for 20 hours. In addition, a 56-hour incubation period with IFN-γ (to determine A_β mRNA levels) in the macrophage cell lines is shown. C = untreated controls. Peritoneal macrophages were exposed to IFN-γ for 18 hours.

shown to increase the steady state levels of class II mRNA, which leads to the increase observed in cell-surface expression of protein. The initial steps in IFN-γ action are unclear, and it is not known whether IFN-γ-induced Ia mRNA expression is a primary response that does not require protein synthesis[2] or a secondary response, that is, mediated by an IFN-γ-induced protein intermediate and therefore dependent on protein synthesis. Furthermore, the mechanism of IFN-γ-induced MHC class II mRNA accumulation remains to be defined, because steady state levels of mRNA can be controlled at or after the level of transcription.

Treatment of murine peritoneal macrophages with IFN-γ induces a coordinate expression of MHC class II gene (Ia) mRNA (E_α, E_β, A_α, and A_β), but leads to a disparate Ia gene expression pattern in various macrophage-like tumor cell lines (J774 A.1, WEHI-3, and P388 D.1) (FIG. 1). Thus, E_α mRNA was not expressed in the absence of IFN-γ in J774 A.1, WEHI-3, and P388 D.1 cells, but was induced on treatment with IFN-γ. Similarly, A_α mRNA could only be detected after IFN-γ

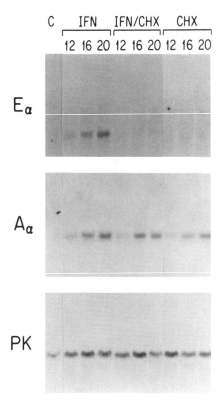

FIGURE 2. Inhibition of IFN-γ-induced E_α mRNA expression by CHX in P388 D.1 cells. P388 D.1 cells were exposed to IFN-γ (250 U/ml) or CHX (5 μg/ml) alone or to a combination of CHX/IFN-γ for 12, 16, and 20 hours. C = untreated controls.

stimulation. In contrast, A_β mRNA was present in uninduced J774 A.1, WEHI-3, and P388 D.1 cells, and IFN-γ treatment for 20 hours did not increase further A_β mRNA levels. Prolonged exposure to IFN-γ (56 hours) was required to induce elevation of A_β mRNA levels in these cell lines. Expression of E_β mRNA in J774 as well as in WEHI-3 cells required stimulation with IFN-γ. Unlike J774 and WEHI-3 cells, E_β was constitutively expressed at a low level in P388 D.1 cells, and IFN-γ exposure for 20 hours did not increase the mRNA levels further. Instead, induction of E_β mRNA by IFN-γ in P388 cells could only be demonstrated after prolonged IFN-γ treatment. Thus, MHC class II genes, which are constitutively expressed in macrophage-like cell lines (A_β in J774 A.1, WEHI-3, and P388 D.1; E_β in P388), show a delayed time course of induction by IFN-γ. These results suggest that Ia mRNA expression in macrophage cell lines is not uniform, but rather is distinct for each member of this gene family. Thus, different mechanisms may account for the regulation of expression of the various Ia genes, possibly indicating that MHC class II genes are regulated not only by cell-type specific mechanisms, but also by gene-specific mechanisms.

To characterize the initial steps in IFN-γ action, we examined the effect of CHX, an inhibitor of protein synthesis, on IFN-γ-induced Ia mRNA expression in murine macrophage cell line P388 D.1. Simultaneous addition of CHX together with IFN-γ for 12, 16, or 20 hours completely blocked the IFN-γ-induced accumulation of E_α mRNA (FIG. 2). Unexpectedly, CHX alone induced A_α mRNA. However, no superinduction of A_α mRNA was observed when CHX and IFN-γ were added simultaneously (FIG. 2). All RNA samples were analyzed for pyruvate kinase mRNA (PK) levels to ascertain that the lack of E_α mRNA was not due to an increased rate of nonspecific mRNA degradation in CHX-treated cells. Direct estimation of E_α mRNA stability by actinomycin D experiments revealed that CHX does not affect the stability of E_α mRNA in P388 D.1 cells. These results indicate that induction of E_α mRNA in P388 D.1 cells by IFN-γ requires *de novo* synthesis of a protein intermediate.

Nuclear runoff assays and inhibition of transcription with actinomycin D have revealed that IFN-γ stimulates the transcription of Ia genes, thus establishing a role for transcriptional activation in the IFN-γ-induced expression of these genes.

REFERENCES

1. UNANUE, E. R. & P. M. ALLEN. 1987. Science **236:** 551.
2. RINGOLD, G. M. 1979. Biochim. Biophys. Acta **560:** 487.

Antibodies Against a Synthetic Peptide Identify Idiotopes on Native Immunoglobulins and Stimulate an Immune Response to Antigen *in Vivo*

F. A. BONILLA AND C. A. BONA

Mount Sinai School of Medicine of the City University of New York
New York, New York

R. G. ANDERSON AND M. Z. ATASSI

Baylor College of Medicine
Houston, Texas

The BALB/c myeloma protein ABPC48 (A48) binds to polyfructose (levan) containing $\beta(2-6)$ linkages, such as bacterial levan (BL) and grass levan, and expresses an idiotype designated the A48Id.[1] Treatment of mice at birth with small amounts of A48 or syngeneic anti-A48Id antibodies results in increased expression of the A48Id in the anti-BL response when mice are challenged at age 1 month.[1] We previously screened

TABLE 1. Reactivity of RaIDab and RaIDab-NL with Various Monoclonal Antibodies[a]

A.	Antibody	Binding of RaIDab	Binding of RaIDab with 20 μg/ml ID 32-44-BSA
	XRPC44	186 ± 20	173 ± 39
	2-1-3	661 ± 5	292 ± 33
	NWSM17-3	672 ± 22	197 ± 21
	10N109-1	745 ± 15	115 ± 8
	ABPC48	968 ± 142	378 ± 11
	MOPC167	2,244 ± 396	760 ± 59
	LPS11-6	4,731 ± 360	3,068 ± 284
	NWSM9-3	5,451 ± 74	3,791 ± 73
B.	Antibody	Binding of RaIDab-L	Binding of RaIDab-L with 10 μg/ml ID 32-44
	2-1-3	5,873 ± 171	1,715 ± 52
	ABPC48	4,882 ± 65	1,513 ± 29
	MOPC167	1,310 ± 87	461 ± 53
	LPS11-6	6,472 ± 134	2,122 ± 43
	NWSM9-3	6,391 ± 439	2,486 ± 238

[a]Results shown are mean ± SEM for triplicate determinations in a solid-phase radioimmunoassay in which plates were coated with RaIDab or RaIDab-L, then incubated with various monoclonal antibodies in the presence or absence of ID 32-44, either conjugated or free. Binding of monoclonal antibodies was detected with a radiolabeled monoclonal rat anti-mouse kappa chain antibody. V gene families used by monoclonal antibodies are: XRPC44, 2-1-3, 10N109-1, NWSM and ABPC48, $V_H X24$; N17-3, $V_H Q52$; MOPC167, $V_H S107$; LPS11-6 and NWSM9-3, $V_H 7183$.

TABLE 2. Effect of Neonatal Injection of Various Antibody Preparations on A48Id Expression by BALB/c Anti-levan Antibodies[a]

Treatment at Birth	n	BL-Specific Plaques	BL-Specific Plaques, % A48Id$^+$	Group
Normal	4	3.11 ± 0.21 (1288)[b]	8 ± 19[c]	A[d]
100 ng normal rabbit Ig	3	3.43 ± 0.12 (2692)	8 ± 11	A
100 ng rabbit anti-PY206[e]	4	3.12 ± 0.14 (1318)	11 ± 10	A
100 ng RaIDab	7	4.25 ± 0.21 (17783)	20 ± 13	B
100 ng RaIDab-L	2	3.84 ± 0.01 (6918)	34 ± 8	B
100 ng syngeneic polyclonal anti-A48[f]	5	2.86 ± 0.22 (724)	65 ± 17	...

[a]BALB/c mice were injected intraperitoneally (i.p.) at birth with various antibody preparations and immunized i.p. at age 1 month with 50 μg of BL. Five days later, spleens were removed and plaque-forming cells measured in the absence or presence of syngeneic polyclonal anti-A48Id antibodies.
[b]Values are mean $\pm$ S.D. of log (BL-specific PFC/spleen). The geometric mean of PFC/spleen is given in parentheses.
[c]Values are mean $\pm$ S.D. of the percentage of BL-specific plaques inhibited by syngeneic polyclonal anti-A48Id antibodies.
[d]Statistical grouping (according to the Tukey test subsequent to the finding of a significant group effect in one-way ANOVA, $p < 0.0001$) with respect to the numbers of BL-specific plaques. Treatment groups with the same letter are not significantly different.
[e]PY206 is a monoclonal antibody specific for influenza virus hemagglutinin.
[f]Data for this group are from Hiernaux et al.[3] and are included for comparison.

168 murine and human myeloma proteins for expression of the A48Id.[1] The phosphorylcholine-binding BALB/c myeloma protein MOPC167 was found to react with syngeneic polyclonal anti-A48Id antibodies.[1] Significant homology between these two proteins occurs only in residues 32–44 of the V_H region.

To assess the contribution of these residues to formation of the A48Id, we synthesized a peptide corresponding to residues 32–44 of the protein encoded by the germline gene expressed in A48 (a member of the V_HX24 gene family).[2] This peptide is designated ID 32–44. We also synthesized this peptide with an extension of Lys-Lys-Arg, designated ID 32–44–KKG. Rabbits were immunized with ID 32–44 coupled to chicken ovalbumin and the antisera were purified by affinity chromatography over a column of ID 32–44–KKG-BSA coupled to Sepharose (preparation designated RaIDab) or a column containing an intact antibody, LPS11-6, coupled to Sepharose (preparation designated RaIDab-L. This antibody was chosen because it reacted well with RaIDab.

The RaIDab preparation was specific for the immunizing peptide, because ID 32–44–BSA inhibited the binding to ID 32–44–KKG–BSA in radioimmunoassay, whereas irrelevant peptides could not (not shown). TABLE 1, part A, shows the binding of RaIDab to various monoclonal antibodies. Clearly, RaIDab are recognizing structures homologous to the peptide, yet the presence of the peptide within a V_H is not sufficient to confer binding with RaIDab in RIA, because RaIDab surprisingly fail to react strongly with A48. The reaction of RaIDab with these antibodies is specific, because it can be inhibited by ID 32–44, conjugated or free.

TABLE 1, part B, shows the reaction of RaIDab–L with various monoclonal antibodies. This preparation displays a pattern of reactivity quite distinct from that of

RaIDab. The most striking difference is the strong binding of RaIDab-L to A48. Thus, immunization with the ID 32–44–ovalbumin conjugate generates antibodies that can bind to structures contained in intact antibodies, but that do not bind to a column of ID 32–44–KKG-BSA. We feel that these results are important in the design and interpretation of experiments aimed at idiotope mapping with synthetic peptides.

TABLE 2 shows that injection at birth of RaIDab or RaIDab-L into BALB/c mice causes a significant increase in the anti-BL response at age 1 month. Antibodies against a synthetic peptide representing a portion of an immunoglobulin variable region (operative idiotope) are thus capable of modulating an immune response mediated, in part, by antibodies bearing a homologous V region structure.

REFERENCES

1. GOLDBERG, B., W. E. PAUL & C. BONA. 1983. J. Exp. Med. **158:** 515–528.
2. OLLO, R., C. AUFFRAY, J. L. SIKORAV & F. ROUGEON. 1981. Nucl. Acids Res. **9:** 4099–4109.
3. HIERNAUX, J., C. BONA & P. J. BAKER. 1981. J. Exp. Med. **153:** 1004.

Diversity of γδ T-Cell Receptors Expressed by Dendritic Epidermal Cell Lines

F. KONING, W. M. YOKOYAMA, G. STINGL, D. COHEN,
E. M. SHEVACH, AND J. E. COLIGAN

Biological Resources Branch and Laboratory of Immunology
NIAID and
Laboratory of Chemical Biology
NIDDKD
National Institutes of Health
Bethesda, Maryland 20892

Subpopulations of T lymphocytes found in the thymus, blood, and skin express the products of the T-cell receptor (TCR) γδ genes.[1] The murine TCR γ gene family has been extensively characterized at the DNA level, and four Cγ genes have been identified.[1] Previous studies[2,3] have indicated that the vast majority of murine γδ TCRs contain a product of the Cγ1 locus (nomenclature of Garman *et al.*[4]), although recent evidence for the expression of Cγ2 has been presented.[5] The Cγ4 gene is only distantly related to the other Cγ genes,[6] and whereas Cγ4 rearrangements and transcripts have been detected,[6] there has been no evidence for the expression of Cγ4 protein.

We have described three CD3 associated, non-αβ TCR structures on dendritic epidermal T-cell lines (DETC).[3,7] One of these receptors (80 kd nonreduced), which is precipitable by rabbit antipeptide sera (anti-Cγ1,2,3) directed against the carboxyl terminus of Cγ1, Cγ2, and Cγ3 chains, is composed of a 34-kd γ chain (probably Cγ1) and a 46-kd δ chain. A second receptor that is precipitable by anti-Cγ1,2,3 can be distinguished from the aforedescribed receptor by its overall smaller size (~70 kd nonreduced) and by the fact that only the γ (32 kd) is readily detectable in reducing gels. A third non-αβ TCR is similar in overall size (80 kd) to the first receptor just described, but whereas it can be precipitated by anti-CD3 (MoAb 2C11), it cannot be precipitated by the anti-Cγ1,2,3 sera.

Identification of a non-αβ 80-kd TCR complex that was nonreactive with the anti-Cγ1,2,3 serum raised the possibility that this complex might contain a Cγ4 chain.

Northern blot analysis demonstrated the presence of Cγ4 and δ mRNA in cells expressing this receptor. To examine for the expression of this receptor, cell lines expressing this receptor (Y245, T195, and T195/Bw hybridoma), along with a cell line (T245) not expressing this receptor, were surface radioiodinated, and immunoprecipitations were carried out with anti-CD3 and with an antipeptide serum raised against the carboxyl terminus of Cγ4. As can be seen in FIGURE 1, the anti-Cγ4 serum did not react with the γδTCR expressed on the T245 cell line, but did precipitate the 37–42-kd disulfide-linked chains from the other cell lines. Thus, as summarized in TABLE 1, our studies indicate the DETC can express a variety of γδ TCRs. The putative δ chains associated with the Cγ4 chains have a lower molecular weight than do those associated with Cγ1 chains and may represent distinct δ-gene rearrangements. The presence of diverse types of γδ TCRs on DETC-derived cell lines suggests that DETC cells may be of particular importance for immune function in the skin.

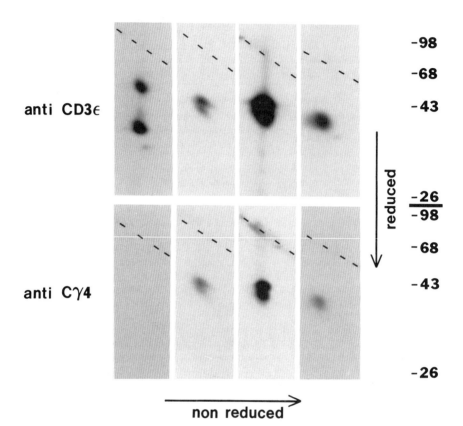

FIGURE 1. Two-dimensional nonreduced/reduced SDS-PAGE gel analysis of anti-CD3ε and anti-Cγ4 immunoprecipitates carried out with digitonin lysates of surface-iodinated T245, T195, T195/Bw, and Y245 cells. The position of the diagonal is indicated by a *dotted line*. The lower molecular weight spot from Y245 lysates precipitated by anti-CD3ε is the 32-kd γ chain indicative of the second receptor on these cells. The position of the molecular weight markers is indicated on the *right*.

TABLE 1. Characteristics of γδ TCRs Expressed by Dendritic Epidermal T Cells

	Northern Blot Analysis			Immunoprecipitation Analysis		
Cell Line	Cγ1,2,3	Cγ4	δ	Cγ1,2,3	Cγ4	Receptor Type
T245 (T93)	+/trunc[a]	trunc	+	+	−	γ1,2,3(34)[b]/δ(46)
T195	−	+/trunc	+	−	+	γ4(42)/δ(42)
T195/Bw	+	+/trunc	+	−	+	γ4(42)/δ(42)
Y245	+	+	+	+	+	γ1,2,3(32)/δ(40)
Y93A	+	+	+	+	+	γ4(42)/δ(40)

[a]Truncated transcripts.
[b]Approximate molecular weights in kilodaltons of the glycosylated chains in brackets.

REFERENCES

1. PARDOLL, D. M., A. M. KRUISBEEK, B. J. FOWLKES, J. E. COLIGAN & R. H. SCHWARTZ. 1987. FASEB J. **1:** 103.
2. PARDOLL, D. M., B. J. FOWLKES, J. A. BLUESTONE, A. KRUISBEEK, W. L. MALOY, J. E. COLIGAN & R. H. SCHWARTZ. 1987. Nature **326:** 79.
3. STINGL, G., F. KONING, H. YAMADA, W. M. YOKOYAMA, E. TSCHACHLER, J. A. BLUESTONE, G. STEINER, L. E. SAMELSON, A. M. LEW, J. E. COLIGAN & E. M. SHEVACH. 1987. Proc. Natl. Acad. Sci. USA **84:** 4586.
4. GARMAN, R. D., P. J. DOHERTY & D. H. RAULET. 1986. Cell **45:** 733.
5. MAEDA, K., N. NAKANISHI, B. L. ROGERS, W. G. HASER, K. SHITARA, H. YOSHIDA, Y. TAKAGAKI, A. A. AUGUSTIN & S. TONEGAWA. 1987. Proc. Natl. Acad. Sci. USA **84:** 6536.
6. IWAMOTO, A., R. RUPP, P. S. OHASHI, C. L. WALKER, H. PIRCHER, R. JOHO, H. HENGARTNER & T. W. MAK. 1986. J. Exp. Med. **163:** 1203.
7. KONING, F., G. STINGL, W. M. YOKOYAMA, H. YAMADA, W. L. MALOY, E. TSCHACHLER, E. M. SHEVACH & J. E. COLIGAN. 1987. Science **236:** 834.

Indirect Evidence of the Nature of the Antigen Receptor on Antigen-Specific Suppressor Cells

Monoclonal Antibodies Against GAT-Specific Suppressor Factors Can Alter the Capacity of H-2 Specific Suppressor Cells to Regulate the Response of CTL to Allogeneic Target Cells

B. H. DEVENS,[a] C. M. SORENSEN,[b] J. A. KAPP,[b]
C. W. PIERCE,[b] AND D. R. WEBB[c]

[a]Department of Immunopharmacology
Roche Research Center
Nutley, New Jersey 07110

[b]Department of Pathology and Laboratory Medicine
The Jewish Hospital of St. Louis
St. Louis, Missouri 63110

[c]Department of Molecular Immunology
Syntex Research
Palo Alto, California 94303

Specific suppression of the immune response by T cells that produce antigen-specific suppressor factors has been documented by many laboratories.[1-4] These studies demonstrate, both *in vitro* and *in vivo,* that negative regulatory mechanisms exist that can modulate immune responses. Although the phenomenon of antigen-specific suppression is well documented, the chemical characterization of antigen-specific suppressor factors (TsF) has proven to be difficult.[3] Nevertheless, substantial progress has been made in the biochemical analysis of TsF in selected systems.

Recently, monoclonal antibodies specific for antigen-specific suppressor factors that regulate the response to the synthetic terpolymer L-glutamic acid[60]-L-alanine[30]-L-tyrosine[10] (GAT) have been produced.[5,6] These antibodies recognize and neutralize GAT-specific suppressor inducer (TsF$_1$) or suppressor effector (TsF$_2$) factors. The antibodies have been shown to recognize GAT-specific suppressor factors from multiple mouse strains, elicited under different experimental conditions. Thus, these monoclonal antibodies have broad reactivity against GAT-specific suppressor factors.

Based on these results, experiments were performed to determine whether these antibodies might recognize general antigen-specific suppressor inducer and suppressor effector determinants. The system studied used a cell-mediated immune response and antigen-specific radiation-resistant suppressor cells. Suppressor cells were recovered after irradiation of 3-day mixed lymphocyte cultures (MLC). These suppressors, when added to fresh MLC cultures, suppress the generation of cytolytic activity.

Treatment of the suppressor cell population with monoclonal anti-TsF$_1$ or anti-TsF$_2$ plus complement eliminated the suppressive activity, as shown in FIGURE 1. These antibodies had no effect on nonantigen-specific suppression generated with concana-

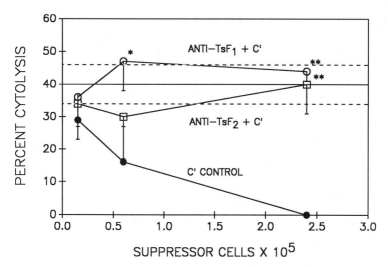

FIGURE 1. Suppressor cells were generated in 4-day mixed lymphocyte cultures (MLC). After the 3-day incubation, the cultures were irradiated with 2,000 rads. The cells were then washed and incubated with antibody, and washed and incubated with complement. Various numbers of suppressor cells, as indicated on the graph, were added to fresh MLC cultures and a 4-hour chromium release cytolytic (CTL) assay was performed following 6 days in culture. The response shown by control cultures without added suppressor cells is indicated by the *solid horizontal line* with the standard deviation from six independent cultures shown by the *dashed lines*. Student's *t* test was used to determine significance, comparing groups with the c' control group. Significance is indicated by * = $p < 0.05$, ** = $p < 0.01$.

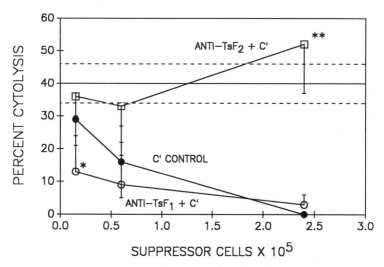

FIGURE 2. The protocol for this experiment is identical to the protocol described in the legend to FIGURE 1 with the exception that anti-TsF$_1$ at the final dilution of 1:10 was added to the cultures used in the generation of the suppressor cells.

valin A (data not shown). Further experiments were performed using these antibodies as neutralizing agents. The addition of anti-TsF$_1$ during the generation of suppressor cells did not affect subsequent suppressor cell activity. The anti-TsF$_2$ addition, in contrast, blocked the generation of suppressor cell activity. However, if anti-TsF$_1$ was added during the generation of suppressor cells, the subsequent addition of anti-TsF$_1$ plus complement did not abrogate suppression, as shown in FIGURE 2. The suppressor activity generated in the presence of anti-TsF$_1$ was still eliminated by anti-TsF$_2$ plus complement (FIG. 2).

The most important conclusion from these studies is that related suppressor inducer and suppressor effector mechanisms may play a regulatory role in both cell-mediated and humoral immunity. Suppressor cells originally identified in the humoral immune response to a synthetic polypeptide (GAT) have a common identity with suppressor cells that regulate the cellular immune response to alloantigen. Secondly, these results indirectly show that Ts precursors display TsF$_1$ or TsF$_2$ determinants on their cell surface and imply a possible role for these molecules in antigen recognition. These data also show the utility of the monoclonal anti-TsF$_1$ and anti-TsF$_2$ antibodies as probes of suppressor cell regulation in various experimental models of immunity.

REFERENCES

1. TADA, T. & K. OKUMURA. 1980. Adv. Immunol. **26:** 1.
2. GERMAIN, R. N. & B. BANACERRAF. 1981. Scand. J. Immunol. **13:** 1.
3. WEBB, D. R., J. A. KAPP & C. W. PIERCE. 1983. Ann. Rev. Immunol. **1:** 423.
4. DORF, M. E. & B. BENACERRAF. 1984. Ann. Rev. Immunol. **2:** 127.
5. TURCK, C. W., J. A. KAPP & D. R. WEBB. 1986. J. Immunol. **137:** 1904.
6. SORENSEN, C. M. & C. W. PIERCE. 1985. J. Immunol. **135:**362.

Characterization of a Mitogenic Antilymphocyte Monoclonal Antibody of the IgM Isotype Obtained by Immunization with Leukoagglutinin-Reactive Human T-Lymphocyte Surface Components[a]

M.-L. HAMMARSTRÖM,[b] T. BERZINS,[c]
M. AGUILAR-SANTELISES,[c] G. ANDERSSON,[c]
P. PERLMANN,[c] AND S. HAMMARSTRÖM[b]

[b]Department of Immunology
University of Umeå
S-901 85 Umeå, Sweden

[c]Department of Immunology
University of Stockholm
S-106 92 Stockholm, Sweden

Human T lymphocytes can be nonspecifically stimulated through the interaction between certain lectins or monoclonal antilymphocyte antibodies (mAbs) and cell surface receptors. Several mAbs directed against the T-cell antigen receptor TCR-CD3 complex and against peptides that have no known role in antigenic recognition (e.g., CD2 and CD28) were shown to be mitogenic.[1-3] Thus, several parallel or interconnected pathways of stimulation might exist. To characterize surface components capable of inducing proliferation in human T lymphocytes, we prepared mAbs against T-cell components reactive with the mitogenic lectin leukoagglutinin from *Phaseolus vulgaris*.[4]

One monoclonal antibody, K46M (IgMκ), obtained in this way gave strong dose-dependent stimulation of human T cells. K46M is a complete mitogen. It induces interleukin-2 (IL-2) production, and Il-2 receptor and transferrin receptor expression and proliferation. K46M-induced proliferation has low requirements for accessory cells. Peripheral blood lymphocytes (PBL), T cells, and E-rosetted cells depleted of adherent cells, OKM1[+], and HLA-Dr[+] cells are induced to proliferation by K46M but not by the anti-CD3 mAb OKT 3 (TABLE 1). The addition of accessory cells giving optimal conditions for OKT 3-mediated activation does not increase the proliferative response to K46M. However, K46M acts as a comitogen to the phorbol ester phorbolmyristate acetate (PMA) in that synergistic effects are seen in cultures in which the two agents are added together (TABLE 1). Approximately 40% of PBL are activated by K46M. The response curves in limiting dilutions experiments are biphasic, indicating that activation of PBL by K46M is not a single hit event, but

[a]This work was supported by the Swedish Natural Science Research Foundation Grant No. B-BU 2032–0108.

rather that different cell populations, including a suppressor cell pool, are activated by this mAb. The proportion of K46M$^+$ cells is low among resting PBL (mean 5%). However, flow cytofluorometry analysis shows that a large proportion of PBL express the antigen(s) in low concentration. The proportion of positive cells increased substantially after stimulation with mitogenic lectins or the K46M mAb (30–95%).

K46M consistently immunoprecipitates two surface peptides from lysates of lectin-stimulated PBL. Their molecular weights are 53 and 42 kd. The 53- and 42-kd peptides were identified as the α- and β-chain of the T-cell antigen receptor. In six of

TABLE 1. K46M and OKT 3 Induced T-lymphocyte Proliferation: Effects of Interleukin 1 and 2 and Phorbolester

		Proliferative Index^a with:		
Cell	Addition	K46M (20 μg/ml)	OKT 3 (50 ng/ml)	Medium Alone
PBL^b	—	10.3	0.9	1^a
	PMA 1.25 ng/ml	17.3	5.1	2.4
	0.63	19.8	7.3	2.5
	0.31	20.0	6.8	0.8
	Rec. Il-2 25 U/ml	11.1	3.4	1.8
	12.5	10.0	1.9	1.5
	Rec. Il-1 25 U/ml	13.5	0.8	0.8
	12.5	17.0	1.0	1.0
	6.3	12.3	1.0	1.0
T cells^c	—	26	2	1^a
	PMA 1.25 ng/ml	123	56	18
	0.63	62	30	10
	0.31	28	6	11
	Rec. Il-2 25 U/ml	50	45	4
	12.5	50	26	3
	Rec. Il-1 25 U/ml	34	2	2
	12.5	30	2	2
	6.3	26	2	1

^{a}Proliferation was measured as [^{3}H]thymidine uptake in cells incubated in the presence of various agents in hepes-buffered RPMI 1640 + 0.4% human serum albumin for 92 hours with a final 16-hour pulse. Proliferative index was calculated as: cpm in culture with added agent/cpm in culture with cells in medium alone. Counts per minute (cpm) for cells incubated in medium alone was $7.6 \pm 0.4 \times 10^3$ for PBL and $1.1 \pm 0.3 \times 10^3$ for T cells.
^{b}PBL = human peripheral blood lymphocytes purified by gelatin sedimentation, treatment with carbonyl iron and a magnet, and ficoll-Paque gradient centrifugation.
^{c}T cells = lymphocytes forming rosettes with neuraminidase-treated sheep red blood cells were enriched, and thereafter adherent cells were removed. Finally these E$^+$-cells were treated twice with OKM1 and anti HLA-Dr mAb plus complement.

eight experiments a 16-kd doublet coprecipitated with the aforementioned peptides. The identity of this 16-kd doublet is not yet known, but it is interesting to note that they have the same molecular weight as do the ζ-peptides of the CD3 complex. Occasionally two bands with 34- and 32-kd molecular weights were also seen.

Only in 2 of 10 experiments were K46M-reactive peptides detected in lysates of resting cells. These were the 53-, 42- and 16-kd peptides and a 20-kd peptide.

K46M also reacts with neutral glycolipid antigen(s) extracted from resting as well as activated lymphocytes. It is therefore likely that the K46M mAb is an anticarbohydrate antibody. Brain gangliosides including G_{D3}[5] were unreactive.

To our knowledge K46M is the only IgM mAb reactive with the TCR-CD3 complex that induces proliferation in human T cells. The absence of Fc receptors for mouse IgM on accessory cells has been suggested as the explanation for the lack of mitogenic effects of earlier described IgM mAbs. In the case of K46M, dependence of accessory cells could not be clearly demonstrated. As several peptides are precipitated by K46M, it is possible that this mAb is efficient in cross-linking different surface peptides needed to form a functional receptor complex.

REFERENCES

1. OETTGEN, H. C. & C. TERHORST. 1987. Human Immunol. **18:** 187.
2. MEUER, S. C., R. E. HUSSEY, M. FABBI, D. FOX, O. ACUTO, K. A. FITZGERALD, J. C. HODGDON, J. P. PROTENSIS, S. F. SCHLOSSMAN, & E. L. REINHERZ. 1984. Cell **36:** 867.
3. LESSLAUER, W., F. KONING, T. OTTENHOF, M. GIPHART, E. GOULMY, & J. J. VAN ROOD. 1986. Eur. J. Immunol. **16:** 1289.
4. DILLNER-CENTERLIND, M.-L., B. AXELSSON, S. HAMMARSTRÖM, U. HELLSTRÖM & P. PERLMANN. 1980. Eur. J. Immunol. **10:** 434.
5. WELTE, K., G. MILLER, P. B. CHAPMAN, H. YUASA, E. NATOLI, J. A. KUNICKA, C. CORDON-CARDO, C. BUHRER, L. J. OLD & A. N. HOUGHTON. 1987. J. Immunol. **139:** 1763.

Biased Use of Certain V_k Gene Families by Autoantibodies

R. MAYER, V. FIDANZA, K. KASTURI, AND C. A. BONA

Mount Sinai School of Medicine
New York, New York 10029

RNAs obtained from 79 hybridomas producing autoantibodies were hybridized with eight V_k gene probes: V_k1, V_k4, V_k8, V_k10, V_k19, V_k21, V_k22, and V_k24. Our results demonstrated that five of these families are used more frequently: V_k1, 14 of 79; V_k4, 11 of 79; V_k8, 7 of 79; V_k10, 10 of 79; and V_k19, 10 of 79. Overall, 52 of the 79 hybridomas studied (66%) used these five families (FIG. 1). In a control experiment of the use of V_k gene families in a panel of 30 hybridomas obtained by fusion of unstimulated lymphocytes from C57BL mice, we observed a more random distribution.

Consistent with these initial results, Southern analysis showed important differences in the autoimmune strains when probed with V_k gene probes (FIGS. 2 and 3). There was no RFLP difference with V_k4, V_k8, V_k21, and V_k22. The tight skin (tsk)

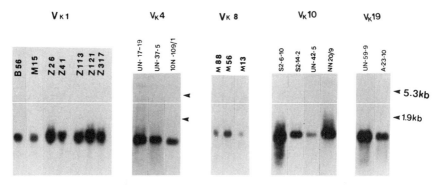

FIGURE 1. Northern analysis. Examples of hybridoma RNAs hybridized with V_k gene probes: V_k1, V_k4, V_k8, V_k10, and V_k19.

mutant mouse showed additional bands in *Eco*RI and *Hind*III digests for the V_k1 and V_k10 probes (7.6 and 4 kb with V_k1 and a 4.4-kb band for V_k10 for *Hind*III digests). The tsk strain also showed an additional 9-kb band for *Eco*RI digests probed with V_k24. The NZB mouse strain showed additional bands of 7.8, 7.0, 3.6, 1.8, and 0.6 kb in *Hind*III digests and two altered fragments of 4.7 and 5.9 kb in *Eco*RI digests for the V_k1 probe. The MRL mouse strain showed a 3.9-kb additional band in *Hind*III digests hybridized with V_k19. The MRL strain also lacked three bands of 5.3, 4.4, and 4.0 kb when compared with the AKR and LG strains in *Hind*III digests probed with V_k1. The SJL strain showed an additional band of 4.4 kb in *Eco*RI digests probed with V_k19.

Our results demonstrated that in a panel of 79 hybridomas producing autoantibodies, which were obtained from autoimmune strains, approximately two thirds use V_k

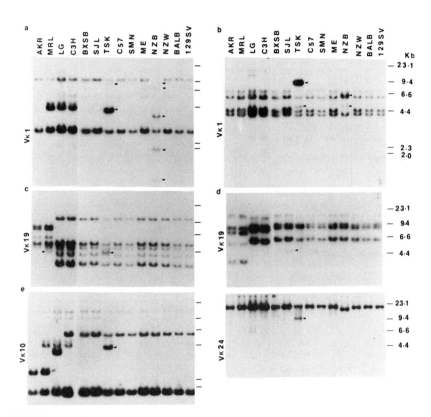

FIGURE 2. RFLP analysis. Autoradiographies of Southern blots hybridized with nick-translated V$_k$ gene probes. The sizes of DNA fragments were determined by comigration with bacteriophage *Hind*III fragments. Kb-kilobases; a, c, and e: DNAs digested with *Hind*III. b, d, and f: DNAs digested with *Eco*RI. *Arrows* indicate the position of additional altered RFLP bands. Abbreviations of mouse strains: MRL = MRL/lpr; C3H = C$_3$H/HeJ; TSK = tight skin; C57 = C57BL/6J; Smn = C57BL/6 SmnJ; ME = motheaten; BALB = BALB/cJ.

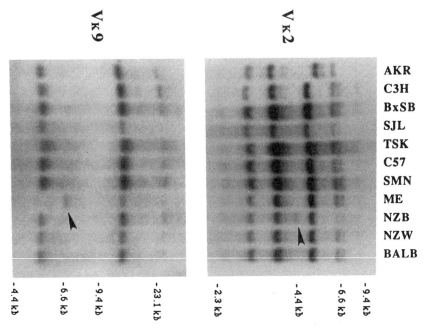

FIGURE 3. Southern blots of *Hind*III-digested liver DNA from 11 strains. Each blot was hybridized with V_k2 or V_k9 probe as indicated.

genes from five families. Southern blot analysis also demonstrated important RFLP differences in autoimmune strains for three of these families. These findings suggest the preferential use of certain V_k gene families by autoantibodies.

REFERENCES

1. BELLON, B., A. MANHEIMER-LORY, M. MONESTIER, T. MORAN, A. DIMITRIU-BONA, F. ALT & C. BONA 1987. High frequency of autoantibodies bearing crossreactive idiotypes among hybridomas using V_H 7183 genes prepared from normal and autoimmune strains. J. Clin. Invest. **79:** 1044–1053.

2. BONA, C. 1988. V genes encoding autoantibodies: Molecular and pheotypic characteristics. Ann. Rev. Immunol. In press.

3. BRODEUR, P. H. & R. RIBLET. 1984. The immunoglobulin heavy chain variable region (Igh-V) locus in mouse I. One hundred Igh-V genes comprise seven families of homologous genes. Eur. J. Immunol. **14:** 922–930.

4. CLARKE, S. H., K. HUPPI, L. RUEZINSKY, L. STAUDT, W. GERHARD, & M. WEIGERT. 1985. Inter and intraclonal diversity in the response to influenza hemagglutinin. J. Exp. **161:** 687–704.

5. CORBET, S., M. MILIK, M. FOUGEREAU & C. SCHIFF. 1987. Two V_k germline genes related to the GAT idiotypic network account for the major subfamilies of the mouse V_k-1 variability subgroup. J. Immunol. **120:** 932–939.

6. CORRY, S., B. M. TYLER & J. M. ADAMS. 1981. Sets of immunoglobulin V_k genes homologous to 10 cloned V_k sequences: implications for the number of germline V_k genes. J. Mol. Appl. Genet. **1:** 103–116.

7. EDELMAN, G. M., D. E. OLINS, J. A. GALLY & N. D. ZINDER. 1963. Reconstitution of

immunologic activity of interaction of polypeptide chains of antibodies. Proc. Natl. Acad. Sci. **50:** 753–756.

8. EDELMAN, G. M. & P. D. GOTTLIEB. 1970. A genetic marker in the variable region of light chains of mouse immunoglobulins. Proc. Natl. Acad. Sci. USA **67:** 1192–1199.

9. GEARHART, P. J. & D. F. BOGENHAGEN. 1983. Clusters of point mutations are found exclusively around rearranged antibody variable genes. Proc. Natl. Acad. Sci. USA **80:** 3639–3443.

10. GIBSON, D. 1976. Genetic polymorphism of mouse immunoglobulin light chains revealed by isoelectric focusing. J. Exp. Med. **146:** 298–303.

11. GOTTLIEB, P. D. 1976. Genetic correlation of mouse light chain variable region marker with a thymocyte surface antigen. J. Exp. Med. **140:** 1432–1437.

12. HERZENBERG, L. A., A. M. STALL, P. A. PARLOR, C. SIDMAN, W. A. MOORE, D. R. PARKS, & L. A. HERZENBERG. 1986. The Ly-1B cell lineage. Immunol. Rev. **93:** 81–102.

13. HUPPI, K., E. JOUVIN MARCHE, C. SCOT, P. POTTER & M. WEIGERT. 1985. Genetic polymorphism at the K chain locus in mice: Comparisons of restriction enzyme hybridization fragments of variable and constant region genes. Immunogenetics **21:** 445–457.

14. KABAT, E. A., K. G. NICKERSON, J. LIAO, L. GROSSBARD, E. F. OSSERMAN, E. GLICKMAN, L. CHESS, J. B. ROBBINS, R. SCHNEERSON, & Y. YASIG. 1986. A human monoclonal macroglobulin with specificity for α(2-8) linked poly-N acetyl neuraminic acid, the capsular antigen which crossreacts with polynucleotides and with denatured DNA. J. Exp. Med. **164:** 642–656.

15. KABAT, E., T. T. WU, M. REID-MILLER, H. M. PERRY & K. S. GOTTESMAN, (eds). 1987. Sequence of immunoglobulin chains. U.S. Department of Health and Human Services Public Health Service National Institute of Health.

16. KELLEY, D. E., C. COLECLOUGH, & R. P. PERRY. 1982. Functional significance and evolutionary development of the 5' terminal regions of immunoglobulin variable region genes. Cell **29:** 681-689.

17. KELLEY, D. E., L. M. WEIDMANN, A. C. PITTET, S. STRAUSS, K. J. NELSON, J. DAVIS, B. VAN NESS & R. P. PERRY. 1985. Nonproductive kappa immunoglobulin genes: Recombinational abnormalities and other lesions affecting transcription, RNA processing, turn over and translation. Cell Biol **5:** 1660–1675.

Contrasuppression As a Determinant of Susceptibility to Autoimmune Injury

CAROLYN J. KELLY, HANNAH MOK,
AND E. G. NEILSON

Renal-Electrolyte Section and the Immunology Graduate Group
University of Pennsylvania School of Medicine
Philadelphia, Pennsylvania 19104

The mechanisms underlying the linkage of various autoimmune diseases to the major histocompatibility complex remain enigmatic. We have been studying the complex mechanism of susceptibility to experimental interstitial nephritis in mice. Following immunization with heterologous renal tubular antigens in complete Freund's adjuvant, susceptible mice develop antitubular basement membrane (anti-TBM) antibodies and interstitial T-cell infiltrates with eventual interstitial fibrosis and progressive renal insufficiency.[1] Susceptibility to murine anti-TBM disease is genetically dominant and maps to the class I locus $H-2K^{s,d}$. Susceptible and nonsusceptible strains mount similar anti-TBM antibody responses to the renal tubular antigen (RTA) but are distinctly different in their effector T-cell responses. In previous work we showed that both susceptible and nonsusceptible mice initially differentiate two different effector T cells after immunization with RTA: $L3T4^+$, I-A restricted T cells, and $Lyt-2^+$, H-2K restricted T cells.[2] *In vivo* studies have shown that in susceptible mice only the $Lyt-2^+$ cells persist, whereas in nonsusceptible mice only the $L3T4^+$ cells remain.[2] This is an important distinction, because although both phenotypes mediate delayed-type hypersensitivity (DTH) to RTA, only the $Lyt-2^+$ T cells typically transfer interstitial nephritis. This selection of effector T-cell phenotype can be duplicated *in vitro* and was previously shown to be regulated by antigen-primed, $Lyt-2^+$, $I-J^+$ regulatory T cells.[3] Previous studies showed that contrasuppressor T cells can play a critical role in the expression of organ-specific autoimmunity.[4] Therefore, we examined the relative roles of suppressor (Ts) and contrasuppressor (Tcs) cells in regulating the selection of effector T-cell phenotype, because such selection correlates strongly with susceptibility to disease.

These studies were performed using a previously described method for *in vivo* induction of antigen-specific effector T cells from a naive spleen cell population.[4] In brief, naive syngeneic spleen cells are cocultured with soluble RTA, growth factors including interleukin-2 (IL-2), and supernatants from syngeneic helper T-cell lines for 5 days at 37°C. T-cell subpopulations are then negatively selected with anti-L3T4 or anti-Lyt-2 antibodies and complement, and the ability of the remaining cells to mediate DTH is assessed by local adoptive transfer in the presence of antigen. Under such conditions, the phenotype of the day 5 effector T cell is $Lyt-2^+$ in SJL and [SJL × B10.S(8R)]F_1 mice (both susceptible) and $L3T4^+$ in B10.S(8R) (nonsusceptible) mice. If *Vicia villosa* lectin-adherent Tcs cells are removed before culture, the phenotype of the effector T cell is $L3T4^+$ in all three strains. If the remaining lectin nonadherent cells are further depleted with anti-$I-J^s$, effector T cells of both phenotypes differentiate and persist in all three strains, a finding consistent with the presence of a lectin nonadherent Ts that suppresses $Lyt-2^+$ cells. Further studies have shown that the function of the lectin-adherent Tcs cell (which is an $Lyt-2^+$, $I-J^+$, T cell) can be replaced by a soluble factor from those cells. This factor is antigen binding, bears I-J determinants, and is H-2K and Igh restricted. Coculture of such TcsF, derived from F_1 mice, with B10.S(8R) spleen cells is a sufficient stimulus to result in selection of an Lyt-2^+ effector T cell. These B10.S(8R) Lyt-2^+ effector cells are also nephritogenic, as they transfer interstitial nephritis into syngeneic mice. Thus the protein(s) contained in these cell lysates are sufficient to "convert" a nonsusceptible phenotype to a susceptible one. These studies suggest that a functional correlate of H-2K-linked susceptibility to disease expression is a regulatory process, contrasuppression, which uniquely distinguishes susceptible from nonsusceptible mice.

REFERENCES

1. NEILSON, E. G. and S. M. PHILLIPS. 1982. J. Exp. Med. **155**: 1075.
2. NEILSON, E. G., E. MCCAFFERTY, R. MANN, *et al.* 1985. J. Immunol. **134**: 2275.
3. MANN, R., C. J. KELLY, W. H. HINES, *et al.* 1987. J. Immunol. **138**: 4200.
4. KELLY, C. J. & E. G. NEILSON. 1987. J. Exp. Med. **165**: 107.

Inhibition of the Na$^+$/Proton Antiporter with the Amiloride Analog 5-(N-methyl-N-isobutyl)amiloride Leads to Superinduction of T-Cell Proliferation Induced via the Alternate (CD2) Pathway

WALTER KNAPP,[a] GOTTFRIED F. FISCHER,[a]
WOLFGANG HOLTER,[a] EDWARD J. CRAGOE, JR.,[b] AND
OTTO MAJDIC[a]

[a]Institute of Immunology
University of Vienna
A-1090 Vienna, Austria

[b]Merck Sharp and Dohme Research Laboratories
West Point, Pennsylvania 19486

The stimulation of cells with growth factors is often accompanied by an increase in intracellular pH (reviewed in Ref. 1). Thus, an alteration of the cytoplasmic proton concentration might be an important step between extracellular first messengers and biologic responses, in particular cell growth. Evidence has been presented, however, that cell proliferation also can be induced without intracellular alkalinization and inhibitors of the Na$^+$/H$^+$ antiporter; the ion channel probably responsible for intracellular alkalinization has not yet shown functional effects on proliferation in lymphocytes.[2-4]

The CD2 antigen on human T cells has recently attracted considerable interest, as on the one hand it apparently functions as an adhesion molecule,[5] and on the other, resting T cells become activated via this antigen on incubation with a combination of CD2 antibodies or one antibody plus the phorbol ester phorbol myristate acetate (PMA).[6,7]

We studied early changes in intracellular pH by loading T cells with the fluorescent pH-sensitive probe BCECF-AM and measuring the fluorescence of cell suspensions in a spectrofluorometer. Cells were stimulated with the phorbol ester PMA, the lectins concanavalin (Con A) or phytohemagglutinin (PHA), or mitogenic CD2 monoclonal antibodies.

We found that PMA leads to an intracellular pH shift in human peripheral blood T cells similar to that described for other cell types.[8] In contrast, we found no such intracellular alkalinizations in response to PHA or Con A, whereas an increase in free intracellular calcium and proliferation induction could be observed. Surprisingly, stimulation of T cells with mitogenic CD2 mAbs led to an increase in intracellular pH (FIG. 1). This increase was similar in extent to that observed on stimulation with PMA. In medium that was nominally free of bicarbonate, this increase was inhibited by an amiloride analog, 5-(N-methyl-N-isobutyl)amiloride (MIA). This finding indicates that the pH shift is mediated by the amiloride-sensitive Na$^+$/H$^+$ antiporter.

In subsequent experiments we studied the influence of MIA on T-cell proliferation induced by monoclonal CD2 antibodies or lectins. The cell cultures were performed in

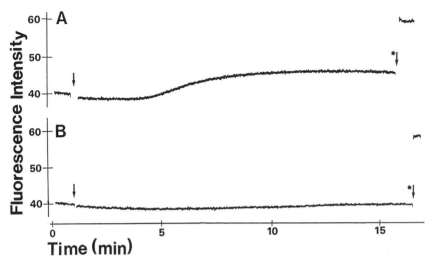

FIGURE 1. Activation with CD2 monoclonal antibodies but not stimulation with PHA is followed by an intracellular pH shift. Traces indicate fluorescence intensities (arbitrary units) of a nylon wool-purified T-cell preparation (6×10^6 cells/ml), loaded with 5 μM of the pH-sensitive fluorescence dye 2',7'bis-(2-carboxyethyl)-5-(and -6-)carboxyfluorescein (BCECF-AM), suspended in simplified medium, and incubated in a quartz glass cuvette at 37°C, as measured in a spectrofluorometer. *Arrows* indicate addition of the stimulants (mitogenic mAbs VIT13 plus X11 in *panel A* and the mitogenic lectin PHA in *panel B*). *Arrows* with an asterisk denote addition of Triton-X-100 at a final concentration of 0.1%. Cells were thereby lysed, and the fluorescence intensity obtained indicated the pH of the medium, which was 7.4.

TABLE 1. Amiloride Analog MIA Enhances CD2 but not Lectin-Induced T-Cell Proliferation[a]

Stimulus	Experiment 1		Experiment 2	
	Medium	MIA	Medium	MIA
Medium	1.5 ± 0.1	1.2 ± 0.3	0.3 ± 0.9	2.8 ± 0.2
9.6	1.1 ± 0.2	1.0 ± 0.2	3.0 ± 0.2	1.1 ± 0.8
VIT13	0.5 ± 0.1	0.9 ± 0.4	3.1 ± 0.2	1.6 ± 0.1
9.6+VIT13	16.4 ± 4.5	70.0 ± 13.2	22.7 ± 3.8	61.0 ± 11.7
PHA	64.5 ± 4.8	78.3 ± 4.6	97.7 ± 11.4	100.7 ± 3.9

[a]Data (cpm $\times 10^{-3}$, mean ± SD of triplicate cultures) are from two independent experiments in which mononuclear cells were stimulated with PHA or mAbs 9.6 and VIT13, recognizing two different epitopes of the CD2 antigen. Cells were cultured with or without 5 μM of 5-(N-methyl-N-isobutyl)amiloride (MIA). The medium was hepes-buffered RPMI 1640 supplemented with 10% fetal calf serum, glutamine, and antibiotics, without sodium bicarbonate. After incubation for 72 hours 1 μC ^{3}H-thymidine was added to each well, and the cells were harvested 18 hours later. Incorporated radioactivity was collected on glass fiber filters and measured in a liquid scintillation counter.

medium not containing sodium bicarbonate in order to assess the functional role of the Na^+/H^+ antiporter. Cells were cultured in parallel with and without MIA (5 μm) and stimulated with mitogenic lectin PHA or CD2 antibodies. Although MIA demonstrated no effects in lectin-induced T-cell proliferation, the CD2-stimulated cells showed a marked increase in DNA synthesis in the presence of MIA (TABLE 1). Our findings indicate that the increase in intracellular pH on stimulation with CD2 antibodies is neither a prerequisite for T-cell proliferation nor a promoter of T-cell growth. Cytoplasmic alkalinization rather seems to function in a regulatory role; in its absence, superinduction of proliferation can be achieved.

REFERENCES

1. SEIFTER, J. L. & P. S. ARONSON. 1986. J. Clin Invest. **78:** 859.
2. YAMAGUCHI, D. T., R. SAKAI, L. BAHN, E. J. CRAGOE, JR., & S. C. JORDAN. 1986. J. Immunol. **137:** 1300.
3. MILLS, G. B., R. K. CHEUNG, E. J. CRAGOE, JR., S. GRINSTEIN & E. W. GELFAND. 1986. J. Immunol. **136:** 1150.
4. MILLS, G. B., E. J. CRAGOE, E. W. GELFAND & S. GRINSTEIN. 1985. J. Biol. Chem. **260:** 14053.
5. SINGER, K. H., L. S. WOLF, D. F. LOBACH, S. M. DENNING, D. T. TUCK, A. L. ROBERTSON & B. F. HAYNES. 1986. Proc. Natl. Acad. Sci. **83:** 6588.
6. MEUER, S. C., R. E. HUSSEY, M. FABBI, D. FOX, O. ACUTO, K. A. FITZGERALD, J. C. HODGDON, J. P. PROTENTIS, S. F. SCHLOSSMAN & E. L. REINHERZ. 1984. Cell **36:** 897.
7. HOLTER, W., G. F. FISCHER, O. MAJDIC, H. STOCKINGER & W. KNAPP. 1986. J. Exp. Med. **163:** 654.
8. MOOLENAAR, W. H., G. J. TERTOOLEN, & S. W. DELAAT. 1984. Nature **312:** 371.

Molecular Genotypes of the Human T-Cell Receptor γ Chain

YIXIN LI, PAUL SZABO, AND DAVID N. POSNETT

Cornell University Medical College
Divisions of Allergy & Immunology and Geriatrics
Department of Medicine
New York, New York

The newly described γ/δ-chain T-cell receptor apparently is associated with early double negative (CD4⁻, CD8⁻) thymocytes and a small population of double negative peripheral blood T cells. The functional significance of this receptor remains unclear. Like the α- and β-chain genes, the γ-chain gene is composed of rearranging V, J, and C segments. The Cγ1 gene consists of three exons (exI, exII, and exIII). Cγ2 cDNA clones, however, have been reported to contain two or three different copies of exon II in addition to exons I and III.[1,2] To what extent this heterogeneity in expressed Cγ2 is

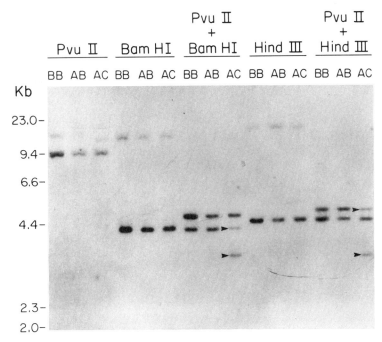

FIGURE 1. Double digestion of DNA from three individuals with the following *Pvu*II-defined γ-chain alleles. One is homozygous for the B allele (BB), the second is heterozygous for the A and B alleles (AB), and the third is heterozygous for the A and C alleles (AC). The probe contained Cγ-exIIexIII sequences. Under these conditions only two *Bam*HI fragments were detected: (1) a 11.5-kb fragment containing Cγ1-exII, Cγ1-exIII, Jγ2, and part of Cγ2-exI, and (2) a 4.0-kb fragment containing the most 3′ Cγ2-exII and Cγ2-exIII.[1]

220   ANNALS NEW YORK ACADEMY OF SCIENCES

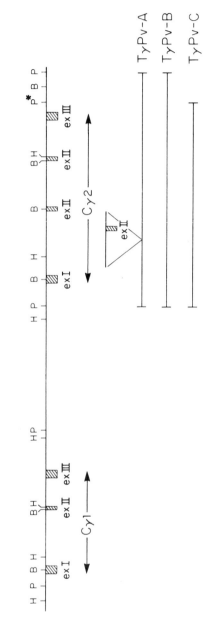

FIGURE 2. Restriction map of the human TCR γ-chain constant region locus. The sites for *Bam*HI (B), *Hind*III (H), and the localization for coding segments exI, exII, and exIII were obtained from Lefranc *et al.*[1] The polymorphic *Pvu*II site is indicated by an asterisk.

the result of alternative Cγ2 alleles or differential RNA splicing of a full complement of Cγ2 exons is unresolved.

Here we describe two new restriction fragment length polymorphisms (RFLPs) of the human Cγ chain defined by a single restriction enzyme, *Pvu*II. They define three alleles. In 36 randomly chosen normal individuals the frequencies of alleles A, B, and C were 32%, 49%, and 19%, respectively. Because these alleles occur at high frequencies, they are useful for haplotype assignments within families and for studies on disease associations with the γ-chain genes. Complete haplotype assignment was possible in some of the families studied and was based solely on the *Pvu*II polymorphisms.[3] Results obtained from hybridization with a constant (C) region probe versus a variable (V) region probe indicated that these polymorphisms are associated with the C and not the V regions. Analysis of double digestion experiments with several restriction enzymes (FIG. 1) showed that fixed *Pvu*II sites flank the Cγ2 gene. In double digestions with *Pvu*II and *Bam*HI the genomic DNA of the C allele could be distinguished from the DNA of the A and B alleles because the 4.0-kb *Bam*HI/ *Bam*HI fragment was shortened to a 3.2-kb *Bam*HI/*Pvu*II fragment in the C allele (FIG. 1, arrows). Thus the polymorphic *Pvu*II site, which distinguishes the C allele from the A and B alleles, maps to the Cγ2 gene segment and is located 3.2 kb downstream of the *Bam*HI site in the most 3′ Cγ2-exII. These results were confirmed using double digestion with *Pvu*II and *Hind*III. In this case a 4.7-kb *Hind*III/*Pvu*II fragment containing Cγ2-exII and Cγ2-exIII sequences was replaced by a 3.1-kb fragment in digests of genomic DNA from allele C (FIG. 1, arrows), but not from alleles A and B. This places the polymorphic *Pvu*II site 3.1 kb downstream of the *Hind*III site within the most 3′ Cγ2-exII and independently confirms the position of this polymorphic *Pvu*II site. A restriction map indicates the location of the polymorphic *Pvu*II site and the fixed *Pvu*II sites (FIG. 2). Because both alleles A and B share the same 5′ fixed *Pvu*II site contained within a *Hind*III/*Hind*III fragment and detected by a Cγ-exon I specific probe, alleles A and B share the same *Pvu*II sites flanking the Cγ2 gene and the difference between alleles A and B must be explained by an insertion of approximately 3 kb in the A allele. As recently shown by Pelicci *et al.*,[4] this insertion contains a third copy of Cγ-exon II and the insertion is located just upstream of the two other exon II segments.

REFERENCES

1. LEFRANC, M.-P., A. FORSTER, & T. H. RABBITTS. 1986. Genetic polymorphism and exon changes of the constant regions of the human T-cell rearranging gene γ. Proc. Natl. Acad. Sci. USA **83:** 9596.
2. LITTMAN, D. R., M. NEWTON, D. CROMMIE, S.-L. ANG, J. G. SEIDMAN, S. N. GETTNER, & A. WEISS. 1987. Characterization of an expressed CD3-associated Ti gamma-chain reveals C-gamma domain polymorphism. Nature **326:** 85.
3. LI, Y., P. SZABO & D. N. POSNETT. 1988. Molecular genotypes of the human T cell receptor γ-chain. J. Immunol. **140:** 1300.
4. PELICCI, P. G., M. SUBAR, A. WEISS, R. DALLA-FAVERA, D. R. LITTMAN. 1987. Molecular diversity of the human T-gamma constant region genes. Science **237:** 1051.

A Microrecombination Event Generates an IgG2b-IgG2a-IgG2b Heavy Chain Gene in a Mouse Myeloma Cell Line

JONATHAN A. BARD, GARY GILMORE, AND
BARBARA K. BIRSHTEIN

Albert Einstein College of Medicine
Bronx, New York 10461

Variants ICR 9.7.1 (9.7.1), ICR 4.68 (4.68), and ICR 11.19 (11.19) were isolated from the MPC11 mouse myeloma cell line (IgG2b, κ) after mutagenesis with ICR-191, an acridine half-mustard.[1,2] All three variants fail to assemble H_2 dimers, halting the immunoglobulin (Ig) assembly process at the HL stage, and do not secrete heavy (H) chains.[1,2] As a group, these variants appear to be unstable, each spontaneously giving rise to secondary variants in H chain production.[3–5] Characterization of these unstable MPC11 variants might give insight into regulation of Ig gene rearrangements.

For short H chain producing variant 11.19 (52,000 MW), initial characterization of its cytoplasmic Ig by Ouchterlony analysis and comparative peptide mapping had indicated a lesion affecting the C-terminal segment of the chain. We investigated the defect that was responsible for short H chain production in two subclones of 11.19, called E5.7A12 and E5.7A14, using mRNA sequencing and DNA restriction mapping analyses.[6]

As shown in FIGURE 1, E5. 7A12 contains a tract of γ2a-derived sequences at the 3' end of the CH_2 domain, which encompasses at least part of the intervening sequences (IVS) between the CH_2 and CH_3 domains (adding 12 amino acids, derived from γ2a IVS, to the protein). A double cross-over or gene conversion event may account for this microrecombination event; it is most likely mediated by a tract of 74 nucleotides of identity between γ2b and γ2a constant region genes in the CH_2 domain and another smaller tract of identity in the IVS region. Contiguous to the 3' end of the microrecombination is a 200-bp deletion that involves the CH_2-CH_3 domain IVS and the 5' end of the CH_3 domain, deleting the amino-terminal 39 aa. of the CH_3 domain. The loss of these 39 aa. coupled with the gain of 12 aa. from the γ2a IVS (see above) accounts for the 52,000 MW size of the H chain produced by E5.7A12.

Further rearrangement may ensue, as evidenced by the isolation of E5.7A14, an H chain nonproducing sister clone of E5.7A12. In addition to the 3' microrecombination/deletion event just described, the H chain gene of E5.7A14 contains a novel restriction map 5' to the enhancer region (FIG. 2). Until the origin of this novel DNA is determined by cloning, we speculate that it may represent an aberrant attempt at variable region replacement or a chromosomal translocation. The defects in H chain assembly and secretion in E5.7 may result in a deficient feedback mechanism, which would normally be mediated by a *complete* Ig molecule and prevent further rearrangements of both H and L genes.[7]

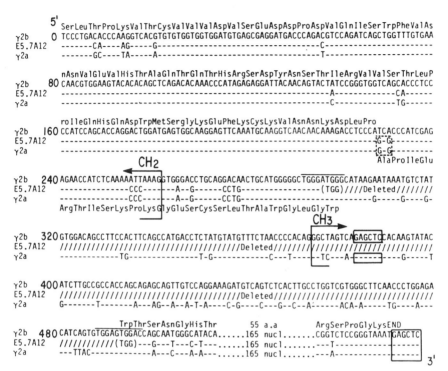

FIGURE 1. Microrecombination and deletion in the E5.7A12 H chain gene. Partial nucleotide sequence of mRNA from E5.7A12 (third line) is compared with the sequence of normal γ2b (second line) and γ2a (fourth line) genes. *Brackets* demarcate the end of the CH₂ domain and the beginning of the CH₃ domain, whereas the sequence between these brackets represents the intervening sequence (IVS). Sequence identity of either the E5.7A12 or γ2a sequences with γ2b sequences is represented by *dashes;* only the nucleotides that differ between γ2b and γ2a genes or between γ2b and E5.7A12 sequences are indicated at the appropriate positions. The predicted amino acid sequence for E5.7A12 is indicated on the first line, if derived from γ2b sequence, or the third line, if derived from γ2a sequences. Although indicated in this figure to be γ2b derived, the amino acids translated from nucleotides 155 to 228, consisting of 74-bp identity between γ2b and γ2a genes, may be derived, at least in part, from γ2a sequences. *Slashes* represent nucleotides that are absent from the E5.7A12 sequence. *Parentheses* around TGG at both the 5'- and 3'-flank region of the deleted segment indicate our inability to determine whether these trinucleotides are derived from γ2b, γ2a, or, in part, both genes, because of the redundancy of this sequence at the flank regions of the deletion. The overlined decanucleotide at the 5'- and 3'-flank region represents the putative sequence involved in the homologous recombination event that resulted in the 200-bp deletion. The boxed hexanucleotide (GAGCTC) represents the 5' and 3' CH₃ domain *Sac*I sites; the 5' CH₃ *Sac*I site has been deleted in E5.7A12 (and E5.7A14) as indicated by the *slashes*. The *dashed boxed* tetranucleotides represent the *Hha*I restriction enzyme site (GCGC) found in the γ2a gene and, because of the microrecombination event, also in the E5.7A12 (and E5.7A14) genes but is absent from the γ2b gene.

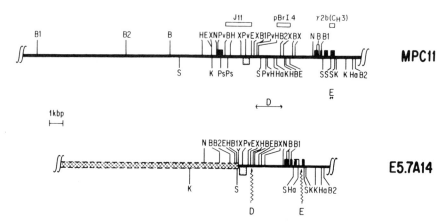

FIGURE 2. Partial restriction maps of the variable region, $\gamma 2b$ gene, and flanking regions of MPC11 and E5.7A14. All maps were generated by extensive Southern blot analyses carried out in our laboratory (with the exception of one *Bam*HI and one *Kpn*I site which were obtained from cloned cDNA sequence). Bars above the MPC11 map indicate some of the probes utilized for generating these maps. *Closed boxes* represent protein-coding regions (exons). *Slashed boxes* below maps represent the position of the Ig H chain gene enhancer. *Labeled horizontal arrows* below the MPC11 map represent the positions and extensiveness of the deletions found in E5.7A14 (D and E) (indicated by *crooked vertical arrows* at the appropriate positions in the variant). The map of E5.7A12 (not shown) is identical to the map shown for MPC11 (using eight different restriction enzymes and four different probes), except for the microrecombination and deletion events that have occurred at the 3' end of the constant region (see FIG. 1 and text). The opened box at the 3' end of the CH$_2$ domain in the map of E5.7A14 represents sequences derived from the $\gamma 2a$ gene as a result of the microrecombination event (see text and FIG. 1). B = *Bam*HI; B1 = *Bgl*I; B2 = *Bgl*II; E = *Eco*RI; H = *Hind*III; Ha = *Hha*I; K = *Kpn*I; N = *Nco*I; Ps = *Pst*I; Pv = *Pvu*II; S = *Sac*I; X = *Xba*I.

REFERENCES

1. Preud'homme, J.-L., B. K. Birshtein & M. D. Scharff. 1975. Variants of a mouse myeloma cell line that synthesize immunoglobulin heavy chains having an altered serotype. Proc. Natl. Acad. Sci. USA **72:** 1427.

2. Koskimies, S. & B. K. Birshtein. 1976. Primary and secondary variants in immunoglobulin heavy chain production. Nature **264:** 480.

3. Eckhardt, L. A. & B. K. Birshtein. 1985. Independent immunoglobulin class switch events occurring in a single myeloma cell line. Mol. Cell. Biol. **5:** 856.

4. Tilley, S. A., L. A. Eckhardt, K. B. Marcu & B. K. Birshtein. 1983. Hybrid $\gamma 2b$-$\gamma 2a$ genes expressed in myeloma variants: Evidence for homologous recombination. Proc. Natl. Acad. Sci. USA **80:** 6967.

5. Birshtein, B. K., J.-L. Preud'homme & M. D. Scharff. 1974. Variants of mouse myeloma cells that produce short immunoglobulin heavy chains. Proc. Natl. Acad. Sci. USA **71:** 3478.

6. Gilmore, G. L., J. A. Bard & B. K. Birshtein. 1988. DNA rearrangements affecting both variable and constant regions of IgH chain genes in MPC11 mouse myeloma variants. J. Immunol. **141:** 1754.

7. Alt, F. W., T. K. Blackwell, & G. D. Yancopoulos. 1987. Development of the primary antibody repertoire. Science **238:** 1079.

Human Fetal Neural Tissue Organotypic Cultures

A Model for Perinatal AIDS Neuropathology

W. D. LYMAN, Y. KRESS, F.-C. CHIU, C. S. RAINE,
M. B. BORNSTEIN, AND A. RUBINSTEIN

Albert Einstein College of Medicine
Bronx, New York

Human fetal central nervous system (CNS) tissue was established in organotypic culture to test the hypothesis that human immunodeficiency virus (HIV) can infect neural tissue during gestation. This infection might account for the neurologic dysfunction seen in children with congenital HIV seropositivity, AIDS, or AIDS-related complex which can include chronic and progressive subacute encephalopathy, pyramidal tract signs, and acquired microcephaly.[1] The pathophysiologic manifestations are seizures, motor dysfunction, and spasms, whereas calcifications in the basal ganglia and cortical atrophy are found histologically.[2]

MATERIALS AND METHODS

Organotypic cultures of human fetal CNS tissue were established by placing sections of frontal cortex (approximately 1 mm thick) from abortuses aged 14 to 19 weeks, on collagen-coated coverslips in Maximov slide assemblies or in 24-well tissue culture plates. The methods used for organotypic cultures of CNS tissue are routine in these laboratories and are reported elsewhere.[3]

CNS cultures were kept in culture for up to 4 weeks for these studies. Sample cultures were processed either for light and electon microscopy or for biochemical analysis on a weekly basis. For microscopic studies, cultures were washed two times in phosphate buffered saline solution before being fixed, osmicated, dehydrated, and embedded in plastic.[3] For Western blot analysis, the cultures were washed as just described, solubilized by briefly boiling in 1% SDS, and then electrophoresed with known amounts of cell-type specific proteins in adjacent lanes. The gels were applied to nitrocellulose sheets and the resolved proteins were transferred to the nitrocellulose using standard methods.[4]

RESULTS

CNS tissue could be successfully cultured, and because fetal cortex has a prominent germinal plate layer and overlaying glial-neuroblast stratum, by orienting the cortical sections with both layers in the same plane, migration of the germinal plate cells was noted. The migration was similar to that noted in normal development as the cells formed rays that permeated the overlaying tissue. Ultrastructurally, the cultures were observed to contain prominent astrocytes and a rich neuropil containing abundant neurites. Prominent features of these cultures were numerous growth cones and

225

synaptogenesis. On Western blot analysis, these cultures contained glial-fibrillary acid protein, the characteristic differentiation astrocyte marker.

Test cultures were incubated in the presence of either conditioned medium from H-9 uninfected cells or medium from H-9 cells infected with HIV and were processed for light and electron microscopy. Results of these studies show that cultures incubated in the presence of HIV for at least 7 days had significant pathology including edema, dissolution of neuropil, and a decrease of glial-like cells with almost complete disappearance of germinal plate cells. HIV-like particles were observed in neuroecto-dermal cells, which might account for the pathology.

DISCUSSION

These experiments may enhance the understanding of HIV-induced neuropatho-physiology and reveal HIV receptors other than the T4 molecule. Such insights may permit the design of improved preventive or therapeutic protocols for combating HIV infection.

REFERENCES

1. ULTMAN, M. H. *et al.* 1986. Develop. Med. **27**: 563–571.
2. SHAW, G. M., *et al.* 1985. Science **227**: 177–182.
3. RAINE, C. S. 1973. *In* Progress in Neuropathology, Vol. 2. H. M. Zimmerman, Ed.:27–68. Grune and Stratton, New York.
4. CHIU, F.-C. & J. E. GOLDMAN. 1984. J. Neurochem. **42**: 166–174

Mechanisms Regulating IL-2 mRNA

JENNIFER SHAW, KAREN MEEROVITCH,
CHRIS BLEACKLEY, AND VERN PAETKAU

Department of Biochemistry
University of Alberta
Edmonton, Canada

The cytokine interleukin-2 (IL-2) is rapidly cleared, disappearing with a half-life of between 3 and 5 minutes after infusion into humans or mice. This is consistent with its role as a transient signal in the immune system, a signal that must be cleared to avoid chronic and possibly deleterious stimulation. We have begun to examine mechanisms that affect the stability of IL-2 mRNA in stimulated T lymphocytes, because a short-lived cytokine might be translated from a short-lived mRNA. The immunosuppressive drug cyclosporine (CsA) has a selective effect on certain cytokine mRNAs, blocking their transcription[1,2] but not affecting generalized transcription in the cell.[3] We have examined the decay of IL-2 mRNA both in mouse EL4.E1 T lymphoma cells and in human peripheral blood lymphocytes (PBL), following the addition of CsA. In both cases, there was a first order disappearance of intracellular IL-2 mRNA, with a half-life of 0.8 hour (EL4.E1) and 1.5 hours (PBL).[4] Thus, IL-2 mRNA has a fairly short half-life in the cell, compared to bulk mRNA (about 10 hours, Ref. 5), but not as short as c-myc, which can be minutes.[6]

The relatively short half-life of IL-2 mRNA, relative to general intracellular mRNA, is itself subject to alterations. Protein synthesis inhibitors have been shown to lead to "superinduction" of various intracellular mRNAs, including IL-2 in human tonsil lymphocytes.[7] We found that cycloheximide (CHX) led to a rapid superinduction of IL-2 mRNA in EL4.E1 cells, human PBL, and the human T leukemia cell line Jurkat. Because we also showed that CHX does not affect the transcription rate of the IL-2 gene,[2] we conclude that it must stabilize the mRNA. This suggests that there is a degradative mechanism for IL-2 mRNA that does not degrade the bulk of cellular mRNA. In addition to CHX, we found that the RNA synthesis inhibitor actinomycin D stabilized IL-2 mRNA. This points to a very high lability in the mechanism that degrades IL-2 mRNA.

Because IL-2 mRNA is relatively short-lived, it is possible to determine whether its synthesis continues after the inducing agent is removed. EL4.E1 cells were induced to maximal IL-2 mRNA synthesis with the phorbol diester PMA (12 hours). They were then washed, and intracellular IL-2 mRNA levels were subsequently determined by quantitative cytodot analysis (FIG. 1). The level of IL-2 mRNA decayed with a half-life of about 1.5 hours, indicating that synthesis is essentially stopped when the inducing agent is removed. The continued transcription of IL-2 mRNA thus depends on a signaling mechanism being continuously stimulated by the inducing agent.

These results have been used to construct a model for the induction and degradation of IL-2 mRNA, which is shown in FIGURE 2. Transcription requires protein synthesis to initiate, but not to continue.[2] Some other type of labile signal, however, is required for transcription to continue, because it stops very soon after the inducing agent is removed. IL-2 mRNA is subject to fairly rapid degradation by a cellular RNase system. That system is, itself, also highly labile, and its ability to degrade IL-2 mRNA is rapidly lost on inhibition of either protein or RNA synthesis. This property is responsible for the superinduction of IL-2 mRNA, in which it resembles other

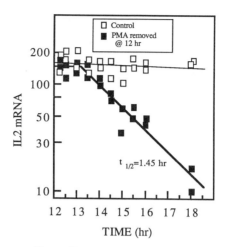

FIGURE 1. Disappearance of intracellular mRNA following removal of inducer. EL4.E1 cells were stimulated for 12 hours with 15 ng/ml of PMA, then washed and re-cultured either with (control) or without PMA. Cytoplasmic RNA was analyzed for IL-2 mRNA by cytodot analysis.

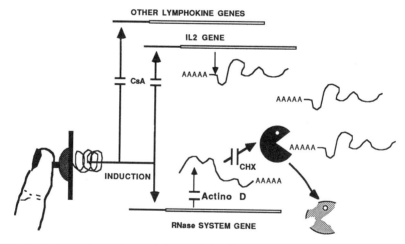

FIGURE 2. A model for the regulation of intracellular IL-2 mRNA levels. IL-2 mRNA transcription continues only as long as the inductive signal ("doorbell") is given. An RNase system that is selective for a subset of mRNAs that includes IL-2 constantly degrades IL-2 mRNA. The RNase is labile, and on inhibition of protein or RNA synthesis, it is rapidly inactivated. CsA blocks the transcription of IL-2 and certain other lymphokines, and leads to its rapid decline when present.

inducible gene products, such as certain liver enzymes and interferon. An RNase that exhibits this kind of sensitivity is RNase L.[8] However, we have no evidence that it is involved in this case. The lability of IL-2 mRNA is consistent with a role as a transient signal in the immune system. When the inductive (antigenic) signal disappears, so does the mRNA and the effector molecule itself.

REFERENCES

1. KRONKE, M., W. J. LEONARD, J. M. DEPPER, S. K. ARYA, F. WONG-STAAL, R. C. GALLO, T. A. WALDMANN & W. C. GREENE. 1984. Proc. Natl. Acad. Sci. USA **81:** 5214.
2. SHAW, J., K. MEEROVITCH, J. F. ELLIOTT, R. C. BLEACKLEY & V. PAETKAU. 1987. Mol. Immunol. **24:** 409.
3. PAETKAU, V. 1985. Can. J. Biochem. Cell Biol. **63:** 691.
4. SHAW, J., K. MEEROVITCH, R. C. BLEACKLEY & V. PAETKAU. 1988. J. Immunol. **140:** 2243.
5. HARPOLD, M. M., M. G. WILSON & J. E. DARNELL. 1981. Mol. Cell. Biol. **1:** 188.
6. DANI, C., N. MECHTI, M. PIECHARCZYK, B. LEBLEU, P. JEANTEUR & J. M. BLANCHARD. 1985. Proc. Natl. Acad. Sci. USA **82:** 4896.
7. EFRAT, S. & R. KAEMPFER. 1984. Proc. Natl. Acad. Sci. USA **81:** 2601.
8. SLATTERY, E., N. GHOSH, H. SAMANTA & P. LENGYEL. 1979. Proc. Natl. Acad. Sci. USA **76:** 4778.

Chemical Cross-Linking of IL-2 to High Affinity Receptors Present on Glycerol-Loaded T Cells and Membranes Prepared from Them Yields Only IL-2/P55 (Tac) Complexes

JOHN J. SIEKIERKA, STEVEN DeGUDICIBUS, AND
JEANNE WADSWORTH

Merck, Sharp and Dohme Research Laboratories
Department of Immunology
Rahway, New Jersey 07065

The T-cell growth factor, interleukin-2 (IL-2), promotes the growth of antigen-activated T cells via interaction with a specific class of high affinity receptors (reviewed in Ref. 1). A second class of IL-2 receptors, which constitutes more than 90% of all IL-2 receptors, exhibits a much lower affinity for IL-2 (K_d = 10 nmol versus 10–50 pmol for high affinity receptors) and does not appear to mediate a growth response.[2] The binding of IL-2 to either receptor class can be blocked by the monoclonal antibody, anti-Tac,[3] which demonstrates that both the high and low affinity forms of the IL-2 receptor share common molecular components. Recent results obtained from affinity cross-linking studies have led to the proposal that the high affinity form of the IL-2 receptor is a heterodimeric molecule consisting of a 55-kd (Tac) polypeptide and a 70-kd polypeptide (reviewed in Ref. 4). Both polypeptides in their monomeric forms bind IL-2 with low affinity (K_d > 1 nmol). It has further been suggested that both the 55-kd and the 70-kd polypeptides contribute to the formation of the IL-2 high affinity binding site.[4]

We have examined the molecular nature of the high affinity form of the IL-2 receptor utilizing an affinity cross-linking approach. We used partially purified plasma membranes prepared from human peripheral blood lymphocytes and the HTLV-I-transformed T-cell lines Hut-102 and MT-2. Plasma membranes were prepared by the glycerol-loading technique of Jett *et al.*[5] and retain high affinity IL-2 binding sites. Scatchard analysis of ^{125}I-labeled IL-2 binding data yielded a K_d essentially identical to that obtained for intact cells (K_d = 20–30 pmol). When ^{125}I-labeled IL-2 was cross-linked to these membranes under high affinity conditions and subsequently analyzed by SDS-PAGE, only a single cross-linked species of 70 kd that corresponds to the IL-2-Tac complex was observed. Similarly, cells that were glycerol loaded, but not lysed, bound ^{125}I-labeled IL-2 under high affinity conditions. Cross-linking analysis again revealed only IL-2-Tac complexes, whereas ^{125}I-labeled IL-2 cross-linked to high affinity receptors present on nonglycerol-loaded cells is found in a 70-kd and a 90-kd complex. The mechanism by which glycerol prevents the formation of the 90-kd (beta) complex is unknown. However, our data indicate that a high affinity IL-2 binding site is present on the p55 (Tac) polypeptide and that a secondary polypeptide may not be required as part of the high affinity IL-2 binding site.

REFERENCES

1. SMITH, K. A. 1984. Ann. Rev. Immunol. **2:** 319–333.
2. SMITH, K. A. & D. A. CANTRELL. 1985. Proc. Natl. Acad. Sci. USA **82:** 864–868.
3. LEONARD, W. J., J. M. DEPPER, T. UCHIYAMA, K. A. SMITH, T. A. WALDMANN, & W. C. GREENE. 1982. Nature **300:** 267–269.
4. SMITH, K. A. 1987. Immunol. Today **8:** 11–13.
5. JETT, M., T. M. SEED, & G. A. JAMIESON. 1977. J. Biol. Chem. **252:** 2134–2142.

Homozygous Deletion of the Immunoglobulin Cγ1 Gene

Analysis of the IgG Subclass Profile of Antiviral Antibodies[a]

C. I. EDVARD SMITH,[b] EVA FRIDELL,[c] ANNIKA LINDE,[c]
TIIT MATHIESEN,[c] AND LENNART HAMMARSTRÖM[b]

[b]Department of Clinical Immunology and Center for Biotechnology
Karolinska Institute at Huddinge Hospital
S-141 86 Huddinge, Sweden
and
Department of Immunology
Stockholm University
Stockholm, Sweden

[c]Department of Virology
National Bacteriological Laboratory
Stockholm, Sweden

There are nine functional gene segments encoding the human immunoglobulin C_H chains. The suggested order of the γ, ϵ, and α functional and pseudogenes on chromosome 14, as previously reported,[1,2] is depicted in FIGURE 1. The various deletions so far observed[3-7] are also presented in FIGURE 1. As can be seen, 8 different deletions have been found, corresponding to 12% of the total number of 66 possible deletions (calculated as the sum of deletions comprising one continuous stretch of DNA; if haplotypes containing two or more noncontinuous deletions are included, the observed number is considerably less than 12%). As previously discussed,[8] the deletions so far reported do not encompass the μ, δ, or the most 5' (J-proximal) of the γ or the most 3' of the α genes. It is not known if this is fortuitous or if the mechanisms underlying the deletions operate less efficiently in these regions of the C_H locus. Although heterozygous gene deletions in the immunoglobulin C_H locus may not be very rare,[4] gene deletions are seldom found as a cause of immunoglobulin deficiency. Thus, in IgA deficiency, either in the form of an isolated defect[9] or as part of common variable hypogammaglobulinemia,[10] gene deletions have not been found. Furthermore, in the case of IgG subclass deficiencies, deletions also seem to be rare.[11] We recently described a patient with a homozygous gene deletion encompassing the γ1 gene[7] (FIG. 1). A total IgG1 deficiency is a very rare disorder,[7,12] and to our knowledge a homozygous gene deletion resulting in this defect, apart from our patient, has not been reported.

Patients with immunoglobulin gene deletions permit analysis of the compensatory mechanisms in the immune response. In normal individuals antibodies against viral antigens are invariably found in the IgG1 subclass with a varying contribution of IgG3

[a]This work was supported by the Swedish Medical Research Council and the Ellen, Walter and Lennart Hesselman Foundation.

232

and IgG4.[13-15] In view of this restriction, we investigated the serum from the γ1-deficient patient and her parents for antiviral antibodies in ELISA as previously described in detail.[13-15] As expected (TABLE 1), we were unable to detect any IgG1 antibodies directed against viral antigens in the patient. Instead, specific IgG3 as well as IgG4 antibodies were found. At the age of 19 months the patient was vaccinated against measles, mumps, and rubella using live virus. Thus, it is likely that only her response to cytomegalovirus (TABLE 1) is due to a natural infection. Apart from the total lack of IgG1 there were no obvious abnormalities. The seemingly good response to parotitis virus may reflect the higher degree of cross-reactivity with other viral antigens that is found using this virus.

Although it has not been formally proven, both parents are likely to carry a heterozygous deletion of the γ1 gene and, in the case of the mother, also of the α1 gene[7] (FIG. 1). However, no obvious deviations were found in their sera as compared with the antiviral isotype profile in normal healthy subjects.[13-15] We recently analyzed the immune response to hepatitis B surface antigen in individuals with or without immunoglobulin C_H gene deletions.[16] IgG1 antibodies had the highest affinity.

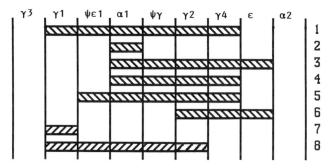

FIGURE 1. Immunoglobulin C_H gene deletions in man. *Patterns 1 and 2* were reported by Lefranc *et al.*,[3] *patterns 3 and 4* by Migone *et al.*,[4] *pattern 5* by Chaabani *et al.*,[5] *pattern 6* by Carbonara and deMarchi,[6] and *patterns 7 and 8* by Smith *et al.*[7]

Furthermore, the affinity of specific antibodies of a particular subclass was similar in both patients with gene deletion and normal healthy subjects. Although affinity analysis using antibodies from the patient with the homozygous γ1 deletion has not been carried out, these findings may suggest a lower affinity, possibly resulting in an impaired qualitative immune response.

CONCLUSION

A patient with two different immunoglobulin C_H gene deletions resulting in a homozygous deletion of the immunoglobulin Cγ1 gene was analyzed for the IgG subclass distribution of antiviral antibodies. In contrast to the response in normal healthy individuals who respond mainly with IgG1 antiviral antibodies, the immune response to measles, mumps, rubella, and cytomegalovirus was restricted to the IgG3 and IgG4 subclasses.

TABLE 1. Antiviral Antibodies in Familial IgG1 Deficiency: ELISA O.D. Values[a,b]

Subject/γ1 Deletion	Cytomegalovirus				Measles				Mumps				Rubella			
	IgG1	IgG2	IgG3	IgG4	IgG1	IgG2	IgG3	IgG4	IgG1	IgG2	IgG3	IgG4	IgG1	IgG2	IgG3	IgG4
Mother/ Heterozygous deletion	>2.0 (>2.0)	0.12	1.12	0.17	0.59	0.15	0.12	0.4	0.52	(N.T.3)	0.15	0.20	1.46	N.T.	0.18	0.05
Father/ Heterozygous deletion	>2.0 (0.57)	0.07	1.55	0.18	1.10	0.09	0.12	0.57	>2.0 (1.11)	0.06	0.16	1.8	1.88	0.057	0.12	0.05
Patient/ Homozygous deletion	0.06	0.00	0.55	0.17	0.10	0.06	0.24	0.22	0.04	N.T.	1.05	>2.0 (0.67)	0.08	0.09	0.24	0.10

[a]Background O.D. values + 3 S.D. <0.2. For IgG3 in measles the background + 3 S.D. was 0.16. Values >0.2 are underlined. The technical details of the assay and the response to cytomegalovirus, mumps, and rubella have previously been published.[13-15] The measles antigen consisted of whole virions and was assayed essentially as previously described.[13-15] All 45 individuals initially analyzed (adult seropositive, vaccinated children, and SSPE patients) had specific IgG1 measles antibodies.

[b]Values without parentheses correspond to a serum dilution of 10^{-2}, with parentheses to 10^{-3}.

[c]N.T. = not tested.

ACKNOWLEDGMENT

The technical assistance of Lotta Tauson is gratefully acknowledged.

REFERENCES

1. FLANAGAN, J. G. & T. H. RABBITTS. 1982. Arrangements of human immunoglobulin heavy constant region genes implies evolutionary duplication of a segment containing γ, ε and α genes. Nature **300:** 709.
2. BECH-HANSEN, N. T., P. S. LINSLEY, & D. W. COX. 1983. Restriction fragment length polymorphisms associated with immunoglobulin C genes reveal linkage disequilibrium and genomic organization. Proc. Natl. Acad. Sci. USA **80:** 6952.
3. LEFRANC, M. P., G. LEFRANC & T. H. RABBITTS. 1982. Inherited deletion of immunoglobulin heavy constant region genes in normal human individuals. Nature **300:** 760.
4. MIGONE, N., G. OLIVIERO, G. G. DE LANGE, D. DELACROIX, F. BOSCHIS, L. ALTRUDA, M. SILENGO, M. DEMARCHI & A. O. CARBONARA. 1984. Multiple gene deletions within the human immunoglobulin heavy-chain cluster. Proc. Natl. Acad. Sci. USA **81:** 5811.
5. CHAABANI, H., N. T. BECH-HANSEN & D. W. COX. 1985. A multigene deletion within the immunoglobulin heavy-chain region. Am. J. Hum. Genet. **37:** 1164.
6. CARBONARA, A. O. & M. DEMARCHI. Personal communication.
7. SMITH, C. I. E., L. HAMMARSTRÖM, J.-I. HENTER & G. G. DE LANGE. 1988. Molecular and serological analysis of familial IgG1 deficiency with a new type of homozygous structural gene deletion. Submitted.
8. SMITH, C. I. E. & L. HAMMARSTRÖM. 1986. Gene abnormalities in immunoglobulin deficiency disorders. Clin. Immunol. Newsletter **7:** 145.
9. HAMMARSTRÖM, L., B. CARLSSON, C. I. E. SMITH, J. WALLIN, & L. WIESLANDER. 1985. Detection of IgA heavy chain constant region genes in IgA deficient donors: Evidence against gene deletions. Clin. Exp. Immunol. **60:** 661.
10. SMITH, C. I. E. & L. HAMMARSTRÖM. 1984. Detection of α1 and α2 heavy chain constant region genes in common variable hypogammaglobulinemia patients with undetectable IgA. Scand. J. Immunol. **20:** 361.
11. SMITH, C. I. E. & L. HAMMARSTRÖM. 1986. Detection of immunoglobulin genes in individuals with immunoglobulin class or subclass deficiency. Evidence for a pretranslational defect. Monogr. Allergy **20:** 18.
12. VAN LOGHEM, E. 1980. Genetically determined deficiencies in IgA and IgG. Hematologica **13:** 185.
13. LINDE, G. A., L. HAMMARSTRÖM, M. A. A. PERSSON, C. I. E. SMITH, V.-A. SUNDQVIST & B. WAHREN. 1983. Virus-specific antibody activity of different subclasses of immunoglobulins G and A in cytomegalovirus infections. Inf. Immun. **42:** 237.
14. LINDE, A. 1985. Sublcass distribution of rubella virus-specific immunoglobulin G. J. Clin. Microbiol. **21:** 117.
15. LINDE, A., M. GRANSTRÖM & C. ÖRVELL. 1987. Serodiagnosis of mumps infection and mumps immunity—a comparison of Ig class and subclass ELISAs and microneutralization assay. J. Clin. Microbiol. **25:** 1653.
16. PERSSON, M. A. A., S. E. BROWN, L. HAMMARSTRÖM, M. W. STEWARD, C. I. E. SMITH, C. HOWARD, M. WAHL, B. RYNNEL-DAGÖÖ, G. LEFRANC & A. O. CARBONARA. 1988. IgG subclasse associated affinity differences of specific antibodies in humans. J. Immunol. **140:** 3875.

The 25,000-Dalton Protein Associated with Class II MHC Antigens Is a C-Terminal Fragment of I_i and Is Intracellularly Derived

LAWRENCE J. THOMAS, QUOC V. NGUYEN,
WILLIAM L. ELLIOTT, AND ROBERT E. HUMPHREYS[a]

Department of Pharmacology
University of Massachusetts Medical School
Worcester, Massachusetts 01655

The 25,000-dalton protein (p25), found in immunoprecipitates with antibodies to class II major histocompatibility complex (MHC) antigens or to I_i, was demonstrated to be the C-terminal fragment of I_i and to be relatively resistant to further proteolytic digestion. p25 was also shown to appear maximally in an intracellular fraction of polyclonally activated B cells 20–40 minutes after [^{35}S]methionine labeling.

p25 was shown to be derived from the C-terminal end of I_i by the following experiments. [^{35}S]methionine-labeled I_i and associated molecules were immunoprecipitated with VIC-γ1 monoclonal antibody to I_i, denatured with 9 M urea, desalted, and reimmunoprecipitated with each of several antibodies. One antibody to a C-terminal peptide of I_i (183–193) reprecipitated p25. Another antibody to a C-terminal peptide of I_i (192–211)[1] also reprecipitated p25, whereas an antibody to an N-terminal peptide of I_i (12–38)[2] did not. All three of these antibodies reprecipitated denatured I_i. In another experiment, while I_i was metabolically labeled with either [^{35}S]methionine or [^{35}S]cysteine, p25 was labeled with [^{35}S]methionine but not with [^{35}S]cysteine. This finding was consistent with the view that the single cysteine (position 28) in I_i is not retained in p25.

Nonionic detergent-solubilized [^{35}S]methionine-labeled I_i and associated proteins were digested with trypsin, chymotrypsin, or proteinase K. Peptides were observed to migrate at or near the position of p25 in 2-D electrophoretic gels. These species were relatively resistant to further digestion after longer incubations with the proteases. These observations were consistent with the view that secondary structures in I_i created a relatively protease-sensitive cleavage site that yielded p25.

Human B splenocytes were polyclonally activated wtih *Staphylococcus aureus* for 3 days, labeled for 15 minutes with [^{35}S]methionine, and chased with cold methionine for 0, 10, 40, and 60 minutes. Subcellular fractions of homogenates were separted on a Percoll density gradient and immunoprecipitated with I_i (183–193) peptide antisera. p25 appeared with I_i in endosomal fractions, whereas lysosomal and plasma membrane fractions did not contain p25. Maximal appearance of p25 was demonstrated at 20–40 minute chase times.[3]

These findings were consistent with the hypotheses that: (1) an alpha helix with an axial hydrophobic strip in I_i (147–169) may block the desetope of the class II MHC molecules from the time of their synthesis until reaching a foreign antigen-containing

---

[a]To whom correspondence should be sent.

endosome,[4] (2) I_i could be removed in a way to catalyze the charging of the desetope with foreign peptides, presumably in the endosome with the production of p25,[5] (3) dissociated I_i might self-associate in a manner not to compete for binding of foreign peptides,[4] and (4) I_i might function to retard the release of class II MHC antigens to the cell surface until "completion" of those receptors with foreign peptides.[3]

REFERENCES

1. GIACOLETTO, K. S., A. J. SANT, C. BONO, J. GORKA, D. M. O'SULLIVAN, V. QUARANTA & B. D. SCHWARTZ. 1986. The human invariant chain is the core protein of the human class II-associated proteoglycan. J. Exp. Med. **164:** 1422.
2. QUARANTA, V. & D. O'SULLIVAN. Relationship between Ia biosynthesis and antigen processing. 6th International Congress of Immunology, Toronto, Canada, July 6–11, 1986.
3. NGUYEN, Q. V., M.-Z. XU, P. S. REISERT & R. E. HUMPHREYS. Structures and trafficking of class II MHC molecules and associated proteins in activated human B cells. Submitted.
4. ELLIOTT, W. L., C. J. STILLE, L. J. THOMAS & R. E. HUMPHREYS. 1987. An hypothesis on the binding of an alpha helical sequence in I_i to the desetope of class II antigens. J. Immunol. **138:** 2949.
5. STILLE, C. J., L. J. THOMAS, V. E. REYES & R. E. HUMPHREYS. 1987. Hydrophobic strip-of-helix algorithm for selection of T cell-presented peptides. Molec. Immunol. **24:** 1021.

Regulation of Self-Tolerance to Insulin

PHYLLIS JONAS WHITELEY,[a] RICHARD SELDEN,[b]
AND JUDITH A. KAPP[a]

[a]Department of Pathology
The Jewish Hospital of Saint Louis
and
Departments of Pathology and Microbiology/Immunology
Washington University School of Medicine
St. Louis, Missouri 63110

[b]Department of Molecular Biology
Massachusetts General Hospital
and
Department of Genetics
Harvard Medical School
Boston, Massachusetts 02114

Development and maintenance of self-tolerance are important but poorly understood features of the immune system. It is essential that we understand the mechanisms of self-tolerance if we are to devise specific therapeutic approaches to control autoimmune diseases such as juvenile onset diabetes, myasthenia gravis, and multiple sclerosis. Studies on H-2-linked Ir genes are relevant to this issue, because it is thought that nonresponsiveness occurs because the nominal antigen looks like self-antigen to the host.[1] Murine antibody responses to various species of insulin are under MHC-linked Ir gene control such that certain strains of mice produce antibodies to insulin, whereas others do not.[2] Beef insulin differs from pork insulin by only two amino acids in the A chain loop, yet H-2^b mice produce insulin-specific antibodies after immunization with beef insulin and fail to produce antibody after stimulation with pork insulin. Our studies of the regulation of responses to insulin have shown that T cells from pork-insulin-primed nonresponder mice fail to support responses to pork insulin because pork insulin primes both helper T (Th) cells and dominant suppressor T (Ts) cells.[2] Under the same circumstances, beef insulin, which stimulates an antibody response in these mice, primes Th but not Ts cells, raising the possibility that responsiveness occurs because no suppressor T cells are stimulated. More importantly, the pork-insulin-primed Th cells from H-2^b mice recognize autologous insulin, whereas beef-insulin-primed helper T cells do not.

On examination of the Th cells in the nonresponder H-2^b mice, we found that the frequency of helper T cells stimulated by pork insulin was equivalent to that stimulated by beef insulin.[3] Thus, there are no quantitative differences in helper activity of T cells from H-2^b mice primed with pork (nonresponder) or beef (responder) insulin, and the nonresponder-derived Th cells are not an aberrant phenomenon. Furthermore, we have cloned T cells that recognize autologous insulin from the lymph nodes of mice primed with nonimmunogenic pork insulin: they are MHC restricted, L3T4-positive T cells that produce lymphokines and provide cognate help to B cells. Thus, there is no defect in the ability of nonimmunogenic pork insulin to combine with Ia or with the nonresponder-derived Th cells to recognize this complex. These cloned Th cells are inhibited by pork-insulin-specific Ts cells. Therefore, our data demonstrate that Th cells that recognize autologous proteins need not be clonally deleted from the system if

TABLE 1. *In vivo* Antibody Response to Insulin in (b × k)F1 Nontransgenic and Transgenic Mice

	Relative O.D.[a]	
Insulin	Nontransgenic Littermates	Transgenic Littermates
None	0.06 ± 0.02	0.06 ± 0.02
Human	0.77 ± 0.29	0.06 ± 0.02
Pork	(0.23, 0.40)[b]	(0.07, 0.06)[b]
Beef	2.5 ± 1.8	>5.0
Sheep	0.89 ± 0.44	1.46 ± 0.4

[a]Mice were immunized with 50 μg of insulin in complete Freund's adjuvant intraperitoneally. After 21 days, the sera were assayed by ELISA for insulin-specific antibody. The data are expressed as a ratio of the O.D. at 405 nm of a 1:100 dilution of the sample to a known standard ± SEM of triplicate mice.
[b]Data are from two mice.

they can be functionally attenuated by suppressor T cells that also recognize autologous proteins.

To further our understanding of the mechanisms involved in the immune system's ability to discriminate between self and nonself, we are studying the induction of self-tolerance to a foreign antigen using transgenic mice that express physiologic levels of human insulin. Transgenic (H-2^b × H-2^k)F1 mice that express physiologic levels of human insulin did not produce antibody to human or pork insulin, whereas their normal counterparts responded to both (TABLE 1). Thus, expression of the human insulin gene not only has rendered these mice tolerant to human insulin but also has altered the T-cell response to another, normally immunogenic insulin. The data support the hypothesis that Ir-gene-controlled antibody responses to certain antigens, such as insulin, involve mechanisms used for maintenance of self-tolerance. Our new model, which uses mice that are transgenic for the human insulin gene, will be useful in studying the mechanisms involved in induction and maintenance of self-tolerance.

REFERENCES

1. SCHWARTZ, R. H. 1978. Scand. J. Immunol. 7: 3.
2. JENSEN, P. E. & J. A. KAPP. 1985. J. Immunol. 135: 2990.
3. WHITELEY, P. J., P. E. JENSEN, C. W. PIERCE, A. F. ABRUZZINI & J. A. KAPP. 1988. Proc. Natl. Acad. Sci. 85: 2723.

MHC-Linked Diabetogenic Gene in the NOD Mouse Is Not Absolutely Recessive

LINDA S. WICKER AND BEVERLY J. MILLER

Department of Immunology Research
Merck Sharp & Dohme Research Laboratories
Rahway, New Jersey 07065

We previously reported that at least three loci, including one that is linked to the major histocompatibility complex (MHC), control the development of diabetes in the NOD mouse (K^d, $I\text{-}A^{NOD}$, D^b) when analyzed by outcrossing to the C57/BL10SnJ (B10) (K^b, $I\text{-}A^b$, D^b) strain.[1] The current study was undertaken to characterize the mechanisms by which the MHC influences the development of diabetes in the NOD mouse. Because the disease is polygenic, it was necessary to produce an MHC congenic strain on the NOD background. To produce the NOD.$H\text{-}2^b$ strain, repetitive backcrosses to the NOD were performed using breeders expressing $I\text{-}A^b$ on the surface of peripheral blood B cells. All progeny were tested weekly for diabetes. At the onset of diabetes or at 7 to 9 months of age, mice were sacrificed and their spleen cells were typed for $I\text{-}A^b$. TABLE 1 summarizes the incidence of diabetes in backcross generations N3 to N9 for NOD MHC homozygous and heterozygous females. The incidence of diabetes in our colony of NOD females is 70% at 7 months of age[1]; by the N4 generation, the incidence of diabetes in the NOD MHC homozygous female backcross mice reached that of the parental strain. In the NOD MHC heterozygous backcross females, 4 of 97 mice developed diabetes as determined by the presence of glycosuria, polydipsia, and weight loss. Histologic examination of pancreata from these four diabetic heterozygotes revealed pathology consistent with overt diabetes. These data suggest that homozygosity at the $I\text{-}A$ region is not essential for the devleopment of diabetes in the NOD mouse.

One NOD MHC heterozygous female from the N6 generation had produced a single litter before developing diabetes, and a pedigree analysis of her progeny was performed. Of her NOD MHC homozygous progeny, nine of nine females and four of five males became diabetic by 7 months of age. In contrast, only 1 of 10 females and 0 of 10 males that were NOD MHC heterozygous became diabetic. Because a high frequency of diabetes was not observed in these NOD MHC heterozygous progeny, this analysis indicates that a recombination event between a putative MHC-linked diabetogenic gene and the K and $I\text{-}A$ regions of the MHC did not account for the diabetes observed in the heterozygous female from the N6 generation. This pedigree analysis supports the hypothesis that diabetes can occur in low frequency in $H\text{-}2^{NOD/b}$ heterozygotes.

Although not all NOD mice become diabetic, insulitis is found in nearly all adult female and male NOD mice[2] and probably represents the initiation of the autoimmune response. Therefore, all backcross mice were assessed for abnormal cellular infiltrates within their pancreata. Moderate to severe insulitis was observed in approximately 85% of NOD MHC homozygous female and male mice, and periislet inflammation was observed in the remaining 15%. Approximately half of the NOD MHC heterozygous females and males displayed moderate to severe insulitis, with the remainder displaying less severe inflammatory lesions. Therefore, it is not surprising that some

TABLE 1. Incidence of Diabetes in NOD/NOD MHC Homozygotes and NOD/b MHC Heterozygotes in (NOD × B10) × NOD Female Backcross Mice

	No. Diabetic/Total	
Backcross Generation	NOD/NOD MHC	NOD/b MHC
Second (N3)	41/84 (49%)	1/21 (5%)
Third (N4)	8/11 (73%)	0/27 (0)
Fourth (N5)	Not tested	
Fifth (N6)	15/22 (68%)	1/32 (3%)
Sixth (N7)	7/8 (88%)	1/10 (10%)
Seventh (N8)	3/3 (100%)	1/15 (7%)
Eighth (N9)	3/3 (100%)	0/5 (0)
Total	77/131 (59%)	4/110 (4%)

Peripheral blood mononuclear cells or spleen cells were incubated with anti-I-$A^{b,d}$, H-$2^{p,q}$ (34-5-3S), Litton Bionetics, Charleston, South Carolina, a monoclonal antibody that recognizes I-A^{b} but is not reactive with I-A^{NOD}. The cells were washed and then incubated with FITC-conjugated goat anti-mouse IgG and analyzed by flow cytometry, as described previously.[1]

NOD MHC heterozygotes proceed to develop overt diabetes, because an autoimmune response is clearly initiated in most of these mice.

REFERENCES

1. WICKER, L. S., B. J. MILLER, L. Z. COKER, S. E. McNALLY, S. SCOTT, Y. MULLEN & M. C. APPEL. 1987. J. Exp. Med. **165:** 1639.
2. MAKINO, S., K. KUNIMOTO, Y. MURAOKA & K. KATAGIRI. 1981. Exp. Anim. **30:** 137.

Receptor-Coupled Effector Systems and Their Interactions in Splenocytes from Athymic Nude Mice[a]

ERIK WIENER AND ANTONIO SCARPA

Case Western Reserve University
Department of Physiology and Biophysics
Cleveland, Ohio 44106

Intracellular signaling systems can often modulate one another. For example, products from the hydrolysis of phosphatidylinositol-4,5-bisphosphate (PIP_2) can increase and/or potentiate cAMP accumulation in rat pinealocytes, vascular smooth muscle cells, and neutrophils.[1-3] In B lymphocytes, antibodies to surface immunoglobulins (anti-Ig) activate inositol phospholipid hydrolysis,[4] but little is known concerning their effects on cAMP levels. We have examined whether activation of PIP_2 hydrolysis by anti-Ig alters cAMP metabolism in splenocytes from athymic nude mice.

Goat anti-mouse IgM both increased the levels of cAMP and modulated agonist-induced changes in the cAMP concentration. Antibody (25 μg/ml) stimulated a rapid transient increase in cAMP from a basal level of 250 fmol/10^6 cells to 400 fmol/10^6 cells within 1 minute, which after 10 minutes subsided to 310 fmol/10^6 cells (FIG. 1). Pretreating the cells with anti-Ig produced opposite effects on the forskolin- and PGE_1-induced cAMP increases. Anti-Ig potentiated the forskolin-induced (114 μM) cAMP increase by 76% (FIG. 2A), but it decreased the response to 50 nM PGE_1 by 30% (FIG. 2B).

The observations just described coupled with those of Bijsterbosch *et al.*[4] reveal a correlation between the changes in cAMP metabolism and activation of PIP_2 hydrolysis; however, they do not prove a causal relationship. Stimulation of PIP_2 hydrolysis activates two parallel intracellular signaling systems; one involves an increase in the cytosolic free $[Ca^{2+}]$ and subsequent activation of calmodulin, whereas the other results in the production of diacylglycerol and activation of protein kinase C.[5] Therefore, if anti-Ig-induced inositol phospholipid hydrolysis modulates cAMP metabolism, then activation of one or both pathways should also modulate cAMP metabolism. The studies whose results are depicted in FIGURE 2 examined whether activation of protein kinase C could modulate the adenylate cyclase system. Treating splenocytes with compounds that directly activate protein kinase C, such as 12-O-tetradecanoyl phorbol-13-acetate (TPA)[6] or sn-1,2-dioctanoylglycerol (diC$_8$),[7] resulted in responses qualitatively similar to those from pretreating the cells with anti-Ig. Preincubating the splenocytes for 3 minutes with TPA (97 nM) potentiated the forskolin-induced increase from 1.7 ± 0.1 to 4.3 ± 0.6 pmol of cAMP/10^6 cells (FIG. 2A), but reduced the PGE_1 response from 0.98 ± 0.06 to 0.51 ± 0.03 pmol of cAMP/10^6 cells (FIG. 2B). Similarly, pretreating the cells with 5 μM diC$_8$ increased the forskolin response from 1.7 ± 0.1 to 5.1 ± 0.2 pmol of cAMP/10^6 cells (FIG. 2A), but reduced the PGE_1

[a]This work was supported by NIH Grant DK-37878. E. W. was supported by National Institute of Health Training Grant HL-07502 in partial fulfillment of a Ph.D. in biophysics from the University of Pennsylvania.

response from 1.15 ± 0.03 to 0.75 ± 0.04 pmol of cAMP/10^6 cells (FIG. 2B). The inactive phorbol ester 4α-phorbol-12,13-didecanoate had no effect on either the forskolin or PGE$_1$ response. These results indicate that the modulation of cAMP metabolism by anti-Ig results from PIP$_2$ hydrolysis and the resulting activation of protein kinase C. Furthermore, activation of protein kinase C results in the modifica-

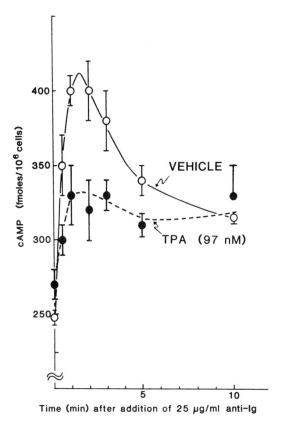

FIGURE 1. Anti-IgM stimulates an increase in cAMP levels. Single cell suspensions of spleens from 6–7-week-old nu/nu mice were prepared in a HEPES buffered physiologic salt solution containing 0.1% BSA (BSS/BSA), were depleted of dead cells and red blood cells on a discontinuous ficolpaque gradient (d = 1.09), washed in BSS/BSA, and resuspended in BSS/BSA supplemented with 10 mM glucose and 500 μM 3-isobutyl-1-methylxanthine at 1.25×10^6 cells/ml. The cells were incubated at 37°C for 10 minutes before incubating the cells with anti-IgM, for the time indicated, in the presence of equal concentrations of EtOH, 0.6%, as vehicle (O) or 97 nM TPA (●) added 3 minutes before the antibody. Values are the means ± SE of a single representative experiment performed in triplicate.

tion of at least two components of the adenylate cyclase effector system with opposite effects.

These observations imply that cytokines and/or prostaglandins secreted by other lymphoid cells can act in concert with anti-Ig and/or antigen to define the state of

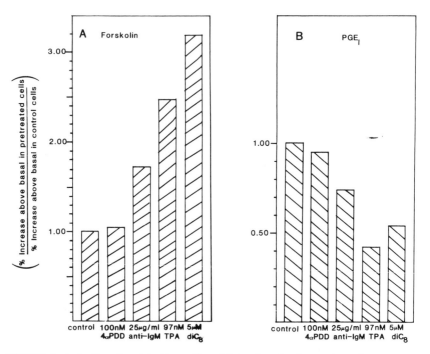

FIGURE 2. Activation of protein kinase C modulates the adenylate cyclase effector system. Splenocytes were incubated for 10 minutes at 37°C before (A) a 10-minute incubation with 114 μM forskolin, or (B) a 2-minute incubation with 50 nM PGE_1. The protein kinase C activators indicated in this figure were added 3 minutes before the cAMP agonists.

B-cell proliferation or differentiation. Furthermore, it also provides a mechanism by which antigen can differentially regulate T and B cells responding to macrophage-produced prostaglandins.

REFERENCES

1. SUGDEN, D., J. VANECEK, D. C. KLEIN, T. P. THOMAS & W. B. ANDERSON. 1985. Nature **314:** 359–361.
2. NABIKA, T., Y. NARA, Y. YAMORI, W. LOVENBERG & J. ENDO. 1985. Biochem. Biophys. Res. Comm. **131:** 30–36.
3. VERGHESE, M. W., K. FOX, L. C. MCPHAIL & R. SNYDERMAN. 1985. J. Biol. Chem. **260:** 6769–6775.
4. BIJSTERBOSCH, M. K., C. J. MEADE, G. A. TURNER & G. G. B. KLAUS. 1985. Cell **41:** 999–1006.
5. BERRIDGE, M. J. 1984. Biochem. J. **220:** 345–360.
6. CASTAGNA, M., Y. TAKAI, K. KAIBUCHI, K. SANO, U. KIKKAWA & Y. NISHIZUKA. 1982. J. Biol. Chem. **257:** 7847–7851.
7. LAPETINA, E., B. REEP, B. GANONG & R. BELL. 1985. J. Biol. Chem. **260:** 1358–1361.

Prolactin: Role in T-Cell Proliferation[a]

LI-YUAN YU-LEE

Departments of Medicine and Cell Biology
Baylor College of Medicine
Houston, Texas 77030

The pituitary peptide hormone prolactin (Prl) has been shown to be capable of restoring the immunocompetence of hypophysectomized animals in mounting both humoral and cell-mediated immune responses.[1] A role of Prl in modulating the immune response through its modulation of lymphocyte proliferative properties has been proposed. I have been studying, as a model system, the rat NB2 T lymphoma cell line which is dependent on picogram amounts of Prl for growth.[2,3] The NB2 cells were established from the lymph node of an estrogenized male rat and contain a large number of high affinity Prl receptors (12,000/cell) which may form the basis of their exquisite sensitivity to Prl.[4] In NB2 cells Prl stimulation is characterized by a rapid

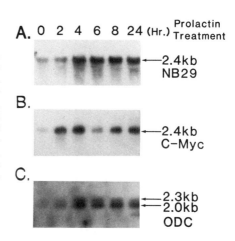

FIGURE 1. Time course of prolactin (Prl) induction. NB2 cells were made stationary by incubation in Fisher's medium for leukemic cells containing 10% horse serum for 24 hours. Ovine Prl was added to 100 ng/ml, and at various times total RNA was prepared as described.[6] Identical blots containing 10 μg/lane RNA were hybridized with nick-translated probes for NB29 (1.5 kb cDNA from S. deToledo), *c-myc* (2.4-kb genomic fragment from E. Murphy), and ODC (1.14 kb cDNA from O. Janne).

induction of several growth-related genes including *c-myc*, ornithine decarboxylase (ODC), and a heat shock protein 70 (Hsp 70)-homologue, NB29.[5] Characterizing the patterns of specific gene expression constitutes a starting point in deriving the molecular mechanisms of Prl action on lymphocyte proliferation.

On addition of Prl to quiescent NB2 cells, a rapid induction of *c-myc* and ODC mRNA was observed by 2 hours, with maximum induction by 4 hours (FIG. 1). The Hsp 70-homologue NB29 mRNA level was maximal by 4–6 hours. Thereafter, the continued presence of Prl is required for maintaining an elevated level of expression of all three genes throughout the cell cycle (20 hours). This represents a first report that the ODC mRNA may be regulated by Prl. To examine whether Prl induced gene transcription and/or mRNA stability, the transcriptional activities of the NB29,

[a]This work was supported by ACS Grant BC–425.

A. Transcription

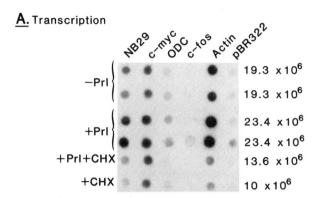

FIGURE 2A. Transcription and mRNA stability of growth-related genes are regulated differentially by prolactin (Prl) and cycloheximide (CHX) in NB2 cells. The transcriptional activities of 45×10^6 nuclei isolated from NB2 cells treated with combinations of Prl and CHX were assayed by a run-on transcription analysis as described.[7] *In vitro* labeled transcripts (numbers in counts per minute [cpm] as indicated) were hybridized with DNA dot filters, each containing 5 μg of NB29, *c-myc*, ODC, *v-fos* (1.3-kb viral fragment from E. Murphy), β-actin (1.15 kb cDNA from M. Buckingham), and pBR322 DNA. Duplicate sets of filters were used for −Prl and +Prl samples.

B. Relative Transcription Rates of Prolactin-Inducible Genes

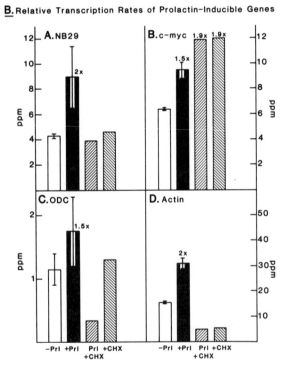

FIGURE 2B. Relative transcription rates of Prl-inducible genes. After correction for pBR322 background counts (average 35 cpm), the hybridized cpm were converted to parts per million (ppm), and the fold of Prl induction relative to control nuclei (−Prl) is determined (+/−).

c-myc, and ODC genes along with *c-fos* and β-actin genes were examined by nuclear run-on transcription assays and compared with the corresponding steady-state mRNA levels (FIG. 2). In the NB2 cells, ODC and *c-fos* transcription rates are low, bordering on the limits of detection. Prl induces a small 1.5- to 2-fold increase in transcriptional activity of NB29, *c-myc,* ODC, and actin genes (FIG. 2A and B). However, these genes are regulated differentially at both the transcriptional and the posttranscriptional levels as determined by treatment with cycloheximide (CHX) (FIG. 2B and C). These genes fall into three categories: (1) *c-myc* gene basal transcription is under *negative* regulation; the addition of Prl and CHX superinduces both transcription and mRNA stability; (2) β-actin gene transcription is under *positive* regulation; the addition of CHX decreases both transcription rate and mRNA levels; (3) NB29 and ODC genes' basal transcription does not require on-going protein synthesis; however, Prl induction of both gene transcription and mRNA accumulation involves labile positive regulatory proteins.

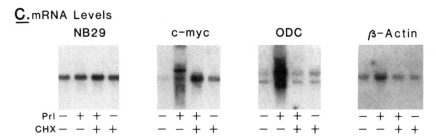

FIGURE 2C. Steady-state mRNA levels. Total cell RNA (10 μg/lane) was also prepared in parallel from a duplicate batch of cells in the same experiment, and steady-state mRNA levels were determined by RNA blot analysis. Note that the level of NB29 mRNA is normally decreased in the presence of Prl and CHX; the elevated level seen in this experiment is not reproducibly observed. The multiple bands seen in lane 2 in the *c-myc* and ODC RNA blots are due to incomplete glyoxalation of the RNA samples.

Thus, analysis of expression of known growth-related genes after mitogenic stimulation by Prl of T lymphocytes has been employed to understand the early events preceding cell proliferation. Another approach currently being employed involves isolating Prl-inducible novel gene sequences from an NB2 cell cDNA library which may be important for lymphocyte proliferation. Furthermore, these studies should generate unique molecular markers with which to examine how the neuroendocrine system interacts with the immune system to modulate its proliferative responses.

REFERENCES

1. NAGY, E. *et al.* 1983. Acta Endocrinol. **102:** 351–357.
2. GOUT, P. W. *et al.* 1980. Cancer Res. **40:** 2433–2436.
3. TANAKA, T. *et al.* 1980. J. Clin. Endocrinol. Metab. **51:** 1058–1063.
4. SHIU, R. P. C. *et al.* 1983. Endocrinology **113:** 159–165.
5. DeTOLEDO, S. M. *et al.* 1987. Molec. Endocrinol. **230:** 1174–1177.
6. CHIRGWIN, J. M. *et al.* 1979. Biochemistry **18:** 5294–5299.
7. McKNIGHT, G. S. & R. D. PALMITER. 1979. J. Biol. Chem. **254:** 9050–9058.

Molecular Profile of Monoclonal Antibody Expressing the A48 Regulatory Idiotope and Having Distinct Antigen Specificities[a]

HABIB ZAGHOUANI, C. VICTOR-KOBRIN, Z. BARAK,
F. A. BONILLA, AND C. BONA

Department of Microbiology
Mount Sinai Hospital
New York, New York 10029

It has been proposed that regulatory idiotopes (RId) are autoimmunogens, germline gene encoded and borne by both the T-cell receptor and antibodies having different antigenic specificities.[1] The anti-β 2-6 fructosan myeloma protein A48 expresses an idiotype defined as regulatory because it is silent in bacterial levan-immunized BALB/c mice but can be expressed on priming with either A48 or anti-A48 Id antibodies after challenging with levan.[2] In previous studies, several A48 Id bearing monoclonal antibodies (mAbs) were isolated by first priming newborn or adult BALB/c mice with the IDA10 monoclonal anti-A48 Id and then challenging with bacterial levan.[3] Most of these antibodies belong to the V_H X24 and V_k10 germline gene families that respectively encode the V_H and V_k of the A48 protein.[4] These antibodies display different types of fructosan or unknown antigenic specificities but nevertheless share a common idiotype.[4] This last observation was made among antibodies sharing other RIds. Thus, we were interested in exploring the molecular basis for RId expression.

Herein we screened 70 mAbs directed against different antigens for the expression of the idiotype recognized by IDA10. From this panel we found five antibodies: Z26, M56, PY102, XY101, and Y19-10, which bound to IDA10. Z26 and M56 are specific for Sm antigen. PY102 and XY101 are specific for hemagglutinin H1 of PR8 influenza virus and hemagglutinin H3 of X31 influenza virus, respectively, and Y19-10 is a rheumatoid factor. As can be seen in FIGURE 1, Z26 and M56 completely inhibited the binding of mAb 3-14-9 to IDA10, albeit at higher concentrations than the homologous ligand. 3-14-9 is an antipolyfructosan that expresses the A48 RId recognized by IDA10.[2] PY102, XY101, and Y19-10 are weak inhibitors (40, 30, and 15% inhibition, respectively). These results are in good agreement with a direct binding assay in which these last three antibodies bound ^{125}I-labeled IDA10 only two- to threefold higher than background, but Z26 and M56 bound sixfold higher than background (data not shown). The binding of IDA10 to each antibody is not inhibited by the corresponding antigen, which suggests that the idiotypes expressed on these antibodies are not antigen inhibitable (data not shown). In a separate experiment we found that the isolated heavy and light chains of these five antibodies do not bind IDA10. This was done by polyacrylamide gel electrophoresis under reducing conditions followed by Western blotting. However, intact antibodies electrophoresed and blotted from the same gel under nonreducing conditions bound IDA10 (data not

[a]C. V. K. is a recipient of an Investigatorship from the New York Heart Association.

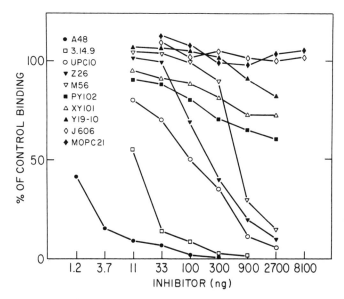

FIGURE 1. Expression of A48RI by antibodies having different antigen specificities. In this solid phase radioimmunoassay, serial dilutions of monoclonal antibodies compete with [125]I 3-14-9 (Id) for binding to IDA10 (anti-Id) coated wells.

shown). These results led to the conclusion that the idiotype expressed on these antibodies is a conformational one.

For a deeper insight into the molecular basis of A48 RId expression, the V_H and V_k families used by these antibodies were investigated in Northern blotting experiments. Cytoplasmic RNA was isolated, Northern blotted, and hybridized under stringent conditions with V_H and V_k P^{32} nick-translated probes, representing the various

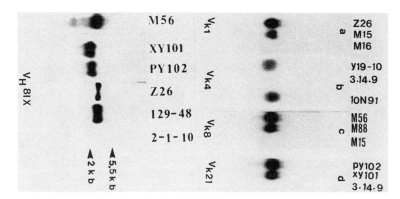

FIGURE 2. V_H and V_k usage by monoclonal antibodies expressing the A48R1d and having distinct antigen specificities. Cytoplasmic poly A^+ mRNA was electrophoresed, Northern blotted, and hybridized under stringent conditions to either V_k (*upper panel*) or V_H (*lower panel*) P^{32} nick-translated probes.

germline gene families. As can be seen in the lower panel of FIGURE 2, hybridization is observed with the V_H81X probe to an mRNA species from all the hybridomas (except Y19-10). The V_H81X germline gene probe is a member of the V_H7183 family. Y19-10 belongs to the J558 V_H family as determined by nucleotide sequencing analysis. The upper panel of FIGURE 2 also shows hybridization of the same hybridoma RNA preparations with the V_k probes. Hybridization is observed to the light chain mRNA of PY102 and XY101 with the V_k21 probe, Z26 with the V_k1 probe, and M56 and Y19-10 with the V_k8 and V_k4 probes, respectively.

In conclusion, the results show that the A48 RId is expressed to varying extents as a conformational determinant on five hybridoma proteins displaying diverse antigen-binding specificities and are encoded by V_H genes deriving from various V_H families in combinatorial association with genes derived from various V_k families. This situation is different from the very restricted V_H and V_k expression that has been observed among fructosan binding A48 RId bearing mAbs. However, ongoing nucleotide sequencing analysis of both the heavy and light chains of these antibodies as well as several galactan and fructosan binding A48 RId bearing proteins may clarify the basis for A48 RId expression.

REFERENCES

1. PAUL W. E. & C. BONA. 1982. Regulatory idiotopes and immune networks: A hypothesis. Immunol. Today 3: 230.
2. RUBINSTEIN, L. J., B. GOLDBERG, J. HIERNAUX, K. E. STEIN & C. BONA. 1983. Idiotype anti-idiotype regulation. V. The requirement for immunization with antigen or monoclonal antiidiotypic antibodies for the activation of β 2-6 and β 2-1 polyfructosan reactive clones in Balb/c mice treated at birth with minute amounts of anti-A48 idiotype antibodies. J. Exp. Med. 158: 1129
3. GOLDBERG, B., W. E. PAUL & C. A. BONA. 1983. Idiotype-antiidiotype regulation. IV. Expression of common regulatory idiotopes on fructosan-binding or non-fructosan-binding monoclonal and immunoglobulins. J. Exp. Med. 158: 515.
4. VICTOR-KOBRIN, C., F. A. BONILLA, B. BELLON & C. A. BONA. 1985. Immunochemical and molecular characterization of regulatory idiotopes expressed by monoclonal antibodies exhibiting or lacking $\beta2$-6 fructosan binding activity. J. Exp. Med. 162: 647.

The Initial Repertoire of V_K Rearrangements Is Distributed over Many Subfamilies

ANN M. LAWLER AND PATRICIA J. GEARHART

Department of Biochemistry
The Johns Hopkins University
School of Hygiene and Public Health
Baltimore, Maryland 21205

Rearrangement of variable genes in B cells is a developmentally controlled process that requires the programmed expression of large gene families on separate chromosomes. During the first stages of B-cell development in mice, rearrangements of heavy chain variable genes (V_H) occur more frequently from the V_H subfamilies closest to the joining genes, particularly the 7183 and Q52 subfamilies. In adult mice, genes from the more 5' subfamilies are rearranged, and the expressed pool of heavy chains becomes more heterogeneous. We have found that two individual genes, 81X of the 7183 subfamily and Ox2 of the Q52 subfamily, are repeatedly rearranged in pre-B cells from fetal liver.[1] To further define the mechanisms controlling variable gene rearrangement, we examined a population of kappa rearrangements from fetal and day 1 B cells. This will allow a comparison of the rearrangement patterns of the heavy versus kappa variable gene families, and will describe the repertoire of antibodies expressed at this time.

We have identified the V_K rearrangements in a group of hybridomas made from fetal and day 1 liver B cells of BALB/c mice. By genomic cloning and nucleotide sequencing of these genes, repeated rearrangements of individual genes can be observed. The 12 rearrangements in this group are members of the following six subfamilies: three V_K21 genes ($V_K21E1.5$ rearranged once to J_K4 and once to J_K5, and $V_K21E1.6$ rearranged to J_K2); three V_K4 genes ($V_K4.58$ to J_K4, V_KH1 to J_K2, and $V_K4.68$ to J_K2); two V_K10 genes ($V_K10ArsA$ rearranged once to J_K2 and once to J_K4); two V_K1 genes ($V_K1.60$ to J_K2 and $V_K1.30$ to J_K2); one V_K9 gene ($V_K9.42$ to J_K1); and one V_K12 gene ($V_K12.48$ to J_K2). Three genes are not productively rearranged, whereas the others are productive and are presumably expressed. These subfamilies have been mapped on the V_K locus by using recombinant inbred strains and restriction fragment length polymorphisms.[2] V_K21 is closest to the J_K genes, V_K4, V_K12, and V_K10 are in the middle of the locus, and V_K1 and V_K9 are distal to the J_K locus.

The repeated use of several subfamilies suggests that the process of V_K rearrangement is not random in fetal and day 1 liver B cells. The targeting of multiple rearrangements to individual variable genes that was observed in heavy chain rearrangements[2] was also seen in two cases of repeats in this group of kappa rearrangements. Although the exact position of individual genes is unknown, the distribution of these subfamilies over the V_K locus suggests that the pattern is more heterogeneous than is that of the heavy chain and is not directed to the C_K-proximal subfamilies.

REFERENCES

1. LAWLER, A. M., P. S. LIN & P. J. GEARHART. 1987. Adult B-cell repertoire is biased toward two heavy-chain variable-region genes that rearrange frequently in pre-B cells. Proc. Natl. Acad. Sci. USA **84:** 2454–2458.
2. D'HOOSTELAERE, L. A., K. HUPPI, B. MOCK, C. MALLETT & M. POTTER. 1988. The Ig_K L chain allelic groups among the Ig_K haplotypes and and Ig_K crossover populations suggest a gene order. J. Immunol. **141:** 652–661.

Different Frequencies of Mutation in Immunoglobulin Genes after Primary Immunization with PC-KLH

S. G. LEBECQUE, N. S. LEVY, U. V. MALIPIERO,
AND P. J. GEARHART

School of Hygiene and Public Health
Department of Biochemistry
The Johns Hopkins University
Baltimore, Maryland 21205

To analyze the mechanisms of hypermutation in immunoglobulin variable genes, we have defined a population of B cells undergoing hypermutation. Adult BALB/c mice were injected with phosphorylcholine (PC)-hemocyanin in *Bordetella pertussis,* and sacrificed 7, 9, and 13 days later. V_H and V_K genes were sequenced from cDNA libraries made from splenic RNA. Two groups of genes were sequenced: (1) genes from the V_HS107, V_K22, and V_K24 subfamilies that encode anti-PC antibodies,[1] and (2) genes from the V_H7183, V_H3660, and V_K21 subfamilies that do not encode anti-PC

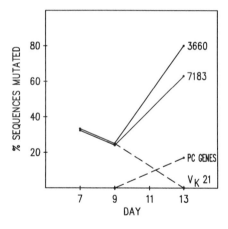

FIGURE 1. Percentage of mutated genes at different times after immunization. Each line represents a different subfamily of genes, except that the PC genes include the V_HS107, V_K22, and V_K24 subfamilies.

antibodies. All the V_H genes that were sequenced were associated with IgG constant genes.

Different frequencies of mutation were observed. Genes encoding PC-binding antibodies had a low frequency of mutation (0.08%). The frequency of mutation was low (0.23%) in the V_K21 genes on day 9 and was not detected on day 13. In contrast, genes from the V_H7183 and V_H3660 subfamilies underwent a higher frequency of mutation, which was 0.46% on day 7, 0.23% on day 9, and 0.68% on day 13. As shown in FIGURE 1, 5 of 15 (33%) sequences were mutated on day 7, and as many as 11 of 16 (68%) sequences had mutations by day 13. A high frequency of mutation on day 14 in genes encoding anti-oxazolone antibodies was also found by Griffiths *et al.*[2] In addition, the ratio of nucleotide substitutions that result in replacement of amino acids versus those that cause silent changes (R/S) in complementary determining regions on day 13 was 7 (22/3) for 3660 and 7183 genes. A high R/S ratio suggests that mutations are selected at the protein level for binding to antigen with increased affinity.[3]

We conclude that mutations occur early after primary immunization and that the frequency increases with time. The low frequency of mutation in genes coding for PC-binding antibodies and in $V_K 21$ genes could reflect the small increase in affinity provided by those mutations. In contrast, the higher frequency of selected mutations in 7183 and 3660 genes could represent increased affinity for undetermined antigens.

REFERENCES

1. GEARHART, P. J., D. M. CARON, R. H. DOUGLAS, U. BRUDERER, M. B. RITTENBERG & L. HOOD. Major effect of somatic hypermutation is to increase affinity of antibodies. Proc. Natl. Acad. Sci., USA, in press.
2. GRIFFITHS, G. M., C. BEREK, M. KAARTINEN & C. MILSTEIN. 1984. Somatic mutation and the maturation of immune response to 2-phenyl oxazolone. Nature 312: 271–275.
3. SHLOMCHIK, M. J., A. MARSHAK-ROTHSTEIN, C. B. WOLFOWICZ, T. L. ROTHSTEIN & M. G. WEIGERT. 1987. The role of clonal selection and somatic mutation in autoimmunity. Nature 328: 805–811.

Multiple Control Regions Regulate the Constitutive and Inducible Expression of Eα Gene

D. THANOS,[a] G. MAVROTHALLASITIS,[a]
M. GREGORIOU,[a] A. BYGRAVE,[a] AND
J. PAPAMATHEAKIS[a,b]

[a]Institute of Molecular Biology
Research Center of Crete
Iraklio, Crete, Greece

[b]Department of Biology
University of Crete
Iraklio, Crete, Greece

Class II major histocompatibility complex (MHC) antigens have important immunologic functions. The corresponding genes are subject to tissue and lymphokine regulation, such as their response to gamma-interferon (IFN-γ).[1]

To study class II gene regulatory sequences we have used 5' deletion constructs on the CAT gene. Analysis of CAT levels from these deletions reveals a multiplicity of control regions within a single cell line as well as cell-type specific patterns (FIG. 1). A positive region maps between −113 and −183 dp in cells of various tissue origins regardless of their class-II-related phenotype: fibroblastic cell lines of human (xeroderma GM4429B) or mouse (LTK⁻, C127, 3T3) origin, human epithelial-like cells (HeLa), mouse macrophage WEHI-3, and B lymphoid lines (A20-2J and Raji). We conclude that this region has a general positive control function irrespective of the class II expression state or inducibility by IFN-γ.

Another positive region encompasses part of the conserved class II region, namely, box A, and functions in class II negative cell types but not in WEHI-3 or A20-2J (FIG. 1, solid line).

In addition, two negative regions mapping 5' to −97 and 5' to −353 bp were identified in class II negative cell lines (FIG. 1, broken line), suggesting that class II genes are under negative control in nonexpressing cells. This analysis points to some regulatory similarities with the human DQβ gene.[2]

Furthermore, we studied regulation by IFN-γ using 5' deletions as well as 3' deletions fused to the human α-globin promoter. Results from transient expression assays (or stable clones cotransfected with pSV2neo) showed that a IFN-γ response region resides between −164 and −43 bp. The conserved boxB (reverse CAT box) was found to be dispensable in the presence of the α-globin promoter associated CAT box. In the latter case the 3' boundary was mapped at −65 bp.

Internal deletion analysis (FIG. 2) further showed that both conserved boxes are required for a IFN-γ response. The requirement of the positive region mapping 5' to −113 bp for induction resembles the case of the H-2Kᵇ gene.[3]

Reversion of the IFN-γ response sequence (FIG. 2, construct R) reduced but did not eliminate induction. Similarly, a corresponding region of the Eβ gene (−77 to −208 bp) confers inducibility to the α-globin promoter in either orientation. This indicates that the IFN-γ response region has characteristics of inducible enhancer-like elements.

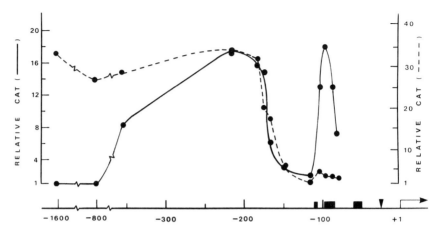

FIGURE 1. Basal levels of CAT activity (1 unit was assigned to the construct showing minimal activity) of the 5' deleted Eα gene in cells expressing (*broken line*) or not expressing (*solid line*) class II genes. Initiation of transcription (*arrowhead*), TATA box (*triangle*), and conserved class II sequences (*filled boxes*) are indicated.

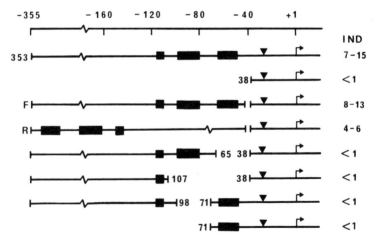

FIGURE 2. Gamma-interferon (IFN-γ) inducibility of internal deletions carried on a −353 to +14 bp fragment fused to CAT. The range of induction ratio (IND) is shown. Other symbols are described in the legend for Figure 1.

REFERENCES

1. KORMAN, A. J., J. M. BOSS, T. SPIES, R. SORRENTINO, K. OKADA & J. L. STROMINGER. 1985. Immunol. Rev. **85:** 45–86.
2. BOSS, J. M. & J. L. STROMINGER. 1986. Proc. Natl. Acad. Sci. USA **83:** 9139–9143.
3. ISRAEL, A., A. KIMURA, A. FOURNIER, M. FELLOUS, & P. KOURILSKY. 1986. Nature (London) **322:** 743–746.

Index of Contributors

DATE DUE

GAYLORD			PRINTED IN U.S.A.